THREAD OF GOLD

Celebrating the unbroken history
of 250 years of Freemasonry
in the Province of Cornwall.

1752 - 2002.

"Now is the time for us to remind the popular world of the Craft's true aims and of its contribution to our local and national history. We should also take the opportunity to show our confidence in the continuing relevance of Freemasonry in today's world". The Grand Master, H.R.H. The Duke of Kent, K.G., speaking at Grand Lodge in March 2001.

A celebration and demonstration of 'Freemasonry in the Community' throughout England and Wales is planned from 25 June to 2 July in 2002.

Her Majesty The Queen at the Royal Cornwall Show in 2000

HER MAJESTY THE QUEEN

With congratulations from the Province of Cornwall for the Golden Jubilee of her reign, 1952 - 2002.

Since H.R.H. The Duke of Kent was installed as Grand Master in 1967 he has led English Freemasonry through some of the most significant changes the Craft has seen.

For 35 years the Grand Master has directed the English Craft and has shown great dedication throughout that period.

We are all immensely grateful, for we have gained much from his guidance, leadership, and experience.

We can all be justly proud to be members of this ancient and honourable institution.

THE MOST WORSHIPFUL BROTHER - HIS ROYAL HIGHNESS

THE DUKE OF KENT K.G., G.C.M.G., G.C.V.O., A.D.C.

GRAND MASTER OF THE UNITED GRAND LODGE OF ENGLAND

THE PROVINCE CONGRATULATES THE GRAND MASTER ON THE 35th ANNIVERSARY OF HIS INSTALLATION.

1967 - 2002

Thread of Gold

A Message from The Pro Grand Master, M.W. Bro. the Most Hon. the Marquess of Northampton, D.L.

I am delighted to send my congratulations to the Province of Cornwall on reaching its 250th anniversary.

There have been many changes in Society during this time but the Grand Principles of Freemasonry - friendship, charity and integrity - are as relevant today as they have always been.

This is a time for a great celebration of history and achievements of Cornish Brethren in the past, but it is also a time to look forward to the future and rededicate ourselves to the high standards that masonry expects of its members.

I have no doubt that masonry in the Province of Cornwall will continue to flourish and I send my best wishes for your future endeavours.

Northampton

Foreword
by The Provincial Grand Master,
Right Worshipful Brother Nicholas J.F.C. Barrington.

I am writing this foreword a few days after the 250th celebrations of the lodge of Love and Honour No. 75 when they welcomed to Cornwall the Deputy Grand Master R. W. Bro. Iain Bryce.

The Province's oldest existing lodge was constituted on 12th June 1751. A year later seven members of the lodge of Love and Honour constituted our Provincial Grand Lodge and William Pye their first Worshipful Master became the Province's first Provincial Grand Master. In July 2002 we will celebrate the Province's 250th birthday at the same time holding a festival for the Royal Masonic Benevolent Institution.

This history is a major part of the Province's 250th celebrations and as the thirteenth Provincial Grand Master it is my privilege and delight to write this foreword as a welcome to a very special book.

This book together with our service in Truro Cathedral on 23rd June 2002 and our festival reception and dinner on 4th July 2002 at the Royal Cornwall Showground will be, I am certain, a fitting tribute to our forebears and encouragement to our successors.

This history cannot refer to every facet of Freemasonry during 250 years. It is not a list of events but rather a story showing the development of Freemasonry in our province over two and half centuries. We only have to think of the changes that have taken place in housing, transport and working conditions. In 1752 mining was a business in which many thousands worked but sadly the last working mine South Crofty at Camborne closed a few years ago.

This book has involved a tremendous amount of work by W. Bro. William Wattters as Chairman of the History Project Committee, W. Bro. Douglas Williams as Editor and W. Bro. the Revd. Raymond Wood together with W. Bro. Robert Lawrence who has photographed the lodge temples and banners. I cannot thank them enough for their efforts but additionally this history could not have been produced without the many brethren of the individual lodges who spent so much time in researching and producing the history of their respective lodges. I am extremely grateful to all of them for their research and co-operation.

I hope that when brethren read this history they will reflect on the achievements of the individual lodges, the continuity and development of our fraternity which can take pride from its involvement in the life of Cornwall during the last 250 years.

I believe that you will be very proud of what has happened in the past 250 years and that it will encourage each and every Freemason in this Province in the future. Long may Freemasonry in this Province continue to flourish - long may it continue to uphold our Masonic values which even in a rapidly changing world have survived the test of time.

I commend this book to you all, whether a Freemason or not. I hope you will enjoy reading it and that it will provide you with some understanding of what has gone before and as a further encouragement as to what we hope to achieve in the future.

June 2001

The Pro Grand Master M.W. Bro. the Most Hon. the Marquess of Northampton, D.L.

The Provincial Grand Master, Right Worshipful Brother Nicholas J.F.C. Barrington.

THE MAKING OF A HISTORY

EDITORIAL TEAM: R.Wor.Bro. Nicholas Barrington (P.G.M.), W.Bro. William Watters P.J.G.D. (Chairman), W.Bro. Douglas Williams M.B.E., P.A.G.D.C. (Editor), W.Bro. the Revd Raymond Wood P.A.G.Chaplain.

Cornwall and Cornish Freemasonry during the past 250 years have been crowded with momentous occasions, inspiring personalities and leaders, together with a rich continuity of service and example. In this provincial history we have set out, with the support of the 81 lodges and so many members and friends, to tell the story of that 'Thread of Gold' that has linked the centuries and our fraternity. So often the history of our province has been intertwined with that of our Duchy.

It was over two years ago that our Provincial Grand Master formed the group that has shaped this book, and its contents, telling of the developments from 1752, and before, when maritime and militia towns were the centres of Freemasonry. Many of the distinguished moments are featured, particularly the visit of the Grand Master The Prince of Wales (later King Edward VII) for the foundation stone laying at Truro Cathedral in 1880. The ancient Duchy Palace at Lostwithiel, the more modern King Arthur's Hall at Tintagel, and the legend of George Washington's Bible in Freemasonry, are among the fascinating illustrated stories told here.

For some years in the 20th century Freemasonry paid the penalty for the public perception of apparent 'secrecy' but the new spirit of awareness and openness, nationally and locally, is changing that aspect. It is important that freemasons continue to demonstrate confidence and pride in an organisation that has a membership of over 300,000 in the United Grand Lodge of England - attracting more than 10,000 new recruits each year - and a membership of about 4,000 in Cornwall and the Isles of Scilly.

The theme of 'Freemasonry in the Community' and work for many non-masonic charities, continues to be at the forefront. We trust this history will add to this bright prospect. We acknowledge the contributions made by our 13 leaders, as described in their biographies and the records of the lodge histories.

DOUGLAS WILLIAMS M.B.E., EDITOR.   September 2001

ACKNOWLEDGMENTS

To photographers and sources including Phil Monckton (Cornwall and Isles of Scilly Press, picture of H.M. the Queen), Neil Lindsay (Wadebridge), Bernard White (Newquay), Bro. Anthony Curd (Newlyn), Trevor Whetter (St. Austell), Alan G. Tomkinson (Looe), Photo-Graphic (Plymouth), Morrab Library (Penzance), Cornwall County Library, Cornish Studies Library (Redruth), Andrew Campbell (Falmouth), W.Bro. Graham Hindle (Callington), B.J. Press (Threemilestone), the West Briton (Truro), The Cornishman (Penzance), Falmouth Packet Newspapers (Falmouth) and the Western Morning News (Plymouth), as well as many individual lodges.

In addition to the leaders of the lodges and of the Royal Arch and Mark degrees in the province there have been significant editorial contributions by the Grand Secretary R.W. Bro. James Daniel, W.Bro. Dr. John Tyerman Williams ('Setting the Scene') and W.Bro. John Cornish ('Freemasons on the March') as well as the photography and professional advice of W.Bro. Robert Lawrence.

We are grateful for the dedicated efforts of Mrs Carole Marland for the text setting and to Rowe the Printers (Hayle) for their co-ordinating role and co-operation.

THREAD OF GOLD

Published in 2001 by the Cornwall Province of Freemasons, Truro.
Printed by Rowe the Printers, Hayle, Cornwall.
Bound by J.W. Braithwaite Ltd., Wolverhampton.

Copyright ©2001 by The Province.

Masonic Images ©2001 Robert Lawrence LBIPP.
No reproduction without prior written permission.

ISBN No. 0 9540850

The Festival Masonic Jewel

Ladies Brooch

The Jewel of the Festival in 2002 for the Royal Masonic Benevolent Institution

(designed by W.Bro. Henry Mitchell PJGD, Past Provincial Grand Secretary).

Deputy G. M. R.W. Bro. Iain Ross Bryce (left) was the guest of honour at the 250th anniversary celebrations of LOVE AND HONOUR LODGE, Falmouth, in May 2001. The PGM R.W. Bro. Nicholas J.F.C. Barrington. (right) brought the congratulations of the province.
With them is the Worshipful Master, W. Bro. Anthony Tregenza.

250th anniversary celebrations of LOVE AND HONOUR LODGE, Falmouth, May 2001

Thread of Gold

CONTENTS

Chapter I
	Setting the Scene	3
	Freemasons on the March	7
	A Treasure Trove	13
	The Carn Brea Obelisk	15
	A Cornishman as Grand Secretary	20

Chapter II
	Provincial Grand Masters Down the Years: Cornwall and International Dates of Interest	30

Chapter III
	Splendour at Truro	73
	Cornish Men and Masons	82
	Special Moments in History	89

Chapter IV
	Royal Arch Chapter	109
	Mark Master Masons	114
	Royal Ark Mariners	118
	Cornish Masons' Role in Transvaal	119

Chapter V
	Glossary	126
	Highlights in the Cornish Craft	140
	Craft Lodges by date of Warrant	144
	Royal Arch Chapters by date of Chapter	147
	Leading Officers during 250 years	148
	Other Masonic Orders in Cornwall	152

Chapter VI
	Masonic Meeting Places in Cornwall	154
	Individual Lodge Histories	155
	Poem: 'True Masonic Nobility.'	360

THREAD OF GOLD

Chapter I

Setting the Scene
Freemasons on the March
A Treasure Trove
The Carn Brea Obelisk
A Cornishman as Grand Secretary

A photograph taken in Coinagehall Street, Helston of the First World War Ambulance subscribed for in 1915 by the Brethren of the Province. The Provincial Grand Master, the Earl of Mount Edgcumbe asked lodges to give the equivalent of 1/- (5p) per member to raise the £140.00 needed.

A general view of the first Provincial Garden Party, held at Killiganoon, near Playing Place, Truro, in 1983, opened by Lady Cornwallis, that raised over £7,000 for charity.

SETTING THE SCENE

What sort of place was Cornwall when Freemasonry was first established there in the middle of the 18th century? What sort of men became Masons in those days? These two questions confront us as soon as we start asking questions about the early days of the Craft in Cornwall. They also remind us that Freemasonry has never existed in isolation from the rest of society. The recent trend in Masonic history emphasizes this important fact. Even the most dedicated Freemason spends more of his time outside the Lodge than in it. We who are Freemasons are many other things as well. We have our own callings, trades and professions. We have families. And, of course, we are profoundly influenced by the world we live in, by the education we have received, by the ideas and customs of our contemporaries. So we come back to our first question: what sort of place was Cornwall in 1751 when the first Masonic Lodge was formed at Falmouth?

TRANSPORT

Even today, Cornwall is different from other parts of England. It was far more different 250 years ago. Difficulties of travel made it remote. What our 18th century ancestors called roads were often rough tracks which heavy rain converted into impassable mud. Roads in Cornwall were particularly bad. Many had not improved since 1698, when Celia Fiennes made her famous journey 'Through England on a side-saddle in the Time of William and Mary' Descending the steep road into Fowey, she wrote, 'In the road there are many holes and sloughs wherever there is clay ground, and when by the rain they are filled with water it is difficult to shun danger.' For this reason, saddle-horses for people and pack horses for goods were used more than coaches. The earliest coaches in Cornwall were all privately owned. The first belonged to the Hawkins family of Trewinnard, St.Erth. Made about 1700, it was in use till 1780. Obviously vehicle-makers then were less skilled in producing built-in obsolescence. The 'Trewinnard Coach' is today on permanent exhibition at the Royal Cornwall Museum, Truro, in the main gallery.

Family excursions in their coach were impressive occasions. Bottrell wrote, 'When the ladies and gentleman of Trewinnard drove out in their chariot, accompanied by a cavalcade of belles and beaux, with hawk and hound, they must have thought themselves as grand and glorious as the Queen of Sheba and King Solomon.' But their magnificence was no protection when they were 'stuck fast in a hole, or jolted out in the mud, when the half-dozen or more men by whom they were attended, with poles and ropes, picks, spades and led horses, contrived to set them in motion again, at about the rate of three miles

Setting the Scene

an hour, at least where the roads were the best.' When even aristocrats had to travel in such conditions, it is not surprising that masonic lodges, like all other assemblies, met only where there were enough potential members in easy, often in walking, distance.

The later part of the century saw improvements in both the construction and the administration of roads. By about 1790, a stage-coach was running every other day from Exeter to Falmouth via Bodmin. The journey began at 3am and was due to end at midnight. Public coach transport within the county also developed. By 1799 stage-coaches ran from Torpoint to Liskeard, Lostwithiel, St.Austell), Grampound, Truro and Falmouth. The frequency with which Falmouth appears as a coaching point is further emphasis. Truro also increased its importance after it became the centre from which many stage-coaches routes radiated, to Launceston, Penzance, Torpoint - and Falmouth again. Even a century later, Wilkie Collins, the author of 'The Woman in White' and 'The Moonstone', could, without obvious absurdity, entitle his book about Cornwall 'Rambles Beyond Railways'. True, a railway between Bodmin and Wadebridge had been opened in 1834 and the Hayle-Redruth line had been working for seven years when Collins made his journey; but the Falmouth-Truro-Plymouth line, though proposed in 1846, was not working till 1863. His title was fair enough.

WORK AND JOBS

Despite its isolation, in some ways Cornwall was more prosperous than it is today. In the century from 1660 to 1760, the population had risen by 50 percent, from 100,000 to 150,000. This increase was mostly in the west, where the growth of mining had attracted a sizable migration from the agricultural east. By the turn of the century, Cornwall had 75 mines, employing about 16,000 men, women and children. By 1837, there were 200 mines, employing about 30,000. The area around Consolidated Mines at Gwennap, some three miles south-east of Redruth, was reputed to be the richest square mile in the Old World. Collins knew that readers would feel cheated if a book about Cornwall did not include a visit to a mine. So his chapter IX is called 'Botallack Mine'. A greater novelist than Collins, Anthony Trollope, also described a Cornish mine, 'Wheal Mary Jane' and made it play a vital part in the plot of 'The Three Clerks' (1857). Trollope also described a more primitive aspect of Cornish life in a short story, 'Malachi's Cove' (1864), set 'On the northern coast of Cornwall, between Tintagel and Bossiney'. Here an old man makes a living by gathering seaweed and selling it as manure. Trollope got to know something of Cornwall when, as a Post Office official, he was reorganizing and expanding the postal services in the whole south west of England; an important part of opening up Cornwall.

CHURCHES AND NOBILITY

Setting the Scene

When Freemasonry came to Cornwall, the Church of England there was was still part of the vast diocese of Exeter. It was not until 1877 that the bishopric of Truro was constituted. Cornish Freemasons made important contributions to the new cathedral, ceremonial and financial. A pier of the central tower of the cathedral records, "This pier was erected to the glory of the Most High, with the offerings of the Freemasons of Cornwall (the Earl of Mount Edgcumbe, Provincial Grand Master) and others, their Brethren in the Craft, who attended when the North East corner stone of this Cathedral Church was laid in Masonic Form by H.R.H. the Duke of Cornwall, Grand Master of England, Thursday, 20th May A.D., 1880." A striking example of the happy relations that have often existed and always should exist between Craft and Church. This is also illustrated by the many clergy, Anglican, Methodist and others who have contributed so much to Masonry in Cornwall by their active support.

Cornwall posessed many well-established county families, such as the Bassets, Borlases, Boscawens (Viscount Falmouth since the reign of George Ist, but ennobled as long ago as the reign of Henry III), Eliots (Earls of St. Germans from the reign of George III), Lemons, Mount Edgcumbes (Earls of Mount Edgcumbe since the reign of George III) and St. Aubyns (created Baron St. Levan by Queen Victoria). Several were and have continued to be prominent in Freemasonry. Sir John St. Aubyn was P.G.M. of Cornwall from 1785 to 1844, when he was succeeded by Sir Charles Lemon, The Earl of Mount Edgcumbe from 1873 to 1917, the Earl of St.Germans from 1941 to 1952, and the Hon. Robert Eliot from 1978 to 1994, while others from similar backgrounds also held high Masonic ranks. For the benefit of non-Masonic readers, I should explain that Freemasonry in England is governed by the United Grand Lodge of England, headed by the Grand Master and his officers. Below this, the country is divided into Provinces, usually coinciding with counties. Each has its own Provincial Grand Master with his officers, who exercise masonic jurisdiction over the private lodges in the province. There were many others classified as landed gentry and county families, who were active Freemasons.

TRADES AND PROFESSIONS

Taking Falmouth as both fairly typical and Freemasonry's first home in Cornwall, we find out of 86 names listed: Trade 48; Manufacturers and artisans 26; Professional 8; Official 2; Gentleman 1; Banker 1. (Bailey's Western and Midland Directory, containing an Alphabetical List of the Names and Places of Abode, Of The Bankers, Merchants, Manufacturers, Gentlemen of the Law and Physic, and other Eminent Traders).

Though Cornwall was remote in many ways and parts of it were very wild, there were several pockets where a lively social and intellectual life flourished. It was at one of these that the first Masonic lodge was founded in 1751. Happily, this lodge still flourishes as the Lodge of Love and Honour, now No. 75 on the register of the United Grand Lodge of England.

Setting the Scene

Falmouth was a natural home for a masonic lodge as it had become established as a local centre of society and fashion. London, of course, had long been the social and intellectual as well as the political and administrative capital. However, even for towns less remote than Falmouth, visits to London were difficult and rare. So many a provincial town became the seat of a very vigorous social life. Falmouth was one of these centres. It had received its Royal Charter as a borough in 1661, just after the restoration of King Charles II. It was important as the most westerly landfall for sailing ships, and it was also the seat of the Royal Cornwall Polytechnic Society.

The 18th century was a great time for clubs and societies. Dr. Johnson, himself an enthusiastic clubman, was uttering a severe criticism when he described an acquaintance as 'a most unclubable man'. Some of the clubs of this period were primarily social. Many were intellectual: literary, musical, artistic and scientific. Freemasonry itself was an example of this tendency to meet both for pleasant fellowship and serious discussion.

As the rest of this work will show in detailed abundance, Freemasonry has continued to exemplify this tendency through two and a half centuries, and is still flourishing today.

W.Bro. Dr. John Tyerman Williams

The success of fundraising for the two hospices in Cornwall - Mount Edgcumbe at St. Austell and St. Julia's, Hayle - over many years, was continued in November 2000 with the presentation of cheques totalling over £4,000 from the Grand Charity. The PGM. R. W. Bro. Nicholas Barrington (centre) gave a £3,100 cheque to Mount Edgcumbe and one for £1,000 to St. Julia's, to Mr Alastair Adams, chief executive (Cornish hospices), and Ms. Sarah Folland, the director of nursing. Mr Barrington said that in 2000 the Grand Charity had given £500,000 to hospices in England and Wales: over recent years the total was almost £4-million. In addition there were the gifts from individual lodges.

FREEMASONS ON THE MARCH
THE STORY OF THE EARLY MILITARY LODGES OF CORNWALL

"These three lodges were formed during a very turbulent period in the history of our country, a time of war, of death and destruction on a grand scale." These were: The 1st Cornwall Regiment of Fencible Light Dragoons - True and Faithful Lodge; The Cornwall and Devon Miners Regiment - The Lodge of Fortitude; The Royal Cornwall Militia - One and All Lodge.

Many lodges in this country owe their existence to the formation of military lodges warranted from the mid 1700s to the early part of the 1800s: this province is no exception. The section *Highlights of the Cornish Craft* in the Year Book traces the origins of some, and from these daughter lodges have been formed. The lodges are very proud of their military heritage and possess various items that have survived over the years. At this particular period of history it was not easy to find time to form a lodge. The country was often at war, or sabre rattling with many countries.

THE 1ST CORNWALL REGIMENT OF FENCIBLE LIGHT DRAGOONS, was raised in 1794, initially as four troops of cavalry later extended to six. The list of the original senior officers reads like a 'Who's Who' of the landed gentry of Cornwall. The commanding officer, with the rank of Lt. Colonel, was Viscount Falmouth, a powerful, wealthy and influential gentleman of the county. Next in command, with the rank of Major, came Sir Francis Basset: even today Redruth, Camborne and Falmouth have Basset Roads and Basset Streets, public houses bear his name, and a restaurant. On top of Carn Brea hill outside Redruth, is the massive granite memorial to that great man and mason. The provincial sword bearer today carries the sword presented to the province by Sir Francis. Next in command came a pair of captains: one was the Hon. Edward Eliot of St. Germans. One descendant became Dep.P.G.M., in 1868, and two others were P.G.M., one from 1941 - 52 and the other from 1978 - 94. Most of the dragoons would have been Cornishmen, used to working with horses; some may have worked on the estates of the senior officers of the regiment. The uniform of the day was the red coat, as worn by most regiments, with black facings (the lapels and turn back cuffs with white lace), the fine cavalryman's helmet with a turban of yellow. He would also have carried the cavalry sword, a particularly powerful weapon. A single blow from this type of sword could, and at times did, completely sever an opponent's arm.

The Royal Cornwall Militia would have been dressed as a foot soldier from a Regiment of Foot. By the time the lodge was formed in 1810 the uniform would have been as illustrated with its own regimental markings.

Freemasons on the March

On the 12 April 1799 a warrant was issued to the Cornish Dragoons and the name of the lodge was True and Faithful, as it remains to this day. It was not consecrated in Cornwall, but later that year in a public house "Scotch Arms" in Newcastle-on-Tyne. The secretaries' books are long gone but those of the treasurers have survived: when they consecrated they did it in style. They employed a military band for the day at a cost of £3.15p they purchased 12 aprons for 50p, (in total) and to be 'made a mason' would require the sum of £2.35p. The ordinary dragoon could not afford this: his rate of pay was about 10p per day but, as the army provided his mount, almost half of that was deducted straight away. By the time he had spent some money on tobacco, a couple of pints of beer, perhaps some extra food, plus the fact that gambling was rife in the army at that time, his money was spent. At that time to be a mason in the army was the preserve of the officers and the senior non-commissioned officers. The regiment soon returned to Cornwall and was disbanded, the officers retiring on half-pay which they could continue to draw for up to two years. The dragoons themselves would have been paid off, but many would have re-enlisted in other regiments, in particular the Regiments of Foot, who were still short of men. At this stage the warrant could have lapsed and been returned to Grand Lodge but the warrant then became a civil one, still in the name of True and Faithful, meeting at The Angel Hotel in Helston. The lodge today has a reminder of its military days with six swords from the regiment on the lodge walls and members perform a 'chant' at the end of the lodge meeting which is also said to be from its military days.

A military unit that did not have the advantage of riding everywhere, was a Regiment of Foot, with men who marched shoulder to shoulder to the front line of the enemy, braving the cannon, musket ball, and ultimately the bayonet. There was a considerable number of these regiments; by the year 1815 they numbered over 100, many having more than one battalion. Vast numbers were required to serve king and country. Of particular Cornish interest is the 67th Regiment of Foot, which dates from 1758, also known as the South Hampshire Regiment, the county where it was raised. The uniform at that time would have comprised the long red coat with the regimental markings, the three-cornered hat had just been replaced by the 'grenadier' style with a tall front bearing the regimental colours. The soldier would have carried the trusty musket of the day 'Brown Bess'. The first commanding officer was Colonel James Woolfe who became one of the great names in military history. During the siege of Quebec he ordered the attack on the defending French from an unexpected quarter, the scaling of the Heights of Abraham. These cliffs, some 170 feet high, were considered by the French to be impregnable. The British troops proved them wrong and after successfully climbing found not one French soldier on guard: they attacked and the battle was won, Quebec had fallen and this ultimately led to Canada becoming part of the British Empire. Unfortunately General Woolfe was killed at the age of 32. The masonic history of the regiment began in 1772 when in July a lodge was constituted in the 67th Regiment of Foot at Chatham, Kent. There is very little information regarding its early years as a military lodge but its masonic chest would have travelled with it during its various postings both in the United Kingdom and overseas, so that when time permitted lodge meetings could take place. The regiment had two periods in the West Indies, not a pleasant posting in those days: in common with all regiments posted there it was ravaged by Yellow Fever and many men died. Many officers knew of the reputation of the West Indies and made sure their last will and testament was left with friends and relatives: the regiment returned from the second period in the West Indies in 1803, its ranks much depleted, but it was soon on a recruiting drive and within a few months was once

A group of officers of Provincial Grand Lodge in 1905 with the PGM, the Earl of Mount Edgcumbe and his deputy V.W.Bro. Philip Colville Smith. On the right, seated, is the Prov. G. Sec. W.Bro. B.F. Edyvean.

A Lewis who was to become prominent in provincial and Mt. Sinai Lodge, Arthur Robinson, is in this young group of four bearing the Volume of the Sacred Law when the Provincial Grand Lodge met in July 1921. They are, from left: Cyril A.J. Rodda, Arthur C. Robinson, Charles F. Jennings and Ronald F. Drewitt.

Freemasons on the March

A Dragoon of the Late 1700's and early 1800's, showing how our 1st Cornwall Fencible Dragoons would have looked. The only missing item is the turban that would have been around the body of the helmet.

again up to strength. They spent the next few years within the United Kingdom, and it was not until 1807 that again they received orders to move to the port of embarkation this time bound for the East Indies, and decided at that time to relinquish their masonic warrant.

Coming closer to home, THE CORNWALL AND DEVON MINERS REGIMENT was raised in 1798 and stationed in many towns in various parts of the South of England but, as peace was believed to have arrived, in the year 1802 was disbanded. It was not long before it was realised that Napoleon was making plans to invade England and again the miners were required to serve. June 1803 saw the regiment, now renamed the Royal Regiment of Cornish Miners, on the move, being ordered to march to Exeter, ready to repel any invasion on the South Coast. The men left Truro on 6 June and marched to Mitchell a distance of nine miles. On day two they marched from Mitchell to Bodmin some 14 miles, day three Bodmin to Launceston 21 miles; day four Launceston to Okehampton 20 miles, and day five Okehampton to Exeter 22 miles. The usual daily mileage was considered to be about nine miles, carrying some 60lbs of equipment so it was clear they were needed urgently at Exeter in case of a landing by the French and that it was a forced march. Not for them the tarmac of today, but the rutted stone and earth surface, very uneven, and they had to carry their packs, muskets, bread ration and water container.

There were further marches to other towns but as the danger of an invasion had receded they were posted to Dover. Most of their time there was spent building and maintaining the massive fortifications, and as miners they were used to blasting, tunnelling and earth moving. Many of their tunnels are there today, a tribute to their skill. In 1807 the 67th Regiment of Foot was off to foreign climes and no longer required its warrant but the Royal Regiment of Cornish Miners was interested in forming a masonic lodge and so a transfer of the warrant took place at the aptly named Ordnance Arms, Dover in April, with 11 members of the Royal Regiment of Cornish Miners being present, the meeting hosted by Town Lodge No. 203, Dover. Now there were not only senior non-commissioned officers as members of the lodge but other ranks (ie Privates) were allowed to join. Times were changing. It was initially known by its number only, but later was named 'The Lodge of Fortitude', as it continues to this day. The membership was soon on the increase and within a year stood at 24. The number of meetings increased and reached three or four a month and were attended by other Dover lodges, with numbers in excess of 40. If one was late, or did not attend, a fine was imposed, but the dignity and decorum which we now take for granted was not always the case. Swearing, gambling, bad manners or interrupting any officer of the lodge, brought a fine at the discretion of the W.M. and majority. Being 'disguised in liquor' in lodge was a problem and there was a sliding scale of punishments for the first, second and third offences. To transgress for the third time meant being excluded and reported to Grand Lodge. In one particular year there were five meetings in December, including Christmas Eve, at which the W.M. was elected.

Freemasons on the March

At one meeting the Regimental Sergeant Major of the regiment was initiated. One can imagine what many of the brethren of the lodge must have thought: here was a man ramrod straight, used to having the junior ranks scared half to death, now coming into their lodge. His eye would have scanned the room and seen many he knew, as every brother in the regiment was present!

The regiment left Dover in 1811, posted to Ireland. There was a sweetener: every volunteer was paid a bounty, and every member volunteered to go. Eventually they returned to England and after a posting to Hillsea Barracks were informed that they were to return to Cornwall. What a great day that must have been. After being away for some nine years, they received their marching orders and set off for home. After crossing the Tamar, one can imagine a great cheer going up from the troops, and an extra spring in their step as they marched to barracks at Pendennis Castle, Falmouth. Not long after their arrival the regiment was disbanded. The authorities of the day, believing that peace had arrived, decided to disband many regiments. Little did they realise that Napoleon had one further surprise up his sleeve and would raise a mighty army. He met his match on the 18 June 1815 at Waterloo. With the disbandment of the regiment the warrant might have been returned to Grand Lodge but this was not the case: a few members transferred to the Queens Head Hotel in Truro and continued working with the old warrant. Then came a very difficult period in the history of the lodge. As a result of the union of the Moderns and the Ancients in 1813, the lodge could no longer initiate civilians, only military personnel, and as the regiment was disbanded not many military men were available. It wrote continually to Grand Lodge seeking guidance and for a Grand Lodge certificate for those they had initiated but to no avail. They did not receive one reply to their many letters sent over a period of 13 years. It is astonishing that the lodge, now with only seven members, survived but in 1826 the military warrant was exchanged for a civilian one and continues to this day, now being numbered No. 131 having its home in Perranporth and still having many items from its military heritage.

This is the uniform that would have been worn by a foot soldier of a Regiment of Foot, and illustrates the 67th Regiment from 1758 until about 1802.

The third military unit was THE ROYAL CORNWALL MILITIA raised in the year 1760, the Territorial Army of the day, part-time soldiers, but in time of conflict called to serve full-time as required. In the case of the militia they were to serve for the duration of the conflict plus, if needed, an extra six months to enable some of the Regiments of Foot, the regular army, time to return from overseas. The militia was equipped, armed, and paid as the regulars plus two additional bonuses. They received a cash bounty and were required to serve outside of the British Isles. The government used the county militia to suppress public disorder, stamping out any attempt at revolt or insurrection and also to be ready to defend the country against invasion. They came under the control of the county's Lord Lieutenant. By the time a number of senior non-commissioned officers applied for a masonic warrant the old-style

Thread of Gold

Freemasons on the March

uniform had gone. They had short red jackets with high collars and instead of the wide lapels a system of button-holes looped in regimental lace and set in singles or pairs according to regiment. The stove pipe hat was about to be replaced with the 'belgic' style, and gaiters had arrived. The weapon of the day for the foot soldier remained the musket, either Brown Bess or the Indian Pattern: these were the mainstay of the infantry from 1720 until 1840.

Today a warrant for a new lodge would require somewhere in the region of 30 brethren. In 1810 this was not the case, as a warrant was granted with just four members, the Regimental Sergeant Major, Quarter-Master Sergeant, and two other sergeants. The record of this lodge starts with an exercise book with the details of the four founders and the agreement they entered into in order to establish the lodge plus details of the equipment purchased. On the cover of this book is a picture of Mr. Punch, pushing a wheelbarrow containing his wife on his wedding day! From the minute book of the lodge one can chart the progress of the regiment as it was posted to various parts of the country. The first recorded minutes state that the lodge met at the George Inn, Stratford, Essex. The members were in Essex, Middlesex, Hampshire, Devon and Ireland over a four-year period, continuing with their masonry, before being posted back to Cornwall. In those early days the lodge decided to send £1 for the relief of Cornish prisoners-of-war held by the French. The rate of pay for a private in any county militia at that time was only 1s. (5p) per day. They also held an emergency meeting of the lodge prior to embarking for their posting to Ireland to make arrangements for the masonic chest, which would have contained the jewels, Bible and warrant, etc. On their return to Bodmin they met in the old coaching house in the main street, the Queens Head, and continued there for some ten years before moving on to the Town Arms public house and eventually what are described as "masonic rooms". In those early days they had lecture nights for instruction and anyone being absent was fined.

In 1830 the lodge changed its name, became 'One and All', as it remains. The reason was that there were many men in the Bodmin area who wanted to become masons but as this was not possible due to the military nature of the lodge, (only military personnel being able to be initiated), the only way was for the warrant to become a civilian one. Once this decision had taken place on the 12th July 1830, civilians were now eligible to become members. The lodge has many items from its early days and in particular the Bible presented to the lodge by a Brother Major W. Bennett of the Royal Cornwall Militia on the 24th March 1810. This beautiful item is always on display in the temple, kept in a glass case next to the secretary's desk, and used only for initiations and the installation of the W.M.

These three lodges were formed during a very turbulent period in the history of our country, a time of war, of death and destruction on a grand scale. Yet out of the midst of all this came numerous lodges, some of which remain in our province. A debt of gratitude is owed to those early military masons who had the foresight to establish their lodges in often difficult circumstances. If they had not persevered our three military lodges and subsequent daughter lodges might not be here today.

W.Bro. John Cornish

A TREASURE TROVE

Over 15 years of dedicated work has brought the development of the Museum at Hayle. With the encouragement of the Provincial Grand Master and his predecessor, and the support of many members, the collection has grown to almost crowd the room in a building in the heart of a once bustling industrial and maritime town, and formerly the original White Hart Hotel. Photographs or engravings of almost every one of the 13 Provincial Grand Masters during 250 years cover part of one wall. Glass cases contain jewels from every corner of Cornwall. Souvenirs, memorabilia and illustrations tell of historic moments in Provincial history and remind us of some of the truly great Freemasons of the past.

The founder, W.Bro. Henry Mitchell P.J.G.D., who served for many years as Cornubian Lodge secretary, and then as Provincial Secretary (1978-88), explained: "When I was Provincial Secretary, moving around the different provinces, I realised we were one of the few without its own museum. So I endeavoured to

A corner of the Museum at Hayle.

A Treasure Trove

get one started. Everyone was keen on it, but the main stumbling block was a suitable site. I had quite a collection of my own, of jewels and artefacts, and asked the management committee here at Hayle if they could help. At this time a room, formerly part of the Tyler's flat, was almost filled by a pool table. This was offered and accepted - and the museum was opened by the then Provincial Grand Master, the Hon. Robert Eliot, on 7 September 1989.

"He named it 'The Henry Mitchell Museum': that was quite a shock and an honour for me. I have been its Curator from the word go, spending the first couple of years putting it all together. Lodge members helped with the decorating and the ladies committee with the carpeting. It was surprising that once it was opened, as it is on most lodge nights, with visitors coming in, the collection started to build up. It is still growing, although we are getting a little short of space now." The museum's nucleus came from Cornubian Lodge No. 450 which includes the old firing glasses engraved with its former No. 659 (the Lodges were renumbered in 1863). There are jewels once worn by former members, presentation pieces of members celebrating 50 years membership, and many other exhibits, including one of the earliest Cornubian Grand Lodge Certificates recording that Bro. Samuel Shepherd Noell, a Mine Agent of Gwinear, was initiated on 25 January 1850. He made no further progress and the explanation of this remains a mystery. The lodge celebrated its 150th anniversary in 1998.

The most treasured exhibit is a unique minute book covering three lodges and a century of masonic history. The first section covers The Ship Lodge of St. Ives (1765-85), of which the celebrated John Knill, whose Steeple stands above the town, was Master several times. When that lodge ceased, the furniture and effects were stored until some 25 years later when it was bought for £8 by the True Friendship Lodge (1815-1828) which was formed at Crowan. Bro. Mitchell explained "As writing books were quite expensive in those days, the secretary of the new lodge simply missed a couple of pages and commenced his own minutes". This happened again some 30 years after True Friendship was erased, when Cornubian Lodge was consecrated in 1848.

"The lodge was warranted in 1838 but owing to a number of the petitioners that included seafaring men and employees of the Harvey Foundry having, by nature of their calling left the district, it was another ten years before the consecration took place. Cornubian then came into possession of the furniture and effects which included the minute book. Once again two blank pages were left and the minutes of Cornubian Lodge commenced." In the minutes of the fourth meeting it records that a resolution was passed to pay Mrs Pool, landlady of the St Michael's Inn, Crowan Churchtown, the sum of £6 for the storage of the furniture. The Cornubian minutes continued in the same book for its first 11 years! Other relics from the Ship Lodge included several silver officers' collar jewels made by Thomas Harper, a silversmith trading in Fleet Street, London. His masonic jewels are much sought after. Harper was also a prominent Freemason and as Deputy Grand Master was one of the signatories of the Articles of Union, the document that brought the two Grand Lodges together in 1813. By permission of the Provincial Grand Master there is also on show the Provincial Sword of State as well as the Provincial Banners, Consecrating Vessels and Ivory Gavels, which has prompted many brethren to regard it as the Provincial Museum. The display of valuable and interesting exhibits continues to grow to preserve the heritage of Cornish, English and Worldwide Freemasonry.

THOUSANDS ATTEND THE CARN BREA OBELISK CEREMONY

That dominating obelisk on Carn Brea is Cornwall's memorial to Lord De Dunstanville. Its foundation stone was laid with full Masonic Honours on Monday 27 June 1836. It was a great occasion, thousands of people assembling on the hill. All the shops in Redruth were closed. Lord De Dunstanville was the best-known of the Bassets of Tehidy, near Camborne, and the monument was erected the year after his death. He had died in London and his body had been brought to Cornwall in a procession which took twelve days to reach Tehidy: there were 20,000 people present at the funeral.

As Sir Francis Basset, Bt. a freemason, he had presented a Sword of State to Provincial Grand Lodge in 1794, which is still in use. His Baronetcy had been the reward for his zeal in marching to Plymouth to meet a threat by the combined French and Spanish fleet. The Miners Militia made a notable contribution to the defences, and he is remembered for his work for miners' welfare. He succeeded his father in representing Penryn in Parliament and his Barony came from Prime Minister Pitt 16 years after becoming an M.P. Due to poor health, the Provincial Grand Master, Sir John St. Aubyn, was unable to travel to Cornwall for the foundation-stone laying and this ceremony was led by his Deputy, Philip Vyvyan Robinson. An inscription on vellum was placed in a cavity of the lower stone, enclosed in a bottle, with coins, to mark "the virtues of Francis, Baron De Dunstanville, of Tehidy Park, and Baron Basset of Stratton." The design of the column is an octagonal shaft, surmounted by an old Roman cross, 95-ft high. The Carn Brea rock was said to have been used by the Druids as an altar of sacrifice.

PROCESSION

Some ten to twelve hundred miners from North and South Roskear arrived in procession, preceded by the Captains and Agents of these mines. "Every rock, every elevation from which a glimpse of the ceremony could be obtained, was covered with people," wrote an eyewitness. The lodge was opened at Andrew's Hotel in Redruth and about noon the procession moved off, headed by a band, with Masons in full regalia and headed by the Tyler with drawn Sword, and the banner of the Provincial Grand Lodge. The architect and builder were in the Provincial parade, with the officers, and among the items carried and used were a Cornucopia with corn, the St. Aubyn Vase containing wine, a goblet with oil, a plumb rule, level, square and Doric and Ionic lights. Ahead of the Captains and Agents of the Cornish mines was the Standard of King William IV, Patron of the Order.

Carn Brea Obelisk

The Monument on Carn Brea

A contemporary report described the scene: "The procession proceeded to the Castle on Carn Brea and from thence along the brow of the hill to the spot where the ceremony was to take place, where it arrived about two o'clock. After it had halted, an avenue was formed through which the chairman of the committee and the Deputy P.G.M. passed, preceded by the Standard of the King, and Grand Sword Bearer, and followed by the Committee, P.G. Officers etc, to the situation appointed for them around the foundation stone. By this time there was not a spot of standing ground unoccupied on the hill: it was indeed 'a mountain of flesh' and considering that the sides of the hill as well as its spacious summit were crowded with people, we think we may safely say that at one time there were on the hill nearly thirty thousand persons; and with the handsome dresses of the ladies and their cheerful smiles, nothing could exceed the beauty and gaiety of the spectacle.

TRIBUTE

"So great a multitude have not assembled in Cornwall for centuries past: it was indeed an imposing scene; but its grandeur was increased tenfold by the fact that this immense concourse of people were not drawn together from idle curiosity, but they came to pay a tribute of respect to the memory of a great and good man, whose virtues had endeared him to all classes as a Nobleman, a Patriot, and a Christian Philanthropist, whose hand was ever ready to administer relief to the indigent and the distressed - who was at once the benefactor, the friend and adviser of the poor."

> 'On Earth how rare!
> On earth how lost!'

The Deputy P.G.M., explaining the ceremonies, which lay ahead, said: "Suffice it to say, they are fully and publicly known, as being symbolical and emblematical; combining morality with science, and characterising the early and actual operations of our Order, in the elevation of those venerable structures of antiquity which distinguish the various nations of the civilised world (hear, hear), many of which have stood the ravages of time, and the ruthless hand of violence, firm and unimpaired to the present day (cheers)". He read a letter from Sir John St. Aubyn which stated how much he lamented being absent from the ceremony "to the memory of my late friend and relative, whose eminent abilities have ever been exerted in promoting the prosperity of his country, in acts of benevolence towards his fellow creatures (cheers)". The position of the stone was proved by the square, level and plumb, and the Deputy P.G.M. and the chairman of the Building Committee Mr. John Samuel Enys, each gave it three knocks with the maul. The corn was strewn and the wine and oil poured on the stone.

The Prov. G. Chaplain said a consecration prayer, and the Prov.G. Secretary Bro. W.B. Ellis of Falmouth addressed the audience in "a powerful and eloquent speech" that further explained the ceremony, and spoke on the antiquity and nature of Freemasonry and the three fundamental principles on which the Order is founded, Brotherly Love, Relief and Truth, applying them to the character and conduct of "their late lamented brother, Lord De Dunstanville." He concluded by saying that "if no monument were erected to his memory, his fame would be pedestal enough; his excellencies were too well-known and appreciated to need a studied eulogy.

> 'Virtue alone outlives the Pyramids
> 'Her monuments shall last when Egypt's fall' (cheers).

There was also an eloquent oration of thanks by the Deputy P.G.M. for the opportunity of paying tribute to a "Nobleman and a Brother, whose name, from the prince to the peasant, is alike revered; and whose virtues thousands at this moment will join me to acknowledge and proclaim" (loud cheers). The speech was ended with a magnificent peroration of praise to the qualities of his Lordship, and after all had left Carn Brea the day ended with a dinner (starting at 4pm) at Andrew's Hotel, and "a very splendid exhibition of fireworks, given by subscription, in the street at Redruth."

Freemasons throughout Cornwall have given many gifts to the First Air Ambulance Service Trust in the county over the years. On this occasion a cheque - the result of a collection at the provincial annual meeting at Newquay in 2000 - was presented by the P.G.M., R.W.Bro. Nicholas Barrington to the Trust's operations manager Mr. Tony Hellyar. The ceremony, at the Camborne Lodge, came during a meeting of the provincial history committee: pictured from left to right, W.Bro. Revd Raymond Wood (P.A. G. Chaplain), Mr Hellyar, the P.G.M., W.Bro. William Watters, Chairman (P.J.G.D), and W.Bro. Douglas Williams, Editor (P.A.G.D.C).

A procession in Launceston in 1922. Some Masons in the district can still pinpoint the bank manager, the farmer, the builder, the coal and seed merchant. Top hats were worn by most in this procession through the town square - most of the shop fronts now bear new names.

WORLDWIDE MASONIC INTERESTS
OF A CORNISHMAN WHO IS
GRAND SECRETARY

Over the 250 years of the Province two Cornishmen have held office as Grand Secretary of the United Grand Lodge of England. The first was R.W. Bro. Sir Philip Colville Smith, appointed in 1917, who is the subject of a separate feature in this history. The current Grand Secretary is R.W.Bro. James Daniel, who succeeded R.W.Bro. Cdr. Michael Higham R.N., C.V.O., as Grand Secretary and Scribe E in June 1998. He has contributed this special article on his early years in his home town of St. Ives, his career in many parts of the world and also offers "eleven wishes" for the future of the Cornish Province.

MEMORIES

Although I was initiated in 1961 as a 19 year old undergraduate at Oxford (in Apollo University Lodge No. 357) it was in Cornwall that I first experienced the fellowship and further education that regular visits to other Lodges affords, and that I realised the relevance of Freemasonry to men from all walks of life and to the community of which they were a part.

I had no family links with Cornish Freemasonry, though I now believe that Captain John Warren of St.Ives (b.1851), a relative of my grandmother (Ada Daniel, nee Warren, of St.Ives - 1887 to 1969) was made a mason in Hong Kong in 1880s, and that my maternal grandfather (James Robb of Glasgow 1845 - 1904) became a mason in Middleburgh, South Africa. I was put in contact with freemasonry in my home town, St.Ives, by my old headmaster at the Board School in the Stennack, W.Bro. F.O. Adams (with whom I stayed in touch through occasional visits to Rotary Club lunches at his hotel, as a guest of my father James Warren Daniel); by W.Bro. Hollister (my father's solicitor), both stalwarts of Tregenna Lodge No. 1272; and by Charles Pearce of Trenwith Lodge, whose parents in Bedford Road I used to visit as a child on Sundays after morning service at Bedford Road Methodist Church. I joined Tregenna Lodge in 1966 (and resigned in 1980, being unable to attend regularly).

Of the 'characters' I met in Lodge at that time I remember particularly 'Lawyer' Perkin (Edwin Chellew Perkin, W. Master in 1955), a retired aero engine fitter, whom I had often seen walking from Victoria Square, just behind my parents' house 'The Friendship' on the Wharf, across the front to the Masonic Hall, wearing his large black hat and 'stripes' and carrying his regalia case. He soon told me of the importance of his masonic position in St.Ives (a Trustee of the Hall), in the Province (P.P.J.G.W.) and in the 'Mark' (Tregenna, P.G. Overseer 1969), about which I knew very little in those days. He was also in

Worldwide Masonic Interests

the Royal Arch St.Ia Chapter and Royal Ark Mariners. Then there was Billy Phillips, a haulage contractor, (W.Master in 1960 and later P.P.J.G.W.), who ran the Lodge of Instruction, and who gave me my first speaking part in Cornish Freemasonry - the explanation of some working tools - and I remember the embarrassment of having to be prompted. Billy died in 1979 but his Past Master's jewel was worn by W.Bro. Geoffrey Veal P.P.A.G.D.C., (W.M.1980 and 1996), who died in March 2001. And then there was the indefatigable 'Bill' Kent (W.M. in 1963 and P.P.J.G.W. in 1993), who knew the ritual backwards and who drove me all over Cornwall to visit other Lodges. He is the present Chaplain of Tregenna and senior P.M. As a builder, 'Bill' was in competition with my family's firm (J.H. Daniel Ltd.), but as a Mason he extended a warm hand of fellowship to a very young and inexperienced member of the Craft, and I am grateful to him.

One evening while I was visiting my parents in St.Ives from Oxford my father introduced me to a fellow senior County Councillor, with whom he was discussing finance and highways - Robert Eliot - whom I later discovered to be the Provincial Grand Master R.W. Bro. The Hon. Robert Eliot, and a fellow member of the Apollo University Lodge. I took a year off while at Oxford and spent it in the Rhineland, where, thanks to our then Grand Secretary, the late Sir James Stubbs, I was introduced to a lodge in Bonn belonging to the Grosse Landesloge, a Christian Grand Lodge under the (recently) United Grand Lodge of Germany, practising what I later realised was a version of the Swedish Rite of eleven degrees. The membership was small and advanced in years. The members were somewhat surprised to receive such a young Mason into their midst, but they made me very welcome. I remember being particularly impressed by the fact that in those days the more senior you were the simpler the regalia you wore. I also became a frequent visitor to 'Freimut und Wahrheit' Lodge in Cologne, and my familiarity with the Schroder ritual they used will help me to enjoy my honorary membership of Pilgrim Lodge No. 238 in London, the only German-speaking lodge in the English Constitution. (I am also now an honorary member of Tregenna Lodge and Trenwith Lodge, among others).

OVERSEAS

My first overseas postings with the British Council, to Kuwait, Berlin and Cambodia, provided few chances for any Masonic activity, though I remember visiting a lodge that met in Hitler's Olympic Stadium in Berlin (the seat of the British Military Government of Berlin, of which I was a junior member) whose membership appeared to be drawn exclusively from the intelligence, security and consular communities. Each time I came home on leave I visited my Oxford and Cornish Masonic roots, and in Oxford I gradually made my way up the ladder of office in the Royal Arch, Mark, Mariners, Knights Templar and 'Rose Croix' - though I could not progress any further in Apollo as residence within three miles of Carfax was a requirement I could no longer meet.

Worldwide Masonic Interests

However, a four year posting to Sri Lanka found me in a Masonic paradise: three Craft constitutions (English, Irish and Scots) working in amity, a K.T. Preceptory, a Rose Croix Chapter and, new to me, the Scottish Cryptic Degrees available through (life) membership of the Scottish Dalhousie Chapter. I joined three (E.C.) Craft Lodges (St.George No. 2170, Duke of Connaught No. 2940, and St. John's Lodge No. 454), and was installed as W.M.of St.George by Sri Kumaranayagam, now the District G.M. (E.C.) of Sri Lanka. Unfortunately I was posted to Munich in the middle of my Mastership, necessitating a round trip of several thousand miles to install my successor - and to learn that R.W.Bro. David Rockwood, the District Grand Master, had promoted me to Past District Grand Pursuivant, a badge which I wore proudly for the next 17 years. While in Munich I became W.M. of Friends in Council Lodge No. 1383, London, to which I had been introduced, while on sick-leave, by the Grand Secretary. I discovered from the lodge history that it had had close connections with the Supreme Council, the ruling body of the 'Rose Croix', but I had no idea then that I was to renew that relationship many years later. I also joined two then ailing R.A. Chapters: Marquis of Dalhousie No. 1159 and Avenue No. 3231, and in no time at all went through their various chairs.

SUPREME COUNCIL

In the 1980s my career took me via a period in Venezuela to our Embassy in Washington where, out of the blue, I received a phone call from Sir James Stubbs, to meet him in New York. There I learnt that the Supreme Council was looking for its next Grand Secretary General. The Supreme Council's interest in me came at an opportune moment. I had spent 25 years essentially on the move and overseas and I was already putting out feelers for a transfer to the Home Civil Service. I flew to London, was interviewed by the Supreme Council and was offered the job. I accepted, transferring in June 1989. This is not the place to record any details of my experience as Grand Secretary General of the Supreme Council. Suffice to say that my nine years at 10 Duke Street coincided with a period of unprecedented growth of that Order and included the Order's 150th anniversary. I found that the job demanded all the skills I had picked up as a diplomat, a manager and teacher. Looking back, I am surprised that I found time to write papers for and accept membership of Quatuor Coronati Lodge No. 2076, and to serve as W.M. of Westminster and Keystone Lodge No. 10 in its 275th year.

By late 1997 I was beginning to find more time for international work, and for further research which, I hoped, would prove valuable to my next major change of focus, a PhD. in Freemasonry and the Victorian period. All that changed when the Craft suddenly needed to find a successor to R.W.Bro. M.B.S. Higham as Grand Secretary and the lot fell on me. I took over as Grand Secretary and Scribe E on 1 June 1998, only the second Cornishman ever to occupy those posts. It is too early to comment on my work at Great Queen Street, but I know that without the experience I gained at 10 Duke Street (at home and abroad) and the friendship, support and advice of fellow Masons in the Craft and the other Orders I could not have survived my first year at Freemasons' Hall.

ELEVEN WISHES FOR CORNWALL

Congratulations to the Province of Cornwall on achieving its 250th anniversary! There can be very few organisations in Cornwall that have reached such an age and have given such service to the county over so many years. For the Province's next 250 years I have eleven wishes: may there be:

- A continuing flow of candidates who wish to share our Craft or 'mystery': the fellowship, the growth in self-knowledge, our traditions and history, and our service to the community.

- A few members in each Lodge who can dedicate enough time to maintain our traditions, uphold our standards, and educate each new member in his duties and assist him to develop his potential as a man and a Mason.

- Worshipful Masters who can lead and inspire their Lodges, and fully enjoy their year in the Chair.

- Sufficient Lodge Secretaries with a light but certain touch, who treasure and maintain the Lodge's history.

- Lodge Treasurers who keep the Lodge's finances in good order and who are not afraid to press late payers.

- Lodge Almoners who keep in close enough touch with members and dependants to know when they need the Lodge's assistance.

- Lodge Charity Stewards whose skill in raising money for charity is equalled by their ability to spot worthwhile causes.

- Provincial Officers and holders of Provincial Grand Rank who take to heart the fact that their seniority not only marks their service to date but also points out their continuing duty to the Craft, especially in the guidance of more junior members and in the promotion of the good name of Freemasonry throughout the county.

- Provincial Grand Masters who can truly be the Grand Master's lieutenants in the Province, leading Cornish Freemasonry from strength to strength, through good times and bad, never putting quantity before quality but living up to Cornwall's motto 'Onen hag Ol', (One and All).

- Wives and families who will appreciate their husbands/fathers' Freemasonry and feel its benefits.

- A Cornwall where thinking people will continue to value the traditional British rights of free association, privacy and tolerance, and who will judge Freemasonry not by the prejudices of the wilfully ignorant but by the lives and actions of Freemasons past and present whom they have known and who have been proud to declare that they are not only Freemasons but members of the Province of Cornwall, now looking forward to its tercentenary in 2052.

Worldwide Masonic Interests

*The Apron of the Provincial Grand Master
R.W.Bro. Nicholas Barrington*

Worldwide Masonic Interests

Grand Secretary R.W.Bro. James Daniel

Shortly before the end of the 2nd World War, in April 1945, Lodge Lyonesse No. 6014 was consecrated at a ceremony in St. John's Hall, Penzance. The consecrating officer was the PGM, the Earl of St. Germans (fourth from left), assisted by the Dep. PGM Canon H.R. Jennings (fourth from right) and provincial colleagues. Later W.Bro. W.J. Hosken (centre) was installed as the first Master.

THREAD OF GOLD

Chapter II

Provincial Grand Masters Down the Years

Cornwall and International Dates of Interest
During the Lives of our Provincial Grand Masters
1752 - 2002

It was a special day for many Freemasons when Bro. Archer Ormonde Binding AFC was invested as PPJGW of the Province of Somerset at the age of 103. His son, W.Bro. John Binding PPG Chaplain (pictured on the far right) was the founder-treasurer of St Enodoc Lodge No. 9226. Bro. Archie was invested with his provincial honour in 1991, the same year as he was proposed as honorary member of St. Enodoc. He flew airships during the 1st World War, when he was awarded the Air Force Cross, and was believed to be the oldest English Freemason when he died at 105. He is pictured here with members of St. Enodoc at his investiture ceremony in his nursing home: left to right, W.Bro. Raymond Wood, P.A.G. Chaplain, 3rd Master; Bro. Charles Matthews, Senior Deacon; W.Bro. Peter Grundy (Worshipful Master); Bro. Bill Terry, Master Elect, and Bro. Binding's son John.

In September 2000 the Grand Secretary, R.W.Bro. James W. Daniel returned to his home county to present the bi-centenary warrant to the Worshipful Master of True and Faithful Lodge, Helston, W.Bro. Gordon Dawson.

One of the many superb stained glass windows in the King Arthur's Hall at Tintagel: Arthur pulls the sword from the anvil on the stone.

Thread of Gold

THE FIRST THREE PROVINCIAL GRAND MASTERS
1752 -1785

It seems only natural that Falmouth, a thriving port with links throughout the United Kingdom and the world, should provide the stimulus and the venue for the 'Mother Lodge of Cornwall.' The historic Packet shipping line and the Post Office provided the leading personalities in the establishment of Love and Honour in 1751, and the first three P.G.Ms of Cornwall. Time and tide, wind and weather, played a significant part in the meetings and attendances at the King's Arms Tavern. One Packet Captain was initiated, passed and raised within a week "being about to go abroad." Another was initiated and raised "as he sails tomorrow" and yet another was initiated and passed because he was "only dependent upon the wind." During this period, in 1755, Isaac Head was appointed P.G.M. of the Isles of Scilly: at this time there was no lodge meeting on the islands. The following year Dolphin Lodge was warranted there, later to become Godolphin.

The Post Office Packets were carriers of the news as well as of the mails. The officers recorded details of any important events which occurred in the countries they visited. Their journals contained news, "later and more authentic" than any which had yet reached London. This was sent to London from Falmouth as soon as the Packets arrived. It is a bygone age of greatness: the year 2000 was the 150th anniversary of the last Postal Packet sailing from Falmouth. From Falmouth's importance, and its worldwide connections, grew Freemasonry in Cornwall.

The first Provincial Grand Master (1752-62) was W. Bro. William Pye, Collector of Customs at Falmouth, and nephew of the Archdeacon of Cornwall. Known as "Mr Collector Pye", he was born at Creed in 1685 and was the official in charge of the port, extending from the East of The Lizard to the West of the Dodman, from 1710 until his death. The Minutes of the Provincial Grand Lodge were kept in the books of the Mother Lodge, and the entry for 28 May in 1752 states: "This day the Rt. Hon. and R.W. Lord Carysfoot, our G.M.'s Deputation to our Bros. Wm. Pye Esq, appointing him P.G.M. for the County of Cornwall was read, and the thanks of the Lodge were ordered to be returned to the G.M. and the rest of the Grand Officers for the honour conferred on us."

He was the 15th P.G.M. appointed in England. It is probable that Cornwall was the first Prov. Grand Lodge to appoint Prov Officers. "If that is so then Cornwall can claim to have the Premier Provincial Grand Lodge of England," wrote a Cornish Masonic historian. Grand Lodge records that William Pye

Provincial Grand Masters Down the Years

was "Petitioner and first Master at the constitution of Love and Honour Lodge, now No 75" on 12 June 1751, was created the first P.G.M. of Cornwall the following year, and in December 1760 again elected Master of his Lodge. There have been three Custom Houses in Falmouth: Pye served in the first one which had been transferred from Penryn in the mid-17th century and used until 1785, another significant date in Packet and Masonic history. This was at Mulberry Square, on the seaward side at the bottom of High Street (now Mulberry Court), and was also his official residence.

In 1745 the Revd John Wesley visited the town, where he was attacked by a mob. William Pye smuggled him into his riverside home, from which Wesley 'escaped' by boat. Pye's selection as P.G.M. was clearly due to the respect in which he was held and his, and the family's, civic and religious tradition. His father, John Pye, was Mayor of Falmouth in 1720, an office William first held in 1742. He purchased the Advowson of Blisland (the right of presenting a priest to a benefice) in 1746. Much of this ancient church dates back to the 12th century. A Revd William Pye was Rector from 1780-1834, and another long-serving member of the family, the Revd Frances Woolcock Pye succeeded him 1834-92, together spanning over 110 years. They are buried in the churchyard at Blisland, and have their memorials there as have many members of the family, including their sons and daughters. At the death of the first Provincial Grand Master it was recorded: "The Collector of Customs died, having held that office 40 years, and behaved in general therein with candour to ye subject and justice to ye Crown." Grand Lodge tells us that P.G.M. William Pye "went abroad" in 1763 and the first Deputy P.G.M., W. Bro. George Bell, was offered the post. There is a little confusion over the precise dates and records of office at this time. The Premier Grand Lodge of England did not begin to keep membership registers until 1768, and prior to this date lodges did not have to send annual returns. Because of the differences in the records this history has relied on the information obtained from Grand Lodge. Previous histories have given a small variation on this version of the succession with Stephen Bell twice holding office. The record by Bro. E S Vincent in 1960 states that William Pye, then Mayor of Falmouth, took office as Provincial Grand Master in 1752 and retained this role for ten years.

He was succeeded by Stephen Bell who had acted as Deputy P.G.M. on the constitution of Love and Honour in 1751. He held office 1762-64. George Bell followed (1764-75), with Stephen Bell returning 1775-85. The Bell family, father Stephen and son George, held office until 1785 and were also in succession the Agents of the Packet Service. The Bells were described as descending from a family of "great antiquity" in the counties of Norfolk, Gloucestershire and Durham. W. Bro. George was an Entered Apprentice at the constitution of Love and Honour Lodge, a fellow craft and then Master Mason on the first night, 12 June 1751. He was married to Henrietta Banfield: his father-in-law was his predecessor as Packet Agent (1723-47). George served from 1747-75 to be succeeded by son Stephen: the appointment was in the family for over 60 years. George Bell was active in developing the Packet service, and considerable expansion followed to the developing Colonies with Stephen. In 1784 there were 17 ships sailing across the Atlantic in addition to the four to Lisbon, from Falmouth. Their destinations included Jamaica in the Caribbean, New York, and Halifax (Nova Scotia): these maritime provinces were also strategic ports in the international competition, particularly with France at this time. Although

Provincial Grand Masters Down the Years

This is known as a saw-pierced jewel, but is not one of the earliest, of which several can be seen in the Masonic Library and Museum at Great Queen Street, London, dating from 1723. This example from Camborne is dated approximately 1780.

It is a Past Master's breast jewel of that time, usually worn with two bars, after six months or more. At that time Masters sometimes held office for four or more periods of six months.

In the centre of the jewel is the past master's emblem of those days.

All the emblems on the jewel relate to the Craft and are in use today, with the exception of the Hourglass and Trowel. The latter was one of the earliest working tools, cementing the bonds of friendship, but was later discarded, The Hourglass was referred to in some of the old lectures but, like the Trowel, was afterwards discontinued.

P.G.M. George Bell never served as Mayor, his son-in-law James Tippett was a lawyer and Falmouth Town Clerk.

Twelve days after becoming a Master Mason he was elected first Treasurer of the lodge, and on 11 June the following year, 1752, appointed first Deputy P.G.M.. Exactly a year later he was nominated Provincial Grand Treasurer, and on 13 June 1754 elected Master of Love and Honour.

The offer of the post of Provincial Grand Master came on 8 September 1763 "William Pye being absent from England." The Master and Wardens were deputed to "wait on him" to fix the date of Installation which was on 31 January 1764. However Grand Lodge records that five years later P.G.M. George owed "25 quarters" (ten pounds) which grew to £11.5s. (30 quarters) in June 1771. Grand Lodge has a gap in the Minutes from September of that year until April 1780. It was in 1775, on the death of his father, that his son, the Deputy P.G.M., Stephen Bell succeded to the leadership of the Province. He had been initiated into Love and Honour in May 1762, aged 20, the same year as his marriage and his appointment as Secretary. He completed the year on 30 December by being elected Master of the lodge. W.Bro. Stephen was Master again in 1763, 1765 and 1767, and was appointed to "wait on George Bell when he was offered P.G.M." in 1763, himself being appointed Deputy six years later. He was Mayor of Falmouth in 1768: records show there was difficulty in obtaining officials. Four were elected Burgesses and "Mr S Bell was chosen as Mayor, whether he would or no."

An Old Past Master's Jewel

On the death of his father in 1775 Stephen became the third Provincial Grand Master of the province, continuing to 1785, the year of his own tragic death. He was appointed Packet Agent, also in succession. A letter was written on his behalf, in 1775, asking for "succession to his father's post, who being old and gouty is anxious to resign in favour of his son." The appointment was his the following year and continued until his suicide. A famed diarist, who visited Stephen in 1782 wrote that Mr Bell "invited us to spend the following day with him, where we were handsomely entertained with music and dancing." His son, George junior fought in the Royal Navy under Captain Pellow of Penzance (later Lord Exmouth). Many members of his family were Packet Captains: he married the daughter (Frances Lovell) of one, Captain Thomas Lovell. Their son, Stephen Banfield junior became a Packet Captain and a grandson was given the literary maritime name of Tristram Shandy.

There is today a Bell's Court in Falmouth where the Cornwall Maritime Museum is located. The family lived in the Court, very close to the former post office which is now called Post Office Yard. When Sir John St Aubyn was appointed in 1785, to succeed the late Stephen Bell, there were six lodges in the province. He was the first Provincial Grand Master who was not a member of Love and Honour. A new era had begun.

CORNWALL

1751	First Masonic Lodge formed in Cornwall - Love and Honour, Falmouth.
1752	Founding of Masonic Province of Cornwall
1754	Captain William Bligh, of H.M.S. Bounty, born at St. Tudy.
1755	William Cookworthy finds china clay at Tregonning Hill, near Helston.
1758	Cornish Copper Company sets up smelter at Ventonleague, Hayle.
1771	Engineer Richard Trevithick born at Tregajorran, Illogan.
1772	Henry Trengrouse of Helston, inventor of the rocket apparatus for sea rescue, inspired to carry out his work. (Anson wrecked at Loe Bar in 1807).
1777	Engineer James Watt comes to Cornwall and builds new steam pumping engines.
1777	Fishwife Dolly Pentreath of Mousehole, last person to speak the Cornish language as native tongue, dies.
1778	Sir Humphry Davy, inventor of miners safety lamp, born at Penzance.
1782	Artist John Opie of St Agnes leaves for London.

INTERNATIONAL

1752	Georgian calendar adopted in Britain.
1756	Black hole of Calcutta.
1757	William Blake born in London.
1758	Horatio Nelson born at Burnham.
1759	Composer G. F. Handel dies aged 74. Robert Burns born in Ayrshire.
1762	Tsar Peter assassinated.
1768	Royal Academy founded.
1769	Napoleon Bonaparte born in Sicily.
1771	Sir Walter Scott born in Edinburgh.
1773	Boston tea party.
1775	American War of Independence begins.
1780	First Derby run at Epsom.
1781	British, under Lord Cornwallis, surrender to General Washington at Yorktown.
1783	William Pitt the Younger, becomes Britain's youngest Prime Minister aged 24.

Provincial Grand Masters Down the Years

Views of Falmouth in the Old Days

Packet Captains and other members of Love & Honour, the first Lodge in Cornwall (1751), the same year the Lizard Light was completed, must have been aware of the impending arrival in their home town of one of the world's most respected freemasons, Benjamin Franklin, as his baggage was on a packet which left weeks before he eventually sailed from New York. Unfortunately, it appears he did not stay to enjoy the friendship undoubtedly awaiting him, as, having being so delayed, he set off immediately for London.

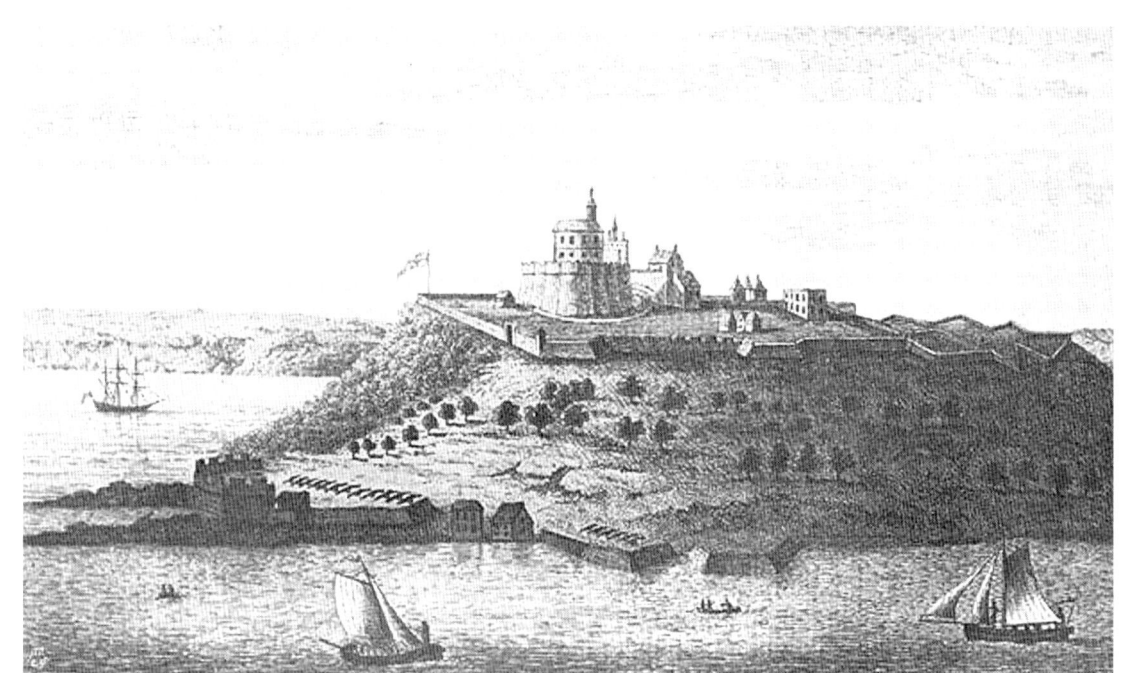

Provincial masons with lodge members at St. Austell - an undated photograph.

Thread of Gold

4th PROVINCIAL GRAND MASTER
1785 -1839
SIR JOHN ST AUBYN Bt.

Sir John St. Aubyn, the fifth Baronet, his great grandson Lord St. Levan, and his Lordship's father-in-law the Earl of Mount Edgcumbe between them held the office of Provincial Grand Master for a total of nearly 120 years. This was a record of distinguished service, in many and varying aspects of public life, with outstanding contributions. The greatly loved and generous Baronet was an active Masonic leader: he held office for 54 years (1785-1839), and no P.G.M. in Cornwall has longer service to his credit. Sir John succeeded R.W. Bro. Stephen Bell, and among his many gifts to the Province was a set of jewels (1794), that are still in use by the Provincial Senior and Junior Wardens. A Masonic jewel, inscribed 'Sir John St. Aubyn Bart, S.G.W. 1781' is in the possession of the present Lord St. Levan.

The colourful Sir John was installed as fourth Provincial Grand Master at Love and Honour, Falmouth by its W.M. but was the first not to be a member of it, and never joined this lodge. He reigned until his death at the age of 82, and was a member of 'True Friendship' Crowan, and the Lodge at Somerset House. Sir John (Past S.G.W.) may well have been one of the founders of United Grand Lodge. The funeral procession from Putney, London, in August 1839, to the Clowance ancestral vault 11 days later, is possibly the most magnificent in Cornish history, displaying the enormous affection in which he was held. A hearse, drawn by six horses, with seven mourning coaches all dressed with feathers and velvet, together with footmen, porters, 'two mutes' and coachmen, were in the procession which left Putney. At Devonport the civic leaders attended, shops were closed, and the tolling bells of churches and chapels as the 30,000 or more assembled in the streets, demonstrated "that a great man was passing to his grave." At Clowance the body lay in state, attended by 12 boys and 12 girls from the Free School, eight poor men, eight male and seven female servants, and 12 poor widows. There were 20-30,000 spectators at the funeral on 29 August, and through this multitude the procession made its way, including 100 Freemasons, carrying their Banner, Sword of State, a Bible on a black cushion, and the P.G.M.'s Jewel.

During his term as Provincial Grand Master he presented an address in 1793 from the Cornish Freemasons to the Grand Master, The Prince of Wales; became the Second Grand Superintendent of Royal Arch Masonry and saw the foundation stone of the Lander Monument laid with Masonic Honours at Truro (1835). Provincial Grand Lodge was held at the family seat of Clowance Park to celebrate his Golden Jubilee as P.G.M.. The 'St. Aubyn Vase' was used during the installation of his successor, Sir Charles Lemon Bt. M.P., F.R.S. In 1845 Lady St. Aubyn presented a portrait of her husband which hangs in the Temple of Love and Honour.

Sir John, who had succeeded to the Baronetcy when he was 14, was an extravagant man. He had numerous children who were all illegitimate: he was married by his brother-in-law the Revd John Molesworth, to Juliana Vinicombe, in 1822 at Holborn when all their children were grown up. Sir John was High Sheriff of Cornwall at the age of 23 and later was M.P. for Penryn and Helston (1807-12) and a Fellow of the Royal Society. He was a patron of the arts, in particular the Cornish painter John Opie, and had a large collection of engravings and etchings. On his death in 1839 the baronetcy lapsed, but was revived in favour of Sir Edward St. Aubyn (his seventh son and fourth of Juliana) in 1866. Sir Edward's son, again a Sir John and an M.P. from 1858-87, was created the first Lord St. Levan.

CORNWALL

1789   John Wesley makes last of his 32 visits to Cornwall.
1792   William Murdoch lights a Redruth home by coal gas.
1793   Sir Goldsworthy Gurney - a pioneer of steam power in road and rail locomotion - born at Treator, near Padstow.
Cornwall Agricultural Association formed, later to become Royal Cornwall Show.
1794   Billy Bray of Gwennap, preacher and chapel builder, born at Twelveheads, between Truro and Falmouth.
1799   John Harvey establishes Harvey's of Hayle.

INTERNATIONAL

1788   Andrew Meikle designs a threshing machine.
1789   Mutiny on H.M.S. Bounty.
George Washington becomes first American President.
Outbreak of French revolution.
1791   John Wesley, founder of Methodism, dies aged 87.
1796   Edward Jenner proves smallpox vaccination theory.
1797   Sailors mutiny at Spithead.
1798   Nelson's victory at Battle of the Nile.
1799   Income Tax introduced.
1801   Act of Union of Great Britain and Ireland.

Provincial Grand Masters Down the Years

Cornwall Continued

1800	Chartist and social reformer William Lovett born at Newlyn.
1801	Trevithick's first road locomotive tried out - 'Going up Camborne Hill' - on Christmas Eve. First John Knill Steeple ceremony at St. Ives.
1802	John Abbot M.P. for Helston becomes first Cornish Member to be Speaker of House of Commons.
1812	Maria Branwell of Penzance leaves for Yorkshire and marries Revd Patrick Bronte. She was mother of authors Emily, Anne and Charlotte.
1814	History of railway in Cornwall begins with first 'train road' between Portreath and Poldice mine.
1815	Sir Humphry Davy invents safety lamp.
1816	Lord Exmouth, Cornish-bred, releases captive slaves by bombarding Algiers from his Fleet.
1825	Philanthropist John Passmore Edwards - who provided 70 public buildings - born at Blackwater, near Truro. (See feature article).
1831	William Bickford of Tuckingmill, patents the miners safety fuse for blasting.
1834	Thirty million pilchards caught at St. Ives in one hour by seine nets. Explorer Richard Lander dies in Africa, aged 30. (See feature article).
1836	Obelisk to Lord de Dunstanville erected at Carn Brea (see feature).

International Continued

1805	Victory at Battle of Trafalgar, but Nelson dies.
1812	Start of Luddite riots. Prime Minister Spencer Percival assassinated
1814	George Stephenson builds his first steam locomotive. Napoleon abdicates.
1815	Corn Laws introduced, prohibiting imports of foreign grain. Napoleon escapes from Elba: French defeated at Waterloo.
1819	Peterloo massacre at Manchester.
1820	Anne Bronte born in Yorkshire, Florence Nightingale born in Florence.
1821	John Keats dies in Rome, aged 25.
1822	Percy Bysshe Shelley drowns off Leghorn, Italy.
1824	Lord Byron dies at Missolonghi.
1829	William Booth, founder of the Salvation Army, born at Nottingham.
1834	Tolpuddle Martyrs. Abolition of slavery in all British possessions.
1837	William IV dies at Windsor: succeeded by Queen Victoria.

5th PROVINCIAL GRAND MASTER
1844-1863
SIR CHARLES LEMON, Bt.

For more than 30 years Sir Charles Lemon, Bt., of Carclew was an M.P., first for Penryn in 1809 when he was 25 at the stirring times of the great movement for reform in Parliament. There were 20 boroughs in the county, 18 of them nomination boroughs, some of them little more than villages. Mitchell, a few miles from Truro, sent two Members by six electors. Intense interest in reform built up in Cornwall, and at the election of 1831, a year before the passing of the Reform Bill, Sir Charles, in his address avowed himself "a candidate zealously interested in the cause of reform, but a man of no Party."

He was described later as a reformer but rather one of the more moderate Whig School and a man "who had inherited the liberal principles of his father as well as his fortune," which had been developed through the mining and commercial ventures of his ancestors.

He was the third and only surviving son of Sir William Lemon M.P. for Penryn and then of the county, serving for 50 years and becoming father of the House of Commons. He died in office in 1824. Sir Charles represented Penryn, first from 1812, again in 1830, was MP for Cornwall in 1831, and after the

Provincial Grand Masters Down the Years

Reform Bill, when the county's representation was changed to two divisions, represented West Cornwall 1832-41 and 1842-57. He was also a Deputy Lieutenant of Cornwall, Deputy Warden of the Stannaries, president of the Royal Cornwall Polytechnic Society and of the Royal Cornwall Geological Society. As a Fellow of the Royal Society and member of other learned groups, he was deeply interested in the researches and advancement of science and the arts.

The second baronet, Sir Charles was born in 1784, married in 1810 and succeeded to the title in 1824. Sadly his 13 year-old son and last remaining child, drowned while bathing when at Harrow School in 1826, the same year in which his wife (daughter of the Earl of Ilchester) died. Their daughter had previously died in Italy. He became the 5th Provincial Grand Master of the Province in 1844, when the 'St Aubyn Vase' was used at the installation. Five years had passed since the death of P.G.M., Sir John St. Aubyn and this was described as "a period of utmost difficulty in the province."

It was a most interesting situation, for with the death of the P.G.M. the province became dormant until a successor was appointed by the Grand Master. Between 1839-43 there were three Grand Masters! In a previous record of Cornish Freemasonry (Bro. E.S. Vincent 1960) it was explained: "The Cornish Brethren, tired of waiting, set about endeavouring to find a P.G.M. on their own initiative. They submitted an invitation, which was accepted, to Sir Charles Lemon of Carclew. "At the time of his acceptance he was not a mason. He was made a Mason at Love and Honour, Falmouth in 1840 and appointed Warden in 1842. In 1843 he was duly elected Master of the lodge."

He was duly installed as Provincial Grand Master at Falmouth by Bro. John Ellis (who had been acting as Secretary) in April 1844. Significantly, perhaps, the first new Lodge formed just prior to his installation was Peace and Harmony, No. 496, at St. Austell. Eight new Lodges were formed before his resignation in 1863. Five years later there were 65 carriages in the funeral procession for Sir Charles, in February 1868, in the four miles from Carclew to Mylor Church. The coffin was placed in the Carclew aisle alongside the remains of his wife Lady Charlotte. "In private life his genial temperament won for him the affection and esteem of a large circle of friends." He had offered to establish a Mining School for Cornwall, and this was opened in 1839 at Truro. "His goodness of heart and genial disposition won for him the esteem and affection of a large circle: it was said that he had the happy art of his excellent father in being able to conciliate all men. When no longer able to give personal aid, he rendered assistance by his purse to charitable and scientific institutions, and to good works generally."

CORNWALL

1846   Queen Victoria and Prince Albert visit St. Michael's Mount.

1851   Newlyn fishwife Mary Kelynack walks to London to see the Great Exhibition

and meets Queen Victoria and Lord Mayor.

1852   Steam Packet Amazon, largest steam-driven vessel built in England, lost by fire

off Isles of Scilly on maiden voyage: 115 of 161 lost their lives.

1854   The 33-ft. lugger Mystery makes longest voyage by small craft: from Newlyn to Melbourne, Australia in 116 days.

1856   Cornwall's first V.C., Joseph Trewavas, born at Mousehole.

Hydraulic jacks of Tangye Bros. Cornwall, launch Great Eastern, the largest vessel in the world, on The Thames.

1859   Brunel rail bridge built over the Tamar.

INTERNATIONAL

1844   Potato famine in Ireland.

1850   Alfred Lord Tennyson appointed Poet Laureate (until death in 1892).

1854   Charge of the Light Brigade at Battle of Balaclava.

1855   David Livingstone discovers Victoria Falls.

1856   Victoria Cross instituted.

1857   Relief of Lucknow.

1859   Isambard Kingdom Brunel dies.

Provincial Grand Masters Down the Years

6th PROVINCIAL GRAND MASTER
1863-1872
AUGUSTUS SMITH

When R.W.Bro. Augustus Smith died in 1872 it was understood that a lofty monument would be erected - after his own design on his grave at St. Buryan to be visible from his home at Tresco Abbey, Isles of Scilly. It was said he had sketched the design of an obelisk that would be a landmark to mariners, as with de Dunstanville at Carn Brea and John Knill at St. Ives, if it was approved. This was not to be. A prominent yet modest stone marks the final resting place. The funeral was an unusual and unexpected finale for a remarkable man who had led the Province for nine years, following the resignation of Sir Charles Lemon. The Provincial Grand Master's body had been brought by train from Plymouth, where he had died. A writer commented at the time: "If anyone had whispered ten days since to the masonic body, and the Scillonians, that their head and chief would pass a portion of his last long sleep in a coach-house in New Street, Penzance, they would have deemed the soothsayer mad. Such, however, was the case. Mount Sinai Lodge would gladly have given fit and honourable rest to the Grand Master within its portals. But the deceased had been so specific that, had he willed this, it would have been plainly set forth."

He had earlier selected an elevated triangular spot in the little churchyard of Old Town, St. Mary's, where Prime Minister Harold Wilson (later Lord Wilson) was buried in June 1995. The Provincial Grand Master aged 68, took cold on his way from London to St. Austell to attend the Provincial meeting (he was unable to do this), then went to Plymouth to be near his doctors after discussing Masonic appointments and business. He died at the Duke of Cornwall Hotel. He had been a giant of a personality, 'Lord Proprietor' of the Islands, and an M.P. for Truro. On the islands he carried out permanent and important changes after becoming lessee under the Duchy of Cornwall in 1834. Two years earlier he was initiated in the Watford Lodge where he became Master. He spent some time in Ireland where he became Master of a Lodge, and came to the Isles of Scilly as Governor. Shortly after he became Master of Godolphin Lodge, St. Mary's. In 1853 he became a member of Phoenix, Truro, being installed Master in 1857. He was "the inspiration of the building of the Public Rooms at Truro."

His first appearance at Provincial Grand Lodge came in 1854 at Callington when he became Prov.S.G.W: he was installed as Deputy Provincial Grand Master at Helston two years later. He presided over six annual meetings of the Craft until the resignation of Sir Charles in 1863, when he was installed at Truro "in the presence of the largest number of Brethren ever assembled together in the Province." During his reign nine new lodges were consecrated. The Provincial Grand Master was a zealous and efficient Mason, particularly in the charities, and was president at the 67th anniversary of the Royal Masonic Institution for Boys. Each annual festival became still more successful than its predecessor. He helped establish a county fund for aged and infirm Freemasons in the Province. This began as the Cornwall Masonic Annuity Fund, was later extended to educational grants and annuities for widows etc, and since 1978 has merged into the Cornwall Masonic Benevolent Fund.

His term ended with several more new Lodges in the Province, and a total of over 900 members. In 1869 Love and Honour became the first Lodge in the Province to receive the Centenary Warrant. During his long association with the Scillies, Augustus Smith made many improvements, completing the church begun by William IV, building a new pier, rebuilding farmhouses, and establishing schools and introducing compulsory education. He chose Tresco island for his home, built a mansion known as The Abbey, and planted magnificent gardens, today one of the treasures of Britain. Born in 1804 in Herts (his grandfather was Receiver General of Customs) he was educated at Harrow and Christ Church, Oxford. A magistrate for Hertfordshire, Buckinghamshire and Cornwall, and a Deputy Lieutenant for Hertfordshire, he was a member of an old-established banking family. He was Liberal M.P. for Truro 1857-1865, he also served as president of the Royal Geological Society of Cornwall 1854-64 and president of the Royal Institution of Cornwall, 1863-65. "Whether in aid of charity, the promotion of science, or other objects for the welfare of the county, Augustus Smith was always found a liberal and hearty supporter."

November 1991 brought the Consecration of one of the youngest lodges in the province, the Greystone Border Lodge No. 9449. The PGM, R.W.Bro. the Hon. Robert Eliot performed the ceremony and the Deputy PGM, V.W.Bro. Sidney Pearce officiated at the installation which followed. The first WM was W. Bro. John Parnall

May 1987 brought the Centenary Festival meeting of Cotehele Lodge No. 2166 of Calstock, with provincial leaders and officers of the lodge led by W.Bro. Rob Rawlings. This was the first meeting as secretary of W.Bro. Dennis Jennings, second from left seated, who succeeded W.Bro. Bill Jane, second from right. Bro. Jane was secretary for 34 years and served for 25 years as charity steward. He died, aged 86, in 1996.

A bible, and two gavels, of One and All Lodge at Bodmin. Each has a story to tell. Published by the Clarendon Press (Oxford) in 1808, the Bible was presented to the lodge by Bro. W. Bennet, a Major in the Royal Cornwall Militia, on 24th March 1810.

A visitor to the lodge from London, some years ago, drew attention to the fact that it was valuable and known as the 'Lovejoy Bible'. It is now kept in a glass display case, paid for from a legacy from the estate of Bro. G. Hamley, and is now used only for initiation and installation ceremonies.

The gavel on the right was presented to the lodge by W. Bro. W.H. Sweet PM, PDGS Deacon, Bengal, in 1928.

On the 24th July 1857, Sir Henry Lawrence K.C.B., was mortally wounded by a cannon ball. This gavel is made from wood of the door of the room in which he sat at the time. It now hangs on the front of the Master's pedestal in the lodge.

Sir Henry, from Bodmin was appointed Commissioner and set up office in the residency at Lucknow in late 1856, following his success in stabilising the Punjab after Sikh wars. He died early in the defence of Lucknow.

The gavel on the left was presented by the Royal Solomon Lodge, Jerusalem, in 1900, to Bro. J.R. Collins, and by him to the One and All Lodge. It also hangs on the front of the Master's pedestal.

Thread of Gold

Provincial Grand Masters Down the Years

CORNWALL

1866   The 'Cornish Nightingale' Fanny Moody born at Redruth.

1867   First broad gauge passenger train from Paddington to Penzance.

1871   First consignment of flowers sent to Covent Garden market from Isles of Scilly.

INTERNATIONAL

1866   Dr. Barnardo opens his first Children's Home.

1867   Nobel produces dynamite.

1871   Trade Unions given full legal recognition.

1872   Voting by secret ballot introduced in Britain.

The 150th anniversary celebration of the St. Martin's Lodge, Liskeard, in March 1995. The P.G.M., R.W.Bro. Nicholas Barrington and his provincial officers are pictured with the W.M., W.Bro. W. W. Nicholas, lodge officers, members and guests.

Thread of Gold

7th PROVINCIAL GRAND MASTER
1873-1917
THE EARL OF MOUNT EDGCUMBE
G. C. V. O. (Deputy Grand Master 1891-96)

No Cornish Provincial Grand Master played such a full and dominating role in the life of his county as the Earl of Mount Edgcumbe, who died aged 84 in 1917. The Earl led the province for more than a generation and was held in affection as well as great admiration. "He was no mere figurehead: he was a living force and few worked harder for, or took more interest in, masonic affairs." Under his guidance the province increased in prosperity and influence. "The Earl was a fine type of the cultured country gentleman, never happier than when among his tenants, administering his extensive estates or superintending the affairs of the Duchy."

He was installed as the seventh Provincial Grand Master in 1873, following the death of R.W.Bro. Augustus Smith, and was appointed Deputy Grand Master of England in April 1891, representing H.R.H. The Prince of Wales (Grand Master), later King Edward VII, on several masonic occasions. The Earl resigned as Deputy G.M. in 1898, and the highlights during his years in office were as chairman of the Jubilee Festival of the Royal Masonic Benevolent Institution at the Theatre Royal, Covent Garden in 1892, and presiding at the annual festival of the Royal Masonic Institution for Girls in 1895. On this latter occasion his province subscribed 700 guineas towards the £16,000 raised, and united with Devon in the joint reception of H.R.H. The Prince of Wales as Grand Master at the opening of the Guildhall, Plymouth.

The centenary festival of The Cornish Lodge No. 2369, London in 1990 with guests and officers at the Cafe Royal in Regent Street including the PGM R.W. Bro. the Hon Robert Eliot and the W. Master W. Bro D.J. Windows

Provincial Grand Masters Down the Years

The Earl was initiated in London in 1856 and joined Sincerity Lodge, East Stonehouse, Plymouth, the following year, being appointed Provincial Grand Warden of Devonshire in 1858 when he also became W.M. of his lodge. Perhaps the greatest day in Cornish Freemasonry came when he presided at the Especial Grand Lodge in May 1880 when the Prince laid the foundation stone of Truro Cathedral. His Lordship was chairman of the Cathedral Committee and also Lord Lieutenant of Cornwall at the time (see special feature on the Cathedral ceremony in this history). He was also present in 1903 for the Benediction of the Nave in the presence of the Prince and Princess of Wales. Among other important ceremonies he performed in the Province were the laying of the corner-stone of the Church of All Saints, Millbrook (1893) and the laying of the foundation stone of the Cottage Hospital at Liskeard, given by Bro. Passmore Edwards (1895), both in Masonic form. Many new Craft lodges were warranted during his regime, and new masonic halls opened at Wadebridge, Falmouth, Camborne, St. Austell, Calstock, St. Germans, Redruth, Bodmin, Penryn, Penzance and St. Ives.

The Cornwall Masonic Charity Association was formed under his presidency 1885. His connection with Freemasonry was confined to the Craft and to the Holy Royal Arch. He was for a long period the longest-serving Provincial Grand Master and Grand Superintendent under the constitution. Several new Chapters were formed during his period in office.

"Few noblemen stood more in the good graces of Queen Victoria....he was essentially one of those men whom the Sovereign delighted to honour." The Earl was a favourite at Court, chosen as a companion of the Prince of Wales when a young man, appointed an Extra Lord of the Bedchamber, and accompanied the Prince on foreign travels. He was Lord Chamberlain of the Household (1879) and from June 1885 to January 1886 he acted as Lord Steward of Her Majesty's Household. The Earl's royal appointments were many, including aide-de-camp to the Queen, Deputy Lieutenant of Devon, special Deputy Warden of the Stannaries and Vice-Admiral of Cornwall (1897) an office held in abeyance since the death of his father in 1861. He was president of the Cornwall Territorial Army Force Association, one time chairman of the Cornwall Quarter Sessions, and the first chairman of the Cornwall County Council an office he held for 18 years. "Thanks very largely to the qualities of chairman possessed and exercised by the Earl, friction and ill-feeling found no place."

To mark his retirement the County Council presented him with a portrait as he appeared at the Coronation of Edward VII, wearing his robe of ermine and purple over the uniform of Lord Lieutenant. Other appointments included President of the Royal Institution of Cornwall (1882-84) and of the Royal Cornwall Polytechnic Society (1992-5), Captain of the Duke of Cornwall's Militia Rangers, and Hon Colonel of the 5th Battalion Devonshire Regiment. His favourite recreation was as a water colourist. "For the advancement of literature, science and art, he rendered every assistance in his power."

Educated at Harrow and Christ Church, Oxford, his public life began in 1859 when he was elected Conservative M.P. for Plymouth (he was then the heir, Viscount Valletort) but moved to the House of Lords on the death of his father two years later. The Earl had married the daughter of the first Duke of

Provincial Grand Masters Down the Years

Abercorn in 1858. She died 16 years later, leaving a son and three daughters (the youngest, Lady Edith Hilaria St. Aubyn). He re-married in 1906 and at the Provincial Grand Lodge at Redruth that year an illuminated address and an album were presented to him. His second wife was his cousin, Caroline Cecilia, Countess of Ravensworth. They were married at Cotehele, but she caught a chill at the opening of Parliament and died in 1909. The Earl died at Winter Villa, Stonehouse in 1917, after being taken seriously ill two months earlier. "By his death there has passed away a nobleman who won the confidence of Queen Victoria and King Edward VII, who held important office in the State and who stood very high in public estimation in the West of England."

CORNWALL

1875	German liner Schiller wrecked on rocks off Isles of Scilly: 42 survive of 355.
1875	Lady of the Isles passenger steamer built by Harveys of Hayle (lost during World War I).
1876	Camborne School of Mines established.
1877	Edward Benson White becomes first Bishop of Truro.
1880	Foundation stone of Truro Cathedral laid by Grand Master, the Prince of Wales (see feature).
1882	First artists arrive to form famed 'Newlyn School.'
1893	Twenty miners drowned in tragedy at Wheal Owles, St Just.
1896	Mount's Bay fishermen 'Riot' against Sunday fishing.
1897	Helston born Bob Fitzsimmons wins world heavyweight boxing title.
1898	Steamer Mohegan wrecked on Manacles: 107 of 157 lost.
1901	First Transatlantic wireless (radio) signal, sent from Poldhu, and received by Marconi at St. Johns, Newfoundland.
1904	Earthquake felt around Penzance bay.

INTERNATIONAL

1874	Winston Churchill born at Blenheim Palace.
1875	Bizet composes opera Carmen; Gilbert and Sullivan write Trial by Jury.
1879	Battle of Rorke's Drift in Zulu War.
1885	General Gordon killed in Fall of Khartoum.
1887	Queen Victoria's golden jubilee celebrations.
	Murders by 'Jack the Ripper' in London.
1894	Manchester ship canal and Tower Bridge officially opened.
1896	Cecil Rhodes resigns Premiership of Cape Colony.
1898	William Gladstone (four times Prime Minister) dies aged 88.
1900	Relief of Ladysmith and Mafeking after Boer siege.
	Poet and dramatist Oscar Wilde dies in Paris.
1901	Queen Victoria dies aged 81. New king, Edward VII, resigns as Grand Master of United Grand Lodge.
1902	Boer War ends.
1903	Ford Motor Company born.
1904	Charles Rolls and Henry Royce found car firm Rolls-Royce Ltd.

Cornwall Continued

1908   Celebrated Cornish carol composer Thomas Merritt of Illogan, dies aged 46. Cornwall wins its first County Rugby Championship Final, 17-3 over Durham.

1909   Bodmin gallows claims final victim, hanged for murder.

1910   Liner Minnehaha hits rocks off Isles of Scilly.
Cornwall Music Festival founded.

1911   Death of Cornishman philanthropist Passmore Edwards.
William Golding, author of 'Lord of the Flies' born at St. Columb Minor.

1916   Author D.H. Lawrence comes to live at Zennor.

1917   February skaters on ice at Pencalenick Pond, Truro.

Past Masters Jewel
presented at
Tregullow Lodge N. 1006

Provincial Grand Masters Down the Years

Before 1931 Past Masters jewels were presented at Tregullow Lodge No. 1006 as funds allowed. The question of whether or not to present a jewel was always a matter of debate.

On enquiry at Messrs. Toye Kenning and Spencer it was learned that the firm had never supplied any other lodge with this design. The earliest were of 9-ct gold and cost about £4 each. This photograph shows one "as first issued."

This jewel was presented in 1900 to Bro. T.R. Mills, great-uncle of Bro. Joseph Mills of St. Day. Two years later there was a ballot on who should receive one, "funds being so low", and one Past Master was obliged to wait 20 years, until 1931. Since then they have been presented annually.

8th PROVINCIAL GRAND MASTER
1917-40
LORD ST LEVAN

A distinguished soldier, Brigadier General the Right Hon. Lord St Levan C.B., C.V.O., (1870-1940), ruled over the Province for 22 years, and was Grand Supt of the Royal Arch for 20 years. It was recorded: "The Province would remember with affection and gratitude the charm of his courtesy and his ever-ready sympathy in every good work." He was the eighth P.G.M. (1917-40), succeeding his father-in-law, the Earl of Mount Edgcumbe, being installed at Truro during the First World War years. His Lordship married Lady Edith Hilaria, and her sister Lady Albertha wed Sir Henry Lopes, subsequently P.G.M. of Devonshire. Following Lady Edith's death in 1931 he married in 1933 Julia, the widow of the 2nd Earl of Dartrey.

No account of him would be complete without some mention of his life as a soldier. After education at Eton and Trinity College, Cambridge, he joined the Grenadier Guards, serving through the Sudan Campaign including the Suakin and Nile Expeditions (as ADC to General Sir Redvers Buller), and was later ADC to the Governor of Hong Kong. He commanded the Guards from 1904-8 and served with the British Expeditionary Force in France 1917-18. He was a JP, a Deputy Lieutenant for Cornwall and Deputy Warden of the Stannaries as well as Honorary Colonel of the Devon and Cornwall Heavy Brigade (Royal Artillery), Hon. Colonel of the Cornwall Royal Garrison Artillery. From 1892-94 he had been Military Secretary to the Governor General of Canada and before the 1st World War was awarded the Red Eagle of Prussia. On the death of his father, the 1st Baron, in 1908, he succeeded to the title, becoming a member of the Household Brigade Lodge two years later, in the same year joining Mount

Sinai Lodge at Penzance. In a further two years (1912) he was elected to the Chair of Mount Sinai. The gavel used at his installation was presented to the Lodge for the purpose, and was the one used by his great-grandfather, Sir John St Aubyn in 1836 as P.G.M. He joined the Cornish Masters' Lodge in 1912 and was elected W.M. the next year. In 1912 he was also made S.G.W. of England and Prov. G.W. of Cornwall. "He proved a most capable ruler in the Chair and presided with a grace and dignity combined with pleasantry, his speeches being characterised by a happy method of phrasing".

The year 1913 was a special one in other ways for it was the Mount Sinai Lodge Centenary - and this was celebrated in the Chevy Chase Room at St Michael's Mount. His Lordship took part in the Especial Grand Lodge to celebrate the Bi-Centenary (1717-1917), held at the Royal Albert Hall. In 1920 he was installed as the 6th Grand Superintendent of the Royal Arch. He took part at the initiation of the Earl of St Germans at Eliot Lodge, and acted as Senior Warden in the Household Brigade Lodge in June 1919, when the initiate was Col. H.R.H. The Prince of Wales and Duke of Cornwall (later Duke of Windsor). The Prince's brother, later King George VI, was initiated in December 1919.

The Prince of Wales subsequently became W.M. of his Lordship's Lodge (Household Brigade), and Lord St Levan was present at Grand Lodge when he was made Senior Grand Warden of England in 1922. In this same year his Lordship presided over the annual festival of the Royal Masonic Benevolent Institution. Cornwall that year contributed £20,397 and took part in the ceremony of laying the Dedication Stone at the Royal Masonic Hospital, Ravenscroft. He initiated the movement which resulted, in 1935, in the handing over to the Dean and Chapter of Truro Cathedral the first bay of the Cloisters of Truro Cathedral, erected by the Freemasons of Cornwall. This was to mark the 50th anniversary of the laying of the foundation stone by the Grand Master (later King Edward VII). In 1937 Provincial Grand Lodge was held at Penzance under the banner of St Levan Lodge, at his request.

Dear to his heart was St Levan Lodge at Penzance which Sir Philip Colville Smith, Grand Secretary of England and Deputy Provincial Grand Master consecrated in October 1929. Lord St Levan was the founding W.M., and the consecration was near to the Feast of St Levan. He presented the lodge with three Tracing Boards and a banner bearing the St Levan Arms. During his lifetime he lived up to the family motto, which translated means "Exact in Himself." He practised freemasonry throughout his life and there were many instances of his unbounding kindnesses and generosity. When he became too ill to attend Lodge meetings his interest remained strong, and it was said of him: "Lord St Levan was an earnest Mason who appreciated more than anyone in the Province the dignity and high importance of Freemasonry and held the view that a good Mason could not be a bad citizen. Even if Lord St Levan was only able, owing to his health, to watch the activities of the Province from the summit of his rocky fastness at St Michael's Mount, they wanted him to remain as P.G.M. and hoped he would preside over their destinies for many years to come."

Provincial Grand Masters Down the Years

Provincial Grand Masters Down the Years

CORNWALL

1916	Cornish blind poet and author Jack Clemo born at Goonharris, St. Austell.
1918	Dodman Point presented to the nation.
1919	Levant mine disaster at Pendeen: 31 men die.
1920	Isles of Scilly steamship company formed.
1924	At Poldhu - England speaks to Australia by wireless transmitter.
1927	St. Ives Society of Artists formed.
1928	First Cornish Gorsedd held at Boscawen-Un, St Buryan.
1929	Midsummer Eve bonfire tradition revived.
1932	Minack open air theatre at Porthcurno opens.
1937	Dylan Thomas and Caitlin Macnamara wed at Penzance.
	Newlyn fishermen take petition to Westminster on board long-liner Rosebud.
1938	Daphne du Maurier publishes novel Rebecca.
1939	Loss of seven lifeboatmen in St. Ives tragedy: one survivor.

INTERNATIONAL

1918	Allied-German Armistice.
	Men over 21 and women over 30 given vote.
	World-wide influenza epidemic hits Britain.
1919	Nancy Lady Astor becomes first woman to take seat in House of Commons.
	Fascist Party founded in Italy by Mussolini.
1920	Prohibition in the U.S.A.
1922	Tomb of Tutankhamun discovered.
1924	Lenin dies.
	British Empire Exhibition.
	Ramsay MacDonald becomes first Labour PM.
1926	General Strike grips nation.
	Future queen, Princess Elizabeth, born.
1927	Talking pictures arrive.
	Baird demonstrates colour television.
1928	Sir Alexander Fleming discovers penicillin.
1929	Wall Street crash.
1930	Airship R.101 crashes on flight to India: 48 die.
1932	Methodist churches united.
1933	Hitler appointed Chancellor of Germany.
1936	George V dies at Sandringham in January, succeeded by Edward VIII who abdicates in December. His brother George VI succeeds him: Coronation in 1937.
1938	Civilian gas masks issued.
1938	Liner Queen Elizabeth launched.
1939	War declared September 3.
1940	Churchill becomes Prime Minister.

9th PROVINCIAL GRAND MASTER
1941-1952
THE EARL OF ST GERMANS
K.C.V.O., O.B.E.

The Earl of St. Germans K.C.V.O., O.B.E., (Montague Charles Eliot) had been in attendance on five Sovereigns. A "wonderful man with a grand character", he and his wife had celebrated their golden wedding anniversary only a few months before his death in September 1960. From 1901, he was Gentleman Usher to King Edward VII, and in the following two years Groom-in-Waiting. Then until 1936, he was Gentleman Usher, 1920-36 also Groom of Robes, and from 1924-36 Extra Groom-in-Waiting to King George V. He served from 1936 as Extra Groom-in-Waiting to King Edward VIII, then to King George VI, and to our present Sovereign, H.M. Queen Elizabeth II. He was an Officer of the Order of Leopold of Belgium. In 1919 he received the O.B.E., in 1923 was made an M.V.O., later a C.V.O., and in 1934 a K.C.V.O.

He succeeded to the title on the death of his brother in 1942. Educated at Charterhouse and Exeter College, Oxford, he became a Barrister of the Inner Temple and was a Director of the Alliance Assurance Company. From 1914-19 he served as a Lieutenant Commander in the Royal Naval Volunteer Reserve. He was initiated into Apollo Lodge, Oxford, joined Eliot Lodge, St. Germans in 1919, becoming its W. Master in 1926. He was made Junior Grand Warden in United Grand Lodge in 1936. When acting for the Provincial Grand Master (Lord St. Levan) in 1937, assisted by Prov Grand Officers, he dedicated the new Masonic Hall at Padstow. This was just a few months before the death of the Deputy P.G.M., Sir Philip Colville Smith C.V.O., P.G.W. and Grand Secretary. As Sir Montague Eliot P.G.W., he became the Deputy P.G.M. later that year, and in 1938 consecrated the Colville Smith Lodge, Falmouth, as well as Tewington Lodge, St. Austell.

Provincial Grand Masters Down the Years

He was installed as the ninth Provincial Grand Master at Truro in May 1941 by the Pro Grand Master the Earl of Harewood, in the presence of over 600 brethren, following the death in November of Lord St. Levan. The following year he dedicated new lodge premises at Tuckingmill for St. Luke's Lodge, in 1945 consecrated the Lyonesse Lodge at Penzance, and presented a Centenary Warrant to St. Martin's Lodge, Liskeard. With the advent of peace, after the war years, several new lodges were consecrated in 1946, Trewinnard, Fistral, Essa and Trenwith. Phoenix celebrated its Centenary the following year: the lodge was warranted in 1810 but the Warrant was not granted in 1910 because of a break of nine years (1837-46) when the lodge did not meet.

The Earl of St. Germans Lodge (No.7031) was consecrated by the Provincial Grand Master in January 1951, the year before his resignation. He took a keen and active interest in the life and welfare of the village and church. He was the Vicar's Warden for many years, and a past president of St. Germans cricket club, taking an active part in his younger years. He was a keen sportsman and a renowned shot. At his funeral service the bearers were tenants, members of his staff and members of Eliot Lodge.

CORNWALL

1944	Sir Arthur Quiller-Couch dies at his Fowey home.
1947	Battleship Warspite wrecked near Prussia Cove on way to breakers' yard.
1950	Harold Hayman becomes first Cornishman to enter Parliament as a Labour MP.
1952	Freighter Flying Enterprise sinks after drama off Falmouth.

INTERNATIONAL

1941	Rudolph Hess lands in Scotland. United States declares war on Japan and Axis powers.
1942	Victory at Battle of El Alamein.
1944	D. Day invasion of Europe (6 June).
1945	Surrender of Germany. Atomic bombs dropped on Hiroshima and Nagasaki. Surrender of Japan.
1946	Coal industry nationalised.
1947	India Independence Act. Princess Elizabeth marries Prince Philip.
1948	Independent State of Israel proclaimed. Assassination of Gandhi.
1950	British troops in action in Korea.
1951	Festival of Britain.
1952	Lynmouth flood disaster.
1952	King George VI, Past Grand Master dies. Princess Elizabeth becomes Queen.

10th PROVINCIAL GRAND MASTER
1952-64
COLONEL EDWARD NEYNOE WILLYAMS

A distinguished soldier, who won the D.S.O. in 1917 and was twice mentioned in Despatches, Col. E.N. Willyams D.L. J.P., of Carnanton, St. Mawgan led Cornish Freemasonry from 1952-64. He was an eminent public figure in the county, was W.M. of the Duke of Cornwall Lodge, St. Columb in 1930 and was appointed Past Grand Deacon in 1942. On the resignation of the Earl of St. Germans (1941-52) he was installed as P.G.M. at Truro by the Grand Master, the Earl of Scarborough K.G. For many years he also served as Provincial Grand Master of Cornish Mark Masonry. In 1962 he laid the foundation stone of the new Masonic Temple at Saltash: a silver trowel was presented to him as a memento of the occasion.

These post-war years continued to mark a rapid growth in the consecration of new Lodges, including Carlyon and St. Mellyon, Pendennis, St. Piran's, St. Gluvias, Penhellaz, Towan and St. George's. Another special day came in 1961 when the P.G.M. consecrated Godolphin Lodge at St. Mary's, Isles of Scilly. It was recorded: "It is pleasing to note that the ancient Master's chair and jewels of the Provincial Officers of the former Godolphin Lodge, which was erased in 1851, are in use by the new Lodge."

Six lodges, Boscawen, Meredian, Dunheved, Restormel, Fowey and Three Grand Principles, were presented with their Centenary Warrant by the Provincial Grand Master. With the consecration of St. Piran's in 1959 the province became entitled to an Assistant P.G.M. The province in 1962, supported the Provincial Grand Master of Devonshire - who presided over the Festival of the Royal Masonic Institution for Girls - by contributing 7,500 guineas.

Provincial Grand Masters Down the Years

One of Col. Willyams' forebears, James Willyams of Carnanton, who was a banker, was among the group of Reformers in Cornwall who promoted the founding of The West Briton newspaper at Truro in 1810. High Sheriff in 1934-35 and a Deputy Lieutenant in 1936, Col. Willyams was educated at Eton and the Royal Military College at Sandhurst. He served throughout the First World War, retired from the Regular Army in 1926, and from 1929-35 commanded the 4/5th Bn D.C.L.I. (T.A). In the first year of the Second World War he commanded No. 3 Stevedore Bn, Royal Engineers in France. The following year he commanded the 6th H.D. Bn the Wiltshire Regiment, and from 1947-58 he was Honorary Colonel of the 4/5th D.C.L.I. In 1956 he retired from the chairmanship of the Cornwall Territorial and Auxiliary Forces Association.

Appointed a magistrate in 1935, Col. Willyams was chairman of the Pydar Bench for several years. He was a member of St. Columb Rural District Council, which ceased to exist with reorganisation in 1934. He was then elected to St. Austell Rural District Council and was its chairman 1945-47, and again in 1949. For many years he was chairman of St. Mawgan Parish Council. In the parish he was a benefactor, was patron of the church, president of the Feast sports, angling and cricket clubs and a manager of the village school. Col. Willyams was taken ill at the annual meeting of the Provincial Grand Lodge of Mark Master Masons at Bodmin in May 1964, and died shortly after, aged 73.

CORNWALL

1953 Posthumous VC to Lieutenant Philip Curtis of D.C.L.I. for valour in Korea.
1954 Lanhydrock house and park presented to National Trust.
1956 Lord Denning opens first purpose-built Cheshire Home at Long Rock, Marazion.
1957 Heavy redundancies at Falmouth and Camborne-Redruth.
1960 Dr. Barbara Moore walks from John O'Groats to Lands End: 'end-to-end' interest revived.
1961 Tamar road suspension bridge opened.
1964 Harold Wilson, at 48 becomes youngest P.M. this century - and spends Christmas at his Isles of Scilly bungalow.

INTERNATIONAL

1953 Coronation of Queen Elizabeth II.
Hillary and Tensing reach Everest summit.
1954 Roger Bannister becomes first to run mile in under four minutes.
Food rationing ends after 14 years.
1955 Commercial television begins.
1957 Suez invasion. Petrol rationing re-introduced.
1958 Manchester United air crash at Munich.
Introduction of parking meters.
1960 First episode of 'Coronation Street' televised.
1961 Gagarin becomes first man in space.
1962 Britten's 'War Requiem' given first performance.
1963 Great 'Train Robbery.'
Beeching report on rail closures.
President Kennedy assassinated.

11th PROVINCIAL GRAND MASTER
1964-78
COLONEL EDWIN PERRY MORGAN
M.B.E., T.D., J.P.

Playing a full role in the community life of the St. Austell area, Col. Edwin Perry Morgan was interested and actively involved in many organisations as well as Freemasonry. He succeeded in combining the office of Provincial Grand Master with the other interests for nearly 14 years (1964-78) and his long career in freemasonry, with his business life and leadership including local education, the arts, to Rotary and service as a magistrate.

Col. Morgan M.B.E., T.D., J.P., who was appointed P.J.G.D. in Grand Lodge and P.A.G. Soj in the Supreme Grand Chapter in 1958, was installed as P.G.M. by the Earl of Scarborough K.G., the Grand Master, at St. John's Hall, Penzance, in November 1964. A few weeks prior to this, as P.G.M. Designate, following the death of Col. E.N. Willyams in May, he presented the Centenary Warrant to St. Anne's Lodge, at Looe. A freemason from 1929 when he joined Saint Andrew Lodge at Tywardreath - he was a member during its 1967 centenary year - he died in January 1980, aged 73. His grandfather, Mr Edwin Broad, was also a member of this lodge. His friendly manner, his natural gifts of leadership and his sympathetic insight, made him a most popular P.G.M., welcomed and admired wherever he travelled in the Province.

During his term as Provincial Grand Master the centenary of many lodges including Tregullow, Tregenna, Zetland, Mount Edgcumbe, Carew, Duke of Cornwall, and his own St. Andrew Lodge, were celebrated, as was the bi-centenary of Lodge of Fortitude (No. 131) in 1972. Several lodges were

Provincial Grand Masters Down the Years

consecrated, including Roseland, St. Denys, Caradon, Breanick, Penwith, Cornish Acacia and St. Budoc's. In April 1966 further honours fell on the province by the investiture of E. Comp Col. Perry Morgan as Grand Sc.N at the Grand Festival of Supreme Grand Chapter.

At a service of thanksgiving in Truro Cathedral to mark the 250th anniversary of the foundation of the Grand Lodge of England, in 1967, a donation of £250 was made to the Dean and Chapter by the P.G.M. for the Cathedral Fabric Fund. In 1971 he attended the annual meeting of the Board of Governors of the Royal Masonic Hospital, and presented the Assistant Grand Master with a cheque for £11,000, the result of a two-year special appeal for the redevelopment and modernisation fund of the hospital. In June 1973 he was installed as Deputy Grand Master in the Mark Degree, to the great delight and satisfaction of the whole Province.

Born in Exeter and educated at King's School, Bruton, Col. Morgan joined the Territorial Army in 1929. He commanded a regiment of light anti-aircraft gunners and served three years in India and Burma during the 2nd World War. When the Territorial Army was reformed in May 1974 he was second-in-command and later Commander of the 456 Heavy Ack Ack, retiring from the Officers' Reserve on his 58th birthday with the rank of Colonel. For almost a half-century he was a member of the Rotary Club of St. Austell, and was secretary and then treasurer of St. Austell Arts Club for nearly 30 years. He was the first chairman of the South Western Arts Association for 12 years, and through his efforts the St. Austell arts club and theatre was founded and built up into the largest of its kind in the South West at that time. In younger years he played hockey for Cornwall, and also enjoyed golf. Col. Morgan, who lived at Carlyon Bay, was a former chairman of Broads (St. Austell) Ltd, joining in 1928 on the 70th birthday of his grandfather, who founded the firm in 1881.

He also followed in these footsteps by becoming a Justice of the Peace in 1953. For eight years he was chairman of the Hundred of Powder Bench, until he retired in December 1973. From 1950-66 he was chairman of the St. Austell and district youth employment committee, receiving the award of the M.B.E. for his services. For three years after the war he was a member of the former St. Austell Urban Council. When he retired in 1962 after nine years as District Scout Commissioner he was made an Honorary District Commissioner in appreciation. He was keenly interested in education, was chairman of the Governors of the old St. Austell Grammar School and a governor of West Hill School.

His name continues in Masonry with the 'Perry Morgan Temple' at Freemasons Hall, Hayle, dedicated with full Masonic ceremonial by his successor, the Hon. Robert Eliot, in January 1979, two months after his installation as P.G.M., and a year before Col. Morgan's death. The Edwin Perry Morgan Mark Lodge No. 1632 was consecrated in 1986, meeting in Perranporth.

CORNWALL

1966	Pleasure boat Darlwin 'vanishes' with 31 lost, between Fowey and Falmouth.
1967	Oil tanker Torrey Canyon wrecked on Seven Stones reef between Land's End and Isles of Scilly.
1969	Four drown at Portreath: huge seas lash breakwater.
1971	Concorde booms over Cornwall cause concern.
1972	Sir John Betjeman speaks at Polzeath on being Poet Laureate.
1973	Prince Charles receives 'Feudal Dues' at Launceston ceremony.
1975	Sculptor Dame Barbara Hepworth dies in fire at St. Ives home.

INTERNATIONAL

1965	Death and State Funeral of Bro. Sir Winston Churchill, aged 91.
1966	England win soccer World Cup.
	Horror of 'Moors Murders.'
	Tragedy at Aberfan: over 140 die when coal slag heap collapses.
1967	Cunard liner QE II launched by Queen.
1968	Start of long-continuing Civil Rights disturbances in Northern Ireland.
	Robert Kennedy and Martin Luther King assassinated.
1969	Open University founded.
	Man first walks on the Moon - a Freemason.
	Death penalty abolished.
1972	Cod 'war' with Iceland over fishing limits.
1973	Britain becomes member of E.E.C.
1974	Richard Nixon resigns as U.S. President.
1975	Margaret Thatcher becomes first woman leader of Conservative Party.
1976	Concorde enters commercial passenger air service.
	Worst drought in Britain for 250 years.

Provincial Grand Masters Down the Years

12th PROVINCIAL GRAND MASTER
1978-94
THE HON. MONTAGUE ROBERT VERE ELIOT

The consecration of the Robert Eliot Lodge in 1992 not only marked the 50th anniversary of the Provincial Grand Master in Freemasonry but was the culmination of his 16 years as leader of the province. It was the 80th lodge in the province and the visit of a star-studded team led by Lord Cornwallis, Past Pro Grand Master provided a dazzling scene. This was the climax of an ambition in 1988 to increase the number of lodges in the province from 67 to 80 and will be one of his memorials. He died the following year to the great distress of the province. Those who worked alongside him during the early 1990s when he suffered severely from his ankles, admired his determination to lay aside his stout walking sticks one by one. At Earls Court, London, in June 1992 at the magnificent celebrations for the 275th anniversary of Grand Lodge and the 25th anniversary of the Installation of the Grand Master, the Duke of Kent, the P.G.M. was unable to take part in the procession. The sight of him, however, making the long walk ahead of the parade to his seat on the platform was a moving one for the many Cornishmen in the audience, and indicative of his determined spirit.

He was the younger brother of the 9th Earl of St. Germans and uncle of the present Earl. He was born and brought up on the Eliot family estate and initiated into Freemasonry in the Apollo University Lodge, Oxford. In May 1937 he was one of the eight pages carrying the train of King George VI at his

Coronation. He was a Grenadier Guards captain in the 2nd World War serving through the Normandy campaign and was wounded in the advance through Holland. He served on Westminster council for nine years, was a Conservative candidate at the 1959 General Election and spent 11 years in Tangier where he ran his own estate agency and was correspondent for Reuters. He was Master of Eliot Lodge No. 1164 in its centenary year of 1967 and flew from Tangier to Cornwall for each meeting. On his return to Cornwall in 1973 settling in Liskeard, he made progress in the provincial hierarchy, swiftly establishing his authority and personality.

In 1974 he was appointed Assistant P.G.M., the following year Senior Grand Deacon and in 1976 Principal Grand Sojourner. His promotion continued that year: in April he was appointed Grand Superintendent Designate and in November was installed as Grand Superintendent by the 2nd Grand Principal Comp, the Hon. Fiennes Cornwallis. He consecrated the chapter of Three Grand Principles (No. 967) in May 1976. In June 1977 he consecrated the St. Levan Chapter at Penzance and in October the Fistral Chapter at Newquay, also the Tewington Chapter in January 1988 and the Duke of Cornwall Chapter in March 1994. He carried out an enormous amount of civic and public work, was a county councillor from 1977-93 serving as deputy leader of the Conservative group. He worked unceasingly for heritage and environmental concerns, for the Oxford Society, the Royal British Legion, the Cornwall Heritage Trust, and was president of the Royal Institution of Cornwall and the Cornwall Family History Society.

In 1978, on the retirement of Col. Perry Morgan, he was installed at Falmouth as Provincial Grand Master by R.W. Bro. Major General Sir Allan Adair, the Past Deputy Grand Master. The following year he dedicated the Perry Morgan Temple at Hayle and April 1982 with a number of brethren flew to Gibraltar to attend their District Grand Lodge and thank members for their excellent support for the Festival. To celebrate the Centenary of the Cathedral and its close ties with the province he led freemasons at a service there in March 1980 and presented a cheque for nearly £7,000. The following year he presided over the festival for the Royal Masonic Institution for Boys.

In 1983 he married Mrs Marie Lusk whom he had met in Tangier when she was working for the United Nations Organisation. He presented cheques totalling £6,000 to the Dean towards the Cathedral Restoration Fund in 1984 and further gifts in 1988 to mark the centenary of its consecration and in June 1992 on the 275th anniversary of the formation of Grand Lodge. The next year he presented a cheque towards the £150,000 half share with Devonshire of the £300,000 required for the site upon which Cadogan Court, Exeter, is built.

During December 1986 the foundation stone of Robert Eliot Court was laid jointly by the P.G.M. and Lord Burnham, chairman of the Compass Housing Association. In July the next year Mr. Eliot welcomed the first tenants and gave them the keys. In 1989 he became the Founder Master of the Aedes Christi Lodge No. 9304 in London, restricted to former members of Christ Church College, Oxford. By this time the number of Cornish lodges was rapidly increasing and he consecrated 13 in the years 1987-1992

Provincial Grand Masters Down the Years

Provincial Grand Masters Down the Years

with the 80th, the Robert Eliot Lodge No. 9483 in October 1992 with all its splendour. At the next Provincial Grand Lodge the Provincial Grand Master was presented with a Claret Jug by Deputy Provincial Grand Master, V.W.Bro. Sidney Pearce on behalf of the lodges in recognition of his half-century of freemasonry. Garden parties, banner dedications and many gifts to non-masonic charities, including Friends of the Royal Cornwall Hospital, the Mt. Edgcumbe and St. Julia Hospices, Cheshire Homes and Cornwall Air Ambulance, were led by him. The Hon. Robert Eliot's reign as P.G.M. was crowded with activity and interest, many memorable moments and great distinction. His friend, W. Bro. Rollo Crabb P.S.G.D. P.A.P.G.M. expressed it in this way in his eulogy at the funeral service at St. Germans Parish Church in June 1994: "He was a very hard worker, he knew how to pick men and how to leave them with the authority of their office. He listened to advice, he made up his mind and he was then resolute and determined in pursuit of his object".

CORNWALL

1979   Distinguished potter, Bernard Leach, dies at St. Ives.

1981   All eight Penlee lifeboatmen lost in bid by Solomon Browne to save those on coaster.

1983   Twenty die when passenger helicopter crashes into sea off Isles of Scilly.

1984   Poet Laureate Sir John Betjeman dies and is buried at St. Enodoc.

1985   Cornwall's first test-tube baby christened at St. Levan Church.

1986   David Penhaligon M.P. killed in road accident.

Tin miners and supporters march in London in support of the industry.

INTERNATIONAL

1979   Lord Louis Mountbatten murdered in his boat off Ireland.

Margaret Thatcher becomes Britain's first woman Prime Minister.

1982   Falklands War won against Argentina.

1983   First £1 coin introduced.

U.K's biggest robbery: £25-million in gold bars.

1984   I.R.A. bomb explodes at Brighton hotel during Conservative conference.

1985   Church of England Synod approves Ordination of women.

Mikhael Gorbachev becomes leader of Soviet Union.

1986   Explosion at Chernobyl nuclear reactor in U.S.S.R.

1987   Cross-channel ferry, Herald of Free Enterprises sinks at Zebrugge: 192 die.

Cornwall Continued

1988	400th anniversary of Spanish Armada: chain of beacons begins at Kynance Cove.
	Camelford water crisis after Lower Moor treatment works accident.
1989	Novelist Dame Daphne du Maurier dies.
1990	Geevor tin mine at Pendeen closes.
1991	Cornwall win their first County Rugby Championship for 83 years: 29-20 over Yorkshire at Twickenham.
1993	Opening of Tate Gallery, St. Ives, by Prince Charles.

International Continued

1987	Fifteen million trees lost in October hurricane.
	Black Monday hits stock market.
	I.R.A. blast at Enniskillen, N. Ireland on Remembrance Day.
	Many die in blaze at King's Cross station, London.
1988	Lockerbie jumbo jet 'plane explosion: 281 die.
1989	Berlin Wall demolished.
1990	Two sides of Channel linked by tunnel.
	B.S.E., 'mad cow disease' brings developing farming crisis.
1991	Operation 'Desert Storm' - Gulf War - against Iraq, successful.
	Last Apartheid laws abolished in South Africa.
1992	Devastating fire at Windsor Castle.
	Betty Boothroyd becomes first woman Speaker of House of Commons.
1993	Nelson Mandela and President de Klerk of South Africa receive Nobel Peace Prize.

Provincial Grand Masters Down the Years

13th PROVINCIAL GRAND MASTER.
1994 -
NICHOLAS JOHN FITZCHARLES CANNINGTON BARRINGTON.

Solicitor, family man and sportsman, the Provincial Grand Master became a member of St. Gluvias Lodge, Penryn, when he was 26. He has brought tremendous energy and enthusiasm to all his interests and firmly believes the emphasis must be on enjoyment in Freemasonry, in work and leisure interests. This he has displayed in his relationships with Craft and Chapter members throughout his eight-year leadership, combining it with a friendly approachable style and administrative skill. Always ready to listen to the views of members, no matter how busy his masonic schedule, he has given renewed pride to the province in taking it into the 21st century. He knows they are all members of a "wonderful fraternity" and has advised them to share it with their friends. "A man is a mason when he learns how to pray, how to love and how to hope, when he has kept faith with himself, with his fellow man and with his God," he has declared at Provincial Lodge.

Cornish born, he has spent nearly the whole of his life in the county, and can trace his first masonic link to his birth at Stratton Hospital in June 1939: the doctor was Dr. Thomas Arthur King, a Past Master of the Granville Lodge at Bude. His home was at Morwenstow and, after primary school there, he went with his brother Jonah to preparatory school in Ireland in 1950, and then to Cheltenham College from 1953 to 57. Qualification as a solicitor came in 1962, after being articled to the Bude firm of Andrew and Jones (he later discovered both were freemasons) and then worked for some time in Okehampton before coming to Falmouth in 1964. The Provincial Grand Master met his future solicitor partner, Ivon Hine (of Ratcliffe, Hine and King) when playing squash for Cornwall, and was invited to join the practice, in which he became a partner in August 1964. The firm later became Hine, Stonehouse and Barrington: he was later the principal partner and then consultant in September 1997.

His closest masonic family tie was through his great-uncle, a member in West Lancashire, who was a Junior Grand Deacon. R.W.Bro. Barrington was initiated into St. Gluvias Lodge in December 1966, proposed and seconded by W.Bros. Geoffrey Druce and Len Burton with whom he played tennis at the Falmouth Club. He was W.M. in 1974 and Provincial Grand Sword Bearer in 1981 with the following three years as Provincial Grand Registrar. From 1979 to 1981 he was assistant secretary of the Cornwall Masonic Grand Charity, through the festival in 1981 with its celebration in London, and then for ten years its secretary. He was a founder member of St. Budoc's Lodge (1972) and of the Robert Eliot (1992), becoming W.M. of the latter lodge in 1997.

In nominating him for the post of Grand Treasurer for 1984-85, the then P.G.M. remarked at Grand Lodge: "Outside his practice he leads a busy and extrovert life. Only last week he led the Falmouth Cricket team to win the Cornwall county championship: the first time the club has achieved this prize for many years. Apart from all this, he devotes a considerable time to Masonic activities..... I am confident that if Grand Lodge accepts this nomination, he will make a constructive and helpful contribution to the deliberations of the Board of General Purposes during his year." In 1991 R.W.Bro. Barrington was appointed Assistant P.G.M. and Deputy in 1994 at the annual meeting: five weeks later came the sad and sudden death of the Provincial Grand Master. Until October of that year he served as Deputy-in-Charge, and was installed, at the age of 55, by Lord Cornwallis Past Pro Grand Master. On the same day he also became the M.E. Grand Superintendent of the Holy Royal Arch Chapter of Cornwall, after serving as Deputy-in-Charge, having been exalted into Volubian Chapter, Falmouth, in November 1974. From a founder-member of Three Grand Principles Chapter No. 967 at Penryn in May 1976 he became M.E.Z. in February 1983, Grand Treasurer 1984 - 85 and Deputy Grand Supt. in 1989. He is also a Past First Principal (1991) of the Cornish First Principals' Chapter. He has consecrated one craft lodge since his installation, the Millennium Lodge, in 2000 at Perranporth.

R.W.Bro. Barrington and his wife Jane have been married for 37 years, have lived at Carnon Downs since 1973 and have two daughters and a son. Mrs. Barrington shares her husband's zest and talent for sport and is an excellent golfer. He is a renowned sportsman in the county and has been deeply involved in club sport since his youth, as a goalkeeper with Launceston in the S.W. League, Rugby with the Falmouth club and hockey for Truro and Cornwall. Cricket has been his passion, first with Bude and Okehampton and then with Falmouth since 1964, being captain for three periods totalling some ten seasons. In 1983 Falmouth won the county senior league under his captaincy for the first time in 37 years. His brother Jonah was six times British and world squash champion and is Past President of the Squash Rackets

Provincial Grand Masters Down the Years

Association. The P.G.M. played for Cornwall during 26 years, was county champion on ten occasions, and county secretary for 15 years. Now he plays golf as a member of the Perranporth and Budock Vean clubs.

The increased openness and awareness of Freemasonry and the efforts being made to counter inaccurate criticism have been stressed by him to members in recent years. He has said they should share and spread the virtues of Freemasonry, its beliefs, the privileges, the happiness, enjoyment and the friendships gained. No one has done more, in his public, leisure and private life, to spread this spirit and inculcate its values.

CORNWALL

1995	Former Prime Minister, Lord Wilson, buried at Old Town cemetery, St. Mary's.
1996	Sailing ship Maria Asumpta, wrecked off Padstow.
1997	March from St. Keverne to London to mark 500th anniversary of Cornish Rebellion.
	Death of St. Austell-born scholar, historian, poet and author Dr. A.L. Rowse C.H., aged 93.
	Cornish sailor Pete Goss becomes national hero after rescuing French sailor off Tasmanian coast.
1998	South Crofty, Cornwall's last tin mine, closes.
1999	Cornwall is centre of attention in August for total eclipse of the sun.
2001	Eden Project opened.
2002	Cornwall celebrates 250 years of Freemasonry in the County.

INTERNATIONAL

1996	Massacre of 16 children and teacher at Dunblane.
1997	Diana, Princess of Wales, killed in Paris car crash.
	Death of Mother Teresa of Calcutta.
1998	Allies act after crisis in Kosovo.
1999	Elections for devolved Scottish and Welsh assemblies.
2000	Celebrations for New Millennium centre on London's Dome.
2001	Terrorist attacks in United States with massive loss of life.
2002	Golden Jubilee of reign of Queen Elizabeth II.

Provincial Officers

Deputy Provincial
Grand Master
V. W. Bro. Frank Crewes
PG Swd.B.

Assistant Provincial
Grand Master
W. Bro. James Kitson
PSGD.

Provincial Officers

Assistant Provincial Grand Master
W. Bro. John Davy PSGD.

Provincial Grand Secretary	W. Bro Barrie Tinker PAGDC.
Provincial Grand Treasurer	W. Bro. W. David Williams PJGD.
Charity Steward	W. Bro. Eric S. Williams PAGDC.
Almoner	W. Bro. Roger W. Freeman PAGDC.
Director of Ceremonies	W. Bro. D. Harry Davey PAGDC.

THREAD OF GOLD

Chapter III

Splendour at Truro
Cornish Men and Masons
Special Moments in History

Splendour at Truro

Some of the splendid scenes at Truro, including the Triumphal Arches, for the visit of the Grand Master (HRH The Prince of Wales) and the laying of the Foundation Stone of Truro Cathedral. The inscriptions include 'Peace, Commerce Plenty', 'God Bless the Prince of Wales', 'Fish, Tin and Copper' and 'Hail Grand Master.' Top right shows enthusiasm outside the City Hall.

Thread of Gold

SPLENDOUR AT TRURO
LAYING THE FOUNDATION STONE OF TRURO CATHEDRAL

Freemasonry and the Church have never forged a stronger bond than on the day when H.R.H. The Prince of Wales, Duke of Cornwall, laid the Foundation Stone of Truro Cathedral. The Prince, as Grand Master, carried out the ceremonies with Masonic ceremonial, assisted by Grand Officers, Provincial and Lodge members, and Clergy. He laid the Foundation Stone of the first Protestant Cathedral erected in England since the Reformation on Thursday 20 May 1880. Since then, to the present day, the Province has maintained its friendship and support towards the Cathedral, which has been reciprocated by the Dean and Chapter.

The restoration of the Cornish Bishopric and the building of the Cathedral for the recently-formed Diocese, are of great significance in the history of Cornwall. It was an historic day in the life of the Church in Cornwall. It was an act of faith that this should be done in a county in which, at that time, 51% of the church-going population were Methodists and only 28% were members of the Church of England. This was also a unique day in the annals of English Freemasonry. As far as we know, this was the only time a foundation stone of a Cathedral had been laid by a Grand Master, supported by Grand Lodge, in full Masonic splendour. Also, this was one of the very few times in its history that Grand Lodge itself has been summoned to meet outside of London.

At the ceremony the Grand Officers of England stood to the right of their Grand Master and the three Bishops, of Truro, Exeter and Madagascar (the son of a former Vicar of Kenwyn) were immediately behind. The Archbishop of Canterbury was unavoidably absent, through illness. It was a magnificent day for Truro and Cornwall. With the Prince was H.R.H. Princess Alexandra, and their two sailor sons, Prince Albert Edward and Prince George. Five 'Triumphal Arches' marked the city route, all of different design by Cornish architect Sylvanus Trevail. The masonic arch at Lemon Bridge was reported to rival anything of the kind ever put up in England, with its classic design based on the Arch of Peace in Milan. The masonic, civic and cathedral interests were personified by the Earl of Mount Edgcumbe, who was the P.G.M., the Lord Lieutenant of Cornwall and chairman of the Cathedral Committee. The Provincial Secretary was W.Bro. E. T. Carlyon. The Bishop of Truro, Rt. Revd Dr. Edward White Benson was later to become Archbishop of Canterbury.

Splendour at Truro

The Royal group had left Marlborough House on the Monday by train for Cornwall, visiting Torquay during the Tuesday and making a brief stop at Plymouth. Grampound Road station was carpeted for the arrival and there were huge crowds. Lord Falmouth and the Hon. Evelyn Boscawen received the Royal party and drove with them in carriages to Tregothnan. It was reported: "Before the Royal party arrived the mansion was well filled with visitors, as well as the members of the family and servants attending each, for whom 96 beds had been provided." After dinner there was a ball in the library. "The ball was a brilliant affair and there is every reason to believe that nothing similar in point of magnitude and elegance had previously taken place in the county." Wednesday was more restful and included a trip on Truro river to Falmouth harbour.

Ten thousand came to Truro by rail on Thursday to join the population of the city in the most spectacular and colourful occasion in its history. Military guards of honour, parades and processions, bands and choirs - and a fine day - completed the pleasure. The principal guests were in uniform or Masonic regalia. The Lord Mayor of London was among them. Some 2,800 men of the Royal Cornwall Miners' Artillery, the Royal Cornwall Rangers and battalions of the County Rifle Volunteers lined the streets together with 280 Metropolitan police who arrived by special train. There were presentations of Loyal Addresses by the High Sheriff (Mr. C. G. Prideaux-Brune), the Mayor (Mr. P. P. Smith), and the Miners Association of Cornwall and Devon.

During the morning a Provincial Grand Lodge was held in the Public Rooms, attended by some 600, clothed in their Masonic attire, with banners of the lodges forming "an imposing spectacle." The Provincial Grand Master accompanied the Deputy Grand Master, the Earl of Latham, and the Provincial Grand Master of Devon, Viscount Ebrington. Later, at the town hall, Grand Lodge was opened by the Earl of Latham and later closed by the Grand Master. In the address presented by the P.G.M. to The Prince of Wales, were these words: "We, the Provincial Grand Master officers and brethren of the Province of Cornwall, desire to be allowed to welcome your Royal Highness on this memorable occasion with a respectful expression of loyalty and fraternal devotion to your person as Heir to the Throne of England, lord of this ancient Duchy and head of our honourable Craft." The address was beautifully prepared on parchment, richly illuminated. The welcome added: "We rejoice in the occasion which has brought your Royal Highness among us to perform our ancient rites at the foundation of a building which we believe will be worthy of the high and holy purpose for which it is to be reared." The Prince joined the masonic body in Lemon Street, in masonic apron and jewels, and walked in procession to the special enclosure at the Cathedral site.

The grandstand was approached by an archway erected at the entrance at High Cross. There was seating for 2,500. The Prince's reception tent was lined throughout with scarlet and white drapery, and the floor was laid with crimson cloth. His pavilions in the Western and Eastern enclosures were octagonal, again lined in scarlet and white, draped with blue and amber with rich fringe gauze and tassels and appropriate banners. The dais for the Princess was equally splendid and the masonic stands, in the North East enclosure, covered at the back with crimson and surrounded by masonic banners. What a sight it all must have been. The Princess and Princes, and all the non-masonic party had taken up their places, and the

Splendour at Truro

Truro Volunteers had played 'Trelawny' before the Grand Master arrived. "Soon afterwards the banner of the Provincial Grand Lodge of Cornwall appeared, and then followed the longest procession of Freemasons Cornwall has ever seen," stated a contemporary report.
"They looked very gay, with the silk banners of their Lodges. For some ten minutes or a quarter of an hour they filed through the western enclosure in a continuous stream…" While this long procession came through the main entrance the clergy, who had assembled and robed in St. Mary's Church, came out of the West door. The scene, being now complete, was described as "strikingly effective, the grouping being most beautiful and picturesque. Upon the canopied dais in the centre of the enclosure had assembled all the distinguished personages who were to take part in the ceremony."

The Bishops of Truro and Exeter said prayers, there were choral groups from Truro, Camborne and Penzance, and the Royal Marine Band for music-making. The clergy totalled some 300. When the Prince had laid the foundation stone, and the Bishop blessed it, he said: "Be it known unto you that we, being lawful Masons, true and faithful to the laws of our country, although not operative masons, have from time immemorial been associated with the erection of buildings raised for the benefit of mankind and the glory of the Great Architect of the Universe. We have among us secrets concealed from those who are not Masons, but they are lawful and honourable and are not opposed to the laws either of God or of man. They were entrusted to Masons in ancient times, and have been faithfully transmitted to us, and it is our duty to convey them down to posterity. We are assembled here in the presence of you all to erect a house for the worship and praise of the Most High, which I pray that God may prosper as it seems good to him." The Grand Chaplain offered prayer, and the Grand Master said: "I now declare it to be my will and pleasure that the corner-stone of this Cathedral be laid." He used an ancient mallet to lay the foundation stone, and a trowel of solid silver. Col. Shadwell H. Clerke, Grand Secretary, read the inscription: "To the Glory of God the Corner Stone of this Cathedral Church of St. Mary in Truro, was placed by H.R.H. Albert Edward, Prince of Wales and Duke of Cornwall, Grand Master of the Ancient Free and Accepted Masons of England, Thursday the 20th day of May, A.D. 1880".

Gold vessels from Grand Lodge were used to scatter the corn and pour the wine. The Grand Master said: "Brethren, we are an ancient fraternity which from its earliest days has been identified with all that is beautiful and grand in architecture, and you will therefore be proud to have aided me, as I have been proud to work with you, in commencing a building, which by the beauty of its design and the solidity of its construction, will, we trust, be an ornament to this city and Province for centuries to come. But, brethren, it is something far more than this. It is a temple to be erected to the glory and worship of our Heavenly Father, the Great Architect and Creator of all things."

There were presentations of purses by the Princess and the two Princes. After the stones had been laid the Prince walked with the Grand Officers to the town hall where he closed the Grand Lodge. The Earl of Mount Edgcumbe presided at the luncheon where there were toasts to the Queen, the Prince and Princess and the rest of the Royal party. The Prince responded with a toast to the prosperity of the county, the city, and the diocese. He remarked: "I congratulate you all upon the complete success of the proceedings of today. I assure you the welcome we have received is one which will always remain vividly in our memories."

Splendour at Truro

Laying the foundation stone of Truro Cathedral.

Splendour at Truro

Splendour at Truro

Watched by Church and Masonic leaders, the Grand Master, HRH The Prince of Wales, carries out the laying of the foundation stone of Truro Cathedral, with full Masonic Honours.

Splendour at Truro

A rare photographic record of the splendid scene at the laying of Truro Cathedral's foundation stone, with Masonic honours, by the Grand Master, HRH The Prince of Wales (later King Edward VII), in May 1880.

Splendour at Truro

The day's celebrations continued with a military review at Treliske (including an elephant that had brought the band in a gilded carriage), a concert, and evening illuminations in the city.

At this time the cost of the Cathedral was estimated at £95,000. The lodges of Cornwall contributed generously to that cost and have continued their interest and support to the present day. The architect was Bro. John Loughborough Pearson, R.A. (1817-1897) of Harley Street, London, who was initiated into Jerusalem Lodge No. 197, London, in March 1880, just two months before the laying of the foundation stone. At the Truro ceremony Bro. Pearson was presented to the Grand Master, who, after having examined the plans of the intended building, said to him: "I place in your hands the plans of the intended building, together with the necessary tools, not doubting your ability and skill as a craftsman; and I desire that you will proceed without loss of time with the completion of the work, in conformity with the plans and designs now entrusted to you." A statue in Bath stone of Mr. Pearson holding these plans can be seen on the external south porch of the Cathedral, immediately above a carving of H.R.H. The Grand Master.

The Prince of Wales returned in November 1887 for the consecration ceremony in the new Cathedral. "The beautiful work of God among us today - the first such founded and built these eight centuries - founded and built for many centuries to come, " said the Archbishop of Canterbury in his sermon. Yet it was a different city scene from 1880: a storm had raged overnight and there was rain during the day. Truro again was dressed with banners and bunting. The Royal Procession made its way from the railway station to the Cathedral, and later to the public luncheon without rain, but the return to the station was in a heavy shower.

There were three services: the Consecration with the Archbishop as preacher, the afternoon service with the sermon by the Bishop of London, and a service of praise in the evening.
The Provincial Grand Master the Earl of Mount Edgcumbe, was at the station to greet His Royal Highness, who responded to a loyal address by the Mayor with these words: "It affords me the most unfeigned satisfaction to be able to attend the great religious service which is held here today, and to be present at the consummation of the important ceremony in which I took a leading part more than seven years ago. The interest which the Duchess of Cornwall and I have felt in the progress of the work has continued unabated since that period and she commissions me to assure you how deep is her regret and disappointment that unavoidably prevents her from accompanying me to the consecration of the first Protestant Cathedral ever erected in England. I join most heartily in the expression of your hope that the western part of the building may ere long be completed and I trust that circumstances will allow me once more to visit a town which can boast of having been mentioned in the Domesday Book eight hundred years ago." The service was attended by Bishops and clergy from around the world. This year, 1887, was the Diamond Jubilee year of Queen Victoria's reign.

There are several other masonic links within the Cathedral, some from the 1900s.

In the south-west corner of the building, under the Cornish Fishermen's window, is a 1910 memorial tablet to King Edward VII, referring to the laying of the foundation stone when he was Grand Master. There are three references to the Provincial Grand Master the 4th Earl of Mount Edgcumbe, and later a Deputy Grand Master. One is on the first pier, from the west of the transept on the south side of the nave, partly hidden by the wooden nave pulpit. This marks the ceremony of 1880 and the efforts of Freemasons in Cornwall. On the West side of the South transept entrance is a memorial tablet to the Earl with his coat of arms above and Cornwall Craft and Holy Royal Arch Chapter badges on the base. It is in memory of "the great services which he rendered to the county, the diocese and this cathedral 1832-1917." A further reference to the Earl is on the tablet in the Chapter House entrance, which commemorates the Hall being given by his two grand-daughters, The Hon. Marjory Parker and The Hon. Hilaria St. Aubyn. The Chapter House was opened on 20 May 1967, exactly 87 years after the laying of the foundation stone.

There is a fine marble tablet within the Nave, with the Truro City coat of arms and the square and compasses, in memory of Thomas Chirgwin J.P. C.C. (1828-1894). He was five times Mayor, P.P.S.G.W. and Provincial G. Secretary of the Province: "This Window and Tablet have been erected by many of his Friends and Masonic Brethren." Richard Trevithick (1771-1833), Cornishman, engineer and inventor, is remembered in the Chapel of Unity, under the Cornish Miners' window, on a tablet of Delabole slate. Trevithick Lodge was consecrated in 1989.

There are three memorials to the Rt. Revd Joseph Hunkin, O.B.E., M.C., D.D., Bishop of Truro 1935-1950. One tablet bears a bronze effigy of him (1887-1950) inscribed "A Man Greatly Beloved." Another tablet bears Greek words from St. Paul's letter to the Ephesians, and may be translated "And Christ shall give thee light": or "And Christ will shine upon you." On the external north east wall, opposite the steps to the Chapter House is a slate tablet stating that the trees and hedges in this close were planted in Bishop Hunkin's memory, "A Lover of Gardens." Several parish churchyards in the diocese have a camellia or other shrub planted in his memory. Bishop Hunkin was initiated into Alma Mater Lodge No. 1492, whilst an undergraduate at Cambridge. He was a founder member of Truro School Lodge No. 5630 in 1936 and its Worshipful Master in 1938. He was appointed Grand Chaplain of the United Grand Lodge of England in 1942.

In July 1935 the Provincial Grand Master the Lord St. Levan, handed over to the Dean and Chapter, the first bay of the cloisters on the north side of the transept, erected by the Freemasons of Cornwall. This was to commemorate the 50th anniversary of the laying of the foundation stone "and to preserve in memory the happy and honourable association of our Craft and the building of this Temple of God". The building was received and dedicated by Bishop Hunkin. The Dean and Chapter intend to complete the cloister if and when the large sum of money required is available. Within the cloister, on either side of the door, are carved shields, one bearing the 15 bezants of the Duchy of Cornwall, and the other bearing the masonic symbols of the square and compasses around a Radiating Sun. There is a commemorative inscription on the east wall of the cloister telling of the Jubilee 1880 - 20 May 1930.

CORNISH MEN AND MASONS

"THE CORNISH CARNEGIE"
JOHN PASSMORE EDWARDS
1823 - 1911.

Cornwall's great philanthropist was the son of a carpenter and market gardener in the village of Blackwater, between Redruth and Truro. Today his memorials stand in over 20 splendid public buildings in the county. Yet this is but a third of all his endowments. There are 70 in all, including libraries, hospitals, convalescent homes, institutes and art galleries, all erected at his own expense within about 15 years. His first gift in Cornwall was an Institute at his home village (1890). In one week in May 1895 five foundation stones were laid or buildings opened. That year saw four in Cornwall, at St. Agnes, Newlyn art gallery, Camborne and Redruth free libraries, as well as buildings in London and the Home Counties. Newspaper proprietor Passmore Edwards, of Bedford Square, London, was initiated in that city's The Cornish Lodge No. 2369 in 1894, when he was aged 70. He joined the Gallery Lodge No. 1928 of London in 1896: it was originally formed by Hansard writers and political journalists at Westminster and remained very much a Press lodge. In 1898 he joined London's Caxton Lodge No. 1853, but there is no record of his becoming W.M. or taking office. He took part, however, as J.W. when the Cornish Masters Lodge No. 3324 was consecrated in 1908 in The Orangery at Mount Edgcumbe, by V.W.Bro. Edward Letchworth, with R.W.Bro. Sir William Treloar, the Lord Mayor of London, as S.W.

Four of the corner stones of his gifts were laid with full masonic ceremonial, two in Cornwall. One of these followed a Provincial Grand Lodge in May 1895. The P.G.M., the Earl of Mount Edgcumbe (Deputy G.M. of England), laid the foundation stone of the Cottage Hospital at Liskeard, under the banner of St. Martin's Lodge No. 510, then in its Golden Jubilee year, preceded by a procession of 200 freemasons in full dress. The other was in 1897 when the stone for the Cornwall Central Technical Schools in Truro was laid in memory of the late P.G.M., Sir Charles Lemon. About 400 freemasons went in procession to the ceremony. Twice Passmore Edwards declined a knighthood, first by Queen Victoria and later by King Edward VII. As he pointed out in his autobiography: "I like to do the work for its own sake." His foundation stones were laid to the praise and affection of crowds from all stations in life but he remained fiercely proud and sympathetic to his simple origins.

Cornish Men and Masons

When he was 20 he obtained a post with a Truro lawyer and walked to work each Monday morning (with pasties for several days), walking back to Blackwater on Saturday evening. Taking up a job on The Sentinel at Manchester was no easy task: he walked to Falmouth, sailed to Dublin, on to Liverpool, and by rail to Manchester. His first attempt as a proprietor and editor in London failed, but in 1876 his future prosperity was established when he acquired The Echo, the country's first halfpenny evening newspaper. He retained control until 1896.

A special Provincial Grand Lodge meeting marked the laying of the foundation stone, in Masonic form, of the Passmore Edwards Cottage Hospital at Liskeard in May 1895. With the civic leaders and members and guests of St. Martin's Lodge are the ladies (on the left) the PGM, the Earl of Mount Edgcumbe, and the donor Bro. Passmore Edwards, an Honorary Member of St. Martin's.

A campaigner from his early years, he knew Dickens, Peel, Thackeray, Cobden and Bright, promoting many causes, and going with Cobden to the first International Peace Congress in Brussels in 1848 and later to Paris and Frankfurt. He opposed capital punishment and in 1880 was elected M.P. for Salisbury, withdrawing five years later. He declared: "In nine cases out of ten, members voted on party lines in

Cornish Men and Masons

obedience to party discipline. An ordinary member is only a cog in the wheel of the party machine." In his time Passmore Edwards was much loved and respected. He said at Liskeard: "By vigilant work and fairly good luck I have become the custodian of a certain number of sovereigns, which came mostly from the labours of working men, and my desire is that these sovereigns, or most of them, should flow back to the fountain from which they mainly derived." He was Truro's first Freeman, in 1893, and also accepted this honour from the boroughs of West Ham, Falmouth, Liskeard and The Stationers Company. A silver casket, presented during the ceremony at Liskeard, bore the words: "To a distinguished patriot and philanthropist who has rendered eminent service to this borough, to Cornwall and to the Country." He died in 1911 aged 88. A close colleague was his architect Bro. Silvanus Trevail, who designed six buildings for him in Cornwall: he was born at Luxulyan and among his other works were many schools, churches and chapels. He was a member of One and All Lodge No. 330, Bodmin.

"GARIBALDI'S ENGLISHMAN".

The name of Colonel John Whitehead Peard has been linked, down the years, with that of the great Italian patriot Garibaldi. He was also prominent in Cornish Freemasonry. The two men, fair-haired, tall, broad-shouldered and bearded, brave and fearless, looked very much alike - so put courage in the hearts of the soldiers in two places at once!

Colonel Peard was born at Fowey in 1811, the son of Vice-Admiral Shuldham Peard and his second wife Matilda Fortescue: his first wife was Elizabeth Bligh, daughter of Admiral Bligh of H.M.S. Bounty. Strong and clever, Peard graduated at Exeter College, Oxford, in 1836 was called to the Bar and practised on the Western Circuit, joining the Duke of Cornwall Rangers in 1859. Many Englishmen went to Italy to help the struggle of the peasants during the revolutionary turmoil which ended with that country free and united. Garibaldi said that but for the help of the "English Thousand" and their gallant Colonel, freedom would never have been won. John Peard was given command of this 'English Legion': he distinguished himself and received the rank of Colonel on the field of battle.

At Garibaldi's side in the triumphal march into Rome was his Englishman: Col. Peard received the Cross of Valour from the new king, Victor Emmanuel. He had made his home at Penquite, Fowey, and there were tremendous scenes of excitement when the international hero, Garibaldi, visited in 1864. The Colonel had joined him in London and travelled to Cornwall by train with him and the Duke and Duchess of Sutherland, with huge crowds at every station. Thousands waited at Par and there were triumphal arches and flags flying in the streets as the horses pulled the carriages to Penquite. Garibaldi spent three days there, with many celebrations, finally leaving from Albert Quay, Fowey, for the Duke's yacht, after saying his last farewells to his friend.

In 1839 Col. Peard had married Catherine Augusta Richards, daughter of the Head of Blundells School. While living at Penquite he had the splendid house at Trenython built at Tywardreath in 1869-70. He died there in November 1880 and was buried in Fowey cemetery. He had served as a Justice of the Peace, a Deputy Lieutenant, High Sheriff in 1869 and was Commodore of Royal Western Yacht Club. The first knowledge of his masonic career was that he came from Exeter as a joining member of Fowey lodge No. 977, which was founded in 1863. He joined in that year, was not a founder, but was W.M. two years later. He visited St. Andrew No. 1151 several times in the 1870s, although he never belonged to that lodge: St. Andrew dates from 1867 and meets in Tywardreath. Col. Peard was Provincial S.G.W. in 1866 (rapid promotion indeed!) and was appointed Dep. P.G.M. in 1879. He was also most active in other branches of freemasonry. He was the second First Principal of Unity Chapter No. 1151: most traces of Unity have vanished since it was erased in 1918. Peard was the second person to be appointed Second Principal of the province. In 1865 he was Commander of the Restormel Conclave of Knights Templar and in 1877 was Prov. Prior, the first to bear that name which had previously been Prov. Grand Commander. He may also have had a Devonshire connection with the Rose Croix, for in 1875 he was a founder member of the Cornwall Chapter No. 61, the first Rose Croix Chapter in Cornwall. He was in the chair in 1876.

SIR PHILIP COLVILLE SMITH
1862-1937

Sir Philip Colville Smith was never a Provincial Grand Master of Cornwall but he has been described as its best-known Freemason, nationally and internationally. For, in 1917, he was appointed to the high office of Grand Secretary of the United Grand Lodge of England and Grand Scribe E of Supreme Grand Chapter, offices he held for the next 20 years. Although these duties occupied much of his time, both in the United Kingdom and overseas in places as far apart as South America, Africa and in Europe, he never lost touch with the county and was regular in his attendance at all Masonic meetings of importance in the province. For 38 years from 1899 until his death he was Deputy P.G.M. and Second Grand Principal in Provincial Chapter. In the same year Sir Philip was appointed Senior Grand Deacon in United Grand Lodge and Second Assistant Grand Sojourner in Supreme Grand Chapter. In 1923 he received the richly deserved honour of C.V.O. and two years later he was created a Knight. Also in 1923, in the Mark Degree, he became Provincial Grand Master for Cornwall, another high office he held until his death.

Cornish Men and Masons

Sir Philip Colville Smith

During his Secretaryship of Grand Lodge there were some significant events in the history of English Freemasonry. In 1933 came the building of the Masonic Peace Memorial in Great Queen Street, London, the heart of the Masonic Order and the headquarters of English Freemasons throughout the world. In 1937, the Coronation year of King George VI and Queen Elizabeth, a Special Grand Lodge was held when the King was invested as Past Grand Master. Among other events were the building and opening of the Royal Masonic Hospital and the new senior school of the Royal Masonic Institution for Girls. Sir Philip, who never married, was called to the Bar at the Inner Temple, but never practised. He devoted his life to Freemasonry and is still remembered as one greatly revered by the Craft. He died, aged 74, in November 1937: a memorial service was held in London and at Truro Cathedral. The following October the new Colville Smith Lodge No 5738, was consecrated at Falmouth.

A brother of a Chief Constable of Cornwall, he was initiated at an early age in Apollo Lodge No 357 at Oxford, later joining Phoenix Lodge of Honour and Prudence No. 331 at Truro - his native city - and in due course became Prov.S.G.Warden. His name can be seen on many foundation stones of Masonic Halls throughout this Province, the first being Camborne (1898) which was dedicated two years later, and Calstock (1900), returning for its dedication the following year. In 1910 the Corner Stone of the new hall at Bodmin was laid by his hand and in 1912 the new hall at Penryn was dedicated by Sir Philip. He dedicated the new hall at Looe (1919), was associated with the laying of the foundation stone at Newquay (1928), the consecration of the St. Levan Lodge, Penzance, the following year, and the dedication of the new Masonic Temple at Union Place, Truro (Fortitude Lodge No. 131) in 1934.

"A MAN GREATLY BELOVED."
Rt. Revd Joseph Wellington Hunkin
1887-1950.

The eighth and longest serving Bishop of Truro "a man greatly beloved" had a strong interest and involvement in Freemasonry. A Cornishman, born in Truro in 1887 and brought up as a Methodist, he was initiated in August 1921 into Alma Mater Lodge No. 1492 in Cambridge. He was a founder member of the Truro School Lodge in 1936, its W.M. in 1938, and was appointed Grand Chaplain in 1942. His enthronement as Bishop, and installation as Dean, in June 1935, brought this declaration: "I have come home. This is my call. I expect no other." And so it proved. He died unexpectedly in October 1950 at the Royal Masonic Hospital in London where he had gone for an operation after suffering badly from toothache. Cornwall was stunned by his death.

In October 2000, Cornish provincial leaders led by the Provincial Grand Master, R.W.Bro. Nicholas Barrington, attended a memorial talk and service at the Cathedral to mark the 50th anniversary of his sudden death, and his contribution to Cornish life. There are three memorials to him in the Cathedral, including a tablet bearing a bronze effigy, and one opposite the steps to the Chapter House, which states the trees and hedges in the Close were planted in memory of this "lover of gardens." Several parish churches in the diocese have a camellia or other shrub planted in his memory. Within a month of his enthronement he received and dedicated the first bay of the cloisters on the north side of the transept erected by the freemasons of Cornwall. This was handed over by the Provincial Grand Master Lord St. Levan to commemorate the 50th anniversary of the laying of the foundation stones (1880-1930) and to "preserve in memory the happy and honourable association of our Craft and the building of this Temple of God".

As a youth the Bishop had attended the St. Mary's Wesleyan Church - alongside the Cathedral - with his family, and the Truro Wesleyan College, now Truro School, preaching his first sermon at Tresillian chapel when he was only 16. He went to The Leys School, Cambridge, a leading Methodist public school, and then to Gonville and Caius College, Cambridge, prepared for the Wesleyan ministry with a year at Headingley College, Leeds, and went as a probationer minister to Bangor in North Wales. Then came the change. "He needed more air and a larger room," it has been written, "and he believed this could be found in the comprehensiveness of the Church of England." He was confirmed as a communicant member, studied at Ridley Hall, Cambridge, was ordained in 1914 and took up his first position at St Andrew Parish Church, Plymouth.

Cornish Men and Masons

The Bishop at the Bishop Rock lighthouse.

The future Bishop became a hero to many in the 1st World War, volunteering as a Chaplain in 1915 and serving in some of the worst battlefields, including Gallipoli, Ypres and Arras. Padre Hunkin showed great courage in ministering among the badly wounded in the mud and the dressing stations, and was described as "one of the greatest chaplains of the war", receiving the Military Cross and Bar and the O.B.E. He was himself gassed while going up with stretcher bearers to fetch back men affected by the poison, but after convalescence returned to the field.

The Bishop and his wife Ruth had two sons, Oliver and Andrew and two daughters Patience and Elisabeth. He was an outstanding scholar, of strong convictions, ever-zealous for the truth, and completely fearless, both physically and morally. After the war he became Dean of Gonville and Caius before becoming Rector of Rugby, Archdeacon of Coventry and Chaplain to H.M. The King, and then coming "home" to Truro. At the outset of the 1939-45 war he hoped to enlist again as a Padre but received this message "I may tell you quite frankly that in my view your post is in the Diocese" from the Archbishop of Canterbury! So he joined the Home Guard in which he served as a Private. This brought him considerable publicity as did his trip to the Bishop Rock lighthouse in 1936 to confirm two of the keepers. He was hauled up by ropes, complete in black frock coat and gaiters.

Soon after his enthronement he became the first 'non-Methodist' to preach at Gwennap Pit, that shrine of Methodism - where John Wesley held the attention of thousands of miners during his visits - on Whitsun Bank Holiday. He worked always for better relations between the two churches in Cornwall, which has continued to this day. All Cornwall lost a friend at his death. "His record was a wonderful one," commented Col. E.N. Willyams (P.G.M. 1952-64). "He was a very brave man in the 1st World War: he has been a great leader of men and his loss will be severely felt in the county."

SPECIAL MOMENTS IN HISTORY

ON MY OATH - WAS IT GEORGE WASHINGTON'S BIBLE?

A Bible, published in London in 1712, has a place of pride in the Duke of Cornwall's Light Infantry Museum at Bodmin. Known as the 'Washington Bible' it is claimed to have been used during a masonic ceremony for George Washington, later to become the first President of the United States of America. The evidence has been challenged, but makes an absorbing story whatever the precise proof might be. This volume of the sacred law is some 8-ins x 10-ins, bound in black morocco with the spine and covers tooled in gold. The title LSMV (Libens Solvit Merito Votum - Lodge of Social and Military Virtue) is on the front cover, with 'No. 207, 46th Regiment'. The spine contains square, compasses, straight edge, mallet, chisel and other emblems, including a pentagon with the capital letter G in the centre, and the date 1712.

George Washington wearing his Masonic regalia.

The Bible was originally owned by a clergyman who, it is claimed, crossed to America on The Mayflower in 1620. It was later passed on to his daughter - which rather confuses the date process. In 1778, during the American War of Independence, it was taken from the burning home of Bartholomew West, just outside New Bedford, Massachusetts, by members of the British 46th Regiment of Foot. "At the time of its taking it is alleged that the Bible contained the signature of George Washington, signed by him when he had been 'Obligated as an Entered

Thread of Gold

Special Moments In History

Major R. Vyvyan-Robinson, MBE., the curator of the Regimental Museum, The Duke of Cornwall's Light Infantry at Bodmin, holds the Washington Bible which is kept on display there

Apprentice Mason, 4 November 1752.' This is disputed by certain Americans who say that it was merely a boastful claim by the British to have captured an American artefact of such historical significance, when all they had in fact taken was an old man's family Bible," Major Hugo White, for several years Curator of the Regimental Museum at Bodmin, has recorded. "One would imagine that neither the 46th Foot nor the 2nd Battalion the Duke of Cornwall's Light Infantry would have fabricated the Washington story. However, one must admit that myths do arise which later become enshrined in regimental history, and certainly nobody alive today has ever seen evidence of the signature. The Second Battalion always claimed that the flyleaf on which George Washington had signed his masonic indentures was ripped out when the Bible was on display in their officers' Mess after Sunday church parade in the early years of the 20th century. The story is, however, somewhat garbled and the event is variously recorded as having taken place in two separate places - Gibraltar in 1905 and Bermuda in 1907."

The 46th Foot had established a masonic lodge when they were in Ireland in 1752, receiving their charter from the Grand Lodge of Ireland, and known as 'The Lodge of Social and Military Virtue.' This had continued to flourish and the Bible plundered at New Bedford was taken into use as the Regiment's masonic Bible. Major White added: "The Bible was captured by the Americans at some time between 1778 and 1782 but before the 46th re-embarked for Ireland at the end of the War it was returned to them by their victors. Later, on the 22 February 1805, the 46th Foot had their baggage, including the Bible, captured by the French in Dominica: it was later returned under a flag of truce." This lodge, No. 207, of the 46th Foot, operated up to 1827, when it became dormant due to lack of members. In 1834 it was

Special Moments In History

revived and continued until about 1902 when it appears to have been finally wound up. The Bible was then removed to the Officers' Mess, where it was kept in the mahogany and glass case in which it is still contained in the Museum. A silver plate on the front of the box states - 'On this Sacred Volume, Washington received a degree in Masonry. It was twice taken by the enemy and both times returned to the Regiment with all Honours of War.'

The Bible has generated considerable correspondence since at least 1884, and in the 1980s the West family made unsuccessful overtures for its return. This Bible is one tangible artefact the Regiment retains in memory of the American War of Independence, and a reminder of a remarkable amphibious operation by the British Army of which the 46th Foot, in particular, were justly proud. It was printed by Thomas Newcomb, 'Printers to the Queen's Most Excellent Majesty' and was rebound at some time in the mid-19th century. George Washington was initiated into masonry on Friday 4 November 1752 at the Fredericksberg masonic lodge, with other ceremonies taking place in 1753. Yet the date of initiation was five months before his 21st birthday! When he was sworn into office as President on 30 April 1789 the ceremony was conducted by the Grand Master of New York and he took his oath on a masonic Bible. He had then been a member of the Craft for 26 years and was a member of the Alexandria Lodge No. 22. The history of the 46th Foot and its lodge were closely bound. It was not until the 1760s and '70s that the Regiment was in the United States.

After returning to Londonderry in 1788 the Regiment saw service in Dominica and later India. The chest, with what remained of its contents, came to England in 1834, and 12 brethren returned the warrant the following year with request for renewal. This was granted but the lodge transferred allegiance to the Grand Lodge of Canada while the Regiment was there in 1857, and in 1896 the 46th - now the D.C.L.I. at Newry - was granted a military warrant by the Irish Grand Lodge under the title of the Dominica Lodge. Much travelled and changed, indeed, and the lodge appears to have become dormant during the 1914-18 war. Through all these vicissitudes the one relic that was retained was the Bible, now at Bodmin. In the glass display case close to the Bible is the masonic gavel of Lodge No. 174, 46th Regiment of Foot, made from a tree planted by General Washington at his home Mount Vernon, U.S.A. And so it would appear the 'Washington Bible' with its remarkable history, remains an enigma wrapped firmly in a legend... and a delightful piece of Cornish history and mystery!

Thread of Gold

Special Moments In History

OLD DUCHY PALACE: A CLAIM ON HISTORY

Can any other lodge in the United Grand Lodge of England claim to meet in a building of such antiquity and history as Restormel No. 856 at Lostwithiel? Can another lodge in Cornwall boast of a visit by a reigning monarch? King George VI (Past Grand Master of United Grand Lodge and Past Grand Master Mason of Scotland), accompanied by Queen Elizabeth and Princess Margaret, were shown over it on 11 July 1950 during a tour of the town. The borough regalia was also displayed, all three signed the lodge minute book, and a memento of their stay is a treasured possession.

The 'Duchy Palace' at Lostwithiel

A photograph of the King, signed by all three Royal guests, together with the extract from the minute book and an accompanying letter from the Private Secretary is permanently displayed in the lodge. Among the records is a copy of a letter to a Mrs Brewer, written in 1950 on behalf of the W.M. and brethren of Restormel, with thanks "for the very kind and practical help you gave in lending and so effectually using your Hoover in cleaning up the carpet etc for the reception of their Majesties, the King and Queen, together with H.R.H. Princess Margaret."

Special Moments In History

Through the ages the building has been referred to as the Old Duchy Palace. Yet it was never a palace (but The Mint) and it is assumed the name originated from the time it was erected. It was said to have been built as a replica of the Palace of Westminster, the Parliament buildings in those days, around 1265-1300 A.D. The medieval Dukes and Earls of Cornwall had their residence at Restormel Castle, near the town. The Shire Hall, or Duchy Palace, was their seat of government and also the home to the Shire Courts and other jurisdictions connected with the County and Duchy.

As well as the Great Hall where the Assizes and County Courts were held, there were the smelting houses for the tin, and Coinage Hall for the Stannaries, the Exchequer Hall for both the Stannaries and the County, and also the prison. In those years the whole suite of buildings extended the entire length of Shire Hall Street, which is commonly known as Quay Street. It was a great complex, covering two acres. In 1265 the town and a great deal of land in the neighbourhood, together with the river and town of Fowey was bought by Richard Earl of Cornwall, the younger brother of Henry III. At this time Lostwithiel was the largest port in Cornwall and second only to Southampton on the South coast. Richard died in 1272 and his son Edmund continued the building work which was completed in 1300. After Edmund's death the Earldom was raised to a Dukedom and granted to the Black Prince, then only seven years old. Since then the eldest son of each monarch becomes Duke of Cornwall.

So from that time up to the 19th century the Duchy as well as the county of Cornwall were administered from the Duchy Palace as the Great Hall and its complex was now known. The Parliamentary Army, under the 3rd Lord Essex, seized Lostwithiel in 1644 during the Civil War. There was a long battle in and around the town which was badly damaged. The Great Hall and most of the Duchy Palace was wrecked and burnt, causing the destruction of many important records of the Duchy. It was never completely rebuilt after the Restoration. The Exchequer Hall, the least damaged part, continued to be the administrative centre for the Duchy as well as the seat of justice. Other parts of the building fell further into ruin, a new Guildhall was built in Lostwithiel, the Duchy Offices were moved out in 1874, and the remains of what had been a 'Great Palace' sold off to various commercial interests in the town.

The first masonic lodge to be consecrated in Lostwithiel was St. Matthew Lodge No. 1158, in October 1861, which met at the Royal Talbot Hotel. It is thought the name came from the Feast of St. Matthew at the time of the consecration, but this remains a mystery. It may be because Matthew was a tax collector and this was a Royal Mint. The first minute book is lost and the parish church is named after St. Bartholomew.

At the January meeting of the lodge in 1880 it was proposed to erase the name St. Matthew from the Charter and "that in future this lodge be known under the name of Restormel Lodge to mark the connection of our freehold lodge buildings 'the Old Duchy Palace' with the Manor and Castle of Restormel, the Property of H.R.H. The Prince of Wales, Grand Master of England." Grand Lodge approved but, curiously, no new warrant was issued and the alterations were inscribed in the top right hand corner of the original warrant and signed by the Earl of Mount Edgcumbe. From among the ranks

Special Moments In History

of Restormel have come two Provincial Grand Secretaries, a Grand Superintendent and at least one active Provincial Grand Warden. Restormel Lodge received its Centenary Warrant in October 1961 and the celebrations included a service at St Bartholomew's Church. Records of its history have been compiled by W.Bro. S.A. Penpraze (P.P.S.G.W.), W.Bro. Donald Dunkley (P.P.G.Supt.Wks.), and the immediate past P.G.M. the Hon. Robert Eliot.

In 1997 the lodge banner was rededicated in a ceremony led by the Provincial Grand Master, R.W.Bro. Nicholas Barrington, and the Provincial G.Chaplain, Revd N.C.T. Olivey. It is believed the banner originated at the time of the renaming of the lodge to Restormel in 1880 and depicts a painting of Restormel Castle which at that time was overgrown with ivy and brambles - a complete ruin. The banner was repaired in 1924 and then restored for the 1997 ceremony. The Duchy coat of arms with its 15 bezants, surmounted with the Ducal Crown, is also displayed, signifying the importance that Restormel and the lodge building had in the early structure of the Earldom and the Duchy of Cornwall. The 'Palace' is now the home of several other lodges: Fowey Craft No. 977 (Centenary Warrant 1964); Fowey Royal Arch Chapter No. 977 (Consecrated 1946), Restormel Castle Council No. 85 (Consecrated 1973), and Edward the Black Prince Mark Lodge No. 1680 (Consecrated 1991).

The signed Minute Book marking the Royal visit to Restormel Lodge by King George VI, Queen Elizabeth and Princess Margaret in July 1950. The accompanying letter is from Balmoral Castle, 2nd October 1950. It states: Dear Sir, "The king has received your letter of 2nd September and was interested to hear of the steps taken by Restormel Lodge No. 856 to commemorate the visit which His Majesty paid, together with the Queen and Princess Margaret to the Old Duchy Palace, Lostwithiel, in July last.
"The King has signed a photograph of himself for your lodge premises in the palace to mark the occasion of his visit, and he has commanded me to send it to you, with an expression of His Majesty's good wishes to the Worshipful Master and Brethren of the lodge." Yours Truly, Edward Ford, Private Secretary.

LANDER MONUMENT

Special Moments In History

The Lander Monument, a dominant feature of Lemon Street, Truro, with its statue atop the mighty column, marks the explorations of two brothers from the city. Richard was more celebrated than John and in his all too brief life made three expeditions to Africa. He traced the lower part of the River Niger and discovered its source, but on his journey in 1834, when he was still only 30, he was attacked by natives and died of his wounds. Two years earlier the townsmen of Truro had marked the discoveries of the Lander brothers with a dinner when a subscription was launched to present pieces of plate to them. After the death of Richard his brother asked that the money be used for some more permanent memorial.

A later Cornish Provincial Grand Master Sir Charles Lemon gave the site and in June 1835 the foundation stone was laid with Masonic ceremony. There was a meeting of the Provincial Grand Lodge at the Red Lion Hotel before the procession left High Cross. "After a service at St. Mary's Church a lengthy procession was formed, headed by a band of music, to the top of Lemon Street, where it was calculated 5,000 people were assembled," it was reported. "The procession was marshalled by Mr. Ellis, the Prov. Grand Secretary, and the various Masonic implements and emblems were carried in formal order." Richard Lander's daughter placed a phial containing a vellum, emphasising that both brothers were being honoured, and current coins of the realm, into a prepared cavity in the foundation stone.

The Lander Monument and statue at Lemon Street, Truro, photographed in 1890.

Special Moments In History

This was on 24 June the Festival of St. John the Baptist, yet it was far from the end of the story. There were delays in the construction, more money was needed, and in May 1836 when the column was nearly at its full height, it "suddenly fell down with a tremendous crash." Three men working there escaped serious injury and in the following January arrangements were made for the "immediate erection" of the column. There was a further appeal for funds, and William Pryor of Truro, who had recently successfully completed the building of the De Dunstanville Monument on Carn Brea, worked speedily. By July the column had "risen into form from the pile of ruins which occupied the site." The column was safely erected in 1837, and in December 1849 it was learned that Neville Northey Burnard, the Cornish sculptor, born in Altarnun, had designed a model of Richard Lander. The 9ft. high statue was brought to Truro by a trading vessel in March 1852. It was of magnesium lime and was raised to the top of the column.

There appears to have been no ceremony of unveiling, masonic or otherwise. Contrary to the usual practice of having the figure gaze into the distance, Lander is shown looking downwards and dressed in contemporary clothes instead of the customary classical robes. So ended an enterprise that had its beginning almost 20 years previously. Burnard, after achieving fame in London, and frequently exhibiting at the Royal Academy, died in the Redruth Union in 1878 and was buried in a pauper's grave in Camborne Churchyard.

JOHN KNILL AND THE SHIP LODGE

Cornish lodges in the earliest days were named after the hotels or public houses in which they were held, such as the King's Arms, Ship and Castle, or King's Head. One of the most interesting was the Ship Lodge, then No. 240, of St Ives, which opened in July 1765 at the Ship Inn.

There is no longer an inn or a lodge of that name in the seaside town. Its first Worshipful Master was Bro. John Knill, famed for his Knill Steeple on the outskirts of the town, with its colourful ceremony, and as Mayor in 1767 and Collector of Customs from 1762-82. At the time of the formation of the lodge he was in his prime but was not a native of the town, being born in Callington. Knill drew up the details for the ceremony, around the 50-ft high pyramid mausoleum, and was present at the first in 1801. It continues once every five years, to the present day. Ten little girls in white and two elderly widows follow where the fiddler leads, round and round the steeple to the tune of the Cornish Furry Dance. Knill is not buried here: he died in London.

There were lodge meetings at the Ship Inn twice a month and the lodge was the sixth oldest in the province after Falmouth, Helston, Truro, Redruth and Penzance. The first officers included such well-known Cornish surnames as Stephens, Lane, Trengrouse and Hicks, but apart from these brethren no other was permitted to become Master. So the controversy at the finish had its origin at the start! There were but seven members of the lodge that had cost a little over £30 to constitute, including fees, jewels, books, candlesticks, pedestal and aprons. Because of the rule there was "great dissatisfaction and ill-feeling" that ultimately brought about the breaking-up of the Ship Lodge in 1780. Among the by-laws were those for no smoking "during the lecture", repealed six years later, and fining 5s. those coming "disguised with liquor." Any Brother, cursing or swearing, was to be first reprimanded, fined 1s. for the second offence, a half-crown for the third, and afterwards a crown and expelled for the night. There were records in the minutes of W.Ms being fined 2s.6d. for neglecting to send the "key to the pedestal" on meeting night. On one occasion so many leaders had to appear as witnesses at Bodmin Assizes that the lodge could not be held!

Bro. Knill figures prominently in the short history but there appears to have been few meetings from 1772-77. When, in 1775, the province said there would be a meeting at Falmouth to decide on a new P.G.M., he commented: "I know not of any particular person who is adapted for the high office". Two colleagues wrote suggesting him for the position, but he replied: "I should on all account decline the great honour if it was tendered to me." R.W.Bro. Stephen Bell was appointed. Then, in 1780, came disputes, some "taking umbrage at some supposed misconduct in the Master not proceeding to the election of a Master, becoming so Impetuous and Turbulent as wholly to prevent the secretary entering the Intended Motion," stated the lodge minutes. The brethren who had erased their names could not be persuaded to return. From July 1765 to October 1780 the lodge met 179 times but there had been only five W.M's: Bro. Knill seven times, Bro. Lane five, and Bros. Stephens, Hicks and Trengrouse four times each.

Prior to the breaking up of the lodge there were but seven subscribing members on the books. Eight from St. Ives were initiated into Druids Lodge of 'Love and Liberality,' Redruth, subsequent to the closure of the 'Ship', including ropemakers, innkeeper, mariner, sailmaker, carpenters and a 'gentleman.' In 1815 the furniture, minute and cash books were at Crowan where Lodge of True Friendship No. 678 was formed. It was warranted the following year. Sir John St. Aubyn of Clowance, who was to become Provincial Grand Master had earlier presented furniture to the Ship Lodge, but his name does not appear in the minutes at Crowan or that he was a member of the lodge. He was appointed S.G.W. of the Grand Lodge of England by his Grace the Duke of Manchester, the Grand Master, in 1786, and appointed the fourth P.G.M. five years later.

The minutes at Crowan continued from the book used at St. Ives, and later went on to Hayle to be used at Cornubian Lodge as were the chairs from the inn at Crowan. With some brethren leaving the area, two dying - including Bro. Henry Glasson soon after his initiation as Master at the age of 25 - the last recorded meeting of True Friendship at Crowan was in December 1819. One prominent member, the treasurer, Bro. Francis Pool, kept the St. Aubyn Arms at Praze, Crowan, "who was thrown from his horse and received such injuries that he never fully recovered." In 1816 the lodge had been held at his home by special dispensation, and continued there for some years.... with the dispensation returned to Grand Lodge in 1819, when a Warrant of Constitution was sent from London... and the last minutes recorded. The minute book became the property of Cornubian Lodge at the time of its consecration.

Special Moments In History

TREGENNA BANNER AND THE STEEPLE

Some members of Tregenna Lodge, No. 1272, St. Ives, claim a greater antiquity for their lodge than a mere 132 years. They affirm that it can be traced back to 1765, the year of the formation of the 'Ship Lodge' which met in the town and which owed its origin to John Knill, the Port Reeve, who is remembered by the Knill Steeple and the ceremony performed around this monument every five years. So the steeple features in the current lodge banner.

The original banner and valuable artefacts of the Lodge having been 'mysteriously lost' even the description could not be recalled nor traced! A new one was completed in 1986 by artist Bro. Marsden Prophet. The centre shown between the square and open compasses is in the likeness of the steeple, which Knill had built in the shape of a pyramid. He had hoped to be buried there, but failed to get the ground consecrated. This Collector of Customs at St. Ives - highly suspected of 'rather dubious practices' - was also eventually elected Mayor and was W.M. of the Ship Lodge. The central feature is the likeness of the original Smeaton's pier and lighthouse, and the black mackerel boat SS 116 is shown alongside the pier wall. The banner was finished 116 years after the consecration of Tregenna Lodge in 1870, and the ship is a reminder of the original lodge. The background of The Island and St. Nicholas' church is included because they are landmarks and navigational points for fishermen returning home.

WHAT'S IN A LODGE NUMBER?

The lodge number and venue of Love and Honour changed several times during the century or so from its formation in Falmouth in 1751 to 1863. Hotel and tavern were the centres until the foundation stone of the present Masonic Hall was laid by the Deputy P.G.M., W.Bro. Sir C.B. Graves Sawle in July 1885, the first meeting being held on May 10 the following year. From 1751 to 1781 and then from 1799-1814 the Lodge meeting place was at the King's Arms Tavern in Market Strand with six numbers in sequence. While at the Royal Standard, between two periods at the King's Arms, the number remained at 95 (1782). It was the final number at the King's Arms, 110, that continued when the venue changed to the Royal Hotel in Market Street (1820) but was altered again to 89 in 1832 before achieving the senior Cornish No. 75 in 1863 which continues to the present day. With eight lodge numbers in its 251 years it must amount to a national record. Brothers must have had to think twice to make sure, when they gave greetings from their lodge!

MOTORBIKES FOR CHARITY

Special Moments In History

Many fundraising projects have aided the 2002 Festival but one of the most unusual was the 315 mile ride by three motor-cyclists around Cornwall. They collected £2,600 during their 14 hours visiting 27 lodge temples, starting and finishing at Saltash and including St. Germans and Penzance en route. The trio were Bros. Terry Martin, Ken Baylis and Dave Thomas from the Essa Lodge at Saltash. In all there were donations from 49 Craft lodges and one Royal Arch Chapter, and these were credited to the individual lodges. The final cheque was handed over at Bodmin to the P.G.M. Nicholas Barrington. The ride began at 7am and ended at 9.45pm "It was probably the worst Sunday for weather we had all year" said Bro. Martin, "but we really enjoyed it."

CALIFORNIA - HERE WE COME!

Six Freemasons went on a visit to California in 1999 when they stayed at Cornish 'twin cities', were hosted by two U.S. lodges and saw the old mining areas where their ancestors worked. The holiday group also went to Nevada City and Grass Valley, major centres for emigrants from the Duchy in the 19th century to work in the Gold Country. Bro. Philip Southwood, led the 14-day trip during his year as W.M. of St. Levan Lodge at Penzance. Nevada is twinned with Penzance and Grass Valley with Bodmin. His father was a member of a U.S. lodge many years ago. The group visited Madison Lodge (Grass Valley) the Nevada City Lodge, and the San Francisco Masonic Memorial Temple was opened especially for them. It is hoped there will be a return visit.

TEN O'CLOCK TOAST TO MARINERS

The 'Ten O'Clock Toast' is a feature of the fishing harbour lodge of Tregenna at St Ives. It has been part of the ritual since the lodge inception in 1870 and took its rise from the previous Ship Lodge of 1765-1786. St. Ives, at that time, was a mercantile port with shipping traversing the globe, particularly the Mediterranean region. Some of the captains and first mates on these vessels were masons, and the only time they could attend lodge was on the rare occasion they were in port. In the old sailing ships of the 1760s these brethren were at sea for months or years. It was felt that when they were away from their loved ones and their lodge, on the open sea, their thoughts, and the thoughts of their brethren could be affirmed by a toast of rum or some other spirit (or beverage) at the time when, possibly, they would change the watch or come off from a watch, which apparently was 10 o'clock. "Therefore, on every lodge evening at precisely 10pm the Brethren toast their absent colleagues," said W.Bro. Tom Bennetts, secretary for some years. "This is always followed by the first verse of the hymn 'Eternal Father Strong

Special Moments In History

to Save', to provide a safe journey while at sea. "This has a touching sentiment, as we all know the hazards of life at sea, and in the history of the lodge have lost brethren from time to time, particularly during the war years. "We have some members who today are employed in the maritime service, and brethren who work abroad or who for some reason cannot be with us. We always sit quietly for a minute at 10 o'clock and then stand to drink a toast to the absent brethren, led by the Tyler. "They all say how comforting this toast to 'Absent Brethren' is, reminding them of home shores and their Tregenna Lodge 1272."

GAVELS FROM THE PRINCE

The three ebony 'Royal' gavels of Tregenna Lodge, St. Ives.

Three ebony gavels and three black candlesticks of Tregenna Lodge, St. Ives, have a Royal connection. In 1748 the Prince George Lodge was warranted in Plymouth and in March 1748 H.R.H. Prince William Henry (Duke of Clarence) was initiated. He subsequently joined a London Lodge, became King William IV on the death of his father (King George IV), and Patron of the Order for England and Scotland. The Prince presented the Plymouth Lodge with these three gavels, inlaid with the square, level and plumb-rule, and also the candlesticks with gilt mouldings, still used today. They came up for sale and were bought by W.Bro. Martin Dunn (the founder - W.M. of Tregenna 1870-71) in Plymouth, during his first year in office at St. Ives.

THE MALVERN LINK 'DOWN UNDER'.

Mount Sinai at Penzance, has enjoyed many links with those overseas, particularly through members who emigrated during the 19th and 20th centuries. This friendship has also worked in reverse for, in 1926 at the request of the W.M. of Ataka lodge No. 3367, in Egypt, Bro. Leslie Herbert Floyd underwent two ceremonies to complete his becoming a master mason. He had come to West Cornwall to work at the Eastern Telegraph Co. at Porthcurno. The most significant, however, and perhaps unique in freemasonry in this country, is the friendship between the Cornish Lodge No. 121, and the equivalent No. 121 in Melbourne, Australia, the Malvern Lodge. This began immediately after the 2nd World War when the Malvern members collected money to help some in the 'old country.'

There was no Malvern lodge in the English constitution so they chose one with the same number as their own, made contact, and sent food parcels; tea chests filled with goods to be distributed, including tinned fruit, butter, tea and meat. So grateful were the Cornish masons that they sent, in return, a set of 'flat pack' deacons chairs with the inscription "Malvern Lodge 121 - Mount Sinai 121". The chairs are still in use. Replicas of these are on display at Penzance and so is the original collecting box, used in Australia, and brought over by Malvern member W.Bro. Dennis Simsion. There have been many exchanges of gifts, including a set of Firing Glasses from Penzance and, on Malvern's centenary, a P.Ms collar with a Mount Sinai centenary jewel attached. The recipients added their own centenary jewel, and the collar is now worn by the Malvern retiring I.P.M.

A telephone link-up between the two lodges was twice arranged and several Cornish brethren have visited Malvern, the first being W.B. Phil Pengelly (P.A.G.D.C.), who presented a 'heavy maul' made of Cornish serpentine, and weighing nine pounds. W.B. Don Matheson, an original member of the 'collecting committee' gave his own P.Ms jewel, which is now attached to the Mount Sinai W.Ms collar, together with the Malvern centenary jewel. The Penzance lodge secretary for 11 years, W.Bro. Vince Sheldon is an hon. member of Malvern.

W.Bro. Len Trotter was the latest visitor from Australia and Bro. Jeremy Pilcher, who visited from Cornwall, was also taken on a tour of the television production set of the 'Neighbours' programme. The friendship between the two lodges remains as strong as ever.

The collecting box and replicas of the Deacons Chairs marking the Mt. Sinai - Malvern link

KNIGHTS OF THE ROUND TABLE
ARTHURIAN AND MASONIC TRADITION AT TINTAGEL.

Bro. Frederick Thomas Glasscock.

That stirring story of the chivalry, fellowship, love and bravery of the Knights of the Round Table of King Arthur burns as brightly today as ever. Cornwall has a special place in the Arthurian tradition because Tintagel is claimed as the natural centre from which the stories should radiate. The ancient castle is the great attraction, and nearby, in the village, is the magnificent 'King Arthur's Great Halls' - a unique building which forms a splendid setting for Masonic ceremonies. From the outside it looks an old Cornish house: inside it becomes vast and spectacular, the superb and colourful creation of Frederick Thomas Glasscock, a custard manufacturer, and opened in June 1933.

Granite from many parts of Cornwall, 72 stained glass windows described as among the finest of the 20th century in the world, and a tremendous granite dais, throne, and Round Table, make the main hall an inspiring sight. All the wall hangings, flags, shields and standards are the original 1930s decorations established by the founder. In the smaller hall are dramatic paintings depicting the scenes of drama of Arthur's life and death. There is the offering of the sword Excalibur, the passing of the King to the Vale of Avalon, the battle between Arthur and Sir Mordred, the vision of Sir Lancelot and the Holy Grail, among them. These were painted by William Hatherell in 1928, when he was 76 and a famed artist. The Great Halls - Glasscock's Dream Halls - were acquired by the Freemasons of Tintagel and are leased to the 'Sword in the Stone Ltd.' which has Mike Godwin as director. "Until you see it you don't believe it" said curator Roger Toy. "Behind this rather grey building and shop are the two halls. People are amazed. Almost every country in the world is represented in the visitors book."

Perhaps this contrast between exterior and interior is part of the symbolism: never judge a book (or anything or anyone) by the cover but by the inner beauty. The scenes on view make the story live again. Local and Cornish workmen were employed, as far as possible, in the work. The spirit of craftsmanship was fostered, and everything in the halls was based upon the Arthurian Romances. As with the windows, there are heavy Pre-Raphaelite overtones and they are now the story boards for the Son et Lumiere, narrated by film and television star Robert Powell, telling the story of Arthur and his Knights of the Round Table. The crowning glory is the windows, created by Veronica Whall in the 1930s. Her father, Christopher, was also a church stained glass expert - of the late 19th century - whose finest work is in the Chapter House of Gloucester Cathedral. She was a pupil of William Morris. Glasscock first commissioned her to design and build the two sets of triptych windows for the Tintagel halls: he was so pleased he ordered 67 more, 49 to light the galleries around the main hall and 18 for the hall itself. There are 125 shields of granite, set along the full length of the Hall of Chivalry and all around the gallery. They represent over 50 quarries throughout Cornwall - most of them now closed, unfortunately, because of cheaper foreign imports. All the shields were cut, set and polished from blocks brought to the halls and raised by derricks into position. The huge canopy over the throne, weighing almost six tons, is supported on nine massive granite pillars each threequarters of a ton in weight. The whole throne complex is estimated to weigh about 23 tons. The granite Round Table, eight feet in diameter and made in five sectors, weighs a ton.

Who was this man with the ambition to create this Arthurian tribute? When he and his partner had sold their custard company to Bird's Custard he decided to come and

Knights of the Round Table

Although not Prime Minister at the time, William Gladstone was at Tintagel in 1888, and is pictured at the front door to the holiday home of Sir Arthur and Lady Hayter. Today it is the front entrance to King Arthur's Great Halls, and the 'home' of the King Arthur Lodge No. 7134.

Then it was Treven House, a private country house, and Mr Gladstone was at Tintagel for a meeting in support of his campaign for Home Rule in Ireland.

Despite the passing of well over 110 years this main door has changed little. The house was built in 1860 on the site of the old town hall.

The Halls Foundation was begun by philanthropist custard millionaire, Bro. Frederick Glasscock in 1933, and the Halls built as a tribute to King Arthur and the Round Table. Mr Glasscock was a Freemason, a member of three London Lodges, and a co-founder of a Chapter at Launceston.

Knights of the Round Table

live at Tintagel where he had spent many holidays. Bro. Glasscock and his wife had a house built and became benefactors to the village. With his fascination for the Arthurian legend came the inspiration to build a large library of Arthuriana now in the Hall of Chivalry. His Fellowship of the Knights of the Round Table of King Arthur was founded in 1927 and by the early 1930s membership reached 17,000, with Chapters and Cells in many parts of the world. It was while returning by liner from the United States after a lecture tour and recruiting drive that he died of a heart attack in July 1934, aged 63, and was buried at sea. He was a keen scouter and an ardent freemason, being a member of three London lodges before coming to Cornwall when he joined the lodge at Launceston. There is something of the masonic symbolism at the halls with the themes of darkness into light. It is a perfect setting for a lodge ceremony. The King Arthur Lodge meets there, and so does St Enodoc for its installation ceremony. Several years ago the Fellowship Bro. Glasscock founded was revived and there are today many members worldwide. It states: "The Fellowship is based on the symbolism and ideals of the Arthurian tradition and more specifically care and consideration for our fellow beings. "Not sectarian, non-political, and without creed or bias it aims to bring together men and women from all corners of the Earth, where a sense of belonging and communication will bring contact, knowledge and pleasure, enriching our lives." Almost 70 years after the founder's death "One Man's Dream" still lives on. A remarkable Freemason.

275th ANNIVERSARY OF GRAND LODGE

More than 650 Freemasons and their families from throughout the Province celebrated two special events with a service in Truro Cathedral on 24 June 1992. Freemasons wore their regalia in the Cathedral and there were processions of the P.G.M. and his officers, and Grand Officers, and of the clergy and choir. The 24 June is St. John's Day, a special one for English Freemasons, as it was on that day in 1717 that four London Lodges came together to form the first Grand Lodge in the world. At that time most Lodges held their summer festival on St. John's Day and masons were known as St. John's Men. The service was another mark of the openness displayed by Freemasonry, emphasised by the Grand Master, H.R.H. the Duke of Kent, and shown in the international meeting of Grand Lodge at Earls Court. More than 50 members from Cornwall attended at Earls Court, which drew 12,000 members from throughout the world. It was the 275th anniversary of Grand Lodge.

In the Cathedral the Provincial Grand Master, the Hon. Robert Eliot presented a cheque for £7,200 at the close of Evensong to the Dean, the Very Revd David Shearlock, for the fabric fund, to mark the occasion. Of this total £6,000 had come from the Cornish Masonic Grand Charity and £1,200 from the individual Lodges of the Province. The P.G.M. said he was proud to see so many at the service. Since the laying of the foundation stone of the Cathedral in 1880. Freemasons have been involved in many ways with the work of the Cathedral.

The Very Reverend David J. Shearlock, the Dean of Truro, received a donation to the Cathedral Fabric Fund, in April 1988 from the PGM the Hon Robert Eliot. This followed Evensong Service at the Cathedral to celebrate the centenary of its consecration. Between the two is the Deputy PGM, V.W.Bro. Sidney Pearce, and on the right Assistant PGM, W.Bro. Rollo Crabb.

By 1937 top hats had given way to the more popular bowlers. In that year the Provincial Grand Lodge was held at Penzance under the banner of St. Levan Lodge No. 5134. This was at the request of the PGM, the Lord St. Levan, while he was still able to perform Masonic duties. It was one of the last ceremonies he presided over for he died in 1940.

THREAD OF GOLD

Chapter IV

Royal Arch Chapter
Mark Master Masons
Royal Ark, Mariners
Cornish Masons' Role in Transvaal

The P.G.M., R.W.Bro. Nicholas Barrington presents a certificate to W.Bro. R. Shapland in 1995 marking the 60th anniversary of his joining Boscawen Lodge.

A cheque for £4,000 is presented in July 1992 outside the then Provincial office at Truro to the Cornwall First Air Ambulance by the PGM, the Hon. Robert Eliot.

ROYAL ARCH CHAPTER
1791-2002

"EMERGED FROM THE MISTS OF TIME"

The first recorded Royal Arch Chapter activity in Cornwall began over 200 years ago. Some of the events of that time are shrouded in mystery and conjecture, and, as is common with history in general, uncertainties occur with increasing frequency, in direct relation to the length of time which is back-tracked. It is known however that Royal Arch Masonry emerged in Cornwall from the mists of time in 1791 when R.W.Bro. Thomas Dunckerley was made the first Grand Superintendent of the Province.

It is not known how often Dunckerley came to Cornwall. He was a serving member of the Royal Navy and was for many years a Chief Gunner, serving on numerous ships on some of which he formed masonic lodges. At one time he was Grand Superintendent of 28 Provinces and Provincial Grand Master of eight provinces. He was active in the development of the Holy Royal Arch as a separate organisation from the Premier or 'Modern' Grand Lodge of that time. At this time there was no Chapter in existence in Cornwall and Dunckerley's first task was to issue a 'Warrant of Dispensation' for three Companions to be the Principals of the Druids Chapter of Love and Liberality at Redruth.

The First Principal was John Knight, a stalwart of Cornish Freemasonry, who had been initiated into Druids Lodge in 1766 and exalted in the Chapter of Sincerity, Peace and Fame in Plymouth in 1775. E Comp Knight went on to become the mainstay of Freemasonry in West Cornwall for some 35 years. He wrote extensively on masonic matters and fortunately was so very meticulous and painstaking that some of his writings are still in existence, both in the library of Grand Lodge and in our own Masonic Museum at Hayle. From 1791 to 1819 over 100 candidates were Exalted into Druids Chapter, many of whom later became founders of neighbouring Chapters, and Redruth during that time was a very important masonic centre.

In 1795 a petition by John Knight to Thomas Dunckerley resulted in the formation of Chapter of Light and Truth at Penryn, but little record remains, and it had a very brief existence. From 1795 to 1810 however it appears there were no candidates exalted into Druids' Chapter from the Penryn area which suggests that this was the period the Penryn Chapter existed.

Royal Arch Chapter

Following the death of Thomas Dunckerley in 1795 the next Grand Superintendent is believed to have been Sir John St. Aubyn who had been P.G.M. since 1785 and continued in both offices until his death in 1839. There is no evidence however that he was ever exalted into the Royal Arch. This was a very important time for Freemasonry generally inasmuch that the schism which existed between the 'Antients' and 'Moderns' since 1738 was healed by the formation of United Grand Lodge in 1813 followed by United Grand Chapter in 1817 (renamed Supreme Grand Chapter in 1822). Locally, the next two Chapters to receive their Charters were Volubian at Falmouth (1810) and Holy Mount at Penzance (1833). During this period in 1828 John Knight died and with his passing also ended Druids Chapter at Redruth. (The Chapter which now meets at Redruth is Rose of Sharon No.1006 which although originally chartered in 1867 came from St. Day in 1895). The third Grand Superintendent was E Comp John Ellis (1848-1861) who had been First Principal of Volubian Chapter and was also Provincial Grand Secretary from 1823-1857.

Although determined to promote Royal Arch Masonry in Cornwall he was unsuccessful in forming any new Chapters. Richard Pearce, who had been exalted by John Knight into Druids' Chapter in 1818 became the next Grand Superintendent in 1861, and the first Chapter to be consecrated by him was Royal Cornubian No.331 in 1862. Others soon followed, St. Martin's No.510 at Liskeard (1864), Unity Chapter No.977 at Fowey (now erased), Rose of Sharon No.1006 (1867), Eliot No.1164 started at St. Germans 1871 but later moved to Millbrook, Mount Edgcumbe No.496 and Hayle Chapter No.450, both in 1874.

With nine Chapters in Cornwall it was considered that the Order of the Holy Royal Arch had gained more than a foothold and that it was time to consolidate by the formation of a Provincial Grand Chapter, and so on 20 February 1877 in the Masonic Hall at Truro the Provincial Grand Chapter was constituted. The whole impressive ceremony, including speeches and orations was reported at length in the Cornwall Gazette and Western Morning News which contain more information than actually recorded in the Minutes. Copies of these newscuttings have been preserved and can be seen in the Masonic Museum at Hayle.

The year 1877 can thus be considered the commencement of the second phase of Royal Arch Masonry in Cornwall. It is also interestingly the year in which the Diocese of Cornwall came into being, resulting in Truro Cathedral being erected on the site of the Church of St. Mary. From this time the Order has flourished in the Province, five more Chapters came into being in quick succession, Zetland, Dunheved, St. Petrock, St. Anne's and Valletort; although Dunheved which had a difficult start was erased in 1899 before receiving its Charter again in 1920.

The Earl of Mount Edgcumbe reigned as Grand Superintendent for the first 44 years of the new Provincial Grand Chapter and he was followed by Lord St. Levan who held the office for a further 20 years. Since then we have had the Revd Canon H.R. Jennings, the Revd T.A. Webber, W. Lloyd White, the Revd James Gillett, The Hon. Robert Eliot and since 1994 our present Grand Superintendent Nicholas Barrington who like his predecessor continues to hold this office with that of P.G.M.

Royal Arch Chapter

All of these illustrious leaders have been supported over the years by many great masons too numerous to list here, but there is one however who stands out like a giant and is worthy of special mention. He is, E Comp Sir P. Colville Smith who occupied the chair of the Provincial Second Grand Principal for no less than 38 years (1899-1937) whilst going on to become Grand Secretary and Grand Scribe E for 20 years. At the sixth meeting of Provincial Grand Chapter in 1889 a unanimous decision was taken that there should be one uniform ritual worked within the Province - a decision which has never been adhered to as there are a variety of rituals currently in use, and an even greater number of 'openings and closings'. The Hon. Robert Eliot when Grand Superintendent was frequently heard to comment, somewhat tongue in cheek, that of the 31 Chapters in the Province there appeared to be 32 different openings and closings! This variety, together with other local traditions of individual Chapters lead however to more colourful ceremonies which makes visiting in the Royal Arch such a pleasant experience.

By 1970 the number of Chapters had grown to 23 and it was decided that one for the senior members of the Royal Arch was needed. Thus in February of that year the Cornish First Principals Chapter No. 3324 received its Charter. It meets three times a year at various locations in the Province. It has worked the ceremony, received lectures and seen demonstrations, the most recent being the working of the 'Fourth Degree of the Antients' by a team from the Province of Monmouthshire depicting Freemasonry

A Chapter meeting in St. Austell in years gone by.

Thread of Gold

Royal Arch Chapter

in the late 18th century. This Chapter serves a very useful purpose in the Province and continues to thrive due to the large number of Joining members from among the annual influx of installed First Principals. There are of course no Exaltations into this Chapter although the by-laws proclaim an exaltation fee of £1,000! Since 1970 a further seven Chapters have been consecrated making the present total of 31, eleven of which have received Centenary Warrants.

The year 1977 is considered the start of the third phase in our history. The first 100 years of Provincial Grand Chapter was celebrated by a Service of Thanksgiving at the Parish Church in Falmouth which was conducted by Companion, the Revd Canon Jack Jose, in October of that year in the presence of a large congregation of masons together with their wives. That year also saw the start of a new minute book for the Provincial Grand Chapter which now contains full details of annual meetings, agendas and statements of account, together with a record of the Special Convocation for the Installation of our present Grand Superintendent in 1994.

In the early days Provincial Grand Chapter met in various masonic centres at irregular intervals of between one and four years, and it was not until 1899 that the first of the annual meetings was held. As the number attending the meetings has steadily increased so other larger accommodation, usually in schools, has had to be found. Provincial annual meetings now alternate between St. Austell and Redruth, preceded by luncheon at a nearby hotel. From small beginnings, membership throughout the Province has gradually increased. The first number quoted for the Province in 1889 was 290, by the turn of the century it had reached 400. Since then the numbers have fluctuated, reaching a peak of almost 1,700 in 1975, and now standing at 1,457. Almost 50 years on, the percentage remains virtually unchanged with 4,344 Craft members to 1,457 Chapter members.

This short history of the Holy Royal Arch in Cornwall has been extensively sourced from Companion F.W. Shepherd's booklet 'Royal Arch Masonry in Cornwall', published in 1977, and notes of a talk on the same subject by E Comp. Bill Watters, with a little help from the library at Grand Lodge. Further information is contained in the Cornwall Masonic Year Book and notable events within the Province are recorded in the *Highlights of the Cornish Craft* which separates the Craft and Royal Arch sections of the Year Book.

Royal Arch Chapter

M.E. Grand Superintendent
E. Comp
Nicholas Barrington

E. Comp
Michael Fouracres PAG Soj.
Deputy Grand Superintendent

Provincial Grand Scribe	E. Comp. Bruce Roberts PG St.B.
Treasurer	E. Comp. Eric Williams PPG Sc.N.
Director of Ceremonies	E. Comp A.J. Groves PAG Soj.

Thread of Gold

MARK MASTER MASONS
ORIGINS ARE "SHROUDED IN MYSTERY"

The origins of Mark Masonry are shrouded in mystery but certainly by the middle of the 18th century the Degree of Mark Man and Mark Master were being worked mainly in Craft lodges sponsored by the Antients. The union of the two Grand lodges in 1813, however, brought this state of affairs to an end.

It was agreed that "Pure Ancient Masonry consists of three degrees, and no more, viz., those of Entered Apprentice, Fellow Craft and Master Mason, including the Supreme Order of the Holy Royal Arch...." This statement meant that the Mark and certain other orders, which had been worked mainly in lodges owing allegiance to the "Antients" Grand Lodge could no longer be worked. It would appear that, up to the founding of the first Mark Lodge, Meridian at Millbrook in 1864 and then the three others, Fortitude at Truro, Cornubian at Hayle and Love and Honour at Falmouth, Mark Masonry was only worked intermittently in Cornwall. In Redruth a Bro. John Knight had been initiated into most of the known degrees in Freemasonry until his death in 1828. For most however the Mark was a closed book. But in the East of the Province, especially those who had access to Devonport, the Mark was becoming an integral part of their masonic life.

For many years Friendship Lodge - now No. 16 T.I. had worked the Mark Degree, issuing its own certificates and operating a travelling lodge which worked, quite unconstitutionally, in craft lodges. Certificates issued by this lodge have been found and one showed it had advanced candidates in St. Martins Craft Lodge, Liskeard as late as 1846 and continuing into 1847. It must have come to the notice of the provincial authorities, for the Worshipful Master of St. Martin's Lodge No. 750 received a communication from the Deputy Provincial Grand Master in November 1847 enjoining him to "attend to the instructions therein contained". Nothing is known of the contents of the letter, but the Mark ceased to work from that date onwards.

The founding of Mark Grand Lodge in 1856, however, meant that those masons who wished to include the Mark in their masonic profile could now do so, although it was not until 1865 that a Warrant was granted for a Mark Lodge to be held in Millbrook under the title of Meridian. All the petitioners for this new lodge were Devonian. In August 1864 an event occurred which at that time seemed of no account, but in the event proved to be one of the most momentous in Cornish masonry. A "Stuff Buyer" arrived in Truro by the name of William James Hughan. He had been initiated into St. Aubyn Craft Lodge No. 954 and advanced into St. Aubyn Mark Lodge No. 64. He came to Truro with an enthusiasm for masonry which was to have a lasting influence not only on Cornish masonry but also nationally. He joined Phoenix Craft Lodge No. 331 and Fortitude Craft Lodge No. 131, becoming Master twice, in 1868 and 1878. He formed a lasting friendship with Thomas Chirgwin and these two revitalised Mark Masonry in Cornwall.

Mark Master Masons

At this time there were only two Mark Masons in Truro apart from Bro. Hughan, Bro. Arthur Champion Willyams whose lodge was Carnarvon No. 7 London and Bro. Elliott whose lodge was Friendship No. 16 T.I. Thomas Chirgwin was advanced in St. Aubyn Mark Lodge No. 64 Plymouth on 27 March 1865. On 11 April 1865, Fortitude Craft Lodge at the urgent request of Thomas Chirgwin petitioned Grand Mark Lodge for a warrant. The warrant was sanctioned and on 18 May 1865 the first meeting was held and William James Hughan was installed as first Master with the three others as founders.

Following the installation 17 candidates were balloted for and five immediately advanced. The founding of Fortitude Lodge No. 78 Truro seemed to answer a need of Cornish Masons, for by the end of William James Hughan's year as Master no fewer than 70 candidates had been advanced. As quite a number of these candidates were from neighbouring towns it would appear that it was part of a pre-conceived plan to establish Mark Masonry in Cornwall. By the end of 1865 Cornubian Lodge No. 87 at Hayle and in 1866 Love and Honour Lodge No. 94 at Falmouth had been consecrated. This meant that in 18 months Cornwall had acquired four Mark lodges. The time was ripe to petition for Cornwall to become a province in its own right. In 1867 the prayer was granted and the Member of Parliament for Truro, Frederick Martin Williams, was appointed as first P.G.M.. All the hard work put in by Bro. Hughan in establishing the Mark Degree in Cornwall was rewarded when at the first meeting of Provincial Grand Lodge he was appointed as Provincial Grand Secretary. In 1867 Meridian Lodge No. 73 moved to Redruth and was re-opened on 16 October by Bro. Hughan. This meant that Mark Masonry became concentrated in the west of the Province, and it was not until St. Anne's Lodge No. 351, Looe, was consecrated in 1885 that Mark Masonry re-appeared once again in East Cornwall. Since the foundation of the province in 1867, Mark Masonry in Cornwall has flourished under the inspired leadership of its ten P.G.Ms, each having strong links with the province and each one contributing in some way to the ethos of the province. Two have been P.G.Ms of both the Craft was well as the Mark, two have been Deputies in the Craft and the Mark, one has been Deputy Grand Master in the Mark Degree and one, Grand Secretary in the Craft.

From its foundation as a province in 1867 the Mark in Cornwall has flourished. By the turn of the century there were some 13 lodges. It was a matter of some regret that from 1890 to 1919 no new lodges were consecrated and two had failed, Fort Lodge No. 206, Newquay and Lebanon Lodge No. 325, Lostwithiel. In 1919, however, St. Columb founded a new lodge and this seemed to galvanize and revitalise the Mark Degree and under the leadership of Philip Colville Smith a further three lodges were consecrated before the decade was out. Again, there was a lull and it was not until 1944 that another lodge was consecrated at Illogan. During the next ten years a further five lodges were consecrated bringing the total in Cornwall to 21. In 1967 the Province celebrated its centenary and to mark this event the Cornish Installed Mark Masters Lodge No. 1332 was consecrated by the Most Worshipful Grand Master, the Rt Hon. the Lord Harris, M.C., V.L. assisted by officers of Grand Lodge, with over 100 founders. The first Master was R.W.Bro.Col. Edwin Perry Morgan the Provincial Grand Master. The founders were drawn from the lodges throughout the province and contained some of the most enthusiastic masons. That it is still one of the strongest lodges is testimony to the firm foundations laid by

Mark Master Masons

the founders. It seemed only right that when, in 1975, a new Mark lodge was being proposed in Falmouth, the name of one of the most important men in Cornish Mark Masonry should be considered, William James Hughan. So on 17 May 1975 the William James Hughan Lodge No. 1437 was consecrated by the Provincial Grand Master, R.W.Bro. J.E. Price assisted by officers of Provincial Grand Lodge. The Mark Degree continued to prosper and consolidate in the province, and in 1986 a Grand Officers' Lodge was consecrated in Perranporth to honour the name of Col. Edwin Perry Morgan M.B.E., T.D., J.P. a Past P.G.M. and Past Deputy Grand Master of Mark Master Masons. The ceremony was performed by the Deputy Grand Master, R.W.Bro.Col. G.S.H. Dicker C.B.E. T.D. D.L. assisted by officers of Grand and Provincial Grand Lodge. The first Master was the Provincial Grand Master, R.W. Bro. T.C.A. Waghorn and the first S.W. his Deputy, W.Bro. F. Tonkin, now our present P.G.M. In 1991 a new Mark Lodge was consecrated in Lostwithiel, in part to replace an earlier one which foundered in the early years of the century, and also to honour the name of Edward, The Black Prince, who was the first Duke of Cornwall. The Mark Degree in Cornwall continues to flourish and this is exemplified by the consecration of a Mark lodge to meet at Tintagel under the name of Tintagel Castle Lodge No. 1800. The province has 30 Mark lodges and has been well served by many dedicated masons for over 130 years.

The words of the Provincial Grand Chaplain, W.Bro. the Revd Stephen Leach seem appropriate, when he said at the consecration of Tintagel Castle Lodge No. 1800 "….Freemasonry is not a social club, but a way of life, a way of service, and a moral code. It is founded on the belief in a Supreme Being who is the Architect and Creator of all that is and who is all-knowing and all seeing, and who oversees all that He has made; the Great Overseer of the Universe. It is in His Name, and to His service that this your lodge is consecrated and set apart."

There is harmony and co-operation between the Craft and the Mark and long may this continue, as we both have one aim in view "to please each other and unite in the grand design of being happy and communicating happiness, and may brotherly love and affection ever distinguish us as men and masons."

Mark Master Masons

Provincial
Grand Master
R. W. Bro. Frank Tonkin

Deputy Provincial
Grand Master
W. Bro. Mark Hocking PGSD.

Assistant Provincial
Grand Master
W. Bro. Geoff Isaac
PGSD.

ROYAL ARK MARINERS

The Degree of Royal Ark Mariner has been under the jurisdiction of the Grand Lodge of Mark Master Masons since 1871, each lodge bearing the same number as the Mark lodge which sponsored it.

However, it was not until 1895, nearly 30 years after the foundation of the Mark Province in Cornwall, that a Royal Ark Mariner Lodge, attached to Boscawen Lodge No. 101, was consecrated. Many brethren prominent in the history of the Mark in Cornwall have been members of this lodge, including Sir Philip Colville Smith and Col. Edward Neynoe Willyams, both of whom were P.G.Ms of the Mark Province. It was, however, not until 1932 that another Royal Ark Mariner Lodge was consecrated by the Provincial Grand Master, Sir Philip Colville Smith, under the patronage of Three Grand Principles Lodge No. 879 at Penryn, some 37 years after the first was warranted.

During that decade there followed two more in quick succession, at Liskeard in 1933 and Penzance in 1935 making a total of four in the province. For many years St. John the Baptist Lodge No. 404, at Penzance was the largest Royal Ark Mariner Lodge in the country. It would be another ten years before - in 1945 - Fortitude Mark Lodge would sponsor a Royal Ark Mariner Lodge and it was in this lodge that Bro.Col.E. Perry Morgan was elevated in 1947. Camborne soon followed their example and a lodge was warranted there in 1946.

The degree now entered a period of consolidation, and it would be 16 years before any more would be consecrated. In 1965 St Michael's Royal Ark Mariners Lodge No. 175, Helston was consecrated and during that decade a further three lodges were warranted. Since then the popularity of this degree has increased and the province now has some 14 Royal Ark Mariner lodges including one for Installed Commanders attached to the Installed Mark Masters Lodge and which, like its sponsor, is one of the strongest lodges in the province which looks forward to hosting the Festival for The Mark Benevolent Fund in 2006.

CORNWALL'S LEADING ROLE IN TRANSVAAL FREEMASONRY

So many Cornish men emigrated to South Africa during the depression in the Duchy's mining industry in the 19th century that it seems almost inevitable they would play a leading role in Freemasonry there. This they did. Transvaal District Grand Lodge celebrated its centenary in 1995 in the knowledge that it was the largest District in English Freemasonry, with responsibility for 125 Lodges in five countries. Down the century it has had 15 District Grand Masters, three of them with Cornish ancestry or links.

One of them was the first District Grand Master (D.G.M.) (1895-1905), R.W.Bro. George Richards, born of humble parents at Treswithian in 1847. His father was a tin miner who left the county around 1870, attracted by the prospect of the new diamond diggings at Kimberley, as it was later known. George Richards, a merchant, was one of the first initiates (in 1876) of the Richard Giddy Lodge in the English Constitution, five months after the Masonic Hall had been consecrated.

Transvaal was annexed to Britain in 1877 but an early application to the United Grand Lodge of England for a Charter was turned down ten years later. Richards, now an ambitious mining executive, joined Johannesburg Lodge - the first English Lodge on the Witwatersrand goldfields - in 1891, and Freemasonry expanded and flourished. As managing director of his own company, he came to England in 1893 and played a significant part in the next stage of the formation of a District Grand Lodge.

The District was inaugurated in April 1895 with Richards as its leader. Within a few months came the Jameson Raid, and Richards, along with Colonel Rhodes and others were named as conspirators. Cecil Rhodes resigned as Prime Minister of the Cape Colony, and Richards was unable to attend the first anniversary of the founding of the D.G. Lodge in 1896 because he was in gaol. From his release, after a few months, until the outbreak of the South African War in 1899, Richards spent most of his time in England, where in 1897 he presented an Address of Loyalty from Transvaal Masons to Queen Victoria on her Diamond Jubilee. Funds were raised during the war to help relieve English Masons in South Africa. Pressure of business, family commitments and business in England, led to his resignation as D.G.M. in 1905 and he died in 1911 on board a ship off Southampton.

Another 'Cornish Mason' was at the helm from 1937 to 1939, R.W.Bro. Charles Maple-Polmear, who was born in Devon but initiated in Cotehele Lodge No. 2166 at Calstock in 1890. He made rapid masonic progress after emigrating to Australia two years later and was already a District Officer before he came to South Africa with the Australian forces during the South African War. He settled in East London, later moving to Johannesburg in about 1908, becoming Deputy D.G.M. in 1927.

Cornwall's Leading Role in Transvaal Freemasonry

In the Royal Arch he was Grand Superintendent for seven years before becoming D.G.M. Maple-Polmear was seriously injured in a car accident in 1939, left his bed to preside over the District annual meeting in April, but died three weeks later. His period of office was a time when Transvaal Freemasons watched the inevitability of war in Europe from 6,000 miles away, and feared for the Craft and its leaders.

Another Cornish-born Mason, R.W.Bro. James Howard Vivian, was D.G.M. from 1950-55. Born in Camborne in 1885 he was educated at Taunton and the Camborne School of Mines. He emigrated to South Africa at 21, achieving success with his own business in general mining supplies. During his five years in office the country was torn by political and social passions and faced overseas sanctions as a result of restrictive legislation and forced removals. Internally there grew a strong republican movement. Vivian served as president of the Board of General Purposes of the District, and went direct from this to District G.M. During the 1939-45 war he was chairman of the Governor General's War Fund which raised over £11 million: for this work he was commended by King George VI.

He served as leader during the movement within the Craft for a United Grand Lodge of South Africa. The D.G.M. worked hard to provide a new building for English Freemasonry in the Transvaal and was present in 1954 when the foundation stone of the Freemasons Hall at Parktown was laid by R.W.Bro.Major General Sir Allan Adair, the Assistant Grand Master. Unfortunately he did not live to see the completion of the building, but a year after his death in 1955 the J.H. Vivian Lodge No. 7440 was consecrated in his memory.

The story of English Freemasonry in the Transvaal is told in 'A Century of Brotherhood' 1895-1995, from which the 'Cornish Connection' in this excerpt is derived.

FRENCH PRISONERS OF WAR BROUGHT THEIR FREEMASONRY TO CORNWALL

From 1740 to 1815 Great Britain and France were almost constantly at war, marked particularly by the Seven Years War from 1756-1763, and the Napoleonic campaigns that were fought in France, America, Holland, Denmark, Spain, in addition to naval operations on the high seas. Freemasonry had been firmly established in Europe, with the possible exception of Spain and Portugal, from the beginning of the 18th century.

The probability that it had spread rapidly on account of Jacobite refugees from Great Britain cannot be overlooked. It should be remembered, too, that although some Popes had issued Bulls against the practice of Freemasonry, these edicts were not taken seriously and it was not until 1821 that previous Bulls were re-introduced with some degree of expectation that they should be respected. In any event the religious foundations of France in particular were at that time in a state of flux. A war period of 75 years brought in its train a prisoner of war problem. The prisoners themselves were military and civilian. The non-service were the French citizens resident in England on the outbreak of war. During the Seven Years War they were gradually rounded up and placed under surveillance.

The number of service prisoners varied considerably during the early period: they were in the main French. As Napoleonic campaigns spread to cover Europe, practically every European nationality was represented. Very naturally the moral quality fell away early in 1800, the sweepings of Europe were being sent to these shores. This is evident from the facts that for the Napoleonic campaigns in Spain less than half of the men under Joseph Bonaparte were French, while for the Russian expedition of the same year there were only 200,000 Frenchmen in an army of 5,000,000. It will be realized, therefore, that all types and conditions of men were arriving here as prisoners. The numbers through the years varied considerably: repatriation by exchange, death and escape were the reliefs from an otherwise overflowing multitude. In all some 200,000 prisoners of war were brought to these shores, and the largest number in captivity at any one period was 72,000 in 1814. During the whole period about 17,000 were exchanged and over 10,000 died. The French authorities did not remit one penny for the upkeep of these prisoners.

The first batches of prisoners were confined in the normal civil gaols, then military prisons, such as Chatham and Plymouth and finally, into castles, amongst them Pendennis, at Falmouth.

This accommodation was, however, inadequate, and it was decided to adapt a number of old hulks as floating prisons; all told 52 such hulks were so adapted, capable of, or at least rated to accommodate 600-800 men. Eleven of these hulks laid at Plymouth. Conditions on them were deplorable.

French Prisoners of War

Brutal discipline, with cramped decks and leaky quarters, rendered them "hell ships" in the true sense of the words, yet attempts were made at regulations and generally speaking these hulks were used for the trouble makers, those attempting to escape and others whose total lack of moral qualities made them a danger on the mainland. Another class of prisoner was made of those who had given their parole not to escape. Life for them was comparatively easy. They were billeted in the towns, received their half-guinea weekly from the British and, in many cases, were in receipt of money from French sources. Provided they reported once a day and did not go beyond one mile of the town boundary, they were to all intents and purposes free to do as they wished. Normally such parole towns were well away from the coast to prevent the possibility of escapes. Although the number giving their word of honour not to endeavour to escape was not large, the proportion of those doing so and using or abusing their conditions of living to escape was comparatively high. Capture meant incarceration in the hulks.

Such then were the unwelcome guests of Britain. Among their numbers, particularly in the period up to about 1790, there were quite a number of freemasons, owing allegiance to and membership of the Grand Orient of France. This Grand Lodge was recognized by the Grand Lodge of England until 1877. Relations were strained from 1871 when the office of G.M. was abolished, being replaced by a President of the Order.

Soon after new constitutions were published as a result of which relations between the Grand Lodge of England and the Grand Orient of France ceased. The form of freemasonry varied over the country, but in the main it fell into three categories. Where the number of masons in a district was small and there was some freedom of movement, visitations were made to English lodges. In some cases the brethren became joining members, in others there were cases of actual initiations, etc. An instance of brethren becoming joining members is referred to in the minute book of the Ship Lodge at St. Ives. The minute reads: "At St. Ives, 18 March 1778, the following seven brethren, being prisoners of war, favoured our lodge with a visit. On 22 April they proposed themselves to become members of the lodge, which was unanimously agreed to!"

It is not clear where these prisoners were supposed to endure detention. Their rules of detention appeared to be as elastic as the bye-laws of the St. Ives lodge. Initiates who were prisoners of war are mentioned in the minutes of Druids' Lodge of Love and Honour amongst others.

Only one French lodge was formed in Cornwall, that at Launceston. Evidence of French prisoners of war, who were Masons, being present in Launceston in 1757 is given by the following extract of Proceedings of Grand Lodge. "A letter to the G.M. Elect dated 22 April of the Bro.L. de Court late Commander of the French merchant ship, St. James, captured on 29 October by His Majesty's ship, Windsor, and now a Prisoner of War at Launceston in Cornwall wishing his Lordship could procure his liberty to return to Bordeaux and promising all good offices to brethren prisoners in France and praying relief. It was read and spoke of when it being observed that no cartel was as yet settled with the French King it might not be possible to relieve our Bro. otherwise than by money. "Ordered that the Treasurer do pay 20 guineas to Commissioner Pye, P.G.M. of Cornwall, to be applied to the relief of Bro. de Court, in case of enquiry he shall find him worthy of assistance."

French Prisoners of War

The first record of a French Lodge established in Launceston is in 1762. It was given the name De La Consolante Maconne (The Consoling Mason). The lodge at Launceston admitted not only Frenchmen but Englishmen as well. Certificates were issued in French or English according to the nationality. Abergavenny and Wincanton are the only other French lodges that made such admissions. It should be noted that there was not an English lodge working in Launceston at this time. The nearest lodge was probably in Plymouth; Cornubian was warranted under the English Constitution at Launceston in 1767 and ceased working in 1780.

A very fine certificate of the French Lodge is held by Grand Lodge. It is in English printed on a parchment, and refers to Rob Martin, Organist of St. Mary Magdalene, Launceston, being accepted and admitted to the Lodge of E.A.F. Master or Scotch Mason; Martin appears to have been a Mason already, as he is referred to as an Officer Prefect, First Elect and English Master. This certificate is dated 18 April 1763, and it is of interest to note that among those attesting the certificate are Thomas Green and William Rowe. How long this lodge functioned is not clear, but its life appears to have been comparatively short. The Cornubian Lodge, formed in 1767, may well have taken its origin from some of the initiates of this French Lodge.

The people of Launceston gained a somewhat dubious notoriety for their tolerence towards the prisoners in their midst. Parish records show that there were a number of marriages and evidences of assistance, and connivances at escape were all too frequent. A request for a Charter to form a lodge was submitted to Grand Lodge in 1809, but was refused on the somewhat doubtful grounds that the population was far too friendly to the French. Mention has been made of initiates and joining members of existing lodges in Cornwall. The returns of Druids' Lodge at Redruth show six such members in 1791. Love and Honour minutes refer, in 1782, to Bro. Peter Cogrel a prisoner of war at Kirgillick who was relieved with a guinea, also Bro. B. Warogener a French prisoner of war with a similar amount. Such records emphasise that however great the bogey of Napoleon and all that he stood for, the bond of freemasonry rose above such fears. Cornwall had suffered much from privateers and raids on her coasts and shipping.

An army militia of five thousand men was raised from a population that bears no relation to to the present. This, too, without the main drain of Cornish manpower, the Navy and the sea. Yet, despite the bitterness and the hatred there must have been, the common bond of freemasonry swept it away. Can we be so sure that we should have acted as they did in acts of very real charity to members of a nation that had made them miserable over a period of 70 odd years? One can imagine, too, that not always were such acts of charity approved by the uninstructed or popular world.

There were 42 known prisoner of war lodges in Great Britain. In addition, lodges at Gibraltar, Malta, etc. Of the British lodges three were at Plymouth, two of them held on hulks the other at the Mill Prison. The jewels and furniture were in the main made by the prisoners themselves. Grand Lodge Museum holds some beautiful examples of the skill and craftsmanship put into them. Their certificates, too, were nearly always hand wrought, some of them works of art. At the conclusion of peace, 67,000 prisoners left these shores for France between 11 April 1814 and 27 August of the same year. Quite a considerable achievement with the transport then available.

From 'Freemasonry in Cornwall 1751–1959' compiled by W. Bro. E. S. Vincent.

A portrait of Sir John St. Aubyn (P.G.M. 1785-1839) by John Opie, which is on display in the Temple at Falmouth.

The provincial jewels were presented by Sir John in the mid-1790s.

THREAD OF GOLD

Chapter V

Glossary
Colour Illustrations of the Cornish and Isles of Scilly Temples
Highlights in the Cornish Craft
Craft Lodges by date of Warrant
Royal Arch Chapters by date of Charter
Leading Officers during 250 years
Other Masonic Orders in Cornwall

GLOSSARY OF MASONIC ABBREVIATIONS

Grand Ranks

RW Bro.	Right Worshipful Brother
VW Bro.	Very Worshipful Brother.
PGChaplain	Past Grand Chaplain
PGSwdB	Past Grand Sword Bearer
SGD	Senior Grand Deacon
PSGD	Past Senior Grand Deacon
JGD	Junior Grand Deacon
PJGD	Past Junior Grand Deacon
G Treas	Grand Treasurer
AGDC	Assistant Grand Director of Ceremonies
PAGDC	Past Assistant Grand Director of Ceremonies
GStB	Grand Standard Bearer
PGStB	Past Grand Standard Bearer

Provincial Grand Ranks

PGM	Provincial Grand Master
DPGM	Deputy Provincial Grand Master
APGM	Assistant Provincial Grand Master
ProvSGW	Provincial Senior Grand Warden
PPSGW	Past Provincial Senior Grand Warden
ProvGJW	Provincial Junior Grand Warden
PPJGW	Past Provincial Junior Grand Warden
ProvGTreas	Provincial Grand Treasurer
ProvGSec	Provincial Grand Secretary
ProvGDC	Provincial Grand Director of Ceremonies
PPGSuptWks.	Past Provincial Grand Superintendent of Works
PPSGD	Past Provincial Senior Grand Deacon
PPJGD	Past Provincial Junior Grand Deacon
PPAGDC	Past Provincial Assistant Grand Director of Ceremonies

Private Lodge Ranks

WBro	Worshipful Brother, one who is or has been a Worshipful Master
WM	Worshipful Master
PM	Past Master
SW	Senior Warden
JW	Junior Warden
DC	Director of Ceremonies
SD	Senior Deacon
JD	Junior Deacon
IG	Inner Guard
Tyler	Doorkeeper
Stwd.	Steward

Royal Arch Ranks

GS	Grand Superintendent
DGS	Deputy Grand Superintendent
PAGSoj.	Past Assistant Grand Sojourner
Soj	Sojourner

Ranks and Titles

The craft inherits literature mostly from the 18th and 19th centuries. English style changes, and the Editor has tried to follow present day custom in such items as the omission of capital letters for words like *masonry, brethren*, and *master*, and omission of full stops after abbreviations, except where there is a specific reason for including them. However, in quotations, the style of the author has been left unchanged if the original text was available.

Present day masonry also inherits a series of long ranks and titles which are usually given as abbreviations. For the brother who understands these, no problem exists in reading, but the less experienced reader may find that their inclusion breaks his flow of understanding.

The Editor has used titles in full, sometimes followed by abbreviations when repeated. On the other hand, masons of all ranks are generally referred to as brother or by the prefix Bro, and masters or lodges are referred to as such, rather than as *Worshipful* or *Right Worshipful Master*. The latter are modes of address rather than the name of the office, and comfort is taken from their omission in the *Constitutions* of all three jurisdictions of the British Isles.

Bodmin

Bude

Callington

Calstock

Camborne

Chacewater

Falmouth

Hayle
Original Temple

Hayle
Perry Morgan Temple

Helston

St. Mary's
Isles of Scilly

THE ROYAL MASONIC INSTITUTION FOR BOYS
(INCORPORATED BY ROYAL CHARTER)

ONE HUNDRED AND EIGHTY-THIRD ANNIVERSARY FESTIVAL

WEDNESDAY, 3RD JUNE, 1981

THE CONNAUGHT ROOMS

LONDON, W.C.2

FESTIVAL PRESIDENT:
R.W.Bro. The Hon. ROBERT ELIOT, PATRON,
PROVINCIAL GRAND MASTER FOR CORNWALL

Provincial Grand Lodge
and Royal Arch Chapter
of Cornwall

Songs Of Praise

Conducted by The Revd. Andrew Wilson, Prov. G. Chaplain

Bodmin Parish Church, at 3pm, on Sunday October 15th, 2000

Welcome by The Rector of this Church, The Revd. Graham Minors

Organist: Roger Freeman

Soloist: Cheryl Taylor

The Cornwall Masonic Male Singers

Our Provincial Grand Master Nicholas Barrington and his wife, Jane,
thank you all for joining them this afternoon to sing our praises to God and
offer our prayers for all those less fortunate than ourselves

The programmes for the June 1981 Cornwall Festival in The Connaught Rooms, London, for the Royal Masonic Institution for Boys, and the most recent Songs of Praise service at Bodmin in October 2000.

HIGHLIGHTS OF THE CORNISH CRAFT.

1751	The Premier Lodge warranted at Falmouth, as No. 146, now 75.
1752	Lodge warranted at Helston as No. 151, erased as 120 in 1774. R.W. Bro. W. Pye appointed 1st P.G.M. (15th in England).
1754	The first Druids' Lodge warranted at Redruth as No. 176; active until 1828, dormant until 1851 when resuscitated as No. 589
1755	Isaac Head appointed Provincial Grand Master for the Isles of Scilly. Lodge warranted at Penzance as No. 271, erased as No. 163 in 1777.
1756	Dolphin Lodge No. 365 warranted in the Isles of Scilly by Isaac Head, P.G.M.
1779	Death of Isaac Head. No successor appointed; the Province of the Isles of Scilly ended in 1783.
1783	Lodge of Love and Honour No. 75 subscribed £25 for the erection of Freemasons' Hall, London, and received a silver medal for its Master to wear in perpetuity. Only three other lodges outside London so distinguished.
1793	Regulations for Provincial Grand Lodge approved.
1794	Sir John St. Aubyn, presented a set of jewels, and Sir Francis Basset, a Sword of State, to P.G.L. which are still in use.
1808	Provincial Grand Stewards for Cornwall first appointed.
1810	Volubian R.A. Chapter chartered at Falmouth as No. 157 and exchanged in 1828 as No. 75.
1812	R.W. Bro. W. Ernshaw (Past S.G.W.) instructed the Cornish Lodges at Falmouth in the revised work, preparatory to the union of the two Grand Lodges.
1815	Provincial Grand Deacons of Cornwall first appointed.
1819	On 14 May at Falmouth, the unified working of the three Degrees was demonstrated as approved by the Grand Lodge in 1816.
1835	Foundation Stone of Lander Column laid with masonic honours at Truro.
1836	The Dunstanville Monument at Carn Brea inaugurated with masonic honours.
1864	Cornwall Masonic Annuity Fund established. Since 1978 called the Cornish Masonic Benevolent Fund.
1869	Centenary Warrant granted to Love and Honour Lodge No. 75, Falmouth. The first in Province.
1872	On 27 August, a foundation stone of the Masonic Hall laid at Liskeard.
1874	On 14 August, a joint meeting of the P.G.Lodges of Devon and Cornwall at Plymouth, for H.R.H. The Duke of Cornwall, M.W., Grand Master of England.
1876	On 10 January, a foundation stone of the masonic hall laid at Redruth.
1877	On 20 February, Provincial Grand Chapter of R.A. Masons constituted at Truro.
1880	On 20 May, Grand Lodge was opened at the Town Hall, Truro, for the laying of the foundation stone of Truro Cathedral, by H.R.H. The Prince of Wales and Duke of Cornwall, the M.W. Grand Master, with full masonic ceremonial.
1885	Foundation stone of the Masonic Hall laid at Falmouth.

Highlights of the Cornish Craft

1888	Foundation stone of an Obelisk at Padstow was laid as a memorial of Her Majesty's Jubilee.
1891	Foundation stone of the masonic hall laid at Wadebridge.
1891	The Earl of Mount Edgcumbe, P.G.M., appointed D.G.M. and 2nd G. Principal in Grand Chapter.
1893	On 21 September, a corner stone of a new Church at Millbrook was laid with masonic rites.
1895	On 21 May, the foundation stone of Liskeard Cottage Hospital was laid, the gift of Bro. John Passmore Edwards.
1897	Foundation stone of the Cornwall Central Technical Schools laid with masonic ceremonial.
1898	Foundation stone of the masonic hall laid at Camborne.
1900	Foundation stones of masonic halls laid at St. Austell and Calstock.
1901	A History of Freemasonry in West Cornwall from 1765-1828 by J.G. Osborn, P.M. 330 published.
1903	The Nave of Truro Cathedral dedicated in the presence of The Prince and Princess of Wales, the P.G.M. and Brethren.
1904	Charity Jewels presented to Brethren acting as Stewards for the first occasion by the P.G.L.
1908	On 29 September, The Cornish Masters Lodge, No. 3324, was consecrated at Mount Edgcumbe, with 22 Grand Officers and 213 Founders present.
1910	On 21 June, the Province of Cornwall attended the dedication of Truro Cathedral and its Western Towers, completing the work commenced at the Especial Grand Lodge in 1880.
1910	Lodge One and All No. 330, celebrated its centenary: the corner stone of the masonic hall laid.
1912	Masonic Hall at Penryn dedicated.
1915	A motor Ambulance was presented by Freemasons of Cornwall to the 25th Field Ambulance.
1917	W.Bro. P. Colville Smith, 331, Dep. P.G.M., appointed Grand Secretary and Grand Scribe E.
1919	On 2 June. H.R.H. The Prince of Wales Duke of Cornwall initiated; the P.G.M. acting as S.W.
1919	Masonic Hall at Looe dedicated.
1927	The P.G.M. presented two Standards to P.G.L., with the arms of the P.G.M., and the arms of P.G.L.
1928	On 29 November, foundation stone of the masonic hall, Newquay, was laid.
1934	Dedication of Masonic Temple at Union Place, Truro.
1935	On 29 July the P.G.M. handed over to the Cathedral the first bay of the cloisters, the gift of the province in commemoration of the 50th anniversary of the laying of the foundation stone.
1937	On 25 May, the P.G.M. laid the foundation stone of St. Andrew's Church, Redruth.
1937	On 11 June, the Masonic Hall at Padstow was dedicated.
1940	The Rawling Memorial Fund inaugurated; now in the Cornwall Masonic Benevolent Fund.
1942	On 19 May, Lodge premises at Tuckingmill were dedicated.
1946	The following Lodges were consecrated: 11 April, Trewinnard No. 6157, 17 May, Fistral No. 6258, 25 September, Essa No. 6278, and 30 September, Trenwith No. 6309.
1951	Cornwall Masonic Study Circle formed at Truro. Open to all members of the Craft.
1954	Two Hundred Years of Freemasonry in Cornwall, 1751-1951 by W. Bro. K. Durston No. 3405 published.

Thread of Gold

Highlights of the Cornish Craft

1959   On 22 January, St. Piran's No. 7620 was consecrated. The province now having 50 lodges was entitled to an Assistant P.G.M.

1960   A Record of Freemasonry in the Province of Cornwall, 1751-1959 published by W. Bro.E.S. Vincent No. 331.

1961   On 2 December, Godolphin Lodge No. 7790, Isles of Scilly, was consecrated; the Master's chair and jewels of the Provincial Officers of Godolphin Lodge erased in 1851, were in use.

1962   The foundation stone of the masonic hall at Saltash was laid.

1967   On May 13, dedication of masonic hall at Perranporth.
On 1 July, a service in Truro Cathedral for the 250th Anniversary of Grand Lodge.

1970   A new Provincial banner was presented by W. Bro. F.E. Caldicott, St. Piran's Lodge No. 7620.

1971   St. Luke's Lodge No. 5371, sold their Tuckingmill premises and use the Camborne hall.

1972   On 25 November, E.Comp. L.A. Richards, P.G.Treas. was appointed Deputy Grand Superintendent. The first such appointment to be made by any Provincial Grand Chapter.

1973   On 3 February, the masonic hall at Cyril Road, Truro, was dedicated.

1974   On 13 June, Eliot No. 1164, celebrated the 100th birthday of W. Bro. Dr. G.R.U. Harman, P.P.S.G.W. He was W.M. in 1911.

1977   On 6 October, P.G.Chapter centenary celebrated and Royal Arch Masonry in Cornwall published.

1979   On 6 January, the Edwin Perry Morgan Temple at, Hayle, was dedicated.

1980   On 12 April, a service was held in Truro Cathedral to celebrate its centenary, and its close ties with Cornish freemasonry.

1981   For the first time since 1922 the Province sponsored a Festival for the R.M.I.B. On 3 June the P.G.M. handed over £750,000. Cotehele Lodge No. 2166 established a record of the highest lodge total of £16,000; another record was a £7 average per member in the province.

1982   On 4 April, the P.G.M. and other Brethren, flew to Gibralter to attend their District Grand Lodge and other meetings. It enabled the P.G.M. to thank them for their support for the 1981 Festival.

1983   On 4 March, at Exeter the deeds of the site for the R.M.B.I. Home for the Elderly were handed to the R.M.B.I. A cheque for £50,000 was presented by the P.G.M.

1983   On 2 July the first Provincial Garden Party was held at Killiganoon when £7,100 was raised for Charity.

1986   A Cornwall branch of the Devon & Cornwall Masonic Study Circle was formed.

1986   On 1 December, the foundation stone was laid for a sheltered housing project, Robert Eliot Court at Trevarrick Road, St. Austell.

1987   On 1 October, Cadogan Court, the RMBI Home for the South West was officially opened.

Highlights of the Cornish Craft

1988	On 10 April, a service was held at Truro Cathedral celebrating the centenary of its consecration.
1991	On 15 June, the Provincial Garden Party at Trewithen Gardens, Probus, raised £5,810.47.
1992	On 10 June brethren attended at Earls Court, London to celebrate the 275th anniversary of Grand Lodge and the 25th anniversary of the installation of the M.W. Grand Master. On 24 June 670 brethren and families attended Evensong at Truro Cathedral to celebrate the formation of Grand Lodge 275 years ago. On 31 October M.W.Bro. the Rt. Hon. Lord Cornwallis, Past Pro G.M. and team consecrated the Robert Eliot Lodge, the 80th in the province.
1994	On 27 October at a Special Provincial Grand Lodge, W.Bro. N.J.F.C. Barrington Dep. P.G.M was installed as Provincial Grand Master by the Lord Cornwallis. Earlier that day at the Special P.G. Chapter, E. Comp. N.J.F.C. Barrington was installed as Grand Superintendent.
1995	The P.G.M's Certificates to brethren completing 60 and 70 years of membership in the Craft were presented for the first time.
1996	On 29 June the 2002 Festival Garden Party was held at Trewithen Gardens. Lady Farnham performed the opening ceremony, accompanied by Lord Farnham, the Pro G.M. The event raised over £8,000.
1997	In September the first of a series of Initiates Meetings took place.
2001	'Love and Honour Lodge' celebrate 250 years at Falmouth. Publication of Thread of Gold, the History of Cornish Freemasonry over 250 years.
2002	Celebrations for 250th anniversary of the province.

CRAFT LODGES, ACCORDING TO DATE OF WARRANT.

	Date	No.	Name of Lodge	Town
1.	20 May 1751	75	Love and Honour	Falmouth
2.	6 July 1772	131	Fortitude	Perranporth
3.	12 April 1799	318	True and Faithful	Helston
4.	8 March 1810	330	One and All	Bodmin
5.	11 April 1810	331	Phoenix	Chacewater
6.	21 December 1813	121	Mount Sinai	Penzance
7.	24 March 1838	450	Cornubian	Hayle
8.	1 March 1844	496	Peace and Harmony	St. Austell
9.	5 March 1845	510	St. Martin's	Liskeard
10.	14 October 1848	557	Loyal Victoria	Callington
11.	14 March 1851	589	Druids'	Redruth
12.	16 March 1857	699	Boscawen	Chacewater
13.	16 May 1859	789	Dunheved	Launceston
14.	22 October 1861	856	Restormel	Lostwithiel
15.	23 November 1861	893	Meridan	Millbrook
16.	9 May 1863	967	Three Grand Principles	Penryn
17.	1 June 1863	970	St. Anne's	Looe
18.	24 July 1863	977	Fowey	Lostwithiel
19.	23 February 1864	1006	Tregullow	St. Day
20.	19 September 1865	1071	Zetland	Saltash
21.	21 September 1866	1136	Carew	Torpoint
22.	2 February 1867	1151	Saint Andrew	Tywardreath
23.	28 March 1867	1164	Eliot	St. Germans
24.	17 June 1869	1272	Tregenna	St. Ives
25.	17 January 1875	1529	Duke of Cornwall	St. Columb
26.	13 May 1875	1544	Mount Edgcumbe	Camborne
27.	18 October 1878	1785	St. Petroc	Padstow
28.	9 February 1882	1954	Molesworth	Wadebridge
29.	25 June 1886	2166	Cotehele	Calstock
30.	15 February 1899	2747	St. Michael	Newquay
31.	21 July 1908	3324	Cornish Masters	Variable
32.	25 October 1909	3405	Granville	Bude
33.	6 August 1924	4668	Trevaunance	St. Agnes
34.	7 August 1929	5134	St. Levan	Penzance

**Craft Lodges
According to Date
of Warrant**

35.	22 June 1932	5371	St. Luke's	Camborne
36.	5 August 1936	5630	Truro School	St. Agnes
37.	3 November 1937	5698	Tewington	St. Austell
38.	4 May 1938	5738	Colville Smith	Falmouth
39.	1 November 1944	6014	Lyonesse	Penzance
40.	6 December 1944	6025	St. Euny	Redruth
41.	1 August 1945	6157	Trewinnard	Hayle
42.	6 March 1946	6258	Fistral	Newquay
43.	1 May 1946	6278	Essa	Saltash
44.	5 June 1946	6309	Trenwith	St. Ives
45.	6 September 1950	7031	Earl of St. Germans	Wadebridge
46.	13 November 1951	7134	King Arthur	Tintagel
47.	2 March 1955	7392	Carlyon	St. Austell
48.	7 September 1955	7422	St. Mellyon	Mullion
49.	6 March 1957	7520	Pendennis	Penryn
50.	5 November 1958	7620	St. Piran's	Perranporth
51.	4 November 1959	7680	Penhallaz	Helston
52.	2 December 1959	7684	Towan	Newquay
53.	13 September 1961	7790	Godolphin	Isle of Scilly
54.	11 September 1963	7936	St. Gluvias	Penryn
55.	11 December 1963	7953	St. George	Looe
56.	11 September 1968	8250	St. Denys	St. Austell
57.	10 September 1969	8302	Cornish Acacia	Hayle
58.	14 June 1972	8445	St. Budoc's	Penryn
59.	14 March 1973	8513	Hamoaze	Saltash
60.	12 September 1973	8538	Penwith	Hayle
61.	14 November 1973	8543	Caradon	Saltash
62.	13 November 1974	8610	Breanick	St. Agnes
63.	9 June 1976	8734	Roseland	Portscatho
64.	27 April 1978	8839	Sir John St. Aubyn	Hayle
65.	13 June 1979	8892	Saint Mary's	Callington
66.	12 December 1984	9147	St. Stephen's	Saltash
67.	11 February 1987	9226	St. Enodoc	Wadebridge
68.	10 June 1987	9245	Three Spires	Perranporth
69.	27 April 1989	9327	Sir Humphry Davy	Penzance
70.	14 June 1989	9339	Trevithick	Redruth
71.	14 June 1989	9342	Agricultural	St. Columb
72.	13 September 1989	9350	Cornishman	Hayle
73.	14 February 1990	9374	Cornish Maritime	Falmouth
74.	12 September 1990	9398	Lodge of the Chisel	St. Columb

Thread of Gold

Craft Lodges According to Date of Warrant

75.	15 February 1991	9425	Beacon	Bodmin
76.	12 June 1991	9446	Cornish Ashlar	Chacewater
77.	11 September 1991	9449	Greystone Border	Launceston
78.	11 March 1992	9472	Eagle	Perranporth
79.	10 June 1992	9481	Cornish Links	Variable
80.	10 June 1992	9483	Robert Eliot	Variable
81.	10 November 1999	9708	Millennium	Perranporth
	16 May 1890	2369	Cornish	London

One of the last public processions of Cornish Freemasons, pictured as they walk down Chapel Street at Penzance to enter St. Mary's Parish Church. This was in 1937 when Lord St. Levan was PGM. Among the well-known local personalities recognised here are Bros. Howell Mabbott (a Penzance mayor), Rev. Sara and Rev. W.B. Dryden (Chaplains), W. J. Hicks and W. J. Hosken (founder-Master of Lyonesse Lodge in 1945).

The car hindering the procession is also believed to be of 1937 vintage!

ROYAL ARCH CHAPTERS, ACCORDING TO DATE OF CHARTER.

	Date	No.	Name of Chapter	Town
1.	14 April 1810	75	Volubian	Falmouth
2.	18 May 1833	121	Holy Mount	Penzance
3.	5 February 1862	331	Royal Cornubian	Chacewater
4.	2 November 1864	510	St. Martin's	Liskeard
5.	6 November 1867	1006	Rose of Sharon	St. Day
6.	1 February 1871	1164	Eliot	Millbrook
7.	5 November 1873	450	Hayle	Hayle
8.	6 May 1874	496	Mount Edgcumbe	St. Austell
9.	3 May 1876	1071	Zetland	Saltash
10.	6 November 1877	970	St. Anne's	Looe
11.	7 November 1877	330	Saint Petrock	Bodmin
12.	7 May 1879	557	Valletort	Callington
13.	1 May 1907	2747	St. Michael	Newquay
14.	17 May 1909	1544	St. Meriadoc	Camborne
15.	5 March 1920	1272	St. Ia	St. Ives
16.	4 August 1920	789	Dunheved	Launceston
17.	1 February 1928	1136	Carew	Torpoint
18.	7 August 1935	3405	Granville	Bude
19.	3 November 1943	5371	St. Illogan	Camborne
20.	6 February 1946	977	Fowey	Lostwithiel
21.	5 February 1947	318	True and Faithful	Helston
22.	8 November 1961	7134	King Arthur	Tintagel
23.	9 February 1966	1785	St. Gwethnoc	Padstow
24.	11 February 1970	3324	Cornish First Principals	Variable
25.	8 November 1972	4668	Trevaunance	St. Agnes
26.	11 February 1976	967	Three Grand Principles	Penryn
27.	28 April 1977	6258	Fistral	Newquay
28.	28 April 1977	5134	St. Levan	Penzance
29.	11 November 1987	5698	Tewington	St. Austell
30.	28 April 1988	8543	Caradon	Saltash
31.	10 November 1993	1529	Duke of Cornwall	St. Columb
	5 November 1924	2369	Cornish	London

LEADING OFFICERS DURING THE 250 YEARS
PROVINCIAL GRAND MASTERS

	1755-1779	Isaac Head, P.G.M. of Isles of Scilly and other islands adjacent. No successor appointed.
1.	1752-1762	William Pye (15th in England)
2a.	1762-1764	Stephen Bell
3.	1764-1775	George Bell
2b.	1775-1785	Stephen Bell
4.	1785-1839	Sir John St. Aubyn, Bt. (1781 Senior Grand Warden)
5.	1844-1863	Sir Charles Lemon, Bt. M.P. F.R.S.
6.	1863-1872	Augustus Smith B.A. M.P.
7.	1872-1917	William Henry, 4th Earl of Mount Edgcumbe G.C.V.O. (1891 Deputy Grand Master).
8.	1918-1940	John Townsend, 2nd Lord St. Levan C.B., C.V.O. (1912 Senior Grand Warden)
9.	1941-1952	Montague Charles, 8th Earl of St. Germans K.C.V.O., O.B.E. (1930 Junior Grand Warden)
10.	1952-1964	Col. Edward Neynoe Willyams D.S.O., D.L., J.P.
11.	1964-1978	Col. Edwin Perry Morgan M.B.E., T.D., J.P.
12.	1978-1994	The Hon. Montague Robert Vere Eliot
13.	1994-	Nicholas John Fitzcharles Cannington Barrington

DEPUTY PROVINCIAL GRAND MASTERS.

1.	1752-1764	George Bell
2.	1764-1771	Thomas Young
3.	1771-1775	Stephen Bell
4.	1775-1779	William Pryce
5.	1779-1786	John Knight
6.	1786-1793	Benjamin Hearne
7.	1793-1812	George C. George
8.	1812-1822	Thomas Warren
9.	1822-1827	Richard Edwards
10.	1827-1845	P. Vyvyan Robinson
11.	1845-1857	John Ellis
12.	1857-1860	Richard Pearce

Leading Officers During the 250 Years

13.	1860-1863	Augustus Smith
14.	1863-1865	Reginald Rogers (and 1867-1868, 1870-1872)
15.	1865-1867	John Roscorla (and 1869-1870)
16.	1872-1873	Lord Eliot; later Earl of St. Germans (1867 Senior Grand Warden)
17.	1873-1878	Sir Frederick Martin Williams, Bt. (1870 Junior Grand Warden)
18.	1879-1880	Col. John Whitehead Peard
19.	1880-1899	Sir Charles Brune Graves-Sawle, Bt. (1887 Past Junior Grand Warden)
20.	1899-1937	Sir Philip Colville-Smith K.C.V.O. (1917-37 Grand Secretary)
21.	1937-1940	Sir Montague Charles Eliot, K.C.V.O., O.B.E.
22.	1941-1951	The Revd Canon Henry Richard Jennings
23.	1952-1964	Arthur J. Roberts
24.	1964-1971	Cyril J. Rickard
25.	1971-1974	Hubert I. Dingle
26.	1974-1982	Cyril Andrew
27.	1982-1986	Laurence R. Francis
28.	1986-1994	Sidney J. Pearce
29.	1994-1994	Nicholas J.F.C. Barrington
30.	1994-	K. Frank Crewes

ASSISTANT PROVINCIAL GRAND MASTERS.

1.	1959-1962	George H. Gardner
2.	1962-1964	Cyril J. Rickard
3.	1964-1971	Hubert I. Dingle
4.	1971-1974	Cyril Andrew
5.	1974-1978	Hon. Robert Eliot
6.	1978-1980	Gerald Barton
7.	1980-1982	Laurence R. Francis
8.	1982-1986	Sidney J. Pearce
9.	1986-1991	Rowland E. Crabb
10.	1991-1994	Nicholas J.F.C. Barrington
11.	1993-1994	K. Frank Crewes
12.	1994-	James B. Kitson
13.	1994-1998	George Helson
14.	1998-	John Davy

Leading Officers During the 250 Years

GRAND SUPERINTENDENTS.

1.	1791-1795	Thomas Dunckerly
2.	1796-1839	Sir John St. Aubyn, Bt.
3.	1848-1857	John Ellis
4.	1861-1862	Richard Pearce
5.	1875-1917	William Henry, 4th Earl of Mt. Edgcumbe G.C.V.O. (1891 2nd Grand Principal)
6.	1920-1940	John Townsend, 2nd Lord St. Levan C.B., C.V.O.
7.	1941-1951	The Revd Canon Henry Richard Jennings
8.	1952-1964	The Revd Thomas Arthur Webber
9.	1964-1969	W. Lloyd White
10.	1969-1976	The Revd James Gillett M.A.
11.	1976-1994	The Hon. Robert Eliot
12.	1994-	Nicholas J.F.C. Barrington

DEPUTY GRAND SUPERINTENDENTS.

1.	1972-1975	Leonard A. Richards (the first in England)
2.	1976-1976	The Hon. Robert Eliot
3.	1976-1981	A.E.B. 'Jim' Greenwood
4.	1981-1989	William L. Watters
5.	1989-1994	Nicholas J.F.C. Barrington
6.	1994-2000	The Revd Raymond J.L. Wood
7.	2000-	Michael J. Fouracres

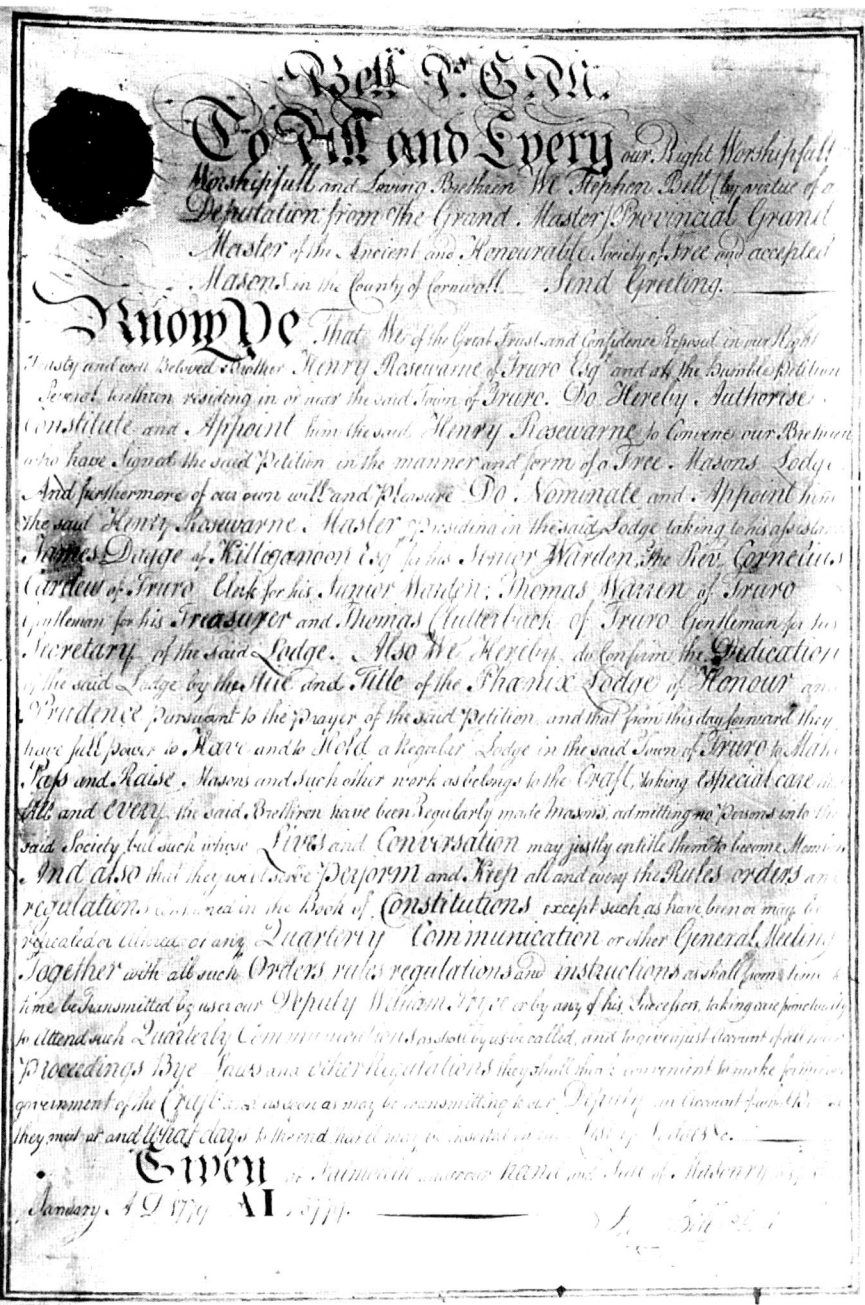

A photograph of the 1779 original Warrant of Phoenix Lodge, possibly the oldest warrant in England still existing. It is signed by P.G.M. Stephen Bell. The lodge was re-warranted in 1810.

OTHER MASONIC ORDERS OPERATING IN OR FOR THE COUNTY OF CORNWALL.

Mark Master Masons and Royal Ark Mariners
30 Mark Lodges and 15 RAM Lodges, meeting throughout Cornwall.

Knights' Templar and Knights of Malta
3 Preceptories/Priories, meeting Hayle, Launceston, Newquay.

Rose Croix
9 Chapters, meeting at Redruth, Liskeard, Saltash, St Austell, Hayle, Falmouth, Helston, Launceston, Newquay.

Red Cross of Constantine
3 Conclaves, meeting at Perranporth, Saltash, Hayle.

Allied
2 Councils, meeting at Hayle, Lostwithiel.

Secret Monitor
Conclaves, meeting at Liskeard, Hayle, Saltash, Penryn, St Columb.

Royal Order of Scotland
1 Provincial Lodge/Chapter, meeting at Exmouth & Keynsham.

Royal & Select Masters
2 Councils, meeting at Hayle and Wadebridge.

Worshipful Society of Free Masons
1 Assemblage, meeting at Bodmin.

Societas Rosicruciana in Anglia
2 Colleges, meeting at Saltash, Perranporth.

Holy Royal Arch Knight Templar Priests
1 Tabernacle, meeting at Hayle.

Further information is given in the Cornwall Masonic Year Book.

THREAD OF GOLD

Chapter VI

Masonic Meeting Places in Cornwall
Individual Lodge Histories
Colour Illustrations of the Cornish Temples
Poem: 'True Masonic Nobility.'

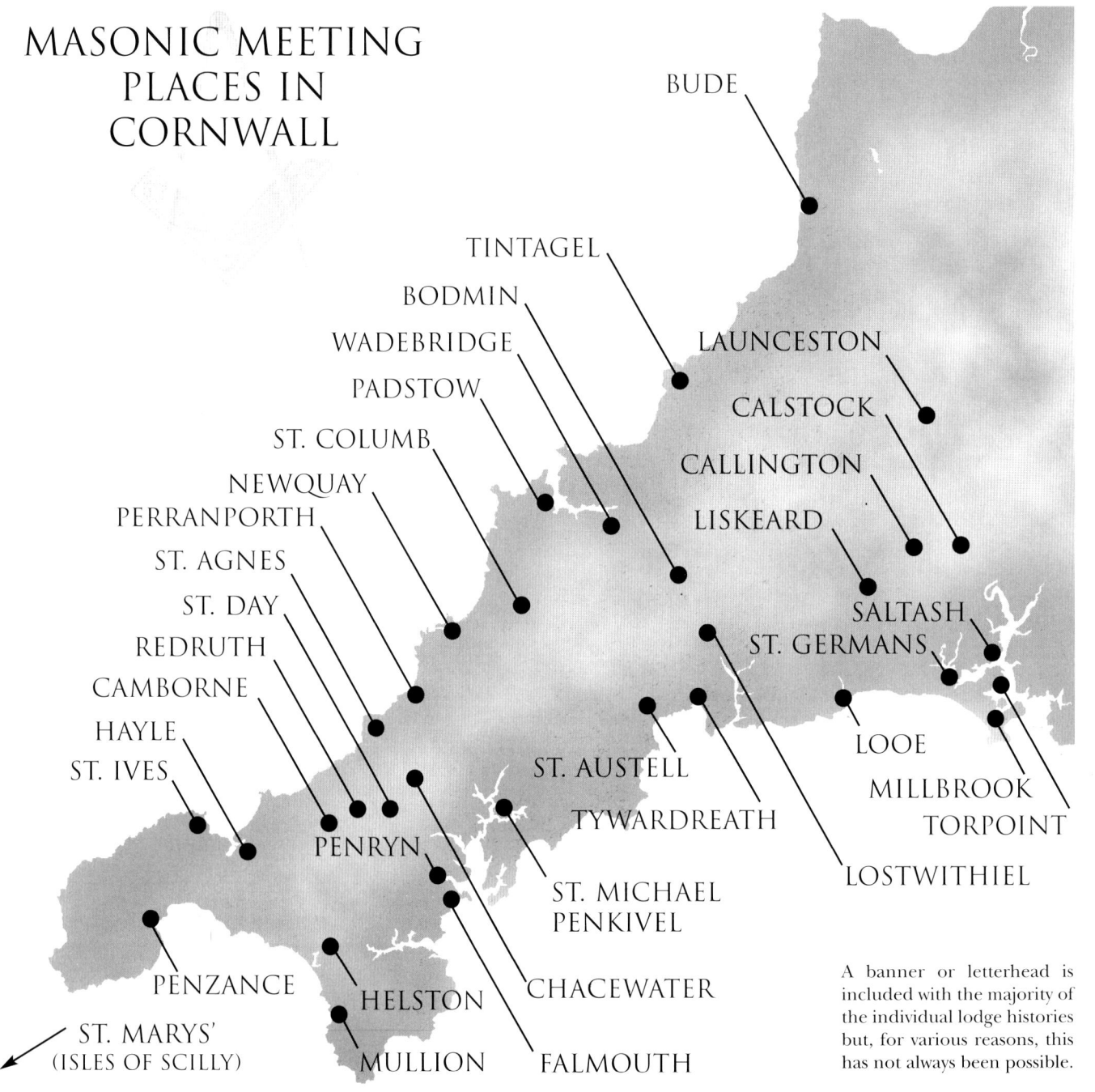

Lodge Histories

LOVE AND HONOUR LODGE No. 75, FALMOUTH.

In 2001 the oldest lodge in the province celebrated its 250th anniversary: it was formed a year before the new province of Cornwall and its first W.M. was William Pye, the first Provincial Grand Master. The first meeting place was the King's Arms Tavern, in Market Strand - "the house of Edward Snoxell" - and its lodge number was 209, soon to become 146, then 116, 94, 95, 110 and 89 before settling as No. 75 in 1863 while at the Royal Hotel in Market Street. Between these two venues there was a short period at the Royal Standard. From 2,500 in 1750 the population of Falmouth has grown to some 20,000.

For upwards of 30 years the meetings were at the King's Arms but moved to the Royal Hotel in 1820 when a fair-sized room in the upper storey was prepared, approached by a very narrow and steep flight of stairs. The first meeting in the new masonic hall was in May 1886: the building was formally declared open by the Provincial Grand Master, the Earl of Mount Edgcumbe in September when Provincial Grand Lodge met there. It has been in continuous use since. The foundation stone had been laid the previous year by the Prov. D.G.M., Sir Charles B. Graves-Sawle Bt. The lodge is a handsome room with a lofty wagon roof. There are portraits of two Provincial Grand Masters, Sir John St. Aubyn and the Hon. Robert Eliot. There are three large statues depicting Faith, Hope and Charity. Two gas chandeliers were previously in St. Gluvias Church (found in 1885 at a junk dealer's premises at Penryn), and the others presented by the Falmouth Corporation.

The Masonic banquet of January 1912 at the installation of W.Bro. Ernest Moss as W. M. of Love and Honour.

During the 18th century one W.M. served for five consecutive years (1793-97) while another for 11 years, although not

Lodge Histories

continuously. The records show that fines were imposed on members for non-attendance, being late, swearing in lodge, drunkenness and gambling. Some new members became master masons in a very short time, days instead of weeks or months, as they were about to join a ship due to leave port. From the time the lodge was founded, until just before the 2nd World War, most freemasons were open about their involvement. At church services, civic parades etc., masons appeared in full regalia. Installation meetings and other major functions were regularly reported in the local newspapers. There was great hardship in Falmouth in the 1840s because of the loss of the Packet Ship service and through competition from the railways, but in 1843 Mylor dockyard was a going concern as an Admiralty establishment. Queen Victoria visited Falmouth in 1841 and 1846, travelling in the Royal Yacht, there being no railway, roads or canals linking the town with London. An earlier monarch had caused celebrations in 1809 with a procession to mark the 50th year of the reign of George III: after a church service and festival the brethren voted £5 for distribution among the poor. A similar sum was granted to an Irish mason five years later after his vessel had foundered off Land's End in a gale. When a Spaniard was initiated in April 1820 two visitors acted as interpreters.

No one knows for certain the precise origin and reason for the beautiful group of statues depicting Faith, Hope and Charity at the Love and Honour Lodge, Falmouth, but it is believed they were placed there by the builders of the Temple

Sir Charles Lemon M.P., became a master mason within three months in 1841, installed as W.M. in January 1843 and as Provincial Grand Master in April 1844 at Provincial Grand Lodge in Falmouth. In 1858 a decision was made to build what is now the Falmouth Docks, with Provincial Deputy Grand Master, Bro. Pearce laying the foundation stone with masonic honours. The oldest building on the site, still in use today, started as a grain store. In February 1863 the memorial stone of the bi-centenary of the Falmouth Church was affixed with Masonic honours. In December there was a serious fire at the lodge with many records, artefacts and portraits destroyed. R.W.Bro. Augustus Smith, the Provincial Grand Master joined Love and Honour in November the following year. The Grand Master, H.R.H. The Prince of Wales, visited Falmouth in November 1887 and laid the foundation stone of All Saints Church, which was consecrated in 1889. The Prince slept on board his yacht in Falmouth harbour, leaving for Truro next morning to attend the consecration of the new Truro Cathedral. June 1896 brought the presentation of a gold watch to Bro. Newman in recognition of his 37 years as lodge treasurer.

The 150th anniversary came in June 1901. In December 1914 it was decided to cancel the usual installation banquet because of the war. During these war years it was arranged that a parcel of food be sent fortnightly to Bro. Capt. J.H. Lowry, a prisoner-of-war in Germany: he received a cordial welcome on his return in January 1919. Visiting brethren from the naval base presented the lodge with an inscribed section of an aeroplane propeller as an expression of thanks for the kindness and hospitality they had received at the lodge during the war. A Roll of Honour containing the names of the 69 brethren of Lodge and Honour who served in the Great War, was hung in the ante-room. These formed 35% of the total membership, and only one, Bro. William Bollocombe, chief engineer in the mercantile marine, paid the supreme sacrifice. Many members have served as Mayor, including T.A. Webber (1924), his father A.E. Webber and uncle T. Webber. Members came from Mount Sinai lodge, Penzance, in 1928, to initiate two candidates, and there was the first exchange with Trevaunance lodge, St. Agnes in 1933. In 1940 members voted 25 guineas to the Mayor's Spitfire Fund and the basement room in the lodge was converted into an air raid shelter. At the end of the war in Europe and the Far East in 1945 it was remarkable that only one member was killed. There had been many visitors from among the servicemen of the United States who were stationed in the town.

During the post-war period there were many new members, several from the Docks and the Telecoms department of the Post Office. In 1950 food parcels from a New Zealand lodge were distributed: this continued until August 1954. In June 1951 came the 200th anniversary of the lodge: the 'family tree' down the years shows the Colville Smith lodge in 1938, Pendennis in 1957 and Cornish Maritime in 1990. The brethren were asked in 1973 to each loan £15 to help clear the bank overdraft: this raised over £2,000 during the year, and in 1978 all the loans were cleared. Tyler of the lodge, Bro. Geoffrey Evans, the Mayor of Falmouth, had the honour of welcoming H.M. The Queen when she visited the town from the Royal Yacht as part of her silver jubilee celebrations. He was Mayor 1976-79, 1993-95 and had his 6th term in 2000-01. There were protracted negotiations from March 1982 with Carrick District Council over the proposed purchase of the lodge premises to make way for a car park, but nothing came of this as it was rejected by the council's own planning committee. A landmark came in 1993 with the death of W.Bro. Mundy, aged 93: he had been initiated at the first exchange visit with Trevaunance lodge in 1933, had held several offices and was a brilliant ritualist. There were moves towards more openness in June 1997 when some of the members of the local Methodist Church were shown around the temple by W.Bro. P. George, as were the ladies in March 1998 when there was also a talk on freemasonry, and questions answered. Membership has shown a decline in the past decade, but the spirit of the lodge has endured. The heritage of the past 250 years, and the celebrations of 2001 are a source of pride and challenge.

The Deputy Grand Master, RW Bro. Iain Ross Bryce, was the guest of honour at the 250th anniversary celebrations on 21 May 2001. He was accompanied by other Grand Lodge officers and brought congratulations from Grand Lodge. It was a unique and splendid ceremony for Love and Honour.

The PGM, RW Bro. Nicholas Barrington, accompanied by his provincial officers, brought the congratulations of the province. He invested W.Bro. John Hall who had written a history of the lodge - as PPJGW.

At the meeting, under W.Bro. Anthony Tregenza WM (son of the lodge secretary W.Bro. Colin Tregenza), a new banner was dedicated by the Prov. G.Chaplain, the Revd Andrew Wilson. There was later a banquet at the Falmouth Beach Hotel.

Lodge Histories

MOUNT SINAI No. 121, PENZANCE.

Even today there is a mystery surrounding the origin of Mount Sinai lodge, the second on the provincial roll. Some notes state the first lodge in Penzance was St. John the Baptist No. 271, constituted in June 1755 but not named until some 20 years later: it was erased in 1777. Others record a lodge chartered by the Ancients in New Granada in 1769, military in origin, that was revived at Penzance in 1813. The first meetings from December 1813 were held either at the 'Ship and Castle' in Market Jew Street or the 'Ship' in Quay Street, but moving three years later to The Star Inn (still with us in the main street), then the Union Hotel (perhaps in what was part of the original Georgian theatre), the Three Tuns Hotel (Green Market), Public Building (St. John's Hall, from 1867), and finally to the present masonic hall in Princes Street from January 1896. The number 121 had been fixed in 1863. From 1753-1800 a total of 17 lodges had been started in the county, 12 under Moderns and five under Ancients, so the rivalry between the two Grand Lodges had penetrated to even the Far West.

The Charter, signed by the Grand Master H.R.H. Prince Edward, Duke of Kent and Strathearn etc., on December 21 in 1813, gave consent to hold the lodge "at the house called or known by the name or sign of the Ship in the town of Penzance.......upon the third Monday in every calendar month". Today it is on the third Wednesday The first Master, named in the warrant, was James Beckerleg, a schoolmaster and "splendid penman". Richard Tonking S.W. and George McDonald J.W. were seafaring men and did not become masters. Tonking was at one time shipwrecked on the Irish coast and the masons of Cork gave him money to reach home. The second W.M., Nicholas Davy, was a joining member. The third John Curnow (1816) had been initiated at the first meeting in 1814 and continued in membership for 48 years, was six times W.M. and served 11 years as treasurer. He was Provincial J.W. and his portrait by Richard Pentreath stands over the Master's chair: he died in 1862 aged 82. W.Bro. Richard Pearce (Deputy Provincial Grand Master) was Master on 13 occasions between 1820-1861 and was also Grand Supt. of the Royal Arch. His grandson W.Bro. Richard Pearce Couch was secretary for 16 years to 1918. A minute by him, written in 1914, solved a riddle that has worried current officers: "It is very much regretted that the first minute book is missing: it would in all probability settle a few points which are now undecided; one of which would be whence came the three handsome and very valuable Chippendale chairs, occupied by the master and his wardens." The chairs are believed to be of Spanish mahogany. The cash books showed the chairs were not bought - and that there had truly been 100 years of uninterrupted working at the time of application for the centenary warrant. The first cash records show: to go to Falmouth £5; to London for warrant £8, and for jewels and furniture £6. 8s. Money held its value for many years: in 1914 an estimate of £70 was accepted for the complete painting and redecoration of the halls!

At the Provincial Grand Lodge at Penzance in 1834 there is reference to the 'St. John's Men' so that "there dined 13 provincial officers, 16 other members of lodges and three St. John's Men, in all 32, and below stairs in the Tyler's room, ten." This could be a link with the St. John the Baptist lodge of earlier times. A toast at the banquet in 1833 was; "May the hearts of Freemasons ever agree however much their heads may differ" and in July the following year a toast was: "May our hopes of reviving the Druids lodge be realised."

Sadly, Druids was erased that year, after 84 years, and the present one rose from its ashes some 13 years later. It is believed the early Penzance masons came from the Druids lodge. The 'Masons Arms' on the South wall of the lodge was discovered by W.B. Frank Latham, stored in an old box a few miles from Penzance. It was painted in about 1753 and appears to have belonged to a Marazion lodge. A poignant, though charming feature from the later years of the 19th century is a collection of Christmas cards from the masters of various lodges, beautifully worked, and still kept in the building. At the August 1830 meeting, with 12 present, there were 'eight black balls' registered against a potential joining member, in a ballot.

It is believed that Lemon Hart, a member of the Jewish congregation at Penzance and founder of the firm that bears his name, was initiated into a Penzance lodge in 1798. He obtained the contract to supply rum to the Royal Navy and later moved to London where he died in 1845. He was born at Penzance and traded in sugar and rum from the West Indies and later inherited his grandfather's wine and spirits business. When a French invasion threatened he raised a company of volunteers in Penwith to help in the defence of Cornwall against Napoleon, and styled the 'Ludgvan Volunteers' of which he was Captain.

'The Ladies' have been involved at Mount Sinai from the earliest times and were introduced "in due form" to the lodge room to see how it was set out, and to the banquet. Sir Charles Lemon, Provincial Grand Master, was in the chair at Provincial Grand Lodge at Penzance in 1847: after toasts "a large galaxy of the fair daughters of Penzance was then ushered in, who, by their cordiality, beauty and grace, greatly enhanced the conviviality of the meeting." So states a contemporary Press report! With the old Prince's Hall transformed into a masonic hall and temple there were celebrations in January 1897 when members processed from their home at the Public Buildings. Because of the growth of the lodge larger premises were needed. Extensive alterations and improvements were carried out at the former Penzance Billiards Club (with the billiards room, now the temple, and the store becoming the dining room). For 25 years before this it had been a concert and lecture hall. The temple floor was raised nearly three feet, the floor covered with cork, old windows replaced by stained glass with emblems of the Craft. A new stairway with mahogany handrail led to the first floor temple and to a second floor which would be used by the Royal Arch and Mark masonry for a time.

Lodge Histories

Lord St. Levan, who was to play such a distinguished role in the province, joined Mount Sinai in 1910 and became S.W. at the installation the following year. In 1911 a gavel was presented that had family associations for him and a P.M., W.Bro. Arthur Pool. It had been given with other furnishings by the Provincial Grand Master Sir John St. Aubyn (Lord St. Levan's great grandfather) to the Ship Lodge, St. Ives (1765-1786). It transferred to the Lodge of True Friendship at Crowan and was used at Provincial Grand Lodge to celebrate the golden jubilee of Sir John's leadership, and remained with Bro. Pool of the Mount's Bay Inn, and his family until 1911. In 1913, to mark his year as W.M. and the 99th anniversary of the lodge, Lord St. Levan gave a silver Loving Cup that continues to be used at all installation banquets. He was appointed S.G.W. of England while in the chair of Mount Sinai. The Deputy Provincial Grand Master W.Bro. P. Colville Smith, presented the centenary warrant in January 1914 to the new Master, W.Bro. Henry Hocking and spoke of the association of the lodge with the municipal and social life of the town. He referred to the laying of the nine foundation stones of the old Guildhall and Market House in 1834 and the foundation stone of the New (Albert) Pier in 1845, with full masonic honours, and attended by thousands. The council granted £4,500 for the building of the Guildhall and voted £1,196 for the new pier. The foundation stone for the latter was laid by Mayor Samuel Pidwell and W.B. Richard Pearce, Provincial S.G.W., "The procession ... exceeded

Cornish Freemasons were among those in the great procession to mark the celebrations at the laying of the foundation stone of the Northern arm of the Penzance pier in July 1845 "with full Masonic honours".

The Mayor, Corporation and the many societies of the town took part in the proceedings, recorded by artist F. Colebrooke Stockdale. It was named the Albert Pier following a visit to Mount's Bay by Queen Victoria and the Prince Consort.

Lodge Histories

anything seen in the county. It was about a quarter-mile long in which were displayed more than 50 banners, and four bands of music." Members also took part in the public processions on the Proclamation of King William IV in 1830 and were at the opening of the West Cornwall Railway in 1852, at the invitation of the borough council. There were huge crowds on these occasions. During its first century the lodge enrolled 677 members.

The unique centenary celebration meeting was at St. Michael's Mount in July 1914 - no doubt anticipating fine weather - with the lodge opened at the Chevy Chase Room, with 29 year-old Herbert Richards Corin, a mining engineer, the initiate. "The initiate was the first and only candidate to whom the light of masonry had ever been revealed within these ancient walls" said his Lordship. There is a question mark over whether the Holy Mount Chapter was consecrated on the Mount in 1831 under Sir John St. Aubyn. The brethren had gathered at Princes Street, went by road to Marazion and over by boat. To gain entry at the Mount gate a small brooch medallion, costing 1s.3d, and marking the occasion, was distributed. The chairs on the right and left of the W.M. were those used by Lord and Lady St. Levan in Westminster Abbey at the Coronation of King George V and Queen Mary. There were plans to join the ladies for group photographs on The Terrace, enjoy trips around the bay on his Lordship's yacht, or walks around the Mount, ending with an open-air concert. Sadly these outdoor events were cancelled because of drenching rain, but there was a service in the Mount Chapel and a "sumptuous tea" in a large marquee before returning home.

One early minute reveals that after lodge had been 'called off' and members enjoying themselves at the Union Hotel......."at about 10pm someone stood up and said 'We haven't closed the lodge yet'" So they closed it at the Union! It appears there may have been a passageway from the top-floor room to the Union Hotel. W.Bro. Vince Sheldon, secretary for 11 years, holds this view: "There is a gap of three feet and it would have been easy to have a walkway from one building to the other." There have been many generous gifts down the years, including the impressive windows given by W.Bro. Thomas Reynolds and the brass knocker with square and compasses on the lodge door by W.Bro. Richard Pearce Couch. One member died in action during the 1st World War and 20 saw service, but within months of its outbreak the brother of a leading member W.Bro. Frank Latham - for many years borough surveyor - was killed by a German shell. Several saw service in the 2nd World War and one member Bro. Frank Holman (R.A.F.) died in action. There has been, since the war, a friendship with the Malvern lodge (also No. 121) in Australia (see feature 'The Malvern Link - Down Under'). Today there are over 100 lodge members and Grand Lodge rank has been bestowed in recent times to W. Bro. Arthur Robinson (P.J.G.D.), and W.Bro. Philip Pengelly (P.A.G.D.C.) At one time there was but one key to the building, held by lodge secretary W.B. Fred Bray - a dominant figure - and the premises continue under the ownership of Mount Sinai. But a joint lodge management committee today carries out the administration of the building in a spirit of co-operation.

FORTITUDE LODGE No. 131, PERRANPORTH.

This was originally a Military Lodge, one of only eight surviving that were formed by the "Ancients" between 1753 and 1813 (two others also being in Cornwall, namely True and Faithful No.318 at Helston and One & All No.330 at Bodmin). The 67th Regiment of Foot was formed in 1758, its first Commanding Officer being the distinguished Col. Wolfe of "Heights of Abraham", Canada fame. It subsequently became the Royal Hampshire Regiment, with a well-documented military history. From 1805 the Regiment was stationed for 21 years in the East Indies.

The lodge was formed at Chatham in 1772 - the warrant was obtained in July for The Fortitude Lodge No.175 - and was attached to the regiment for 35 years. In 1781 there were 17 names on the lodge membership return. Although the regiment was stationed at Chatham it moved from town to town, as required. In 1785 the soldiers embarked for the West Indies where they remained until 1794.

After their return to England they went to Ireland, and in 1796 went back to the West Indies, going to Jamaica in 1801. After being stationed at Winchester, Dunkeld, Guernsey and Manchester the regiment moved back to the West Indies in 1807, the third time in 20 years. The transfer to the Miners Regiment in 1807 took place in the Ordnance Arms at Dover at a meeting of the Town Lodge. Costs were £46.12s.6d, then a considerable sum that was not repaid for several years. First use of the title "The Lodge of Fortitude" appears in October 1807 (previously only known by lodge number). Membership rapidly increased, with frequent meetings.

However, Napoleon had not completed his designs and a Bill was passed raising troops between the ages of 17 and 45 unless they were members of any Volunteer Corps. The regiment thus became embodied again in 1803 as the Royal Miners Regiment and from 1804 to 1811 was deployed almost continuously working on the fortifications of Dover.

Lodge Histories

The Warrant of the Lodge of the 67th Regiment of Foot was transferred to the Miners Regiment in 1807 and remained under its wing until disbandment in 1814.

In 1811 the War Office offered a bounty of two guineas to volunteers for service in Ireland for which the Miners Regiment volunteered to a man and they served there until late 1812 when they returned to Portsmouth. The Napoleonic War concluded with the Treaty of Paris in 1814, by when the regiment had returned to Cornwall at Pendennis Castle, and was disbanded. The lodge moved to Truro where it held its first meeting at the Queen's Head Hotel in July 1814, nine members being present. However a Military Warrant was held by the lodge for 54 years from formation in 1772 until exchanged for a civil one.

From the Union in 1813 the lodge was now No. 213 debarred from initiating civilians under its military warrant. It continued to move from place to place, including Ireland, finally going to Pendennis Castle in April 1814 and to the Queen's Head Hotel, Truro, in July of that year. This caused severe difficulty to the lodge after the regiment was disbanded and its membership dwindled to just seven stalwarts. Pleas to Grand Lodge for dispensation were ignored for 13 years, even when other matters in the same letters were acknowledged. Brethren had to take turns in the offices - Bro. Roger Candy was Master 15 times between 1808 and 1832. But for their loyalty and determination the lodge would undoubtedly have folded until in desperation in 1826 they petitioned to exchange the military warrant for a civil one. This was accepted with alacrity and is the one now being displayed by the lodge at its meetings. The lodge became No.131, in 1863.

The pedestal of the lodge was used to contain fines for lateness and bad language - the amounts varied at different times. The lodge has notable jewels for its Deacons, Inner Guard and Tyler. One of only three sets (including one in Grand Lodge) they were made by the eminent Thomas Harper and were purchased on the transfer of warrant to the Miners Regiment. The lodge also has particular music, including for Installations, which are attractive but of which the origins are unknown.

Its new banner (costing £8 16s 8d) was produced in 1880 in four weeks for the laying of the foundation stone of Truro Cathedral by the M.W. Grand Master, H.R.H. The Prince of Wales. It was a spectacular occasion in which several members took part, including W.Bro. William James Hughan who acted as Grand Registrar. The lodge has had several distinguished joining and honorary members, including Sir Philip Colville Smith, Grand Secretary and Deputy Provincial Grand Master. The lodge moved from hotel to hotel while in Truro, until the leasehold of a property in Old Bridge Street was purchased in 1887 for £110, the brethren subscribing in £5 shares. The freehold was bought for £100 eight years later and the premises rebuilt in 1896 at a cost of £441. Fortitude remained here for 46 years, then exchanging buildings with the British Legion.

In December 1943 a Corporal Karl Reisman of the U.S. Army asked the lodge secretary for advice - he had been elected but had been drafted before initiation. Subsequently the lodge received official permission to admit him, witnessed by many other of his serving countrymen. At about this time the lodge premises, then in Union Place, Truro were requisitioned for the Royal Observer Corps. As military lodges could expect to be on the move they had little use of impedimenta such as Wardens' chairs. The lodge therefore did not have these until 1952 when W.Bro. C.H. Prowse of Mount Sinai lodge was prevailed upon to make them.

These fine chairs bear examination for their elegance and symbolism. Other modern keynotes include the institution of Ladies' Evenings in 1953, the consolidation in 1957 of Truro masonic interests on one site at St. Mary's House, Kenwyn (formerly the Bishop's Palace) and the sponsorship in 1959 of a daughter lodge, St. Piran's No. 7620 (the 50th in the Province). St. Piran's lodge shared premises until 1967 when it built its own premises at Perranporth. St. Mary's House, known by many brethren as accommodating for several years the provincial offices, was sold in late 1997.

The lodge has had close links with the City of Truro, providing many Mayors (including the first, Thomas Chirgwin) since its creation in 1877 and at one time adjusted its meetings to avoid clashes with council meetings. From 1866 until the death of W.Bro. Bert Davey in the late 1960's the lodge had only three Tylers. At one time the lodge had two W.Masters each year, but there is no record of two separate installation ceremonies. The bi-centenary warrant was granted in 1972 when the Deputy Grand Master Sir Allan Adair came with several Grand Lodge and provincial officers for the presentation and banquet

There have been several notable members in the long history. W.Bro. Stanley Pascoe was secretary for 28 years W.Bro. Tom Waters treasurer for over 20 years, (he became Deputy Provincial Grand Master of Mark Master Masons in Cornwall), and W.Bro. Jack Price who was the author of the lodge history from 1772-1972 and became Mark Provincial Grand Master. V.W.Bro. Frank Crewes, W.M. in 1975, is the present Deputy Provincial Grand Master (from 1994), and previously served as Provincial Secretary.

Lodge Histories

TRUE AND FAITHFUL LODGE No. 318, HELSTON.

The records of the True and Faithful Lodge begin in 1799 but from Grand Lodge archives it is found that a lodge was warranted on April 14 1752 and its constitution was paid for by the members on June 18. The lodge met at the Kings Arms, Meneage Street. Like all early Cornish Lodges, with one exception at Falmouth now No. 75, it had a brief existence and was erased as No.120 in 1774. We know nothing more relating to the craft in Helston until 1799 when we find a lodge in an unlooked for quarter and note its constitution and first meeting. W.Bro. Strachan, Grand Registrar (Eng.) in his work 'Northumbrian Masonry' (G. Kenning 1898 page 99) states that on November 5 1799 the Provincial Grand Lodge of Northumberland held a special meeting in the St. Nicholas Lodge and instituted a warrant called True and Faithful No. 582 in the Cornwall Regiment of Fencible Light Dragoons quartered then in Newcastle-on-Tyne. The following is an extract from the Newcastle Advertiser dated Saturday 9 November 1799: "On Tuesday last a Provincial Grand Lodge was held in St. Nicholas Lodge at Mr. Henzells in the Flegh market by order of J. Erington Esq., Provincial Grand Master for Northumberland for the purpose of consecrating a new lodge to be held at Mr. Whitfields the Scotch Arms Newgate Street, on which occasion a grand procession took place accompanied by an excellent band belonging to the Cornwall Fencible Light Dragoons."

The Regiment returned to Cornwall in 1800 and was disbanded. On 10 July a petition was made to Grand Lodge which asked that the lodge recently warranted in the Regiment should become a civil lodge and be held under the same name and number at the Angel Inn, Helston. The petition was granted and so we now have 'The True and Faithful Lodge' No.582 holden at the Angel Inn in Helston. The new lodge was opened on 19 November 1800 with 11 members. This date was also significant in the fact that the lodge furniture in part was delivered and paid for. January 1801 shows the lodge settling down, the previous 11 brethren paying 2/- each and new annual subscription for liquidating the debt of Grand Lodge. Brethren proposing a candidate were required to pay a fee of 10s.6d. prior to the lodge. The tyler received 2s.6d for supplying the apron to the new candidate. March 1801 saw the joining fee raised from 5s to 7s.6d. There were three joining members: one was Sir John St. Aubyn, Past Master of Lodge No.75 Falmouth, S.G.W. of the Grand Lodge of England 1781 and in 1785 appointed Provincial Grand Master of Cornwall. He remained a subscribing member until 1833. Two Ashlars were purchased in 1801 and are in the lodge at this present time. The lodge continued to meet at the Angel Hotel on a regular basis.

In 1813 the lodge was re-numbered 600 and in 1832 No.400. The first recorded minutes date from 1828. Previous minutes were presumed lost. There were occasions when the lodge regular meetings were adjourned due to lack of members attending. In 1832 the J.W. was fined five shillings for being absent without good reason and junior officers one shilling. During 1834-43 the lodge did not meet at all. The original charter was lost and a confirmation warrant was applied for and granted in 1844. The lodge once again met regularly at the Angel until 1855 when it was removed to the Star Inn. In 1863 the lodge found a new habitation on the Tubban in a detached building previously used as a commercial academy. Considerable opposition was raised against the move but it eventually proved successful. On the death of the trustees of the building the property reverted to the Duke of Leeds who in 1891 granted a lease for 60 years. The lodge eventually obtained the freehold in 1901 for £150. In 1863 the Lodge was renumbered No. 318 which it now retains and ranks fourth in age on the provincial roll of lodges. In the by-laws of the lodge when revised in 1869 "the lodge shall meet each month on the Friday on or before a full moon". The day changed to Tuesday in 1895. In 1900 £300 was spent on the interior: to complete the work shares were bought by the brethren.

An entry in the minutes of 1918 states the swords of the original Cornish Light Dragoons were refurbished and hung on the wall of the lodge room. They were again refurbished at a much later date and re-hung in the form of a triangle. A reference was also made to the tracing boards which were hung on the north wall. These boards are in use to this day. From 1920 there were many candidates proposed and accepted. Emergency meetings were convened, at times twice a month. In 1922 the W.M. and brethren were invited to the stone-laying ceremony at the Helston Cottage Hospital. April 1923, the lower room (dining room) was put in hand to be built. The extension was completed in December 1923 when an opening ceremony was performed followed by a banquet and dancing. The lodge held its first ladies festival in 1928. The lodge had previously applied to Grand Lodge for a centenary warrant. In September 1928 Grand Lodge requested the lodge minute books to support the petition: a warrant was granted in 1929. The lodge continued to meet regularly and to prosper. In March 1960 it was agreed that the regular meetings be held on the first Tuesday of each month excluding July and August, and not on the Tuesday on or before a full moon. From a report from the lodge building committee, work was put in hand to renovate and decorate the lodge room and extend it into a small ante-room: the work began in July 1960 and was completed in December. It is regretted that many old artefacts were lost or mislaid during the renovations. Due to increased cost of maintaining the fabric of the Masonic Hall and increased high running costs, a management committee was formed between the two Helston lodges. From 1799 the lodge roll has contained the names of many eminent men of the locality and continues to meet in that love and harmony found among masons.

To mark the 200th anniversary of True and Faithful, in September 2000, the Grand Secretary V.W.Bro. James W. Daniel, presented the bi-centenary warrant to the W.M., W.Bro. Gordon Dawson. The special meeting was attended by the Provincial Grand Master, R.W.Bro. Nicholas Barrington, his Deputy V.W.Bro. Frank Crewes and the assistants W.Bros. James Kitson and John Davy. A brief history

Lodge Histories

from 1799 was given by lodge secretary, W.Bro. Ivor Jones and there was an oration by the Prov.G. Chaplain, Bro. the Revd Andrew Wilson. Later, at a celebration dinner, a birthday cake was cut by the oldest serving member W.Bro. Willie Pascoe and the youngest Bro. Brian Keverne. The Grand Secretary thanked the lodge for its hospitality and wished it a successful future.

A touch of history at Helston, from 1799, with the crossed sabres of the Cornwall Regiment of Fencible Light Dragoons. They were the property of the original Helston 1799 lodge and now hang as a triangle on the wall, mounted on their shields.

ONE AND ALL LODGE No. 330, BODMIN.

One and All has a long and sometimes quite colourful history and is the fifth oldest lodge in the province. The date of the warrant on which the lodge was formed is 8 March 1810. It was a warrant of assignment (being No. 8 of 22 such warrants issued) and assigns the warrant of a lodge meeting at the Crown Inn in Nantwich in the county of Chester which was No. 543 and forfeited on 10 February 1809, to the Royal Cornwall Regiment of Militia to hold a lodge at their headquarters and to be No. 618. This lodge was military and transient. This information and the peculiar nature of the warrant did not come to light until 1980. As a result of subsequent action in the lodge a photo-copy and a transcript of it now hangs in the North West of the lodge. The original is in the Grand Lodge collection. Of the 22 warrants of assignment that were issued, ten are still in use, six are in the Grand Lodge collection and six are unaccounted for. The present warrant of the lodge is dated 12 July, 1830, when it became One and All lodge and is a renewal warrant bearing the No. 625. The founder members of the Lodge were all members of The Royal Cornwall Regiment of Militia.

The first recorded minutes show that a meeting was held at the George Inn, Stratford, Essex, in May, 1810, when the warrant was read by the Grand Secretary. Until 4 July 1814 meetings were held at various places;and although the lodge was itinerent at this time, in fact, only ten meetings ever took place outside Bodmin. The Lodge was later No. 413 and the present number 330 was not in use until the 3rd August, 1863. The transition from a military lodge only able to initiate candidates from within the armed forces to a civil one was accomplished in 1830, 20 years after its formation, the reason cited being that the nearest lodge was 22 miles away in Truro. Bodmin at this time was isolated until the arrival of the railway serving the town. A history of the period states "the streets were ill-paved and badly lighted. Worn flagstones and rough cobbles made pedestrian traffic dangerous, and dark corners full of rubbish abounded." Not ideal conditions for travel in the dark in winter. From 1834 onwards the lodge had great difficulty. Five meetings were cancelled in 1835, 11 in 1836 and

Lodge Histories

nine in 1837, there being insufficient brethren present and sometimes when the lodge was opened the attendance was seven or eight. Clearly some members, however, made great efforts to attend. A framed apron, formerly hanging in the lodge bears the notice; "This apron was worn by Bro. I. E. Harvey who was initiated in the lodge on the 29 June 1812 and was in the habit of walking to and from Saltash to attend his masonic duties."

In its early years the lodge had many connections with the Molesworth family and a memorial window exists in the ante-room to W. Bro. Sir Hugh Henry Molesworth. It seems that Sir William Molesworth was WM in 1833, 1834 and again in 1839, but may have been no more than a figurehead, as the minutes record various attempts to get him to visit the lodge! He was obviously held in high esteem as a minute from 11 January 1841, notes that he be "waited on" by a deputation with a requisition that he might accept a nomination and recommendation from One and All that he be appointed Provincial Grand Master . Hugh Henry Molesworth was initiatied in July, 1843 and became W.M. in 1849. The minutes show that in 1847 seven meetings were cancelled and 11 in 1848 but in this year the strength of the lodge was fairly strong as 75 members were present at the funeral of a Bro. Gatty, who appears to have been responsible for providing the lodge refreshments for a number of years.

On 10 October 1870, the lodge met at the Freemasons' Hall, Turf Street, Bodmin, for the first time. The dedication by the Provincial Grand Master took place on 7 July 1874. In August, 1910, during the centenary year, the laying of the foundation stone of the present hall in St. Nicholas Street took place. In the absence of the Provincial Grand Master this was carried out by his Deputy W.Bro. P. Colville Smith. The eventual cost of the present hall was £1,502.5s.6d. The 'Western Morning News' carries a report of the ceremony, which included the presence of the Cornish Masters Lodge, a procession comprising the Bodmin Territorial Band and the church choir with processional cross, the Mayor and Corporation with mace bearer and town crier followed by the masonic brethren with their banners. The volume of the sacred law was borne by four master masons' sons in front of the Deputy P.G.M. and there were prayers by the Provincial G.Chaplain (the Revd H.R. Jennings, Vicar of Millbrook). Addressing the large assembly present, the Deputy P.G.M. said: "Men, women and children here assembled today, know all of you that we be lawful masons true and faithful to the laws of our country, established of old with peace and honour in most countries, and engaged by solemn obligations to erect magnificent buildings to be serviceable to the brethren and to fear God, the great architect of the universe. We have amongst us concealed from the eyes of all men secrets which cannot be divulged, but these secrets are lawful and honourable, and not repugnant to the laws of God or man. Unless our craft were good and our calling honourable, we should not have lasted for so many centuries, nor should we have been honoured with the patronage of so many illustrious men in all ages."

The dedication of the new hall took place in January 1911, and was carried out by the Deputy P.G.M., after which Bro. M. F. Edyvean was installed as W.M. During the 1914-1918 war, the ante-room was used as a rest and recreation room for wounded and convalescent soldiers. During 1921 and 1922 there were 17 emergency meetings to cope with the work of the lodge, caused by the large influx of prospective members. Exchange workings took place with Molesworth lodge of Wadebridge in 1929 and 1930. During the Second World War the gates and railings of the lodge were "surrendered" in the national interest and have never been replaced. The central heating of the lodge was installed in 1951. In more recent years in addition to the lodge and Saint Petrock Chapter the hall has also become the home of the Saint Nicholas Lodge M.M.M. No. 1188 and Saint Nicholas Lodge R.A.M. No. 1188. One and All has been the mother lodge of some notable freemasons eminent in the province including W.Bro Hubert Dingle (Deputy P.G.M.), and a large number of Grand Officers. The lodge is looking forward to its bi-centenary in 2010.

Lodge Histories

Brother William Henwood, who was initiated in One and All Lodge, Bodmin, in October 1830. He was one of the founders of the St. Martin's Lodge, Liskeard No. 510 in 1845 and this photograph was presented to One and All in 1896.

This is a copy of the original front cover of the first Minute Book, dated March 11 in 1810, of the present One and All Lodge, Bodmin, which received its warrant that month. It shows "Punch Going to be married"!
(see feature 'Freemasons on the March'.)

PHOENIX LODGE OF HONOR AND PRUDENCE No. 331, CHACEWATER.

The titles of some of the old lodges reflect, in some measure, the aspirations of their founders. Modern lodges, on the whole tend to be a little more prosaic in their choice. Phoenix lodge seems to fall into the former category: there is something in the character of a phoenix in the lodge itself, since it has twice risen, seemingly from the ashes, to regroup and start afresh. It was first warranted No.429 on 1st January 1779 and met at the Red Lion Hotel in Truro but had only a very short life, being finally erased in February 1788.

There must have been some interest in freemasonry kept alive in Truro among the former members for in 1806 the lodge was reopened. It decided to meet on the quarter-days and a petition was sent, asking for a renewal of the original warrant. This was refused, on technical grounds, and the lodge did not revive.

The brethren had not given up hope entirely, for in 1810 a warrant was granted and Phoenix was constituted with the number 620 on the roll. The ceremony when the warrant was handed over was attended by the Deputy Provincial Grand Master accompanied by provincial officers. "After the usual ceremonies the brethren proceeded to St. Mary's Church for a service at which the sermon was preached by the Provincial G. Chaplain. The brethren then returned and the installation of Dr. Richard Taunton as Master was proceeded with." During the ceremony an incident occurred which, in the light of today's openness bears recording: "the ladies, being anxious to see the form of the lodge, were admitted, the usual charge called, the Entered Apprentices Song given, after which they returned for refreshment."

In the early 19th century, it was not uncommon for candidates to be proposed, balloted for and initiated on the same evening. On one occasion 12 certificates were issued on one night.

Lodge Histories

By 1811 it had settled into monthly meetings: in 1813 the day was changed to the first Tuesday in the month, but, from 1814 onwards the meetings started to become irregular and from December 1815 to June 1817 no meetings were held at all! The lack of finance appeared to be the motivating factor behind the lack of members and the low state of lodge funds caused a good deal of anxiety.

In 1820, the lodge attended church with the Mayor and Corporation at the Proclamation of King George IV "to the throne of these realms." After an initiation in May of that year the lodge did not meet for some two years; again finance seemed to be the problem. It appeared to be at a very low ebb for there were only 11 members and only three or four meetings held between 1827 and 1830. The lodge after a brief period of activity again slumped into a moribund state, meeting only intermittently. In May 1837 brethren again attended church with the Mayor and Corporation for the proclamation of Queen Victoria and then went into a 'dormant' period for nine years.

The lodge was resuscitated in 1847 and new life seemed to infuse the brethren: by 1848 the lodge had 23 members and £16 in the account. It continued to meet at the Red Lion Hotel, but dissatisfaction had been expressed at the service provided and in 1850 the lodge moved to Pydar Street. It was at this time that jugs adorned with Masonic emblems for use by the lodge were bought and the lodge started to acquire equipment and furnishings to enhance the ceremonies. In 1856 the annual festival was called at the Masonic Rooms, Truro, and in 1858 at new rooms in St. Mary Street or High Cross. It was about this time that a number of masons joined who were to have an important influence, not only on Cornish Masonry, but also nationally.

Among the first of these was Bro. Augustus Smith who became W.M. in 1857 and Provincial Grand Master in 1863. He was followed by Bros. William James Hughan, Sir Frederick Martin Williams M.P., who was Deputy P.G.M. and the first Provincial Grand Master in the Mark, and Philip Colville Smith who was Deputy P.G.M., and Grand Secretary. There were many others too who made an important contribution to masonry in Cornwall; amongst the foremost of these was Bro. E.D. Anderton who was Provincial Secretary. The Anderton Memorial Fund for the education of the children of Cornish freemasons was set up in his memory in 1902, now incorporated into the Cornwall Masonic Grand Charity.

The mid-19th century was a period of consolidation and growth. The resurgence seemed to coincide with the election of Thomas, 2nd Earl of Zetland as Grand Master. In 1861 the brethren of Phoenix felt confident enough to petition for a Royal Arch Chapter: as a result Royal Cornubian Chapter was chartered. By 1869 the lodge eventually moved to a newly-built hall leased from the Truro Public Rooms Company, due mainly to the generosity of the Provincial Grand Master R.W.Bro. Augustus Smith. In July 1870 the lodge room was dedicated. On the day the streets were crowded with people and decorated with flags and bunting. A great gathering from the province and the Provincial Grand Master of Devonshire attended. The hall was of such a size that the provincial meetings could be held there, and

Phoenix acquired a permanent home for the first time. By purchase and gift the temple became well furnished.

The year 1880 was a great year for Cornish Freemasonry for on 20 May the foundation stone of Truro Cathedral was laid by the Grand Master, H.R.H. The Prince of Wales, with full masonic ceremonial. Five members of the lodge were honoured by assisting in the proceedings and Bros. Juleff and Julian took an active part in the laying of the stone. As the century moved to its close the lodge continued to prosper: Bro. Colville Smith, who had joined the lodge in 1889 was invited to take the chair in 1909 for the centenary of the founding of the lodge in 1910.

As it transpired there were no celebrations and he didn't take the chair as hoped! This was because the lodge was dormant between 1839 and 1847. Music has always played an important part in the ceremonies, although there was a period when the province frowned on this, but the problem resolved itself when a copy of the musical score was sent for approval.

The lodge was more fortunate than many for only three members lost their lives on active service during the Great War. After the war the lodge took some time to get back to normal, although when peace came the candidates list which had all but dried up during the conflict came on stream once again. In 1936 Phoenix supported a petition for the formation of Truro School Lodge. Over the years several brethren of the lodge have served not only the lodge well but also the province in differing capacities and others have been further honoured by being appointed to Grand Rank. During the 1939-45 war members of the lodge played their part in the life of the province and to the successful resolution of the conflict.

In 1947 the lodge at long last was able to celebrate 100 years of continuous working, although it was 168 years after the foundation of the first Phoenix lodge and 137 years after the foundation of the present lodge. The Phoenix had indeed risen with renewed vigour! In celebration of this event an 'Historical Sketch' by W.Bro. A.H. Luke Past Provincial S.G.W. was published. In recent years the lodge has moved from Truro to Chacewater.

Lodge Histories

CORNUBIAN LODGE No. 450, HAYLE.

The warrant for the constitution of Cornubian Lodge was granted in 1838. During that year a number of historical events took place including the coronation of Queen Victoria who had ascended the throne the previous year. It was the year the River Thames froze over and in April the 'Great Western', the brainchild of Isambard Kingdom Brunel, crossed the Atlantic to begin a passenger and freight service to America. The founders were Richard Nicholls, gentleman of Treglisson, William Crotch, innkeeper of the White Hart, Hayle, Nicholas Harvey, engineer of Hayle, Sharrock Dupen, steam company steward of Hayle, John Trebilcock, gentleman of Angarrack, Richard Stephens and Thomas Rawlings. Soon after the lodge was warranted, a number of the petitioners left the district which resulted in an insufficient number to form a lodge. There was then a ten year period before the lodge was consecrated in 1848 with Bro. Nicholls installed as the first Master. From its foundation the lodge had met in a room on the ground floor of the new White Hart Hotel, but a minute of January 1869, records that it was resolved to take over the offices in the old White Hart lately occupied by Messrs. Sandys Vivian & Co., solicitors, and an agreement was reached to lease these for ten years at an annual rent of £25. Eventually at its 350th meeting the lodge took up residence in its new abode after extensive alterations and redecoration at a cost of approximately £500. In 1922, the lodge acquired the property and the adjoining houses surrounding it from Messrs. Harvey & Co. for £875.

This Grade II building where the lodge now meets was the original White Hart Hotel, built in 1824 by Henry Harvey, the son of John Harvey, the smith from Gwinear, who set up a smithy and fitting shop at Carnsew with financial help from Sir John St. Aubyn. This was the forerunner of the great foundry and engineering works, known world-wide. Henry Harvey a dynamic personality built the hotel for two reasons - first, to provide a living for his daughter Jane, when her husband, Richard Trevithick, the renowned Cornish inventor and engineer was abroad selling his pumping engines, and secondly, to provide accommodation for businessmen visiting the foundry. Jane Trevithick retired from the hotel in 1837 when it was taken over by William Crotch, an astute and enterprising man who seeing the future possibilities of the development of Hayle persuaded Henry Harvey to build a larger hotel. One can gather from the early writings that William Crotch was the prime mover in bringing freemasonry to Hayle. He was initiated in Phoenix Lodge (which then met at Truro) in 1812 and was the first S.W. in Cornubian Lodge.

We now go back many years to the Ship Lodge at St. Ives (1765 - 1786) and True Friendship at Crowan (1816 - 1828) and their connections with Cornubian Lodge. The Cornubian minutes of September 1848 record that Mrs. Pool of the St. Michael's Inn, Crowan Churchtown was paid £6 for the storage of furniture formerly used by True Friendship Lodge which had previously met there. Prior to this the furniture had been used by the Ship Lodge St. Ives, where it was bought with a donation from Sir John St. Aubyn, the 4th Baronet. This furniture which included the Master and Wardens' chairs is still in use in the Cornubian temple. With the furniture was the minute book and other documents. The minute book contains not only the minutes of the Ship Lodge, but after a couple of blank pages it also holds the minutes of True Friendship, and as books in those days were expensive, Cornubian Lodge followed suit, left another couple of blank pages and recorded their minutes. This book is in the Hayle museum and is a record of freemasonry in West Cornwall from 1765. Cornubian Lodge started life as number 659: when the lodges were re-numbered in 1863, it became 450. Very old " firing glasses" in the museum are engraved with the old number. A minute of July 1883 records that it was resolved to buy a collection of masonic books and the bookcase which contained them from the widow of the late W.Bro. John Coombe for a sum not exceeding £40. The collection was acquired and has been enlarged until it now numbers over 2,000 books, with some of the older editions very valuable. The Coombe Library, as it is now called, is in the capable hands of W.Bro. Len Davies who is the present librarian. The following extracts from the minutes may bring home to us just how life went on at the beginning of the 20th century. It was resolved that the remuneration of the Tyler should be £1 per quarter and the use of the dwelling house rent free. It was resolved that the lodge should be lit by incandescent gas mantles instead of the present gas burners (electricity was installed in 1930). Motoring was then in its infancy and a letter of sympathy was sent to W.Bro. Dr. Thomas Mudge who had sustained a broken kneecap on the occasion of his first run. In 1924 W.Bro. Francis (Frank) Harvey, Provincial S.G.D. retired as treasurer of the lodge after serving 60 years in office. As a mark of appreciation he was presented with a silver Loving Cup. This was in addition to a silver salver which had been presented to him when he had served as treasurer for 40 years.

The new dining room was officially opened in December 1934 by W.Bro. William Wagner, P.G.St.B., the secretary of the lodge since 1890. He died in office in 1937 being secretary for 47 years. As a token of sympathy, W.Bro. W.V. Wagner, his son and W.Bro. T.E.A. Stowell, Provincial S.G.D., his son-in-law, presented the lodge with a magnificent silver Loving Cup in his memory. The inscription on the cup is headed "Remember William Wagner" followed by his masonic career and appointments. The cup is still used at each installation ceremony at the festive board. At the meeting in January 1945, it was resolved to give encouragement to the younger brethren who were desirous of forming a 'daughter lodge'. At this time there were 161 members in Cornubian. Trewinnard Lodge was consecrated in April 1946 by the Provincial Grand Master the Earl of St. Germans. The lodge was named after the Manor of Trewinnard with a number of the members of the Trewinnard family becoming honorary members. Another stalwart

Lodge Histories

of Cornubian Lodge, W.Bro. W.T. Blewett, P.G.St.B., was installed as the first Master. A great occasion for the Lodge was the celebration of its centenary in 1948. The honour of being W.M. fell to W.Bro. R.W. (Bobby) Trevithick. The ceremony was attended by the Deputy P.G.M., V.W.Bro. Canon Jennings in the absence of the Provincial Grand Master who was indisposed. At the meeting in June, 1951 the lodge was presented with a set of tracing boards by Mrs. Eddy, in memory of her late husband, W.Bro. William Arthur Eddy who passed away just a month after his installation in 1949. At the Provincial Grand Lodge meeting in 1954, W.Bro. Sidney Blewett was appointed Provincial G.D.C., a position he held for some 17 years. He was honoured by the Grand Master by being invested P.A.G.D.C. in Grand Lodge. In 1960 and 1963 two of the adjoining properties owned by the lodge were sold, the proceeds to be used for repairs and maintenance to lodge property. At the meeting in October, 1966 it was reported that a committee to be known as the Hayle lodges premises committee had been set up.

An item from the minutes in 1965 reported that two cabinets had been acquired to display items of Masonic interest and to be placed in the committee room on the ground floor and to be administered by W.Bro. H.W. Mitchell. These two cabinets were the forerunner of the comprehensive masonic museum at Hayle which is situated in what was the bedroom in the old tyler's house. It was opened by the Provincial Grand Master the Hon. Robert Eliot in September 1989. During 1973 the newly set up Cornubian and Trewinnard premises committee reported that the new kitchen had been completed and could now cater for more than 100 meals. The complete rebuilding of the tyler's flat was nearing completion and the re-siting and enlarging of the bar would follow early in 1974. At this time there were nine lodges meeting in the complex - three craft lodges and six other lodges. This total has now risen to 15 lodges meeting regularly at Hayle. With the ever increasing number of lodges using the complex, the idea of a second temple was mooted. A general meeting was called in March, 1978 attended by members of the three craft lodges, and it was resolved to provide an additional temple over the dining room where the great height of the room made it possible to add another floor. The dedication of the new temple was carried out by the Provincial Grand Master the R.W.Bro. the Hon. Robert Eliot in January 1979 when he named it the Perry Morgan Temple to honour the late P.G.M., who died in January, 1980.

In March, 1978 the W.M., W.Bro. T. Lobb proposed the lodge approve the petition presented to them to form a new craft lodge to meet at Hayle: this was unanimously approved. It was to be known as the Sir John St. Aubyn Lodge, No. 8839 and was consecrated in June, 1978 by the Deputy P.G.M. in charge, V.W.Bro. Cyril Andrew, with W.Bro. H.W. Mitchell installed as its first Master. At the installation meeting of the Hon. Robert Eliot as Provincial Grand Master in November, 1978, W.Bro. H.W. Mitchell was appointed Provincial G.Secretary and was further honoured at Grand Lodge in April 1979 when he received the rank of P.A.G.D.C., and in 1987 he was promoted to P.J.G.D. Also in 1987, W.Bro. G.C. Mason received the rank of P.A.G.D.C. In 1988 the lodge premises built in 1824, was designated a "building of historical interest" mainly through its connection with Richard Trevithick. It is now a listed Grade II building, which means that no alterations can be made without permission. Now ensued a long period of normal routine lodge business with a steady flow of candidates and many interesting lectures. Fund raising helped the management committee when £1,000 was raised to put on a new roof and £2,000 for a chair lift. The Square and Compass Club was set up to raise money for charity and good causes. Much was done to improve the property. To celebrate the 150th Anniversary, a service of thanksgiving was held in August 1998 at St. Erth Church when brethren in full regalia were accompanied by their wives, members of their families and friends. The service was conducted by the Revd. Fred Harwood, P.P.G.Chaplain. The P.G.M., R.W.Bro. Nicholas Barrington and Mrs. Barrington as well as V.W.Bro. J.W. Daniel, the Grand Secretary and Mrs. Daniel were among the guests. After the service there was a celebration at the Tregenna Castle Hotel, St. Ives.

W.Bro. Roger Freeman (Provincial Almoner) was appointed to PAGDC in 2001.

Watched by an old pedlar (but not by his pony), Cornish Freemasons walk in public procession.

PEACE AND HARMONY LODGE No. 496, ST. AUSTELL.

The first record of a masonic meeting in St.Austell is in a minute book at the lodge and bears the date of 23 March 1844, but there must have been a series of meetings prior to this as it appears by the minutes recorded of that meeting that the lodge was in full working order. The minute and treasurer's books are complete from that date to the present. The lodge was represented for the first time (and then by dispensation) at the Provincial Lodge at Falmouth in April 1844, when Sir Charles Lemon was installed Provincial Grand Master. The consecration of Peace and Harmony was fixed at this meeting to take place in the ensuing July, and the ceremony was performed by the Deputy P.G.M., W.Bro. John Ellis, the lodge bearing in the books of the Grand Lodge the number 728 until a revision in 1863, when it was given its present number.

On its constitution in 1844 the lodge met at the Queen's Head Hotel, and this was its place of meeting until 1850, when after being dormant for a few years the lodge was opened in December 1854, at the White Hart Hotel where it remained until the Masonic Room was built in Cross Lane. The lodge was regularly held there from 1873 to the end of the year 1900, when the present Masonic Hall, in South Street, was built, and the lodge first met there in December of that year.

Most, if not all, of the founders were initiated in the One and All Lodge, at Bodmin:- John Francis Hodge, ironfounder, W.M. Edwin Eveleigh, S.W. John Nott, printer, J.W. Charles Barker, Preventive Service, David Rogers Stickland, innkeeper, John Burrows, currier, Tyler, William Betty, musician, John Rogers, gentleman yeoman, Charles B. Graves-Sawle, Esquire, Edmund Carlyon, solicitor, Treasurer, William Medland, maltster, Secretary, William Gary (initiated in London in 1808), clerk, Horatio Nelson Burrows, gardener.

W.Bro. Edmund Carlyon had a record unique in the lodge. He was initiated on 9 October 1843 in the One and All Lodge, became a founder of Peace and Harmony in 1844, was its first treasurer and was W.M. in 1847, 1848 and 1858, received provincial honours in 1847 in the form of J.G.W., Provincial Grand Registrar in 1855, and Provincial S.G.W. in 1904.

Lodge Histories

The Provincial Lodge of Cornwall met at St. Austell on five occasions, first in 1855 under Sir Charles Lemon, when 11 lodges were represented. Though Sir Charles was Provincial Grand Master until 1863 this was the last time he presided. In 1872 24 Lodges were represented. R.W.Bro. Augustus Smith was to have presided but a sudden illness whilst at St. Austell prevented him from doing so. He never recovered from this illness and died shortly afterwards. Again in September 1883, there was a provincial meeting, the number of lodges in the province having risen by this time to 29. The next meeting of the provincial lodge at St. Austell, was on 25 August 1891, and date of the last meeting in the lodge was 22 September 1903.

The Mount Edgcumbe Chapter of Royal Arch Masons was constituted at St. Austell in 1874; and in 1881 a Lodge of Mark Master Masons was warranted and named St. Austell Lodge, No. 275. Peace and Harmony Lodge has blossomed over the years and in November, 1937 gave birth to her first daughter, Tewington Lodge No. 5698, consecrated March 1938. A further daughter was born in 1955, Carlyon Lodge No. 7392 consecrated November 1955, the youngest daughter being St.Denys, No. 8250, consecrated January 1969.

The masonic hall at 25 South Street, St. Austell, accommodates four craft lodges and five others. Mount Edgcumbe Chapter No. 496 and the St. Austell Lodge of Mark Master Masons No. 275 have already been mentioned. In addition to these are, the St. Austell Lodge of Royal Ark Mariners No. 275 warranted June 1962, and consecrated September 1962. The St. Austell Chapter, Rose Croix No. 744 warranted March 1973 and consecrated October 1973; Tewington Chapter No. 5696 warranted November 1987 and consecrated January 1988. The hall, now over 100 years old, was purpose built.

Before the road developments, steps led to the entrance with beautiful pillars, inside a winding stairway to the temple. Below the temple is the dining room, to the left on entry, a club area, sadly no longer in use. Above the club a caretakers flat, which is now let to help raise funds towards the upkeep of the building. The block work at the front of the building is carved on the outside with various masonic symbols and the dates 5900 A.L. and 1900 A.D. The windows are beautifully leaded with stained glass, again displaying numerous and various masonic symbols etc. It is a most attractive masonic building.

Lewises (the sons of Freemasons) who carried the Bible in procession to St. Martin's Church, Liskeard at the provincial lodge meeting in October 1907. They are left to right: Stanley Maggs, George Morcom, Percival Christopher Mitchell and Samuel Herbert Coath.

Lodge Histories

ST. MARTIN'S LODGE No. 510, LISKEARD.

When St. Martin's was founded in 1845 there were only eight lodges in Cornwall. Nine brethren drawn from One and All, Bodmin, and Lodge of Charity, Plymouth, made the petition and a warrant was granted. The legal profession seemed to have an important influence in its formation, the first W.M. and wardens being solicitors. Unusually, the lodge met seven times prior to its consecration, during which time seven brethren were initiated and six joining members and a serving brother admitted. There is no mention of the consecration meeting in the lodge minutes, but it is recorded that "Provincial Grand Lodge met at Liskeard on 19th August 1845 and that the Lodge of St. Martin was constituted. Bro. Edward Lyne, solicitor, was installed as W.M. and his officers appointed". The event was fully reported in the Cornwall Gazette and the whole town was involved in some way, from the town band to the Mayor and Council. The lodge held a service in the Parish Church of St. Martin, the sermon being preached by the Provincial G Chaplain, the Revd H. Grylls, Rector of St. Neot. On returning from the church the lodge was constituted at the Fountain Inn after which a banquet was held at Webb's Hotel.

The lodge originally met on the second Tuesday in each month, the initiation fee was five guineas and the subscription 1s.6d per month collected previous to closing the lodge. A reminder of this custom is still to be found in some lodges where item "to collect subscriptions" appears on the summons. By the end of 1846 the membership had increased to 33, but attendance at lodge meetings was sparse, sometimes with only enough officers to work the ceremony. At first equipment was minimal, but gradually over the years the lodge acquired, by purchase and gift, various items. Refreshment was provided from the first for both members and visitors, one shilling being allocated each lodge night. Charity has always been one of the corner stones and instances are recorded where relief was granted to brethren and families. In common with many lodges at the time it was part of the tyler's duty not only to set up the lodge and clear it away afterwards but also to make sure the brethren were properly clothed. It was also his task to deliver the summons; for all this he was paid two shillings per night. In common with many lodges at this time multiple ceremonies were worked in an evening, on one occasion the lodge opened at 7.30pm and closed at 10.45pm after conducting three. In 1863 came the last closing up of numbers of the lodges: St. Martin's whose original number had been 750 now received 510. In 1864 it

Lodge Histories

felt confident enough to sponsor a Royal Arch Chapter in Liskeard and in the following year it was consecrated.

As the mines in the area closed and industry generally declined from the 1860s, there occurred an increase in initiations into the craft prior to some of these brethren emigrating to seek work in America, Australia and South Africa. As the lodge grew so additional officers were introduced, stewards in 1870, a D.C. in 1872 and an assistant secretary in 1910. The brethren of St. Martin's were active in visiting lodges in the vicinity, but mainly those accessible by rail, for the roads were notoriously bad in poor weather. In its history the lodge has met at only four venues, the Fountain Inn (1845-50), Bro. Lyne's premises until 1851 and then the London Inn until 1872 when the masonic hall was opened. This was an important event in the life of the lodge: again the whole town seemed to be involved. The hall was dedicated by the Earl of Mount Edgcumbe on his first official engagement as Provincial Grand Master. A procession was formed in which the Mayor, attended by his mace bearers joined, and they all proceeded to Wadham House where a bazaar in aid of the building fund was held. A public luncheon was held later that day and the bazaar was so successful it was continued into the following day raising £220. The lodge furniture was mainly provided by the brethren and by their efforts the mortgage was paid off in 1895 in time for the lodge's jubilee. In 1881 the meeting was changed to the Tuesday on or near the full moon; at this time the installation was changed from the Festival of St. John (27 December) to the regular meeting in January. In 1890 the regular lodge night was changed once again, this time to the first Tuesday in the month. By the turn of the century the lodge had grown and prospered and the hall which had been opened some 28 years previously was proving to be too small, so plans were drawn up to enlarge the temple by incorporating the ante-room. This was done, and in 1902 the temple was totally redecorated, a striking feature at this time being a triple-curtain comprising the three masonic colours of blue, crimson and purple, which extended across the whole of the east end of the lodge with the lodge banner hanging on the crimson centre-band. The two ornate fireplaces are a reminder that before central heating was introduced in 1933 the lodge was heated by open fires.

For many years the lodge took a prominent part in the life of the town: in 1876 a dispensation was applied for to enable the brethren to wear their regalia in the Mayor's procession at the opening of the Royal Cornwall Show and in 1895 the 'corner stone' of Passmore Edwards Cottage Hospital was laid by the P.G.M. attended by members of provincial lodge, Bro. Edwards, and civic leaders. In 1897, presumably to celebrate the diamond jubilee of Queen Victoria, St. Martin's held a church service: the procession was headed by the band of the Volunteer Battalion, D.C.L.I. playing the Freemasons' March, and immediately behind came the sword bearers followed by members of Cornish lodges carrying their banners. The Provincial Grand Master and his deputy walked at the rear of the procession with provincial officers. Four Lewises carried the open Bible on a velvet cushion. Important events in the life of the lodge, certainly up to the end of the Great War, have included the presence of the Mayor and Council. St. Martin's has often had excellent relations with the parish church, the lodge numbering members of the clergy amongst its members. Among its prominent members were W.Bro. W. Hammond (Prov. Secretary and Prov. Grand Scribe E. and later Grand Librarian), W.Bro. R. Faull for many years treasurer - secretary of the Cornwall Masonic Charity Association and W.Bro. R.A. Courtney, twice W.M. of St. Martin's, all of whom were appointed to Grand Rank. In later years there was W.Bro. R.E.

Lodge Histories

Crabb who became W.M. in 1970 and was appointed Assistant Provincial Grand Master in 1986. The Great War of 1914-1918 proved a watershed, not only in the life of the nation, but also locally, and to Liskeard and St. Martin's lodge in particular. Many members rallied to the colours and their contribution is commemorated by a tablet in the lodge room. In the years following the Great War there was a marked increase of interest in freemasonry with 32 initiations from 1918-1921, probably the greatest increase the lodge has known. In 1923 the lodge room was beautified by the addition of four stained-glass windows, one of which was given by members of the lodge, the other three as gifts to the lodge by W.Bro. and Mrs. Richard Faull, W.Bro. A. Hancock and Miss M.L. Hancock, and W.Bro. J.G. and Mrs. Chynoweth respectively. These windows and the new marble tesselated pavement, the gift of W.Bro. A.H. Philp, were unveiled by the Provincial Grand Master Lord St. Levan. With the declaration of war in 1939 St. Martin's men again played their part and as the war drew to a close the lodge celebrated its centenary. The centenary warrant was presented by the P.G.M., the Earl of St. Germans and a history was presented at the centenary meeting by W.Bro. A.H. Philp. In the years since then the lodge has continued to grow and prosper; this was crowned in 1995 when the lodge celebrated 150 years of working and the P.G.M., R.W. Bro. Nicholas Barrington attended with his officers.

The procession to church at Liskeard in October 1907 on the day of the laying of the hospital foundation stone.

Lodge Histories

LOYAL VICTORIA LODGE No. 557, CALLINGTON.

Loyal Victoria Lodge was warranted on 14 October 1848 and opened at Callington in 29 January 1849. In common with many of the early lodges, it started its meetings in the local hostelries. Three of these were favoured, the Bull's Head Inn, the Sun Inn and Goldings Hotel; however, twice in the 1870s the National School was used for installation meetings. Of these only the Bull's Head still survives. The founders were drawn from across the social spectrum from 'gentlemen' to a miner. Unlike today when upwards of 25 or 30 are needed to form a lodge, Loyal Victoria had only eight founders. They were drawn from two lodges, Friendship No. 238 (now 202) Stonehouse and Bedford No. 351 (now 282) Tavistock, both in the province of Devonshire. Bro. John Ellis, Deputy Provincial Grand Master for Cornwall read and handed over the warrant in January 1849 - Loyal Victoria's number was then 815 - at the Bull's Head Inn.

In the years following its consecration there were times when the lodge could not meet through lack of members, but looking at the times when this occurred it was either in the winter or summer months so it is possible that the weather and the harvest may have been a factor as to why the lodge had so few members at those times. Today multiple ceremonies are a rarity in most lodges yet in the years following its consecration these were more common than single ones. During the early years the lodge met on the Monday on or before the full moon in every month. This was, presumably, to provide the members with light to go home by; this state of affairs was perpetuated in the provincial year book up to 1939, although the date had been fixed as the first Monday in the month for some years before. It is quite normal today to expect to see visitors at lodge meetings, yet in the 19th century when transport was more difficult to come by, and travel difficult, it is surprising how many visitors attended lodge meetings. On one occasion in the 1850s only four members of Loyal Victoria turned up, but, with the assistance of three visitors a ceremony was worked. It was quite interesting to see from the list of joining members and visitors, not only the countrywide but also the worldwide aspect, because Loyal Victoria had members joining from Australia, Canada, the West Indies and the U.S.A. When one brother, who had been initiated in South Africa in a lodge under the Grand Lodge of Holland and who wanted to join Loyal Victoria, permission had to be obtained both from province and Grand Lodge.

Lodge Histories

The charitable aspect was particularly evident, especially during the 19th century, when not only members of Loyal Victoria Lodge and their dependants petitioned for relief, but the lodge pledged its votes in the various masonic charities to assist members and dependants of other lodges. One of the most important decisions taken during the early years of the lodge was to have a hall of its own. It took 27 years for this project to come to fruition. The new masonic hall was finally opened in 1876 and in the spirit of the times was embellished on the outside with masonic symbols and armorial bearings, and on the inside an inner door to the lodge was finely carved with masonic symbols as was the fireplace which dominated the side wall. It was not long after this that a Royal Arch Chapter was formed as Valletort from the title of the eldest son of the Earl of Mt. Edgcumbe. These were the years of consolidation and growth and between 1871 and 1881 some 87 members were either initiated or joined the lodge. This growth continued although not at such a pace right up to the outbreak of the Great War, which proved a watershed for Loyal Victoria as indeed for many lodges. When the world was again plunged into conflict in 1939, many members of the lodge again fought for their country. Only one member of Loyal Victoria Lodge was killed during this conflict, Bro. A. Hancock who was killed at sea in 1940.

When the conflict ended the lodge had a great celebration to look forward to, its centenary. This was celebrated in 1949 with some style, allowing for the fact that rationing was still in existence. The Provincial Grand Master The Earl of St. Germans presided over the proceedings with his officers and the banquet was held at the Blue Cap Hotel, one of the venues Loyal Victoria used prior to their acquiring their own premises. The lodge embarked on its second century with renewed vigour and has been, for many years, attracting candidates who have taken their masonry seriously and resulted in work of a very high standard. In 1876 the lodge was looking forward to moving to its new purpose built premises in Haye Road, Callington. By the time the lodge had celebrated its centenary it was looking for new premises yet again, as by now the old building was too small for its purpose. As luck would have it, the United Methodist Chapel in Tavistock Road came on the market. By 1953 negotiations were complete and the lodge moved to its new and present location. The new premises were not only more spacious but also had the advantage of possessing a magnificent pipe organ, an instrument which has enhanced the ceremonies for over 40 years. It was, quite a wrench for the lodge to leave its old premises and while much was moved, some important fixtures had to be left behind, such as the fireplace and the carved doors.

When the Women's Institute, who bought the Old Masonic Hall, refurbished their premises in the 1970s they gave the fireplace back to the lodge, and it was placed in storage until it could be re-positioned in the lodge. It was soon realised that Loyal Victoria would not be able to use it so, rather than letting it deteriorate further, it was given to the masonic hall at Hayle. In the years since its move, Loyal Victoria has progressed and maintained its balance of a cross-section of the community. This is what gives the lodge its character and has been a source of strength. It is a family lodge as many sons have followed their fathers into the lodge. In the late 1970s a number of brethren from various lodges wished to form a new lodge and asked Loyal Victoria to sponsor it, so in 1979 Saint Mary's Lodge was formed to meet at Callington. Loyal Victoria celebrated its 150th anniversary in 1999.

In the days when Masonic processions took place, a sight which is understood to be unique to the Province of Cornwall, was that of the four 'Lewises' (sons of Freemasons) taking part. They carried the Bible. This was at the annual meeting of Provincial Grand Lodge, held at Redruth on 30th July in 1917. The minutes of the meeting reads: "…and on returning to the Druids Hall, the four Lewises, Frank Leslie Gee, George Herbert Vincent, Arthur John Paul, and Joseph Charles Everitt, who had carried the Volume of the Sacred Law in the procession, were introduced into the Lodge. "The acting Provincial Grand Master addressed the Lewises and presented them with copies of the Holy Bible, suitably inscribed and signed by His Lordship" (the Earl of Mount Edgcumbe, the Provincial Grand Master.)

DRUIDS' LODGE OF LOVE AND LIBERALITY No. 589, REDRUTH.

The present lodge is the second one to hold that name in Redruth. The first was founded in 1754 with the number 176; it continued to operate until about 1825, when due to a variety of reasons it became dormant. It was revived in 1851. The first Druids' Lodge met at the London Inn, Fore Street. As with many lodges during this period the membership tended to be small, some 15 to 20 members. They were mostly young men by today's standards, the oldest being only 39. The occupations were mainly from the business and professional classes and gentlemen of private means from the Redruth and St. Agnes areas. In 1773 the lodge decided to add 'of Love and Liberality' to its name, presumably to reflect the hopes and aspirations of its members. By 1814 the membership stood at 58. One name from Druids' past, stands out as a beacon, Bro. John Knight. He was initiated into Druids' in 1766 and until the warrant was returned, held every office in the lodge several times. He was a very experienced mason, who was in several lodges not only in Cornwall but also in Devonshire. He managed to keep the lodge in being and functioning well into the 19th century, but an ageing and failing membership took its toll and in 1825 the warrant was returned and masonry ceased in Redruth.

The election of Thomas, 2nd Earl of Zetland as Grand Master of the United Grand Lodge in 1844 was fortuitous and under his leadership freemasonry was enjoying something of a surge in membership. So it was that in the year of the Great Exhibition of 1851 in London, moves were set in motion for the revival of masonry in Redruth. On 26 April 1851 the founders' dreams were realized and in Andrew's Hotel the warrant for a new Druids' Lodge of Love and Liberality was handed over, with the number 859. In common with many lodges in the mid 19th century Druids' met in one of the local hostelries. This was, however, proving to be unsatisfactory. They moved from the hotel to lease premises in the Clinton Passage area of the town. In 1863 Grand Lodge closed up the numbers on the roll and Druids' number changed from 859 to 589. The problems with their premises continued, and a founder who also had lasting influence on the lodge was Bro. Thomas Mills in that he was the driving force in seeking a permanent home for the lodge. In 1874 a freehold site was purchased in Green Lane for the erection of a purpose built Masonic Hall. In January 1876, with great rejoicing and splendour, the brethren of Druids' in masonic regalia paraded to Green Lane headed by a band and the Tyler with drawn sword.

Lodge Histories

Choristers of Redruth Church Choir sang an ode and members of the public enjoyed the event as with due masonic ceremony the foundation stone for the new hall was laid by W.Bro. John Penrose. The silver trowel used on that occasion is on display in the lodge. By 1878 the hall was completed and in August of that year was dedicated by the Provincial Grand Master The Earl of Mount Edgcumbe. The acquisition of a permanent home enabled the lodge to grow and expand and in the years following, the meetings at which the lodge did not have a candidate were few and far between.

The first decade of the new century was a busy one for the lodge, the meetings well attended and on occasion multiple ceremonies performed. Many of the older members were by now passing away: others however, who were to play an important part in freemasonry in Redruth were coming into the lodge. During the Great War the lodge made contributions to various charities, in particular to the Disabled Soldiers Fund and to the Masonic War Hospital. During the war years very little had been done to the building: as a result in 1919 the lodge building committee reported that the building needed urgent repairs. A contractor was engaged and the work put in hand immediately. The building, however, was in constant need of re-decoration and updating, so it was decided to try to build up a fund to help defray the costs. The lodge in supporting its widows did not forget to support the Masonic Hospital or the various appeals made by the province, in particular that to the Cathedral in 1930. Over the years the lodge had grown and expanded and by the mid 1930s had well over 100 members and it was not uncommon for over 90 members to sit down to dine after a lodge meeting. In 1936 the lodge was invited by Bro. The Revd Ladd-Canney to attend the laying of the foundation stone for the extension to St. Andrew's Church. The lodge responded by donating to the church a pillar to be placed in the North East corner at St. Andrew's carved with masonic symbols and the name of the lodge.

One member who served the lodge long and well was W.Bro. Andrew Kistler, the secretary for 63 years. He was born in Redruth in 1840 and joined Druids' from Boscawen lodge in 1871 and became W.M. in 1882. In 1926 in recognition of his long service to freemasonry he was appointed to Grand Rank. There were lodge highlights during the 1939-45 war when members away on active service returned or when, Druids', in common with many Cornish lodges, allowed American servicemen to receive ceremonies in the lodge. One of these servicemen was Alvin Benjamin Rubin, attorney-at-law from Louisiana. Although, in 1944, the war had still some time to run, the freemasons of Redruth were looking to the future and petitioned for another lodge to meet at Redruth and in May 1945 St. Euny Lodge No. 6025 was consecrated. Druids' Lodge has been fortunate in attracting members who have made a significant contribution to masonry, not only in Redruth but in the province. In 1945 Cyril Andrew joined the lodge, by 1956 he was W.M., and went on to be the Deputy Provincial Grand Master . When he died in 1994 he had been a member of Druids' for some 49 years, and his daughter presented the lodge with a framed list of his masonic achievements. Following the war the lodge looked forward to celebrating its centenary: in 1951 the celebrations took place. W.Bro. H.J. Paul gave a talk on the history of the lodge. A dinner was held and the evening rounded off with a musical programme by the members of the lodge. The 1950s were the high point of membership for in that decade the total reached 120. It was decided in 1972 to transfer ownership from Druids' to the two Redruth lodges (Druids' and St Euny) and have a joint management committee. This proved to be a step in the right direction.

That masonry is strong and flourishing in Redruth was exemplified by the foundation of a daughter lodge, Trevithick, which also meets at Green Lane, Redruth. In common with many lodges Druids' saw a drop in the number of its members during the 1980s and 90's, but in 2001 celebrated 150 years of continuous working.

Lodge Histories

Past Masters of Mount Edgcumbe Lodge, Camborne, photographed in May 1964.

Lodge Histories

BOSCAWEN LODGE No. 699, CHACEWATER.

The lodge was consecrated in 1857 to meet at the Britannia Inn, Chacewater, an association that has lasted - apart from a ten year break in the 1980s - to the present day. Indeed one licensee installed a hatch to enable serving from the inn, and several have been members. Although the lodge has on occasion been known as teetotal, perhaps not always strictly so, nevertheless the association is remarkable in still continuing to the present time. The observant person may notice the masonic symbols visible on the front of the building, one of the last survivors anywhere of a very old masonic tradition. Originally it was a single storey timber building behind the inn on the present site, rebuilt in the 1870s. Although there was no formal sponsor, Phoenix lodge members played a large part in its formation and it is fitting that they have shared a masonic home here since Boscawen returned to Chacewater in 1991 after a ten year sojourn in Truro. The then Deputy Provincial Grand Master (W.Bro. Ellis) visited the site to approve it, writing that he wanted to be back in Falmouth that day - a journey from Falmouth to Truro and Chacewater and back to Falmouth then taking a lot longer than it does by car today.

Originally bearing the number 1000, it was named after the Hon. Revd J.T. Boscawen, Vicar of Lamorran on the Tregothnan Estate: this became clear from the banner presented by him in 1869 bearing his crest with the heraldic crescent of a second son. The warrant is endorsed since a delay in obtaining it meant that the master designate had moved away and a new one had to be elected. The consecration was evidently a very lively affair, ushered in by discharges of cannon fire regularly from 5am and a procession headed by an effective (probably very noisy) band from Truro. After a banquet 50 ladies joined the brethren for wine, dessert and toasts and in the evening there was a display of fireworks and flaming tar barrels. Initiation was four guineas and the proposer paid a deposit of one guinea. The Vicar of Chacewater later became a member and eventually W.M. and presented a Bible that is still in use at lodge meetings. The lodge met at 1pm, dinner at 3.30pm for the members to be home before fully dark. In 1890 the date moved to Monday nearest full moon (in 1899 the provincial directory shows eight lodges then similarly organised). Within two years the lodge was able to host the provincial meeting at the national school-room and afterwards at a marquee on a brother's lawn.

In 1864 a new harmonium was acquired, the first of four from Mr. Mills of St. Day, a great uncle of

Lodge Histories

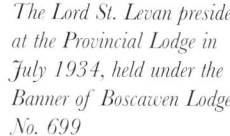

The Lord St. Levan presides at the Provincial Lodge in July 1934, held under the Banner of Boscawen Lodge No. 699

the secretary of Tregullow Lodge. In the 1870s a Bro. Kellow, who had emigrated to America, asked assistance to join an American lodge: his Grand Lodge certificate bore the number 1000 but his clearance certificate that of 699! No doubt the secretary pointed out the renumbering that had taken place in 1863. In 1872 a Bro. Moyle (not the first W.M.), then living in Devon, presented a handsome ballot box: five years later he applied to rejoin but this was rejected, whereupon he asked for his ballot box back, which was unanimously agreed! That now in use is the original, still bearing its first number. In 1874 it was agreed with the brewery to rebuild the hall which was eventually dedicated, with a right of way, in 1881, the lodge having met in the Wesleyan chapel rooms in the meantime. The minutes show some difficulties with the licensee: in 1889 the toilets were shared and in 1891 there were difficulties over his pigeons.

During the 2nd World War, D-Day Landing preparations in the area led to temporary eviction from the restricted zone. The dining room was used by the Home Guard. Earlier military reference may be made to collar jewels of the Royal Irish Regiment (17th of Foot) which had its own lodge; after withdrawal from Afghanistan and India the lodge collapsed and Sergeant Major Wing, sole masonic survivor, retired to Truro with the warrant and jewels, becoming a member of Fortitude Lodge. On his death his widow sought to sell the silver which was bought as a 'job lot' by a Bro. Ninnes who presented it to Boscawen lodge and is largely still in use. On the return of the lodge, with Phoenix, to Chacewater in 1991 the brethren found the hall largely unchanged but lacking modern amenities. Considerable refurbishments were carried out which make this small but historic masonic hall a delightful meeting place.

Lodge Histories

DUNHEVED LODGE No. 789, LAUNCESTON.

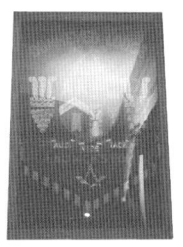

It is probable that a non-regular masonic lodge existed in Launceston, the ancient capital of Cornwall, some years before 1765, for in 1767 a Cornubian Lodge No. 410 was warranted by the Grand Lodge of the 'Moderns'. It later became No. 345 in 1770 and No. 268 in 1780, but ceased working in 1783. From 1757 to 1820 Launceston was a parole town for French officers who were prisoners-of-war and who had given their word not to escape. These officers were billeted in certain towns and among them were quite a number of freemasons, members of the Grand Orient of France which was then recognized by the Grand Lodge of England. In some cases these brethren became joining members of English lodges and some became initiates. A French lodge was established in Launceston in 1762 and was given the name "De La Consolante Maconne" (The Consoling Mason). This was the only French lodge formed in Cornwall and admitted not only Frenchmen but also Englishmen. It is possible that some of these English initiates joined or founded the early Cornubian lodge.

Following the erasure of Cornubian two attempts were made in 1808 and 1810 to obtain a warrant for another lodge in Launceston, neither being successful. During this time most local freemasons had become members of Loyal Victoria lodge in Callington and when Dunheved was eventually formed in Launceston all but one of the founder members were from Loyal Victoria. The petition was granted in May 1859, and the lodge was consecrated in January 1860 as Dunheved No. 1091. On 28 June of that year Provincial Grand Lodge met in Launceston, probably to mark the fact that there was once more a masonic lodge in the town. The consecration was carried out by the Deputy Provincial Grand Master W.Bro. Richard Pearce, and Bro. Charles Thomas Pearce was installed as the first W.M. at the King's Arms Hotel. Beginning with only seven founder members, candidates were soon forthcoming and after seven years the membership had risen to 20. Meetings were held on Thursday, on or after the full moon in every month, the moonlight doubtless making the journey to and from lodge less hazardous when travelling over rough roads. A consequence of meetings being held in conjunction with a full moon was that it was possible to hold 13 meetings in a year and days of installation sometimes took place in December and sometimes in January. In 1863 the lodge was renumbered from 1091 to 789. Membership continued to grow in the 1870s and one of the initiates during that time was a Lt.Col. J.H. Deakin who later became M.P. for Launceston. It was Bro. the Revd D.W. Horlock who introduced into

Lodge Histories

the lodge the Oxford working still in use. Bro. Horlock left for Canada in the 1880s and while there formed a masonic lodge in Vancouver. On his return to this country he held a living near Oxford, visiting his old lodge at Launceston from time to time: he was the first member of Dunheved lodge to hold Grand Rank, being appointed Grand Chaplain.

In October 1877 the date of the lodge meetings was changed from Thursday to Tuesday, on or after the full moon, and in the same year the initiation fee became £8 and dues were raised from five shillings a quarter to seven shillings and sixpence, with an annual dining fee of ten shillings. This was the year when the lodge moved to its new site in Tavistock Road. Three years earlier it was decided that Dunheved should have its own premises and, following a gift of £100 towards the cost from Bro. Col. J.H. Deakin and the conveying of the site unconditionally to the lodge by Bro. J.K. Lethbridge, plans for the new hall were drawn and a tender of £675 for the construction was accepted. The foundation stone was laid in May 1876. In July 1877 the new hall was dedicated by the Provincial Grand Master the Earl of Mount Edgcumbe and to mark the occasion Provincial Grand Lodge met in Launceston. During the year the lodge was embellished by a tessellated pavement given by Bro. T.P. Trood, the sword of Napoleon III was presented by Dr. Scoffern and each brother of the lodge was asked to assist in the furnishings by presenting a chair. In 1884 a joining member was Sir Hardinge Giffard, Q.C., the then M.P. for Launceston who later became Lord Halsbury, Lord Chief Justice. In 1901 W.Bro. A.K. Lee was W.M. and he went on to serve the lodge as its secretary for 27 years from 1904 to 1931. In 1901 and 1902 the grounds of the masonic hall were extended by the purchase of land lying to the north and south of the premises and in 1902 a club was formed and registered for the use of members. In 1909 the mortgage on the property was finally cleared. The total cost of the lodge and its grounds had then amounted to £811. Between 1906 and 1910 several candidates from neighbouring Bude were initiated, and in 1909 the brethren in the Bude district succeeded in their petition to form Granville Lodge at Stratton. In 1911 the installation of electricity replaced the gas lighting. In 1916 W.Bro. J.K. Braddon became W.M., an office he again occupied in 1946. W.Bro. Braddon was D.C. for many years and attained Grand Rank in the craft and in the Royal Arch. A Launceston journalist who achieved great distinction in his profession, Bro. Sir Alfred Robbins, was made an honorary member of the lodge in 1919: he was for some years Editor of 'The Times'. He bequeathed to the lodge his unique collection of masonic jewels which are displayed on the north wall of the temple.

The Volume of the Sacred Law used in Dunheved was printed in 1647. It bears the names of some of the Kingdon family. The lodge gavels, made of Tasmanian wood and silver, now in use in Dunheved were a gift from the sister lodge in Tasmania in 1929. Dunheved reciprocated by presenting the sister lodge with three volumes of Gould's History of Freemasonry. In 1929 the day and meeting of the lodge was changed to the Tuesday on or before full moon each month, still retaining the old attachment to the state of the moon! In 1935 W.Bro. Glasscock, a joining member of Dunheved who had built the King Arthur's Hall, left in his will a complete set of lodge furniture to Dunheved. On the formation of the Truro School Lodge in 1936 it was loaned to them for a short period before eventually being given to them. When King Arthur Lodge was formed in 1952, Dunheved, being the sponsors, asked that the furniture might be given back to it. This was done and is now in King Arthur's Hall at Tintagel.

Lodge Histories

An unusual custom at installation is the placing of camellias at the festive board. These came from Trelaske, and the custom is carried on today. In 1937 it was decided to change the day of the meeting once again, due to Tuesday being the day each week of the cattle market, so the second Wednesday in each month became the new day. The following year saw the Provincial G. Lodge again meeting at Launceston. The brethren attended St. Mary Magdalene's church in procession, as in 1926, wearing full regalia and preceded by the lodge banner and four Lewises carrying the Bible. The last time Provincial G. Lodge met at Launceston was in 1969 when W.Bro. S.G. Adams was W.M. On that occasion W.Bro. A.E.B. Greenwood was invested as Provincial S.G.W. W.Bro. "Jim" as he was affectionately known, went on to distinguish himself in masonry, receiving Grand Rank in the Craft and in the Royal Arch. He was also the Deputy Grand Superintendent in the province for five years. In 1991 Dunheved sponsored Greystone Border Lodge No. 9449 which was consecrated in November of that year at the Masonic Hall, Saltash.

A quiet corner of old Launceston, at Newport, the town of the Dunheved and Greystone Border lodges.

RESTORMEL LODGE No. 856, LOSTWITHIEL.

Lodge Histories

This ancient lodge "holden at the Old Duchy Palace, Lostwithiel" was consecrated on 6 November 1861. The original Charter, marking the foundation of the lodge, hangs in the lodge room. It was issued by Grand Lodge in the name of St. Matthew Lodge No. 1158 - but it is difficult to find any reason why the name of St. Matthew was attached as the Patron Saint of the parish church is St. Bartholomew. However, St. Matthew was the Patron Saint of tax collectors and the Old Duchy Palace was at one time the Royal Mint: perhaps this is the reason for the name. R.W.Bro. Richard Pearce, Past Deputy Provincial Grand Master officiated at the consecration and he was joined by 27 other installed masters. W.Bro. Robert Edyvean was installed as the first W.M. at the consecration that began at 1pm. They then adjourned to the banquet and the brethren "departed at an early hour after an afternoon spent in harmony and brotherly love, with a lively sense of the perfect manner in which all arrangements for the ceremony had been arranged."

The lodge was fixed to meet at the Talbot Hotel on the first Wednesday in every month. The discrepancy in the name 'St. Matthew' - which was on the register of Grand Lodge - was altered in name and number to Restormel on a proposition in open lodge on 3 December 1879....... 18 years after the consecration. The resolution, which was carried in open lodge in January 1880 was "that the name by which this lodge is designated, viz St. Matthew (which was ignorantly adopted at the consecration)... be erased from the Charter and that in future the lodge be known under the name of RESTORMEL to mark the connection of the freehold lodge buildings, The Old Duchy Palace, with the Manor and Castle of Restormel, the property of H.R.H. The Prince of Wales, Grand Master of England."

The change of name was granted by Grand Lodge but apparently no new Charter was issued. An endorsement was made on the original Charter by the Provincial Grand Master. This appears on the right hand top corner, and the new number 856 added in the same size figures above 1158.

Lodge Histories

The lodge's first minute book was lost but the new one, starting in January 1881, first shows the changes as well as the change of day to the first Thursday from May 1884. On the purchase of the Duchy Palace the meetings were held there from December 1878.

For a number of years the lodge opened at an early hour, especially for the Festival of St. John, the installation meeting, in one instance at 11.30am but more usually at 12-noon or 12.30pm. There was a very short meeting, however, in September 1887, opening at 7pm and closing at 7.30pm! The first candidate initiated was Joseph Stephens in November 1861. Candidates in the early years were few and far between: from June 1863 to October 1865 no record can be found of initiates. The initiation fee was £5 and annual dues £1. In 1864 all brethren were required to sign the lodge bye-laws. These included the entry: "Any officer of the lodge being absent from his Office on the lodge night when either of the ceremonies were being worked, a fine of one shilling was imposed, unless he had previously written to the Master satisfactorily excusing his absence."

Until the late 1950s a similar fine was imposed on brethren who were not 'word perfect' at the lodge of instruction. No books were allowed at lodge of instruction and all brethren who had been given work had to attend and carry out their allotted offices. At present some 140 brethren have passed through the chair of the lodge, some on more than one occasion.

It can be very proud of some of the achievements of a few of the brethren in their respective rise in masonic honours. The late W.Bro. Robert Pease, initiated in June 1892, served as Provincial Grand Secretary. The Grand Superintendent of the Holy Royal Arch (1952-64) Most Excellent Companion the Revd T.A. Webber, was an active member of Restormel for many years and was, for a considerable time, the lodge Chaplain. W.Bro. W. Lloyd White, served as Provincial Grand Secretary, and was also Grand Superintendent 1964-1969. Many of the older members owe a debt of gratitude to W.Bro. E.W. Clook Past Provincial S.G.W., for many years lodge secretary until his sudden death in 1976. W.Bro. S.A. Penpraze was secretary for several years, and served the province as Sword Bearer, Deputy D.C. and J.G.W. W.Bro. S.E. Best M.B.E., Past Provincial J.G.W. retired from his second period of office as secretary in January 2000.

Restormel celebrated its centenary in October 1961 when the W.M., W.Bro. W. West, officers and brethren, assembled at the Drill Hall at Lostwithiel, the lodge building not being large enough to accommodate the number present. Also present were 29 members of visiting lodges together with the Provincial Grand Master R.W.Bro. Col. E.N. Willyams. A centenary jewel was presented to the W.M. by the 'Grand Old Man' of the Lodge, W.Bro. G. R. Stephens Past Provincial J.G.W., who had been a member for nearly 50 years. A service was held at St. Bartholomew's Church, officiated over by W.Bro. Revd Albert Sykes Past Provincial G. Chaplain, and Bro. Revd R. M. Rowe the Provincial Chaplain.

Lodge Histories

The building in which the lodge meets is the subject of a special feature in this book and is part of the Shire Hall or Duchy Palace, a whole suite of buildings extending the length of Shire Hall Street, which is commonly known as Quay Street. It was the seat of Government of the medieval Earls and Dukes of Cornwall. The Lord Warden of the Stannaries held his Courts here to decide disputes among tinners. The Duchy officers came to the Shire Hall to conduct 'Coinage', the inspection of tin. Freemasons in 1878 bought that part of the building known as the Convocation Hall and converted it into the present lodge rooms. The two large Gothic windows were inserted in the wall in 1853, and refurbished in 1989. Beneath the lodge building are two vaulted rooms, below street level, one used as a kitchen and the other as a dining room and lodge club room. During the 1939-45 war these vaulted rooms were used as an air raid shelter.

(See feature article on Duchy Palace and visit by King George VI)

In 1910 Lodge One and All, Bodmin No. 330 celebrated its centenary and to mark the year the Corner Stone of a new Masonic Hall was duly laid by the Deputy PGM W. Bro. P. Colville Smith on August 16 "in the presence of a large assembly of Brethren,"

Lodge Histories

MERIDIAN LODGE No. 893, MILLBROOK.

In the mid 19th century Freemasonry in England was experiencing a renaissance following the election of Thomas, 2nd Earl of Zetland as Grand Master in 1844. In Cornwall too, the number of Freemasons and Masonic Lodges was also increasing and in 1861 a number of masons decided to found a lodge in Millbrook. Eight brethren petitioned for a lodge to be called Meridian to meet on the first Monday of the month. In December 1861 a warrant was granted and in May of the following year Meridian Lodge No.1195 was consecrated by the Deputy Provincial Grand Master V.W.Bro. Augustus Smith, assisted by officers of the provincial lodge. By some mischance the minutes of the first meeting were not recorded, two blank pages being left in the minute book. The first meeting was in The Coopers Arms, later meetings being held at the Commercial Inn. The lodge had hardly begun to make itself felt when, in 1863, Grand Lodge closed the numbers up and Meridian's number changed to 893, reflecting the number of lodges which had closed since the last reorganization of numbers some 20 or 30 years previously. In 1865 it was decided to obtain equipment for the lodge and chairs were purchased for the use of the Master and wardens at a cost of £5. It was during this time that the officers of the lodge were elected on the first Monday in June and installed later in the month; some years later the installation was changed to July. In common with many rural lodges the seasons and the weather dictated attendance figures at the meetings, and in January and February 1869, meetings were not held.

In 1873 the Provincial Grand Master the Earl of Mount Edgcumbe became a joining member of the lodge, and W.M. in 1875. During this time the lodge was looking for a more permanent home. In 1874 the National School in New Street offered suitable rooms at an annual rental of £1 per annum and so the lodge moved to more spacious premises. These, however, proved inadequate and in 1880 the lodge was offered, by the Mount Edgcumbe Estates, the present building, which it rented until 1946. In September 1893 provincial lodge met at Millbrook to assist the P.G.M. to lay the foundation stone of the new church of All Saints in Millbrook. To mark the occasion £5 was voted from lodge funds towards the

Millbrook church building fund. In 1897 India suffered a great famine and great hardship was being experienced in the sub-continent. Meridian members decided to hold a ball to raise funds for famine relief and the sum of £18.12s.3d was forwarded. Meridian had never formed a Royal Arch Chapter of its own, but in 1900 Eliot Chapter No. 1164 moved from St. Germans to Millbrook, so that masons from Millbrook no longer had to go outside the town to complete their masonry. By the end of the first decade of the new century the harmonium was no longer serviceable and so in 1909 a new organ was purchased which still serves the lodge well. In 1912 the lodge reached a significant milestone when the golden jubilee was celebrated in some style and with a celebratory banquet.

Lodge banners were used far more than they are today, especially at provincial lodge, so in 1912 a new one was purchased at a cost of £9.15s and this is still in the lodge. In 1915 the province decided to purchase a motor ambulance for use in France and hoped that every lodge would contribute one shilling per member. Meridian responded gladly and £4.5s.6d was forwarded and the list of all who contributed is recorded in the minute book. In 1917 the death of the P.G.M. was received by the lodge with great sadness and the province and the lodge were plunged into mourning for a great mason. In 1919 a framed photograph of the Earl was presented by W.Bro. J. Cheves. Relations with other lodges meanwhile had, over the years, proved difficult for Meridian, situated as it was in the extremity of the province, but, in 1924 the master and wardens of Carew lodge made their first official visit. In 1935 a letter was received from the masonic brethren on board H.M.S. Norfolk, based in Devonport requesting that they receive a Bible presented to them by lodges when they visited the USA. They asked Meridian Lodge to present it to Grand Lodge on their behalf: it is now in the Grand Lodge library.

As the 1930s drew to a close the world was again plunged into war and in September 1939 all meetings were cancelled. An emergency meeting held later in September considered the situation and resolved to meet again in November, and normal working was resumed. In common with most other lodges many members were called away on active service, but the lodge managed to maintain meetings throughout the war. Just as during the previous war an Earl had died so, during the second great conflict, his son and heir also died and the Mount Edgcumbe Estate was ravaged by death duties. As a result of this tragedy the lodge was able to purchase the freehold of the lodge building. The acquisition of the freehold was not the end of the problem, however, as the lodge soon found out, for the building still required a great deal of maintenance. In 1947 a new staircase was presented on behalf of W.Bro. H. V. Wilton who had been secretary for over 27 years. In 1954, after a period of building work, the renovation of the Temple was finally completed and the lodge could look forward to a few years respite in the round of repairs. In recognition of the long association of the lodge with his uncle, William, 4th Earl of Mount Edgcumbe, the 6th Earl presented the lodge with a portrait of the late Provincial Grand Master. In 1960 the date of the installation was changed from the second Monday in July to the second Monday in October. This was the first major change in the lodge meeting dates since the early years of the century. In 1962 Meridian achieved a notable landmark when the centenary was celebrated in some style, commemorating also the brethren who had contributed to the success of the lodge and the promotion of freemasonry in Millbrook. The celebrations were attended by the Provincial Grand Master R.W.Bro. Col. E.N. Willyams.

St. Michael's Mount boatmen in traditional uniform. Sir John St. Aubyn Bt., and Lord St. Levan, who lived on the Mount, were Procincial Grand Masters.

THREE GRAND PRINCIPLES LODGE No. 967, PENRYN.

Founded 1863

The first record of freemasonry in Penryn came when the Peace Joy and Brotherly Love Lodge was constituted in 1782, meeting at the King's Arms Hotel, Broad Street. It was fairly common in those days for lodges to meet at a suitable inn. Meetings were very irregular although from 1795 and 1807 it appears to have been very active with a number of influential brethren. On three occasions during this time the Provincial Grand Lodge meetings were held in Penryn, but in 1808 the lodge "ceased to meet" and was erased a year later.

During the life of this lodge another was started in 1799 under the name of Three Grand Principles No. 577 meeting at the Golden Lion in High Street, as it was called in those days. Later it was renamed Higher Market Street: the inn also changed its name to the Red Lion. The building is now listed and in a conservation area but still bears the masonic symbols over the doorway. Very little is known about the original Three Grand Principles Lodge, it lasted only 39 years, but freemasonry became firmly established in Penryn in 1863 with the revival of this lodge and the first meeting at the King's Arms hotel in July 1863. It continued to meet here for the next 18 years, before moving to the Temperance Hall in Commercial Road for four years.

The masonic hall in Quay Hill was the venue for the next 27 years: the site is now the memorial gardens. Finally, in 1912, the lodge moved to the new purpose-built hall in New Street and has remained there. The cost was £846.16s.0d and was built by the Barnicoat family.

In 1868 a return to Grand Lodge showed there were 23 members, but in 1870 the total was 34. In April 1880 it was decided to procure a banner for the laying of the foundation stone ceremony at Truro Cathedral. This was presented by the W.M., W.Bro. T.B. Hart. During the ceremony, one of the brethren, a Bro. Ackerly, died. The new building was designed and built in 1912, £405 was raised by 17 subscriptions from members. It was dedicated on 6 November in the presence of W. Bro. Colville Smith. Electric light was proposed in May 1919. A new lodge banner and carpet were obtained in 1922 and by 1925 all of the loans for the building had been repaid.

Lodge Histories

Meetings continued throughout the 2nd World War and during an air raid on Penryn in 1941 the lodge's previous home (the old church institute) was destroyed and 18 people killed. The iron railings in front of the lodge were removed in November 1942 in support of the war effort. In 1947 the first ladies night was held at the Budock Vean Hotel. The freehold of the lodge was purchased in August 1961 and the centenary celebrated in September 1963 in the presence of the Provincial Grand Master R.W.Bro. Col. E. Willyams.

The centenary warrant was presented to the W.M., together with a centenary jewel. An oration was delivered by the Provincial G. Chaplain, with the history of the lodge given by W.Bro. P.T.Dancer (he had been treasurer for over 22 years and achieved Grand Rank in May of 1964 while, in 1966 he achieved recognition for playing the lodge organ for 40 years!) In 1975 the third lodge banner was dedicated by W.Bro. the Revd D.W. Phillips (Provincial G.Chaplain) in Latin. The minutes express that Three Grand Principles much appreciated the short and simple ceremony. In the same year approval was given for a Chapter in Penryn. Over the next few years the installation banquet "travelled" around Falmouth, including the Green Lawns Hotel, the Penmere Manor Hotel, the Royal Duchy Hotel, as well as the Falmouth Hotel.

Three Grand Principles lodge has made a major contribution to freemasonry in Penryn, having moved from inn to inn in the early days until the building of the existing masonic hall, which is now home to a number of lodges and other masonic degrees.

The chair used by the Grand Master at the Truro ceremony in 1880, after restoration work in 1994 by W.Bro. Tony James.

Lodge Histories

ST. ANNE'S LODGE No. 970, EAST LOOE.

St. Anne's Lodge petition was submitted in April 1863, largely comprised of members of St. Martin's Lodge, Liskeard, and was approved and recommended by V. W. Bro. Augustus Smith, Deputy Provincial Grand Master and the warrant was granted on 1st June. The meeting place was the Ship Hotel in the borough of East Looe on the first Wednesday of every month. Eleven members of St. Martin's and two fellowcrafts met at the newly formed lodge of "St. Anne" (or St. Anne's as it is now referred to) in December. St. Mary and St. Nicholas are the patron Saints of the two boroughs of East and West Looe and it is premised that St. Anne was chosen for the new Lodge so as not to cause any undue friction between the rival towns. St. Anne was the patron Saint of the Chapel or oratory which stood in the centre of the old bridge connecting the two distinct towns. The lodge was formally consecrated by the Provincial Grand Master R.W.Bro. Augustus Smith on the 26 July 1864 and by this time the membership had grown to 28. It appears from the records that the lodge initially rented a cellar from a Mr. Cook close to the Ship Inn and after some disagreements and temporary removal, the masonic hall, in his premises, was opened in 1871. By December 1874 plans were afoot to relocate to premises in Fore Street owned by a Mr. Crossman, which were adapted to suit the needs of the lodge. St. Anne's remained there until 1917. A building fund was established in 1911 with the view of establishing freehold premises. A deposit of £530 was paid on the chapel in Castle Street in March 1919 with Barclays Bank advancing the purchase price.

The lodge had occupied the Fore Street premises for over 40 years. The chapel was renovated and adapted and St. Anne's held their first meeting in their new building, now called the masonic hall, in November 1919, with the dedication by a provincial team led by the Deputy Provincial Grand Master W.Bro. Philip Colville Smith in January 1920. The surnames of the members of the lodge at this time comprised the 'old' families of the borough many of them recognisable today. Tamblin, Pearn, Oates, Pengelly, Shapcott, Bishop and Cook among them.

Lodge Histories

In 1921 the membership of the lodge reached 100 and a second lodge was muted but failed to gain support. By 1928 electric lighting replaced the old gas mantles. In 1934 part of one of the cottages in the curtilage of the property was converted to form a kitchen on the lower floor. A financial crisis came in 1939 when the accounts could not be found or audited and there appeared to be a loss of some £160 or more: this led to a number of years of financial prudence. It was not until 1953 that further alterations to the building were made and the P.G.M. performed the official opening in October. Music had been introduced early on with the purchase of an Albany model organ by subscription list back in 1896 and since then the lodge has had a number of organs. In 1882 a copy of the 'Claret's' ritual was obtained to be the definitive working used until Emulation replaced it in February 1920. The banner was reported to be showing signs of wear in 1871 and again in 1882. In 1888 the lodge purchased a new one and in July 1935 a banner was presented by Bro. N.L. Ennor, the embroidery having been carried out by his wife. Over such a long history there are many occasions of note and humour, some sad and some which are perhaps better 'glossed' over. It is interesting to note the minutes refer every year, up until 1892, to the poor financial condition of the lodge. The insurance of the lodge furniture cost £50 in 1869, a huge sum. In 1920 a decision was taken to send the lodge agendas to members unsealed because of the increase in postal rates. One marathon meeting in 1877 performed four ceremonies, opening at 6.45 p.m. and closing at 10 p.m. Fortunately there has not been a repeat of such a feat!

The beautiful kneeling stool of St. Anne's Lodge of Looe, showing the ancient bridge on which stood the Chapel of St. Anne's. The Tapestry was made by Mrs. Joyce Gibson, the wife of W.Bro. Tommy Gibson who was W.M. in 1966 and lodge director of ceremonies for 25 years. It took a year to complete. A competition to guess the number of stitches raised funds for the 2002 festival. Recently Mrs Gibson has made the tapestry for the other stool incorporating the masonic symbols.

The bridge connected the two boroughs, was over 380 feet long and varied in width from ten feet three inches to six feet eight inches. It originally stood on 18 arches including two square openings made for the more easy passage of rafts and timbers. Bro. Gibson says: the indulgence for building the bridge was granted on 22 October 1411. On its centre stood a Chapel or Oratory dedicated to St Anne, Mother of the blessed Virgin Mary, and was licensed for divine service by Edmund Lacey, Bishop of Exeter, on 18 November 1436." The foundation stone for the new bridge was laid in 1854 and was opened the following year. It is some 100 yards further up-river and cost under £3,000.

FOWEY LODGE No. 977, LOSTWITHIEL.

The present Fowey Lodge was not the first to meet in the town. The United Lodge of Friendship No. 106. originally established in Birmingham in 1758 was removed to Fowey in 1813 and remained until 1826. The first recorded meeting was on 5 October 1863 at the Ship Hotel, with four candidates. The jewels on the collars of the three principal officers were presented that December by William Rashleigh P.M. of Lodge No.2. Edinburgh and a P.G.Deacon (Scottish Constitution), member of a well-known local family and land owner. These were made of solid silver and are on the collars today. At a regular meeting on February 1st, 1864 Bro. Revd G. Ross, Vicar of Tywardreath, was thanked for his gift of the W.M's chair. The following day the lodge was consecrated by the Provincial Grand Master R.W. Bro. Augustus Smith and other provincial officers: Bro. Thomas Geach was installed as the first W.M. In the early years it was quite usual to have several ceremonies in one evening with multiple candidates, the installation meeting usually lasting some seven hours. The Treffry family has had a very close association with the lodge since its earliest days. Many of the members and P.Ms bore this surname and when the lodge premises were a matter of some discussion, Bro. Revd Dr. Treffry was petitioned in 1865 for a building site for a new temple. The lodge moved to premises in Church Street (which no longer exists) from the Ship Inn in November 1868. Early features include lodge representation at a visit by H.R.H. The Prince of Wales in 1874 to the joint meeting Provincial Grand Lodges of Devon and Cornwall, and Provincial G.Lodge was held at Fowey in 1879.

Another early notable joining member was Col. John Whitehead Peard, son of Capt. Shuldon Peard who commanded the 'White Fleet of the Sea Fencibles' responsible for the defence of the coast from Rame Head to the Isles of Scilly. John Peard was appointed Deputy Provincial Grand Master in 1879, lived at Penquite House, and completed the building of Trenython House in 1880 (see feature article). In 1881, Mr. C.E. Treffry offered to co-operate with the members of the lodge to build a new masonic temple and in August 1882 the first meeting was held in New Freemasons Hall, Lostwithiel Street. The

Lodge Histories

annual rent was £30, membership at this time was 72 and, as could be expected, many of the members' occupations were connected with the busy sea port. The Fowey Hotel was opened in July 1882 and the installation of Bro. John DeCressey Treffry was held there in January 1884.

The charity records show much support for widows of brethren lost at sea and donations of £5 upwards were common. Also a contribution was made to the cost of a masonic lifeboat and relief of sufferers from the loss of H.M.S The Captain. Other contributions included a gift in 1880 to the "Sailor's Window" in the Church in memory of W. Bro. Revd Dr. Treffry Past Provincial G. Chaplain. The Great War brought many difficulties to the lodge, many brethren were killed in action and the hall was taken over by the War Office for use by the 12th Worcester Regiment for many months. In January 1918, Sir Charles Hanson M.P., Past Grand Warden following his term as Lord Mayor of London, was installed as W.M. of the lodge. He was already the W.M. of the Grand Masters Lodge No. 1 and dispensation was obtained for his installation at Fowey. In 1923 the meetings were changed to the second Wednesday of the month and ceased meeting in July, August and September. During the 1939-45 war, the lodge met at 3 pm and after the war candidates came along in increasing numbers, the lodge roll increased to 126, the highest it has ever been.

The centenary meeting was held in the town hall in 1964, followed by a service of thanksgiving at St. Fimbarrus Church. The brethren were welcomed by a peal of bells rung by brethren of Restormel and One and All lodges. In August 1982 a meeting was held to mark 100 years at the masonic hall, with W.Bro. W.M. Owens, the W.M. The Past Masters initiated Mr. L. Colwill, who was manager of the Fowey Hotel where the banquet was held. The lodge moved from Fowey to the Old Duchy Palace in Lostwithiel in 1989, where it continues to meet. The original banner was refurbished and rededicated at the installation meeting in February 1992. Other notable events include the consecration of Fowey Chapter in 1946.

Lodge Histories

TREGULLOW LODGE No. 1006, ST. DAY.

In the mid-19th century the old Gwennap parish, in which St. Day was situated, had a population of over 10,000 and had been the world's richest copper producing area. By 1860, however, Cornish copper mining was coming to an end, and the population decline began. Despite this, and the fact that within two miles there was a lodge at Redruth and one at Chacewater, a lodge was formed at St. Day in 1864 and its W.M. installed in June of that year. Its name was Tregullow and it would appear had no mother lodge. The petition was dated 1 January, the Provincial Grand Master R.W.Bro. Augustus Smith endorsed it on 1 February and the Grand Master granted the warrant during that month. The first meeting was on 28 June in the Hotel St. Day when the W.M., Thomas Mills, read the warrant. This venue continued until July 1865. Of the seven petitioners, four were members of the Druids Lodge (Thomas Mills having been a founder-member there), another was of Boscawen, one of Phoenix and the seventh appears to have been initiated outside the province.

A contemporary report of the consecration confirms that it was entirely through the efforts of Frederick Martin Williams (Phoenix Lodge, Truro) that Tregullow was formed and that his "zeal on behalf of the fraternity and his thoroughly genial and brotherly spirit is known and appreciated throughout Cornwall." The Freemasons' Magazine also refers to the "building itself, which is nearly completed" and in which "there seems to be every requisite to work the Craft and higher degrees of Masonry, having a suite of rooms, all confined exclusively to the purposes of Freemasonry." The first returns to Grand Lodge in 1865 lists 21 names including gentleman, auctioneer, surgeon, engineer, mine agent, accountant, clergyman, solicitor, organist and chemist. The distinguished mason W.Bro. W.J. Hughan acted as S.W. in February 1865: he was then described as of Fortitude, but in 1866 as secretary of Phoenix. Meetings by then were at The Lodge Rooms, St. Day, forming part of what is the present Masonic Hall, being leased at a £12 rental from the West Cornwall Bank. In 1867 W.Bro. E.H. Hawke presented a set of engraved firing glasses and the square and compasses. One of the glasses was presented to the Grand Lodge museum in 1870 and another to W.Bro. Sir Anthony Hawke in 1931: the remainder are in a case in the lodge ante-room. Because of financial problems Tregullow met for a time in temporary rooms and in 1871 the installation was at Druids lodge at Redruth, returning to their own

Lodge Histories

lodge room for the February 1872 meeting. The year in Redruth was a busy one, nine candidates being initiated, and at the final meeting the ballot was taken "for Sir F.M. Williams J.G.W(Eng) as W.M. Elect." His installation took place at an emergency meeting in April 1872. There was no official senior provincial officer present, but among the visitors was W.Bro. Hughan P.M. Fortitude, Past Provincial G. Secretary. In January 1875 the installation was "not carried out" owing to the illness of the Master-elect Bro. E. Rogers. This went ahead at an emergency meeting the following month but - as with the previous year - there is no indication of any dispensation being applied for (or given) for this change of date.

The August 1876 meeting brought the decision to procure a banner with the Arms of the Grand Lodge of England and those of Sir F.M. Williams "mingled thereon." An offer to rent the lodge rooms from the Redruth Brewery Company at £12 a year was accepted in 1881: these were all the current rooms including the one underneath, now used as a school room. The Vicar of St. Day, Bro. Revd J.J. Murley asked that the laying of the foundation stone of the new Sunday School should be a "masonic demonstration" and this ceremony took place in December 1882. There were 23 members of Tregullow and 28 visitors forming a procession to the church "bearing their respective badges of office and the working tools, together with the corn, wine and oil, preceded by the Redruth D.C.L.I. Volunteer Band which played the masonic march, the banners of Love and Honour, Boscawen, Chacewater and Tregullow, waving in the breeze." Brethren from nine lodges attended, including one from Shanghai and one from Montana. Two globes were presented to the lodge in January 1896 by Bro. Samuel Richards: one remains, but is not in use. A pair of terrestrial globes replaced them in the 1950s. The two pillars, each of the Corinthian order, were presented by W.Bro. W.T. Peters in 1897. Tregullow remained as tenants of the brewery until 1906 when the lease fell in on the death of the "last life". The freehold was bought for £250, with £200 borrowed from the provincial fund and the rest raised through shares. The debt was finally cleared in 1923.

Having secured the freehold, and already being well furnished with "every requisite to work the craft and higher degrees" the members settled down to the normal month by month working. W.Bro. T.T. Mills was thanked in 1909 for his gifts to furnish the ante-room and in 1914 there was the first "salutes" recorded to provincial officers at the installation. W.Bro. P. Colville Smith, the Deputy Provincial Grand Master attended with the Provincial G. Secretary W.Bro. E.A.P. Broad, P.A.G.D.C. Up to this date the province had never been represented at a Tregullow installation. The lodge was invited to be represented at the unveiling of a tablet at the town clock, in memory of the late W.Bro. Mills "a leader in all things in St. Day." It came from the St. Day Community Council, was accepted and W.Bro. Strongman represented and spoke on behalf of the lodge. Electricity was installed in 1935, at a cost of £300, and the following year the adjoining property was purchased, doubling the size of the temple and the dining room below. For three months the lodge met at Redruth and for the re-opening ceremony in 1938 there was a visit from the Deputy Provincial Grand Master the Hon. Sir Montague Eliot. In 1964 W.Bro. Frank Wills from Ontario presented two brass door knockers, engraved with the square and compasses. In 1968 he presented frames for the warrant.

The centenary warrant had been presented at a special lodge in January 1966 by the Provincial Grand Master R.W. Bro. Col. E. Perry Morgan. There was the presentation of a centenary jewel to the

The Grand Lodge certificate in 1872 of Bro. John Chapple of Tregullow Lodge No.1006, at St. Day. It was returned to this country by the Casilia Lodge in Chile following his death in Valparasio in February 1892. A letter of thanks was sent by the Cornish Lodge "for the very kind manner they showed toward Bro. J. Chapple… in relieving his wants and carrying out the last sad Offices of respect to departed merit and depositing his mortal remains in a manner worthy of our Order." A message telling of his death in hospital, and his burial, was written across the certificate.

Thread of Gold

Lodge Histories

W.M. by the oldest member of the lodge W.Bro. W.J. Gerrans. A set of ballot balls, made from copper and tin from Wheal Jane, were presented in November 1974 by the mine owners, Consolidated Goldfields Company. In May 1984 the kitchen was refurbished and the temple re-curtained at a total cost of some £900. From its inception in 1864 to 1999 - a span of 135 years - the lodge enrolled 748 members, an average annual intake of over five. Four members held Grand Rank and five were appointed Justices of the Peace. Strong connections with mining continued up to the 1920s. The minute books record the names of visitors from more than 50 lodges scattered thoughout the hard rock mining fields of the world. In 1899, of the 14 initiates, seven were described as "goldminer." Over a dozen states of the United States of America were represented, as well as lodges in South Africa, India, Mexico, Australia, West Africa, Chile, Malta and Shanghai.

Tragedy at the mine. This Memorial Card was issued in 1876 following the death of Bro. Joseph Cock, aged 57, a member of Tregullow Lodge, at Wheal Maiden House, St. Day.

"May we who survive him anticipate our approaching fate and be more strongly cemented in the ties of union and friendship," it declared.

In Memory of
BROTHER JOSEPH COCK,
Of the Tregullow Lodge, No. 1006,
Who died at WHEAL MAIDEN HOUSE, ST. DAY, April 10th,
A.D. 1876, A.L. 5880,
AGED 57 YEARS.

May we who survive him anticipate our approaching fate, and be more strongly cemented in the ties of union and friendship.

ZETLAND LODGE No. 1071, SALTASH.

The year 1865 proved to be a most auspicious year for masonry in Saltash, for in November the first craft lodge was founded. The founders decided to name it after the Grand Master of the day, Thomas 2nd Earl of Zetland. The lodge was consecrated by the Provincial Grand Master R.W. Augustus Smith M.P. at the Green Dragon Inn, Fore Street and the warrant handed over to the first W.M. W.Bro. John Richards. During the first ten years of the lodge existence, 77 candidates were admitted to the lodge, either as initiates or joining members. In 1867 Bro. Foxwell, when Master-elect, presented the lodge with a handsome Bible still treasured and used by the lodge. In 1868 the lodge moved to the Railway Inn, the first of a number of moves until they acquired their own premises.

Zetland Lodge soon realized that their masonry was not complete and so in 1877 sponsored a Royal Arch Chapter under the same name, so that masons from Saltash did not need to go outside the town for their Royal Arch Masonry. It was during this period and beyond that a number of masons were initiated, who were to play an important part in promoting masonry not only in Saltash but also in the province.

Among the first of these was Bro. Joseph Rawlings, who served as secretary of the lodge for six years and later the province as Provincial G.D.C. A few years later saw the initiation of Bro. Fred Avery Rawling, who achieved the chair in 1894. He later became Provincial S.G.W. and subsequently a Grand Officer serving the province as secretary from 1928 to 1940. In 1895 the province honoured Saltash and Zetland Lodge in particular by holding a meeting of Provincial G. Lodge in the town. A newspaper report of the time states that "the principal street of the little town was gay with flags and streamers, the church bells were rung and altogether Saltash was quite gay". About noon the proceedings were suspended and the brethren marched in procession to the church, headed by the Plymouth Borough band. The Bible was carried by four Lewises, who were each presented with a Bible by the Provincial Grand Master the Earl of Mount Edgcumbe.

Lodge Histories

In common with many lodges, Zetland Lodge now started to experience difficulties over its meeting places as well as finance. These, however, were gradually resolved over time and after 1903 when the lodge altered its meeting night from Monday to Wednesday, things started to settle down.

In the aftermath of the 1914-18 war some problems which had dogged the lodge were finally resolved, most important of which was the problem of ownership of the lodge building. In the years that followed, Zetland acquired equipment and furnishing which have enhanced the ceremonies in the temple and the building received much needed refurbishment, including the installation of electric light. In 1925 Queen Victoria Lodge No. 2655 visited Zetland Lodge for the first time on a fraternal visit and so successful was this that they made it an annual event which continues today.

It was in the 1920s and 1930s that a number of masons were initiated who have proved such an asset. Amongst the most significant of these was Bro. Arthur Chastey Luxton: he was initiated in 1937, was by profession an architect, and designed the present masonic hall in Dunheved Road. During the 1939-45 war many servicemen passed through Saltash. It was during the mid-1940s that a number of American servicemen, who had been previously accepted by American lodges, were, at the request of some of the American Grand Lodges - and with the agreement of United Grand Lodge - initiated into certain English lodges. Zetland was privileged to initiate three of these American servicemen in successive months during this time. It was in the 1940s also that two masons were initiated who were to serve the province well in differing capacities during the ensuing years, Bro. T.C.A. Waghorn and Bro. A.R. Batters. Both were to work extensively for Masonic Charities and Bro. Waghorn proved to be a notable Masonic scholar and later led the Mark Province as its Provincial Grand Master.

At the close of hostilities the Saltash lodges tried to get back to some sort of normality. It was indicative of the health of Freemasonry in Saltash that in 1946 a second lodge was founded as a daughter lodge of Zetland under the name of Essa - the old name for Saltash. As the forties gave way to the fifties and the lodge looked forward to celebrating its centenary an event occurred which at the time seemed disastrous, but as events eventually proved was a blessing in disguise.

In 1959 the lodge was officially informed that the Tamar Bridge Authority had been empowered to obtain the masonic hall by compulsory purchase and when notice to quit was eventually received a temporary meeting place had to be found. Different places were suggested and tried - the Baptist Church which was used at first proved unsatisfactory. Eventually, a neighbouring lodge - Queen Victoria Lodge at St. Budeaux - offered a temporary home. Unfortunately this was in a different province and permission had to be sought. The response was favourable and so in 1961 the lodge met for the first time in Devonshire. In the meantime negotiations on a price for the old masonic hall were being conducted by a local solicitor and in April 1961 satisfactory compensation agreed.

On the purchase of a parcel of land adjacent to Dunheved House, Bro. Luxton was asked to draw up plans for a new masonic hall and in October 1962 the foundation stone was laid by the Provincial Grand Master R.W.Bro. Col. E.N. Willyams. By the middle of the following year it was completed and on Saturday 20 July 1963 the new masonic temple was dedicated by the P.G.M. assisted by many Grand and P.G. officers.

Lodge Histories

The lodge could now look forward with confidence and anticipation to the centenary and in November 1965 this was celebrated with some style. The Provincial Grand Master R.W.Bro. Col. E. Perry Morgan attended, supported by his deputy and assistant to present the centenary warrant. In 1974 a second daughter lodge for Zetland was founded, taking the name Caradon. In the years following the opening of the Tamar Bridge, the town of Saltash grew enormously and the influx of new housing greatly increased the population. Freemasonry in Saltash was considered healthy enough and strong enough to support another lodge, so in 1984 the petition for a third daughter lodge was signed and in February 1985 St. Stephen's lodge was consecrated. In 1986 after much discussion and deliberation it was decided to reduce the number of meetings from twelve to ten, the months of January and April being omitted and the bye-laws of Zetland were amended. This was only the second major departure from the original aims of the lodge, the first being the change in the day of meeting some 83 years before.

This portrait, which hangs on the East wall at the One and All Lodge at Bodmin, is of Thomas the Earl of Zetland, who was the Grand Master 1844-1870, prior to HRH The Prince of Wales, *later King Edward VII.*

Lodge Histories

CAREW LODGE No. 1136, TORPOINT.

The lodge was consecrated in November 1866 at the Mechanic's Institute, Torpoint in the presence of the Provincial Grand Master R.W. Bro. Augustus Smith, his Deputy V.W.Bro. Roscorla, together with R.W.Bro. Huyshe the Provincial Grand Master of Devonshire. Bro. Frederick Brine, a serving Major in the Royal Engineers was installed as the first W.M. It was agreed to meet on the third Monday of every month, and to help defray any debts on the lodge to establish a share list. These were £1 each, five shillings to be paid on allotment and the same sum on each quarter as required. All initiates and joining members were expected to bear their fair proportion of the debt. The lodge seems to have had some financial problems during the early years, but by 1870 the situation improved as jewels were presented to various P.M's and a donation made towards a bed at the Royal Albert Hospital in Devonport. There were many candidates and joining members and there was a unique occurrence in 1868 when a joining member was elected to S.D. on the same evening.

A dispute arose in February 1873 when a letter was received from the secretary of the Mechanics Institute requesting the use of the lodge rooms at a fixed rental. This was refused and a second letter followed, resulting in a deputation from the lodge meeting the institute committee. At the April meeting the lodge refused to give up a key to the ante-room, and consequently received notice to quit the premises. After a search for suitable rooms, the Good Templars building, (now the St. John Ambulance hall) was chosen at a rent of £5 a year. The stay at the Good Templars was to be a short one as growing membership needed larger premises. A committee was formed in 1874 to establish a fund for the building of a lodge hall. The lodge was thriving and at the 1874 installation, and in other years, permission was given by the Torpoint Ferry committee to run a special late ferry to enable brethren to return to Devonport. Plans were submitted for the new building in July 1875 on land opposite the Good Templars hall. In August 1876, it was the unanimous decision of the brethren to change the day of the meeting from the third Monday to the third Wednesday and to begin at 6.30pm in winter, and 7pm in summer.

From its consecration brethren from Devon had formed a large proportion of the membership of Carew, as it was thought that the population of Torpoint at that time, was not big enough to support its own lodge. Also many of the brethren were members of the Armed Forces and Civil Service and were often posted abroad, resulting in necessary changes in the officers. In 1877 came the initiation of Bro.

John Pearce who missed only four meetings in 39 years. For 17 of these he ran a small boat to and from Torpoint in all weathers. Although the lodge faced financial problems at times because of the cost of repairs, the records show that generous donations were made to various charities. In 1907 General Sir Reginald Carew-Pole became a joining member and presented the lodge with the two Wardens' pedestals. During the Ist World War several brethren joined the Armed Services but the lodge seemed to have a good share of candidates with two and even three being made members on one evening, resulting in the lodge closing well after 10pm. A Royal Arch Chapter was formed in 1928. In the 1930s lodge funds were again in a critical state, and as the front of the building was in need of repair an overdraft was obtained. A change came in 1938 when the W.M. Elect Bro. F.P.G. Hawken was taken ill, resulting in the installation taking place in January 1939 at a special emergency meeting.

At the outbreak of the 2nd World War the lodge was at last free of debt. Once more brethren were in the Armed Services, and meetings were held on the Saturday prior to the third Wednesday. Sometimes ceremonies would be interrupted by air-raid warnings. As during the previous war, two ceremonies were worked on occasions. A further calamity occurred when the ceiling in the temple collapsed, and meetings had to be held in the refectory. The lodge also gave permission to house people made homeless by enemy action. During these years the P.M's, by their attendance, were greatly responsible for the unbroken continuation and existence of the lodge. With the coming of peace the lodge was honoured in 1945 when Grand Rank was conferred on W.Bro. Allerton who had been initiated in 1902, and held every office in the lodge. In January 1948 a Mark lodge was formed at Carew and in 1950 the lodge once again moved from home, although this time only temporarily, because of repair work being carried out. Zetland lodge allowed Carew to use their temple for a few meetings. The following year Carew lodge bought the freehold of the land on which it stands. Since then much of the repair work has been carried out voluntarily by the members and the close proximity of the Royal Dockyard has produced many excellent craftsmen who have used their skills in the maintenance of the building. Two notable events of recent years were the formation of a 'daughter lodge' Hamoaze No. 8513 in March 1973, and the conferring of Grand Rank in 1987 on W.Bro. Bryan Nickels (P.G.Std.B.) another stalwart who served as charity steward, treasurer and secretary.

Lodge Histories

SAINT ANDREW LODGE No. 1151.
TYWARDREATH.

The lodge was consecrated in 1867 following a preliminary meeting in the town hall, Tywardreath, presided over by the Rector of St. Sampson's, Golant and Vicar of Tywardreath, W.Bro. the Revd George Ross. He would be the first W. Master and the petition was signed by him together with seven members of Fowey Lodge and two of Peace and Harmony. Two events took place in 1867 which had a direct bearing on Cornwall and some future lodge members. Diamonds were discovered in South Africa and the North American colonies were united under the name of The Dominion of Canada. The emigration that resulted no doubt prompted W.Bro. Ross to inform a meeting that he was willing to initiate candidates who were "leaving quickly for foreign lands". The regalia was purchased with a request for "twelve months credit" and the consecration ceremony took place on June 11, conducted by the Provincial Grand Master R.W.Bro. Augustus Smith. Some 80 attended the banquet at 3s.6d per head, inclusive of wines and/or "a glass of grog with water." Entertainment was provided by the Battery Volunteer Band and Ringers, presumably from St. Andrew's Church. The first initiate was a William Job. Some four years later he came to a sudden and mysterious end in California. No trace could be found of him or his effects and the St. Andrew secretary wrote to the Madison Lodge, California, for information. A reply confirmed his sudden demise - with no news of his effects - and it can only be assumed he had disappeared amidst the Gold Rush of that period.

There was also great mining activity for tin and copper at this time in the Tywardreath and St. Blazey district and the lodge register has the record of many occupations as purser of mines, mine engineer, mine agent and miner. W.Bro. Ross initiated his eldest son, the Revd George Gould Ross, and the custom of attending church in masonic clothing was introduced about this time, undoubtedly stemming from the influence of the clergy in the lodge. Of the first five W.Ms, three were vicars. In 1872 W. Bro. Ross presented the maul used by St. Andrew Lodge to this day. It was first used by Prince Albert, the Prince Consort, on 24 July 1841 to lay the foundation stone of Wanstead Orphan Asylum:

subsequently it was loaned to lay a foundation stone of Truro Cathedral by the Grand Master, The Prince of Wales. In the year of this gift there were two significant national events: the secret ballot at elections and the publication of Darwin's 'The Descent of Man.' Three years later, 1875, the lodge bought its own property at Back Lane, Tywardreath for £27.10s. and in April 1876 the working of the lodge was moved from the Town Hall to the new premises.

Lodge Histories

This wooden maul at St. Andrew Lodge, Tywardreath, continues to be used during some ceremonies. An inscribed silver band, including three shields, encircles it.

The first shield is surrounded by a Crown, the second by a deer and the third by the three feathers of the Prince of Wales, later King Edward VII.

In 1880 came the inauguration of a building fund with 14-guineas deposited in the Post Office. In order to allow a candidate, a Revd Eade, to be initiated - and catch the last train back to Newquay - the lodge was tyled at 6pm. March 1894 saw the acceptance of a tender to construct a new lodge at Station Road for £256.10s. This was opened in 1895 and in November of that year the founder, W.Bro. George Ross died. For 20 years he performed the duty of Installing Master, with his last performance in 1888. He retained the office of chaplain until 1892, the year of his last recorded appearance in the lodge (he was made an honorary member). He was then at Holsworthy and one can only imagine the difficulties, well over a century ago, of getting from Holsworthy to Tywardreath and back in one day. He attained the rank of Provincial G. Chaplain and his name heads the roll of P.Ms. Many members have received provincial honours down the years and St. Andrew was the mother lodge of the 11th Provincial Grand Master R.W.Bro. Col. E. Perry Morgan.

The wording on it tells that it was used by HRH Prince Consort in laying the Foundation stone of the Orphan Asylum at Wanstead, Epping Forest on 24th July 1841.

It was presented to the lodge No. 1151 by founder member and first W.Master, the Revd. George Ross P.M and P.G.C., on 25 January 1872.

This maul was also loaned for use by HRH The Prince of Wales in laying the foundation stone of Truro Cathedral, on May 20 1880.

In 1967 the lodge celebrated its centenary year, with W.Bro. Charles Leslie Lobb as W.M. A history was compiled at that time by W.Bro. M.E. Attwood and reprinted in 1995, with all proceeds to the 2002 Appeal. Between 1967 and 1972 the lodge regularly welcomed three, sometimes four, candidates but much of the lodge's time and energy was

Lodge Histories

spent in raising monies to keep the fabric of the lodge building in good repair. In July 1972 a special meeting was held to unveil a specially commissioned photograph of the R.W.Bro.Col. E. Perry Morgan, P.G.M. and P.M. of St. Andrew lodge. At a regular meeting in July 1973 a new banner was dedicated by the Provincial G.Chaplain, the Revd Canon G.W.S. Harmer. Between the years 1973 and 1975 the lodge building was enlarged with an extension to the ante-room and the provision of a new kitchen and new toilets. The money was mainly raised by interest-free loans which were all paid back in a relatively short period of time thanks to some very energetic fund raising.

At the Provincial Grand Lodge meeting held in April 1978 R.W.Bro.Col.E. Perry Morgan resigned as P.G.M., "after nearly fourteen years of devoted service to the province." A special meeting was held in October 1979 at St. Andrew to mark his 50th anniversary in freemasonry. At this time he was in very poor health and there was some doubt that he would be able to be present but his determination got him to the lodge. Over 80 brethren attended and the Provincial Grand Master R.W. Bro. the Hon. Robert Eliot accepted the gavel of the lodge. The Past P.G.M. was unable to reply but gave his written notes to the P.G.M. who read them to the assembled brethren. His notes contained details of his initiation on 10 October 1929; his installation into the chair of St. Andrew Lodge in 1946. He was a member of both the Royal Arch and the Mark degrees as well as other degrees and became Deputy Grand Master in the Mark. He was installed as Provincial Grand Master for this Province in November 1964. In 1966 he became Grand Scribe Nehemiah in Supreme Grand Chapter.

From 1980 to the early 1990s the furniture in the temple continued to be replaced. The seating was replaced when the Congregational Church in St. Austell closed and the pews were installed to take the place of the 'tip-up type' cinema seats which 'clonked' every time the brethren stood up. The old pedal organ was replaced by an electronic one which was donated by a member. Another gift to the lodge was a new secretary-treasurer's desk, made by a brother and assisted by another member in the frontal decoration. The 'pavement' was replaced by a hand-made carpet completed by a brother and his wife. The box of working tools was given in memory of a past master. The tracing boards were refurbished and new canopy tassels were made.

The lodge building has continued to be refurbished over the past few years. In 1996 gas central heating was put in and in 1997 a new kitchen was installed. Well in excess of £5,000 was spent in 1999 on double-glazed windows; refurbishment of the main doors; redecoration of the temple; external redecoration and regalvanizing of the lodge gates. Most of the work was of a 'self-help nature' saving thousands of pounds in labour costs.

Lodge Histories

THE ELIOT LODGE No. 1164, ST. GERMANS.

Founded 1867

Three members of the Eliot family have been W.M. of this lodge, the founder-Master Lord Eliot in 1867, his nephew the Hon. M.C. Eliot (later Earl of St. Germans and Provincial Grand Master 1941-52) in 1926, and the Hon. Robert Eliot (Provincial Grand Master 1978-1994), during the centenary year of 1967. The latter, during his year, travelled well over 36,000 miles to attend lodge, each round trip being over 3,000 miles. He left his home in Tangier, Morocco, usually on the Monday evening, flying via Gibraltar to London, and coming to Plymouth by rail on Tuesday morning. There were celebrations for the centenary of a lodge that had its humble beginnings in the Long Room at the top of the local inn, the Eliot Arms. The heart of the village is the tall Norman church which looms over the former priory of Port Eliot, the home of the family for over 400 years. Near the centre of the village is the lodge and masonic hall. The 3rd Lord St. Germans was Lord Lieutenant of Ireland in 1854 when his third son, who later became Lord Eliot, was initiated into Irish freemasonry in Dublin. Among his achievements was the setting up of the lodge and becoming its first W.M. during a year that saw the formation of the Dominion of Canada.

Ten men had gathered to inaugurate the new lodge, the 22nd in the province, with the original application made in February 1854, but not granted until 1867. The lodge of St. Anne's, Looe, was the sponsor and the Provincial Grand Master R.W.Bro. Augustus Smith led the consecration with his provincial officers. Bro. John Hawke was tyler from 1867 to 1902: in 1873 it was decided to pay him 4s per month in the winter "provided that he lit the fire three times a week to keep the damp out." He also served as Provincial G.Tyler. There was an early 'furious pace' with many candidates, and in May 1876 the lodge night was changed from the Wednesday 'before full moon' to the Thursday After some lean years affairs improved with the turn of the century, with the first ladies night in 1909. It was held at Saltash, then Plymouth and now Looe. In those early days it apparently consisted of a whist drive, and sitting at tables of four for high tea. In May of jubilee year, 1917, a candidate was taken ill during his ceremony and the meeting had to be abandoned. At this time more candidates were coming forward from Plymouth and Devonport and several are listed as Innkeepers. The proceedings regularly ended at 9.30pm as this was the "last possible moment if the last trains were to be caught," but due to the General

Lodge Histories

Strike of April 1912 the meeting was cut short so they could catch the only train at 7.55pm. In 1947 Norman Bate of Liskeard was proposed in February and completed the ceremonies by October: he was 75 at the time. The main interest in the 12 years to 1966, the centenary year, was the two-phase extension of the lodge building which was first used in 1870. The first part was opened by Bro. Lightfoot, at the time a member for 64 years: Bro. Cross, who died in 1958, was a member for 68. In this year the lodge changed from candles to electricity. W.Bro. Dr. George Harman "father of the lodge" and W.M. in 1912, unveiled a tablet marking the completion of the second phase in July 1964: on the same night his grandson Bro. J. Tetley was a candidate. Nearly £3,000 was spent on the lodge in five years.

In 1960 the Saltash Craft and Mark lodges were welcomed while their masonic building was pulled down and rebuilt. In 1964 W.Bro. Harman was congratulated on his 90th birthday and two years later on his diamond wedding. Two members, W.Bro. F.A. Rawling (W.M. in 1891) and W.Bro. Pearse Gundry (1937) served the lodge as secretaries for over 75 years, from 1892. A piano was loaned in 1911 and an American Organ presented two years later. The centenary W.M., in his history, commented that "all the financial affairs of the lodge, from the beginning until recently, are veiled in mystery, because no copies of the treasurers' account and reports have been preserved." Between the two world wars very little seems to have been spent on the lodge and in 1947 it was agreed to pay £500 to the trustees of the St. Germans estates for the building and some ground: the contract was handed over on the 80th anniversary that year by the Earl, the Provincial Grand Master. The installation of the Hon. Robert Eliot as W.M. was held in the large dining room at Port Eliot and he was presented by the senior member, W.Bro. Harman, aged 92. Dr. Harman, who had been initiated on 13 April 1905 - and knew some of the founders personally - died in December 1975. His grandson is still a member. In September 1995 the Provincial Grand Master R.W.Bro. Nicholas Barrington, attended a regular meeting of the lodge for a unique presentation. Three brethren were presented with a framed certificate in recognition of their 60 or more years membership. He referred to their contribution to Freemasonry, and to their public careers, and expressed his thanks. The three were: W.Bro. Leslie Francis Paul (initiated September 1925), W.Bro. Frank Hughes Kimber (May 1928) and W.Bro. John A. James Venn (September 1935). W.Bro. Kimber had been made an honorary member in recognition of his many years as lodge almoner. Sadly all three brethren have since died.

Launceston

Liskeard

Looe

Lostwithiel

Millbrook

Mullion

Newquay

Padstow

Penryn

Penzance

Perranporth

Redruth

Lodge Histories

TREGENNA LODGE No. 1272.
ST. IVES.

Some members of Tregenna claim a greater antiquity for their lodge than 132 years, affirming that it can be traced back to 1765, the year of the formation of the Ship Lodge, which met in St. Ives, and which owed its origin largely to John Knill, the Port Reeve, remembered also by the Knill monument and the quinquennial Knill festival. Although the Ship Lodge No. 240 ceased to have any effective existence in 1780, and was erased in 1828, it lived on as True Friendship Lodge No. 678, meeting at Clowance, and was later resuscitated as Cornubian Lodge No. 659, later meeting at the White Hart, Hayle. The founder members of Tregenna Lodge were all members of Cornubian, so there appears to be a direct line of descent from the original Ship Lodge to the present Tregenna.

The formation of Tregenna Lodge was the outcome of a meeting at the home of Bro. Martin Dunn, in St. Ives, on 16 May, 1869, when four other members of Cornubian were present. Tregenna was consecrated on 18 March, 1870, by the Deputy Provincial Grand Master W.Bro. Reginald Rogers. Bro. Dunn was the first Master and both he and the I.P.M, W.Bro. John Coombe held additional offices (treasurer and secretary respectively). The first regular meeting was in April in new rooms, near Fore Street, and described in the minutes as The Wharf and Market Strand, thought to be on or near the site of the present Salvation Army Citadel. The room actually used was a net loft, and the first initiate - who became Master only four years later - was a boot and shoe manufacturer (the only one of this trade in the lodge records). During the earliest decades the majority of members were mine agents, mine assayers, master mariners, mariners and farmers, leavened by the occasional "gentleman". This reflected the then thriving occupations and industries of the district and form an interesting contrast with the occupations of members today. Emergency meetings were very frequent and as many as four meetings a month took place. The fact that many members were seafarers accounted for some of these - but quite as many seem to have been merely excuses for getting together. No summonses of meetings accompany minutes until September 1952.

The decorum and dignity expected today were not always apparent. One man requested admission stating he was a member of a Plymouth Lodge. The I.P.M. was not satisfied with the responses to the examination and the Master refused to admit him. The minutes state that during these tests he behaved in a very improper manner "by loud and noisy speaking which disturbed the lodge considerably and

Lodge Histories

prevented any business being transacted therein for some time." The brethren asked for a stop to be put to it, and finally "the visitor left stating that if he could not be admitted he did not see why he should keep his obligations." Perhaps because of their heavy labours the brethren of these earlier years seem to have enjoyed very convivial "after proceedings." At different times a number of licensed premises were kept by various members of the lodge and it was to one or other of these that they went after the lodge closed. They met "in great harmony" at The White Hart on one occasion, and following an installation "there was a bountiful repast to which the brethren did ample justice": the cost of this was £12.18s. A footnote in the minutes records that the lodge has three black candlesticks with gilt mountings, and three ebony gavels inlaid with the Square, Level and Plumb-rule, bought by W.Bro. Dunn from St. John's Lodge, Plymouth, which had been presented to Prince George Lodge No. 86 by the Duke of Clarence (later King William IV) on his initiation. These candlesticks are still in use in the lodge. In 1880, the year of the laying of the foundation stone of the Cathedral, Provincial G. Lodge was held at St. Ives for the first time. The meeting was in the Wesley Hall, and the banquet at the New Board School cost 6s per head, inclusive of wines. There was a procession around the town in full Masonic regalia, there were triumphal arches, and the procession was led by the two Hayle bands engaged at £2.10s each (military bands having proved too expensive). That the lodge still had seafarers as members is shown by an entry recording the replacement of a Grand Lodge certificate in May 1887, the original being lost when a vessel foundered, while another had to be replaced because the original had been eaten by rats aboard ship.

The first honorary members were the Master of the Cornish London Lodge (1890) and Bro. John Passmore Edwards in March 1896, when the foundation stone of the Passmore Edwards Institute, now the town library, was laid. The first installation banquet at the Porthminster Hotel, in this year, cost £15. The three principal officers' chairs, still in use, were made in 1898 and cost £6.12.6d. A new organ was bought for 17-guineas in 1901 and a new clothes brush. Perhaps this reflects the state of the roads at the time! The two pillars in the lodge were presented in 1909, a year which saw the retirement of W.Bro. J. Wearne, Past Provincial J.G.W., who had been Master in 1875 and who was secretary for 36 years. He was elected to honorary membership and his portrait, painted in oils, presented.

The Great War years brought the death of shipowning magnate Bro. Edward Hain, and in the immediate post-war years, a great increase in candidates. The date of the annual installation was moved to November in 1919, as it is today, but no reason for the change is recorded. The formation of the St. Ia Chapter came in 1921, and the Tregenna Mark Lodge founded in 1923. After years of debt on the lodge building Tregenna was once again solvent in 1924 and the following year bought the house next to the lodge for £510. In 1926 there was a further change in the day of meeting, with the second Monday in each month substituted for the Monday nearest the full moon. In 1928 came the purchase of "the studio" for £410 to complete the block of property now held by Tregenna. The studio was let to artist Borlase Smart and the cellar to Lanham's business. There was a deep shock in November 1931 when W.Bro. R.T. Read, after delivering the address to the newly-installed Master, collapsed and died at home before the banquet. He was the oldest member, the senior Past Master and had served as treasurer for 40 years.

Lodge Histories

Losses due to submarine attacks can be traced in lodge records during the 2nd World War including the S.S. Tregenna in October 1940. The following year one of the most notable members became the first to be honoured by Grand Lodge, W.Bro. W.J. Jacobs (P.G.Standard Bearer): the members presented him with his regalia. July 1954 marked his 50th year as a member: two years earlier he was presented with his portrait in oils, painted by Leonard Fuller, to celebrate 30 years as secretary. He died in September 1960. This well-loved mason was a powerful influence and skilled guide in lodge. In 1961 the first ladies night took place and is now an annual event. In April 1962 the Masters and officers of the daughter lodge, Trenwith, worked a ceremony in Tregenna Lodge, the first and only time there has been an exchange working. Exchanges with other lodges have taken place, including Trewinnard and Cornubian. In 1966 W.Bro. D.M. Uren became W.M. for the second time - 32 years after he was first installed (because the Senior Warden had to leave the district). The long-awaited social club was opened in 1967 and in 1970 came the celebrations for the centenary. There have been only 16 secretaries from 1869-2002, including W.Bro. J. Wearne (36 years) and W.Bro. W.J. Jacobs (33 years). R.W.Bro. James W. Daniel, the Grand Secretary and Grand Scribe E. since 1998, joined Tregenna Lodge in 1966 and was elected an honorary member in 1999.

On The Wharf at St. Ives at the turn of the 19th-20th Centuries. Tregenna Lodge was warranted in 1869.

Lodge Histories

DUKE OF CORNWALL LODGE No. 1529, ST. COLUMB.

In the 1870s St. Columb was a thriving market town of great importance, being the centre of a large agricultural community. Cattle and farm produce were brought in to the town to be sold not only at the weekly market but also at the annual Fair in November. To supply the needs of the community there were a number of small shops and it would appear that a great deal of business was transacted. Their success was in part due to the fact that St. Columb was on the Turnpike and was a stopping place for the mail coach. To cater for the traveller and his horse there were a number of hostelries, the largest being the Red Lion Hotel which had an Assembly Room where a variety of business meetings and functions were held. It was at this hotel in 1875 that a number of gentlemen met to consider the formation of a masonic lodge in the town and it was decided to petition the Grand Master for a warrant constituting a lodge to be called the Duke of Cornwall Lodge and meeting at the Red Lion Hotel on a Wednesday 'on or after the full moon'.

On 17 August 1875 the Duke of Cornwall Lodge 1529 was consecrated by the Provincial Grand Master R.W.Bro. the Earl of Mount Edgcumbe assisted by provincial officers. Bro. Rowe of Bodmin enhanced the occasion 'by his impressive renderings on the harmonium'. Bro. Thomas Hawken of One and All Lodge was installed as W.M.and W.Bro. Thomas Geach, P.M. of St. Matthew Lodge No. 856 was appointed as the I.P.M. It is interesting to note that Bro. Thomas Hicks was appointed S.W. and treasurer and Bro. Henry Whitefield as S.D. and secretary. During the next few months many candidates were proposed and were grocer/general merchant, Independent Minister, High Bailiff, farmer and merchant of Padstow. By the end of the year in the new lodge were a schoolmaster, butcher, accountant, farmers, innkeepers and master mariners who lived in St. Columb and neighbouring parishes. Two of the candidates were described as 'gentlemen' and one as 'of no occupation'. The first joining member in November was described as 'Esquire'. Subsequently many more candidates were proposed, some were withdrawn, one rejected and some were re-nominated after rectifying unfortunate mistakes in balloting procedure.

Lodge Histories

Extract from the Minute Book of The Duke of Cornwall Lodge. No. 1529.

Proposed by Bro. George Bray. S.D. and Seconded by Bro. W. Hortop. D.C.

That an Address be presented to H.R.H. the Prince of Wales and Duke of Cornwall, K.G. etc; etc; Most Worshipful G.M. of England, Expressive of the Horror and Indignation felt by the Members of this Lodge at the Recent Atrocious Attempt on the Life of His Royal Mother and their Thankfulness for Her Happy Deliverance through the Merciful Intervention of T.G.A.O.T.U.

St. Columb. 8th March 1882.

Deep concern was felt throughout the nation at the "atrocious attempt" on the life of Queen Victoria in 1882.

This message was sent by members of the Duke of Cornwall Lodge No. 1529 to the then Duke of Cornwall, Prince of Wales, the Grand Master (later King Edward VII).

This extract from the Minute Book is framed in the lodge at St. Columb.

Lodge Histories

The first annual banquet in celebration of the Festival of St. John was held at the Red Lion Hotel in November 1875, tickets being 5s exclusive of wines. The Red Lion, Railway and Commercial and Barley Sheaf Hotels catered for annual banquets, the innkeepers at the time being members of the lodge. It is recorded that quarterly suppers were held at the Kings Arms and occasional social functions were held in the town hall and drill hall. In more recent years, to accommodate larger numbers, the annual banquets have been held at hotels in Newquay.

In January 1877 it was unanimously agreed 'that the place of holding the Duke of Cornwall Lodge be removed from the Red Lion Hotel to a building in Victoria Street'. This building was a former chapel and, in order to complete the purchase of this and carry out alterations and additions, the committee was authorised to borrow the sum of £200 either by way of mortgage or bonds, but first it was agreed that brethren of the lodge and their families be invited to subscribe to the loan. In November 1877 at the celebration of the Festival of St. John the Provincial Grand Master and officers of the province performed the dedication service which was witnessed by a large number of members and visiting brethren. The banquet was held in the town hall. It was agreed to purchase an Alexandra harmonium 'if funds permit' in 1884 and two years later a committee was given power to carry out structural repairs 'as cheaply as possible consistent with good workmanship, also if funds will admit such decorative repairs as are necessary'. It transpired that the floor of the lodge was in a dangerous condition and it was agreed that it had to be done despite the cost. In 1898 a new carpet was purchased but four years later it was found to have been damaged by moths. In 1892 one lodge meeting was cancelled because of a very small attendance and in 1904 many members were unable to attend the annual festival on account of inclement weather, many roads being snowbound. The shortest meeting recorded is that of June 1912 which opened at 7.30pm and closed at 7.40pm. In 1904 the secretary was instructed to issue a more elaborate summons.

About 20 members in full regalia attended a memorial service for King Edward VII in St. Columb Parish Church in 1910 and in 1921 the lodge arranged a church service to which neighbouring lodges were invited. In July 1917 a tender was accepted for alterations to the balcony to make it an ante-room. Being war time a permit was required for materials but some battens were obtained at a sale and a door and a table were donated. It was not until 1918 that 'the lodge was in the pleasant position of financial freedom'. The use of the lodge premises was granted to the Mark Masons in 1917 and in 1919 it was proposed that a Mark Lodge be attached to the Duke of Cornwall Lodge. In June 1920 the St. Columba Lodge of Mark Masons was consecrated. During the 1st World War help was given in many ways by the lodge. It responded to appeals for the Belgian Relief Fund, for aid in P.O.W. camps and contributed towards a motor ambulance provided by the province. A good response to appeals was also made during the 2nd World War.

In the autumn of 1932 meetings were held in the Church Hall while extensive alterations were made, the balcony in the lodge being removed and the new ante-room being built, the lowest tender of £587.15s being accepted. In addition to this central heating was installed at a cost of £80. New iron gates were made by Bro. W. Higman and he was given premission to exhibit them the following year at the Royal Cornwall Show. In 1933 W.Bro. A. Rawlings Provincial G.Secretary opened the new ante-room with a silver key presented to him by the contractor Bro. J. Bond. In 1935 the lodge was registered as a club enabling intoxicating liquor to be consumed on the premises. Bro. E.N. Willyams, a joining member, became W.M. in 1930 and in May 1952 was installed as Provincial Grand Master by the Earl of Scarborough. In 1946 the W.M. and secretary of the Duke of Cornwall Lodge No.1839 (London) were elected honorary guests. The lodges still have close ties, and in 1999 one of the members of the London lodge was elected as an honorary member 'for his work in fostering closer ties between the two lodges'. In 1955 the property adjoining the lodge was offered free of charge. It was gratefully accepted and the derelict cottages were demolished and the site made into a car park. The centenary of the lodge was celebrated in October 1975 when a service of thanksgiving was held at St. Columb parish church, attended by the Provincial Grand Master R.W.Bro. Col.E. Perry Morgan and officers of provincial grand lodge, together with many members and visiting Brethren. The opening address was given by the W.M., W.Bro. Cedric Burnett. In 1989 permission was given for a proposed new lodge to be formed at St. Columb and in November 1989 the Agricultural Lodge of Cornwall No. 9342 was consecrated. Since that date the following have been consecrated and also meet at St. Columb, Lodge of the Chisel No. 9398, Duke of Cornwall Chapter No. 1529 and the Pydar Conclave O.S.M. No. 395. To meet the needs of the increased membership, alterations and an addition to the lodge building were made in 1995, the cost of just under £10,000 being met through donations from the members and lodges meeting at St. Columb. The work was completed by skilled craftsmen, all members of the Duke of Cornwall Lodge. In 1997 Bro. Roger Pugh, the then lodge organist, presented the lodge with an electronic organ which was received with grateful thanks. There is a close tie with St. Denys Lodge No. 8250, St. Austell, of which some brethren were founder members. In May/June each year the Masters and officers of the two lodges carry out an exchange working that is always very well attended.

Four Cornish Freemasons, the Holman-Climax male voice quartet, combined masonry with music when they visited Australia. All are members of the Mount Edgcumbe Lodge at Camborne and were guest 'Down Under' in 1997 at the bi-annual Kernewek Lowender - a great celebration by the Cornish folk there - at Moonta, Wallaroo and Kadina

Their hosts were the South Australian Cornish Association and the area at the Yorke Peninsula, near Adelaide, is known as the 'Cornish Triangle' and 'Little Cornwall' because of the great emigration from the county some 150 years ago.

All four hold office in the lodge: top tenor Richard Lindsay, second tenor Ivor Glasson, baritone Peter Williams (W.M. in 1990), and bass Derrick Richards. They had many days of music-making at the festival - even teaching local children some Cornish songs.

In Moonta they were guests of the Duke of Edinburgh Lodge, the oldest surviving lodge building in Australia. They attended the meeting and then entertained members with several songs, including such popular Cornish items as 'Hail to the Homeland', 'The White Rose' and 'Lamorna'. Later in Melbourne, they met the Grand Master of Victoria.

Lodge Histories

MOUNT EDGCUMBE LODGE No. 1544, CAMBORNE.

Freemasonry came later to Camborne than to its two near neighbours. Redruth four miles to the east, had its first, Druids' Lodge of Love and Liberality, in 1754 and Cornubian Lodge at Hayle, six miles west, received its warrant in 1838. This was, no doubt, because both those towns are older and both have close contacts with the sea; conditions that apply to all the older lodges in the province. Redruth was an old mining centre with its outlet at nearby Portreath, and Hayle an old seaport and engineering centre. Camborne was a much younger town and in the late 18th century was little more than a small village consisting of the Church of Saint Martin, a hostelry, a wheelwright and a smith's shop with a few thatched cottages, altogether known as Camborne Church Town. In the next 50 years tin of great value was found to exist in large quantities bringing workers into and around the town in such numbers that by the year 1831 the population had increased to nearly 8,000.

The first traceable Camborne Freemasons were initiated into the old Druids' Lodge of Love and Liberality at Redruth in August 1790, to be followed by 17 other Camborne men before 1822. There were also some who travelled the six miles from Camborne to Hayle to be initiated and to attend the meetings and by 1875 there were several Cornubian (Hayle) members living in Camborne and its surrounds. In all, there was a fair number of freemasons of several lodges residing in the Camborne area and in due course they naturally had thoughts of forming a Camborne lodge of their own. A minute book of Provincial Grand Lodge has a record of a petition for the formation of a new lodge at Camborne being made in January 1866. The Provincial G. Secretary wrote to the Provincial Grand Master who ultimately "declined to grant the Prayers of the Petitioners for the present". No reason was given for the refusal and this is somewhat surprising as by this time Camborne and district had become an important area in the world of mining and engineering. The famous Dolcoath mine had been producing copper from the 1750s and even earlier, and by the 1840s and 1850s was producing large quantities of tin. Dolcoath later became not only the deepest and most productive mine in Cornwall but was probably the most important tin mine in the world. Dolcoath miners are depicted in a stained glass window in the Jesus Chapel in the North West of Truro Cathedral. Camborne rapidly established itself as an important mining and engineering area and so it was, in 1875 another effort was made to form a lodge in the town.

Lodge Histories

It followed, and may have been the result of a visit by The Prince of Wales, Grand Master, to a very large gathering of brethren from Cornwall and Devon at Plymouth in 1874. Three petitions soon appeared and the Provincial Grand Master, The Earl of Mount Edgcumbe, approved them all - as Fort Lodge No. 1528 at Newquay, Duke of Cornwall No. 1529 at St.Columb and Mount Edgcumbe No. 1544.

The consecration took place on November 3 with 14 consecrating officers, 33 founders and some 50 visitors representing most of the lodges west of Liskeard and few from outside the province. The banquet was held at what is now Tyacks Hotel. Freemasonry had finally come to Camborne in the year 1875. A feature of the earlier minute books is the frequency of reference to a member leaving for or returning from anywhere and everywhere in the world that mining was practised and to greetings and subscriptions from members overseas. As to age, it seems fairly certain that there were many younger men admitted in the first half century, often students from the Camborne School of Mines. Cornwall has been an exporting county from which many young men from the mines and foundries emigrated to put down their roots in many parts of the world. The lodge met from the day of its consecration until September 1899 at the hall in Fore Street, but was never entirely satisfied with its rented building. In 1885 a building sites committee was established to seek a new home to be owned by the lodge. The possibility of finding the money for such a project fluctuated and a site in Basset Street was thought to be too expensive. Eventually a site in Cross Street was found to be available on an 80 year lease. Financial worries were partly overcome by a loan from the C.M.A.&B. fund of £500 and this enabled the lodge to accept a tender for the building. There was an impressive and well attended stone-laying, by the Deputy P.G.M., W.Bro. P. Colville Smith and by W.Bro. B.F. Edyvean, Provincial Grand Secretary, in November 1898. The first meeting in the new premises took place on the election night in October 1899 and at the December 1899 meeting there was an offer from W.Bro. Colville Smith of a stained glass window. This was accepted with thanks and he was offered honorary membership. It also produced a letter to W.Bro. Edyvean if he would be willing to contribute a similar window. His window is still there to show that he responded favourably!

Since the erection of the building it has been under constant repair and redecoration. Major work was undertaken in 1914 when the ceiling and walls were re-designed by W.Bro. F.G. Gardenner. The same design remains today and this, together with its colour scheme and the stained glass windows, make the Camborne Temple one of the more attractive in the Province. The lodge has met regularly once a month, which would mean 1,500 meetings to the year 2000 but a total of some 200 in excess of that figure have actually taken place. For many years the additional meetings were known as Emergency meetings and were usually called to deal with the rush of candidates that were forthcoming or to complete a brother's membership before he left for foreign parts. By 1900 the total membership exceeded 200 and the lodge was the largest in the province. This level continued until about 1930 but the number is much less today. These former totals led to attempts to form associated lodges and chapters and daughter craft lodges. The Earl of Mount Edgcumbe, the P.G.M., presided at one provincial meeting at the Wesleyan School and he had one of the vestries fitted for himself as a retiring room. The walls of this room were decorated to the height of the door with fluted crimson satin and it was divided in two by a handsome Japanese screen. It was decorated by ornaments, pictures and plants. The upper schoolroom

Lodge Histories

was used for the assembly and the lower one for the luncheon. A rather delicate compliment was paid to his Lordship as he sat at the table faced with a boar's head, that being the crest of the Mount Edgcumbe family. Both large rooms were festooned with bannerets and further adorned with flowers, plants and inscriptions. Outside the streets had been decorated with flags, there was an arch of welcome over the street from the station. The Royal Standard, recently presented to the town by Mrs Basset, floated over the White Hart Hotel. Halfway through the provincial meeting a procession was formed and the brethren walked to St.Martin's Church headed by the Volunteer Band

The Provincial G. Secretary at the time was W.Bro. Thomas Chirgwin, five times Mayor of Truro whose memorial tablet and window can be viewed in Truro Cathedral. One of the Provincial J.G.Ds at the meeting was a Past Master of Mount Edgcumbe, W.Bro. J.C. Burrow who was widely known as a photographer. Those who are fortunate enough to observe some of his pictures taken underground at Dolcoath can only wonder at the photographic expertise of this photographer of the 19th century. In 1927 the meeting of the Provincial G. Lodge was not the grand occasion as in 1888 but there was still the march in full regalia to the Church. On that occasion four Lewises (sons of masons) carried the Bible: they were J.I. Thomas, R. Taylor, G. Laity and E.T. Sara. They were introduced into the lodge, addressed by the P.G.M. and presented with copies of the Bible inscribed and signed by the P.G.M. It was probably some of the unusual and interesting methods of ritual and high standards at Mount Edgcumbe which attracted in 1977 the Grand Secretary, R.W.Bro. Sir James Stubbs to pay the lodge a visit. The late W.Bro. Frederick W. Shepherd, published a history of the lodge, for its centenary year in 1975 and a copy was sent to London. As a result Sir James expressed a wish to attend a meeting. An emergency meeting was soon arranged on a Friday evening before Provincial Grand Lodge so that Sir James could attend two meetings in Cornwall at the same time. After much discussion, the lodge committee laid on a Cornish menu for the banquet, of which the main course was Cornish pasty, followed by fresh fruit salad and saffron cake. There has been a masonic lodge in the town of Camborne since 1875 and its present home, in Cross Street to where it moved in 1899, has celebrated its 100th anniversary.

ST. PETROC LODGE No. 1785, PADSTOW.

The mother lodge, the Duke of Cornwall Lodge No. 1529 at St. Columb, was consecrated on 17 August 1875, and several of its members came from the Padstow area. The journey home after lodge, on horseback or by carriage, would have been quite an adventure. The dates of meetings were governed by the full moon, so that the horses might be able to see their way home even if their riders could not. Hence it was not long before those from Padstow petitioned to form a new lodge and a warrant was granted on 18 October 1878. It was originally intended to call it the Padstow Lodge but Grand Lodge objected to it being named after the town and this was amended to St. Petroc Lodge. It was opened and consecrated in November 1879 by the Provincial Grand Master the Earl of Mount Edgcumbe, the lodge being a house in Church Street and meetings being held on the Tuesday before full moon of every month. The first premises appear to have been purchased using a loan of £200 from Bro. James Nicholls, the J.D., together with a loan of £100 from the East Cornwall bank. Of the 11 founders, nine came from the Mother Lodge, one from Phoenix Lodge, Chacewater, and Brother Nicholls from the Fort Lodge, Newquay, and they all paid two guineas (£2.2s) founders fee to include their first years' subscription. The initiation fee was fixed at five guineas, joining fee at two guineas and subscription at one guinea per year.

Perhaps the most remarkable feature of the first year was the vast amount of ceremonial work carried out by the W.M. He performed a total of 14 ceremonies. In August 1882 a resolution was passed that meetings be held on the first Tuesday in the month regardless of the moon. In these early years the banquet after installation was held at Wills Hotel (the site is now occupied by the Harbour Inn) at a cost of five shillings per head, but teetotallers in the lodge objected and asked for wines to be excluded and the cost was reduced to three shillings and six pence. To commemorate the Queen's Jubilee a unique event occurred on 1 January 1898 at a regular meeting which was opened at mid-day. After business the lodge was called off and a procession formed in regalia, led by the Padstow Artillery Volunteer Band and proceeded to the site of the Victoria Jubilee masonic obelisk, where the foundation stone was laid. The

Lodge Histories

obelisk was completed the following year from De Lank granite at a cost of £465. The height of the monument was 70 ft and situated on high ground proved a valuable landmark to shipping as well as commemorating Queen Victoria's Jubilee. The Revd S. Paynter a London freemason who retired to St. Issey paid for it. In September 1892 the lodge organ was loaned to the parish church whilst the church organ was replaced by a new one. The church donated a guinea to the benevolent fund with grateful thanks. The lodge had bought the organ for 14 guineas in 1887 and it is still in the lodge, but no longer in use. On 11 April 1900 a terrible disaster befell the Padstow Lifeboat and deepest sympathy was tendered to those who had been bereaved together with a donation of ten guineas. In 1894 Mount Sinai Lodge asked to borrow the lodge banner to put on show but the request was rejected on the grounds that it was not in good enough condition. This set the lodge on the path of designing a new banner. Much thought and research went into the design: it was first shown in 1896, and is still in use.

An amusing incident was recorded in September 1904, when W.Bro. Hawken, who was a builder and decorator, stated that his man had painted the lodge by mistake when he should have painted the house next door. There is no record of payment for the unauthorised work. At the November meeting in 1914 it was agreed that, because of the war, the usual installation banquet not be held but that the brethren be asked to contribute to a war fund the sum that would have been spent on this gathering. Mention was made at the meeting held on 7 May 1918, that Bro. Arthur Sluman was a Prisoner of War, but it was subsequently ascertained that he had been killed in action. He was the only war casualty from the lodge during the Great War. There were 42 members at the end of 1901 and 62 at the end of 1918. In the spring of 1926 final plans were agreed for a new building scheme for the lodge, at a cost of £250. At a meeting held in August 1935 it was decided to make an offer for the Methodist Church in Ruthy's Lane and after some months an offer of £275 was accepted. The cost of the conversion amounted to nearly £600 making nearly £1000 in all. The bank overdraft rose to £750 plus £100 each loaned by three members, and the new lodge was dedicated in June 1937.

During the 2nd World War there were only eight initiations and by the time peace came numbers had dropped from 70 to 60. But in the six years to 1951 there were 19 new initiates and eight joining members. This increased lodge funds and for the first time for many years the accounts were clear of debt. Having lost one member killed in the 1st World War the lodge lost Bro. F.S. Moore killed on active service in November 1939. He was the first member to be initiated from the R.A.F. in September 1934. In April 1967 it was decided to close down for August and September and this continues today. St. Gwethnoc Chapter was consecrated on 6th May 1966, and became a new landmark to freemasonry in Padstow. Bodmin had previously named their chapter Saint Petrock so this name was not available. In 1971, after 75 years use the banner was cleaned and over-threaded and in October 1971 was re-dedicated. In the following year Bros. J.R. and M.J. Reed presented a chair for the D.C. in memory of the late W.Bro. Mark Bate, who had been D.C. for 19 years prior to his death in 1971. In October 1973 Bro. J.R. Reed presented and installed a new organ. In the same year W.Bro. F.H.R. Harte celebrated 50 years in freemasonry.

St. Petroc's became 100 years old in November 1979 and the centenary was celebrated on Saturday 23 February, first in the lodge followed by a church service with the ladies and finally with a dinner at the

Wadebridge Showground. Since that celebration the assistant secretary has read the ancient minutes of 100 years ago and continues to do so at every meeting. This was a prosperous time and generous donations were made to the charities. The 1981 festival reached well over £9,000. In 1992 at the end of November, Padstow suffered the tragic loss of two local fishermen at sea, only days after three local men drowned in the estuary. The installation meeting of the lodge was only two days after the second tragedy and at the dinner that evening a collection from members and guests produced £500 to which the province added £500, in total £1,000 for their widows and dependants. The 1990s showed a decline in the number of new candidates and membership numbers have gradually fallen away. Fellowship and morale continued to be good and carol services in the lodge became an annual event. A third organ, this time an electric one, was given by W.Bro. C. Haughton. In 1999 W.Bro. E. Morton-Nance reached the age of 90, and a special meeting was held in the lodge chaired by the Deputy Provincial Grand Master, V.W.Bro. Frank Crewes when he was invested as Past Provincial S.G.W. The Cornwall masonic year book was fronted by a colour photo of W.Bro. Morton-Nance wearing his Cornish Tartan which he designed 50 years ago. Over the years the lodge has been honoured by the investiture of five Grand Officers, four P.G.St.B. and one P.A.G.D.C. only two of whom were initiated in the lodge. In addition five members have served the province as 'active wardens' and one member (W.Bro. N. Girling) was presented with the Provincial Grand Master's Certificate of Service to Freemasonry.

Lodge Histories

W. Bro. Ernest Morton-Nance, who was promoted to PPSGW on his 90th birthday in 1999, wearing the Cornish Tartan he designed 50 years ago. He has served as Deputy Grand Bard of the Cornish Gorsedd, and is a member of the St. Petroc Lodge and St. Gwethnoc at St. Petroc Chapters.

Lodge Histories

MOLESWORTH LODGE No. 1954, WADEBRIDGE.

Following a petition presented to Grand Lodge by One and All Lodge and recommended by the Provincial Grand Master, the Earl of Mount Edgcumbe, a warrant for Molesworth Lodge was approved in February 1882 and the consecration took place in the assembly rooms of the Commercial Hotel, Wadebridge on 8 February 1883. Two attempts to purchase buildings in the town having been turned down, a plot of land 80ft by 40ft was bought in 1887 and plans for a new temple were drawn up. The foundation stone was laid by W.Bro. B.F. Edyvean of One and All, on behalf of the P.G.M., in February 1891. The first meeting in the new temple was held in July the following year. In 1893 Provincial G. Lodge was held in Wadebridge. In 1909 the lodge accepted a quote from the Wadebridge Electric Light Company and electricity was installed in the temple. The oil lamps were sold to Burlawn Wesleyan chapel. Provincial G. Lodge was held at St. Ives in 1913 and St. Petroc Lodge suggested to Molesworth Lodge that they combine to hire a motor car to travel to St. Ives. This was politely refused as many strongly objected to this mode of conveyance. The lodge tyler agreed to take the lodge banner as usual, but under no circumstances would he travel by car. In 1921 the lodge received the jewels of the late W.Bro. Sholto Henry Hare. He was initiated in 1885 and became W.M. in 1892: the chairs of the senior and junior wardens were among many of his gifts. The first meeting of 1933 was held in the Molesworth Hotel due to structural alterations to the masonic hall in connection with the lodge jubilee celebrations. An extension on the west side provided a cloakroom, electric heating was installed and many other improvements made. A new lodge banner was dedicated, following the installation ceremony, by W.Bro. F.A.Rawling of Eliot Lodge.

In 1936 many brethren left the installation banquet early: a severe snowstorm north of Wadebridge made travel very difficult, causing visitors from Bude to stay the night at Otterham, while brethren from Launceston were unable to travel beyond Camelford. Another strip of ground was purchased to provide access to the east wall in 1937. On the outbreak of the 2nd World War, the lodge was designated a clearing station for evacuees and, although wider powers were later given to the W.M. on meetings, installations etc., during the state of emergency, attendances were severely disrupted for the next four years. Food rationing ruled out installation banquets and were replaced by light suppers in local cafes. To reduce the premium for war damage insurance the Sholto Hare jewels were placed in a bank strongroom. In 1947 another strip of land, this time on the north side of the lodge, was bought for a possible future extension. In 1961 a scheme was put forward to provide a kitchen and dining room: in 1966 this was carried out, the cost being borne by collections, donations and interest-free loans. It was officially opened in December and this ensured that the lodge would be able to dine, with a full meal, on its own premises. It was also agreed to form a masonic club.

In 1970 the lodge suffered the loss of W.Bro. G.H. Gardner, who had been made an honorary member in 1966 following a very distinguished career in freemasonry and one of great service to the lodge in many offices, and to the province, he ultimately becoming Assistant P.G.M. The dining room annexe and the kitchen extension were further enlarged by the removal of an interior wall, the cost again being met by donations and loans. In 1982, to mark the forthcoming centenary W.Bro. M. Collings and Bro. D.B. Knight presented an electric organ to the lodge and in February 1983 the centenary was celebrated in an impressive and enjoyable manner. While the ladies enjoyed refreshments in the dining room, the brethren attended the lodge meeting at the Royal Cornwall Showground, both groups being later taken to St. Breoke Church for a service. The day was rounded off with a banquet at the Hotel Bristol, Newquay. On the death of W.Bro. Percy Dunn, a member for 61 years, the lodge received a legacy of £500 from his estate, and the sale of his regalia provided the lodge with a new clock. W.Bro. E.B. Davey was W.M. in 1962, and over the years was involved in most of the lodge activities. In 1967 he was accorded a special vote of thanks for his work and keen interest in the new extension, and for his generous loan to clear the cost of the building. When the masonic club was formed he became its first secretary, a post he held for 13 years. For his many services he was granted honorary membership. In 1984 he was appointed to P.G.St.B. in Grand Lodge: sadly he died while on a cruise in 1998. The lodge membership stands at about 70 and is proud that two members are Grand Officers, W.Bro. H.J. Fry and W.Bro. W.K. Buse, both Past Grand Standard Bearers.

Lodge Histories

COTEHELE LODGE No. 2166, CALSTOCK.

The latter part of the 19th century was a time when the Tamar Valley was a hive of industry, with mining, brick works, ship-building, quarrying and lime-burning. The only means of transport in this area was the River Tamar and horse drawn vehicles. The roads were mud tracks. Drunkenness was common among men and Friendly Societies abounded to provide a better code of living. At this time various brethren of the area decided there was a need for a lodge of freemasons to be formed at Calstock, between Tavistock in Devon and Callington in Cornwall. Members of Loyal Victoria lodge in Callington were approached to support the petition. The consecration took place on 18 April 1887 by the Provincial Grand Master, the Earl of Mount Edgcumbe supported by the provincial officers. A large number of brethren came from the three towns - Plymouth, Devonport and Stonehouse - and the owners of the steamship 'Aerial' ran their vessel on a special excursion from Plymouth to Calstock. Many brethren from Callington and Tavistock were also present at the ceremony at Cotehele House.

The large hall was admirably arranged as a lodge and was crowded with brethren. A hymn written for the occasion and set to music by Bro. W.H. Rogers of Colyton was sung by the choir and the ceremony was followed by a luncheon where the P.G.M., presided and 100 brethren were present. The Earl returned to Mount Edgcumbe on his steam launch 'Armadillo' accompanied by brethren from Cornwall who were landed at Saltash in good time to catch the down train from Plymouth. The visiting brethren from the three towns returned home on the 'Aerial', all having had an enjoyable trip on the river.

The lodge got off to a good start and at the room in Fore Street, Calstock, continued to prosper. Eventually new premises were built on the site of a quarry at Sand Lane, Calstock and the foundation stone was laid in August 1900 by the Deputy Provincial Grand Master, W.Bro. P. Colville Smith. It was built at a cost of £800, raised by donations and loans from the brethren. The prosperity of the area continued until the 1914-18 war years but with the coming of the railway in 1908 there was a general decline in the river traffic and industry. During the war two of the brethren were killed on active service and the two lodge pillars in the West of the temple were dedicated to their memory. The lodge continued between the two wars despite many difficulties for these were years of decline in industry in the parish, resulting in high unemployment and many brethren seeking work abroad. On occasions brethren from Bedford Lodge No. 282, which had originally provided 12 founding members of Cotehele, took part in the ceremonies. The 1939-45 war also took its toll, with the deaths on active service of two brethren. A dedication and memorial service took place in their memory in January 1952, when the three chairs of the W.M. and two wardens were dedicated by the Provincial G. Chaplain.

There was a resurgence of interest in the lodge after the war, membership increased and the standard of work improved under the guidance of W.Bro. Richard Petherick, M.B.E., who was lodge secretary for 23 years. W.Bro. W.O. Jane became lodge secretary in 1953, continuing until 1987 with an unbroken record of over 500 consecutive lodge meetings. W.Bro. G. Start became D.C. in 1961 and the high standard of work in the lodge was due, in the main, to his efforts. In 1967 the lodge was refurbished at a cost of £1,200 again met by donations and loans. In 1976 W.Bro. W.F.J. Raxworthy was elected charity steward. At the time the lodge was endeavouring to raise money for the 1981 provincial festival: the total stood at £1,000. It was decided to raise as much as possible whilst still supporting the other masonic charities and by March 1981 this had increased to £16,000, then the highest amount given by any of our lodges as a contribution to a festival. It was decided to set a target of £5,000 to enable the lodge to celebrate its centenary in a practical way: at the anniversary in 1987 the lodge presented £10,500 to the Royal Masonic Benevolent Institution towards the new Cadogan Home at Exeter. In 11 years, therefore, the lodge had raised almost £30,000, a marvellous achievement with great credit due to W.Bro. Raxworthy. He now lives in Australia and is an honorary member of the lodge.

In April 1981 the lodge was presented with an electric organ by W.Bro. L.M. Pridham in memory of his late wife. Since the lodge has been formed some 400 candidates have been initiated. Among them was Bro. Charles Maple Polmear of Bere Alston, who emigrated to South Africa and later became District Grand Master for the District of Transvaal and its Grand Superintendent in the Royal Arch. The lodge has been indebted over the years to the late W.Bro. A. Speare and his team for various work carried out to improve the building and its facilities. His widow generously presented to the lodge a new heating system in his memory, which was gratefully accepted at the 1999 carol service. Since the centenary an extension has been built at the rear of the lodge, as a refectory, at a cost of £20,000.

Still looking in remarkably 'mint' condition these roof timbers of the Temple at Cotehele Lodge are now over a hundred years old. Since the centenary in 1987 an extension has been built at the rear of the lodge for a refectory at a cost of £20,000. The brethren backed the development with their commitment and the work has now been totally paid for.

ST. MICHAEL LODGE No. 2747, NEWQUAY.

Lodge Histories

The circumstances surrounding the necessity for the foundation of this lodge may be considered both unusual and rather sad. In 1875 the Fort Lodge No. 1528 was consecrated at Newquay, but by the late 1890s there existed such discord between certain members that it became impossible to continue. A petition for a new lodge in January 1899 contained the names of 21 of the 23 members. Four others also signed the petition which was recommended by the Provincial Grand Master the Earl of Mount Edgcumbe the following month. The new lodge was warranted as St. Michael in the February, and the consecration took place in July, by dispensation, at the Oddfellows Hall, which was then in Marcus Hill, the lodge room being, to apply the term used by contemporary press reports, "....insufficiently commodious to hold the numerous brethren present". The lodge was consecrated by V.W. Bro. E. Letchworth, Grand Secretary of the United Grand Lodge of England assisted by W.Bro. P. Colville Smith, Senior Grand Deacon, as Senior Warden, and W.Bro. E.M. Milford, (Past Provincial S.G.W.) as J.W. This was the first time in Cornish Freemasonry that a lodge had been consecrated by a Grand Secretary in the province. Bro. S. Rickeard was installed as W.M. W.Bro. Lieutenant-Col. G.J. Parkyn, who had overseen the transition from Fort Lodge to St. Michael, and who appears to have been its chief architect, was honoured: he received the rank of Grand Sword Bearer that year. The lodge held its regular meetings at the masonic hall in Gover Lane which was later acquired for St. Michael in 1901. Due to the fact that there had been no ballots for either initiates or joining members since before May 1897 in the Fort Lodge, the early days of St. Michael Lodge proved to be very busy.

In July 1904 the lodge was granted a dispensation to initiate Mr. John Knowlden Willis, who was under 21 years of age. At the following meeting the lodge recorded its hearty approval and congratulations on his gallant attempt to save the life of a French chef who had drowned at Fistral beach the previous day. In September 1905, Provincial G. Lodge was held in the Victoria Hall, Newquay, under the banner of St. Michael lodge. The brethren marched in procession through the streets, which had been decorated with flags by the public, to the church then occupying the site currently held by the

Lodge Histories

Woolworths store. In the procession, the Lewises carrying the Bible were Masters W. Huxtable, G. Hardwick, A. Butler, and Rickard, the whole being led by the Volunteer Band playing masonic music. October 1910 saw the illumination of the lodge room by electricity. In 1912 the lodge expressed their acknowledgement of the valuable services of Bro. J.R.C. Woodward in rescuing a child from falling over the cliff at the scene of the wreck of the schooner Bessie at Newquay on the night of 5 March. During his year of mastership, Bro. Woodward survived the loss of the Newquay lifeboat in January 1917 whilst on service.

During the Great War many members of St. Michael went to serve, and in common with all sections of society, several lodge members suffered the loss of their sons. Although Bro. H. North was the only lodge member killed in action, other brethren suffered the effects of gassing and wounding, from which they never fully recovered. In October 1918, by dispensation, the brethren of St. Michael attended a service at the new St. Michael's church in masonic clothing, having marched from the masonic hall, for the institution of Bro. the Hon. Revd Yarde-Buller into the new parish of Newquay. A member of St. Michael Lodge, he was appointed Provincial G.Chaplain in 1920. The years 1918 - 1920 saw a great increase in candidates from the average three or four per year to 14, 29 and 12 respectively. Following a sharp decrease in membership from 70 in 1913 to 38 in 1916, the years immediately after the war witnessed a leap to 132 by 1921. With this growth, by 1919, the lodge was planning to extend the building in Gover Lane. This move seems to have been insufficient to accommodate the still increasing membership as by 1921 a new site was being sought: from November, 1921 the installation meetings were held at various venues.

At the Provincial G. Lodge at Newquay in 1922, W.Bro. A. Butler, the only member thus far to have served as W.M. for two separate years, was appointed Provincial J.G.W. Following the sale of the Gover Lane building and site in 1926, the lodge met at the Hotel Victoria. The foundation stone of the present premises was laid in November 1928 by V.W.Bro. Sir Colville Smith, K.C.V.O., Grand Secretary, Deputy Provincial Grand Master. The building was completed in time for the lodge to hold its January meeting in 1930 in the new temple. The dedication ceremony was conducted by R.W.Bro. Brigadier-General Lord St. Levan, Past Grand Warden, the Provincial Grand Master in May 1930: over 300 attended. In 1934, W.Bro. A. Butler was appointed Assistant G.St.B. Within 21 years of the armistice, the nation was again at war and once more brethren were to lose sons in action. The lodge mourned the loss of Bro. J.T. Pender and also Bro. Major L. Bellingham who was a former member. Other brethren were held as prisoners-of-war. As in the former conflict, the charitable needs of the time received the due attention of the lodge. With the influx of Allied military personnel, the dance-hall beneath belonging to the lodge was requisitioned. The lodge welcomed many visiting brethren from the armed forces. Again there was a considerable increase in both the years immediately following the war, notwithstanding the consecration of the first daughter lodge (Fistral Lodge No. 6258) in 1946. This increase in masonic activity resulted in the consecration of a second daughter lodge (Towan Lodge No. 7684) in 1960.

At Provincial G.Lodge in 1941, W. Bro. A. Bond was appointed Provincial J.G.W. In September, 1948 the lodge received various gifts of furniture including the fine pair of pillars which adorn the temple. The building attained its present form with extensions to the front and western side during the early 1960s.

Lodge Histories

The first past masters' working took place in 1959, conducted by W.Bro. J.J. Hoskin: this has since become an annual occasion. The first instance of an exchange working was with Mount Edgcumbe Lodge in 1923. Further exchanges did not occur until 1964 when there were two, with St. Petroc's Lodge and secondly with Carlyon Lodge. W.Bro. J.J. Hoskin was appointed P.G.Std.B. in 1961. In April 1990, 12 Newquay masons including ten from St. Michael Lodge, visited Lodge Brittany No. 226 under the Grand Loge Nationale Francais by invitation of their W.M. On this unique occasion, by dispensation, the Newquay brethren performed the ceremony. At the provincial lodge in 1989, W.Bro. G.S. Horner was appointed Provincial J.G.W., and W.Bro. W.F.J. Brock received the Provincial Grand Master's Certificate of Service. In 1996 W. Bro. Brock was appointed P.A.G.D.C. Up to November 1998 St. Michael lodge had initiated 480 candidates and there were 137 joining members and 22 honorary members. The lodge celebrated its centenary in October 1999 when the new lodge banner was dedicated and the centenary warrant was presented by the Provincial Grand Master, R.W.Bro. Nicholas Barrington.

A splendid array at Penzance in 1908 when the Provincial Grand Lodge officers gathered on the steps of St. John's Hall. In the centre is the P.G.M., the R.W.Bro. the Earl of Mount Edgcumbe.

Lodge Histories

CORNISH MASTERS LODGE
No. 3324.

The idea of an Installed Masters lodge was first put forward in 1908 by the provincial secretary, W.Bro. W. Hammond at a meeting of the provincial committee. The petition forms were issued to the then current 30 lodges which produced 213 founders including ten from the Cornish lodge in London. In early July of that year, Love and Honour No. 75 became the sponsor, the petition was duly signed in open lodge, forwarded to Grand Lodge and on 21 July a warrant was issued. It had been agreed that the Provincial Grand Master the Earl of Mount Edgcumbe should be the first Master and that the consecration would take place in the Orangery at Mount Edgcumbe on 29 September 1908. When a large gathering of Masons assembled they were told that the Earl was 'kept in bed by illness' and was unable to be present. The lodge was duly consecrated by the Grand Secretary, V.W.Bro. Edward Letchworth with R.W.Bro. Sir William Treloar, Lord Mayor of London, as S.W. and Bro. Passmore Edwards as J.W. but no installation could be performed. That ceremony took place on 15 December and the lodge was launched.

The basic principles for the formation of the lodge do not appear to have been clearly defined, but over the years it has devoted itself to the pursuit of masonic knowledge. To this end, lectures and the reading of masonic papers have been the main items on its agenda, but for a period it performed ceremonies in other lodges: at one time it attempted to assume the mantle of initiating the first candidate of newly formed lodges. This practice has ended but there have been performances of ceremonies by invitation. Demonstrations from other rituals have been received, the Bristol working, the longer installation ceremonies such as the Exeter working and that in practice at Helston. There have been talks on the formation of the United Grand Lodge together with its organisational aspects as well as those appertaining to provincial lodge and lodges in general: all this in an attempt to expound upon the philosophy of freemasonry beyond the meaning of the ritual itself. At one period there was a correspondence circle associated with the lodge but, since the formation of the Cornwall branch of the Devon and Cornwall Masonic Study Circle, it no longer operates; the lodge sponsored the formation of the Study Circle lodge known as Cornish Ashlar. A pleasant feature of the lodge activities follows the summer meeting - which is kept as short as possible - with a social activity, including the ladies. This began with the August meeting in 1909 and has continued on a fairly regular basis since then and now follows the May meeting. Records include river trips, concerts, visits to stately homes, museums, a dairy, in fact wherever the current Master and his lady wish to invite the brethren and their ladies. In 1910 the meeting was followed by attendance at the laying of the foundation stone of the Bodmin masonic hall.

In the early days, when there was a relatively small number of lodges, the membership climbed to about 300, then dropped to 200 at which figure it remained for many years. After the 2nd World War the number started to decline until now the number stands at about 90. Progression to the chair is by the normal lodge practice except on certain occasions when a particular member of distinction, such as the Provincial Grand Master takes precedence. A member who joins and is in good attendance can soon expect to join the stewards list and make steady progress to the chair. This is not the normal practice of Masters lodges in other provinces where the Master is either nominated by the senior members or the committee, who then makes his own selection of most officers. Keeping a record of attendance is difficult since many masons seem to have a dislike of others being able to read their signatures! All but one of the P.G.Ms have been through the chair of the lodge as well as some deputies, provincial secretaries, treasurers and D.Cs.

The lodge meets throughout the province, the choice of venue left to the W.M., with the exception of the March meeting which usually meets in the nearest masonic hall to the hotel accommodating the Provincial Wardens lunch. In 1909 W.Bro. Hammond reported he had seen in London a 'Masonic chair of great age' and the W.M., the Earl of Mount Edgcumbe sanctioned its purchase for the use of the lodge. This chair appears to have moved about via several lodge rooms, i.e. Liskeard, Falmouth, Truro, as noted in the minutes and is now located as the Master's chair in the Perry Morgan Temple at Hayle.

The great gathering for the consecration of the Cornish Masters Lodge No. 3324 in The Orangery, at Mount Edgcumbe in September 1908. The Earl, the PGM, was unwell and not installed as the first W.Master on this occasion, but the consecration ceremony took place. No lodge in the province was missing from the Roll of Founders: there were 30 lodges at this time and 213 founders. The lodge was consecrated by V.W.Bro. Edward Letchworth (Grand Secretary), pictured centre, with R.W.Bro. Sir William Treloar, Lord Mayor of London, as S.W., and Bro. J. Passmore Edwards, the philanthropist, as J.W. The installation took place in the December.

Lodge Histories

GRANVILLE LODGE No. 3405, BUDE.

Who first thought of forming a lodge at Bude or Stratton is not known but, it can be assumed that W.Bro. John Wonnacott, the first W.M., and the landlord of the Tree Inn, had a lot to say in the matter. A booklet on the history of Dunheved lodge from 1860-1960 tells that between 1906 and 1910 several brethren from Bude were initiated into Dunheved. At a meeting held in July 1906, a petition requesting the foundation of a new lodge was signed but was not approved. The pressure continued. In November 1909 the brethren of Dunheved signed another petition for a new lodge to be called the Granville lodge, and to hold its meetings in the Church Rooms, Stratton. On this occasion, success crowned their efforts, Dunheved became the mother lodge, and the consecration took place on the 10 December 1909, performed by the Deputy Provincial Grand Master, W.Bro. P. Colville Smith. Five of the founders had been W.Ms of nine other lodges so the formation was in experienced hands.

Dunheved gave much valuable support and it is right to acknowledge the influence of Obedience Lodge at Okehampton which came from the fact that it was easier for Bude men to travel to Okehampton by train from Bude than it was to go to Launceston by horse transport. In 1933 Bude suffered serious flooding which included the lodge premises and many records were badly damaged, but no trace of the first minute book, or the early accounts', were found. Yet there is ample proof of what took place in those early days and the warrant, was undamaged by the flood. The first two years of the lodge were very busy, with 15 meetings in the first year when there were 12 initiates with two more proposed. There were six joining members and 36 visitors. For the first two years, the lodge continued to meet at the church rooms at Stratton but in March 1911 seven members gave notice to propose that the lodge be moved from Stratton, "to a suitable building at Bude, to be erected by the brethren". Four founders and one joining member wrote giving their support, but one founder resigned. Yet another emergency meeting was held and the motion was carried and given provincial approval. In July 1911, plans of the building were shown to the brethren and they were invited to take shares. Since it was of timber construction above masonry foundations, it was quickly built and was used for the first meeting in November. It was agreed to pay a rent of £12 a year. In June 1922, things began to happen very fast. A distinguished member died and left £100 to the lodge conditional on the brethren purchasing the masonic hall within a year of his death. It was said that a letter "galvanised the lodge into action". Within a few months, the lodge bought the building for £357 and the freehold land from the Acland Estate for £75. Over the years, the hall has been extended and largely 'encased' with block walls. It is now a very attractive hall with very adequate facilities (the land and building value was in the 1998 accounts at £175,000). In the early days the hall was also used for social events such as whist drives and dances, but that ceased in 1931.

The lodge has many very valuable chairs on the platform: an expert has said that they are irreplaceable. Some were given by a brother in memory of his father who was a founder member. Some were collected over the years by a brother who was an estate agent and auctioneer. The chairs used by the D.C. and the deacons were presented by lodge members. The Bible has been in the lodge since its consecration, and an oak gavel was salvaged from Freemasons Hall in Bristol after it was bombed in the war. The "emblems of mortality" are reported to have come from the battlefield at Stamford Hill where Sir Bevil Granville was one of the principals involved: the battle site is one-and-a-half miles from the lodge. The wall behind the W.Ms chair is adorned by some very old prints dated 1809 and 1813. The hall is also used for Granville Chapter No. 3405 (consecrated in 1935); Sir Bevil Granville Mark Lodge No. 1231 (consecrated in 1959); Sir Bevil Granville Lodge of Royal Ark Mariners No. 1231 (consecrated in 1980). The lodge has a full set of minutes, summons and accounts from 1926. Some were damaged in the floods but have been carefully dealt with and are readable. In 1943 W.Bro. Alfred Banbury received Grand Rank: he was presented with his regalia as acknowledgement of his work. He was the secretary of the lodge for 33 years and had been absent only five times. The practice of presenting grand lodge regalia has continued. In May 1991, the Provincial Grand Master gave dispensation for the lodge to "open and close" only for that meeting, to allow the brethren to be joined by their ladies to view the temple, hear a little about the various offices, and to see the Grand Lodge video, as part of the era of 'openness in masonry'. There was a £20,000 insurance claim following the flood of 1993, and an additional £7,000 spent. A joining W.Bro. who did much work for the lodge before moving to The Canaries found masonry there but only in the Spanish language. So, together with others, he founded two lodges using English Emulation: he also liaised with Spanish lodges. Another joining member who had been a mason for well over 50 years was the owner of a silver match box presented to him by his mother lodge in recognition of an absolutely word perfect ceremony.

Lodge Histories

TREVAUNANCE LODGE No. 4668, ST. AGNES.

For many years prior to 1924 a number of freemasons living in St. Agnes were members of Boscawen at Chacewater, and these were instrumental in requesting the sponsoring of a daughter lodge. The name is derived from that part of St. Agnes known as Trevaunance Cove, comprising the beach and surrounding countryside. The warrant was granted in August 1924 and the consecration in April 1925 by the Provincial Grand Master, R.W.Bro. Lord St. Levan, assisted by his provincial officers, was held in St. Mary's Wesleyan hall, at Truro. There had not been a consecration of a craft lodge in Cornwall since 1909. W.Bro. A.S.B. Sawle was installed as the first W.M. by the Deputy P.G.M. and Grand Secretary, V.W.Bro. P. Colville Smith.

The first regular meeting was in the church hall in April 1925, with 17 present including five visitors: the first two candidates were proposed. This building was far from ideal and negotiations began to buy the present masonic hall which had been opened in 1835 as the Methodist New Connexion Chapel ('salem') but had closed through lack of support after World War I. The cost was £240, trustees were appointed, and the first meeting was in December 1925 in the large room on the ground floor: the lodge continued here until 1934. In 1926 the members decided there should be no form of entertainment in the building and in the April the first installation meeting in Rosemundy was attended by 29 of the 30 members together with the P.G.M. The following year brought the first inter-lodge working, with Fowey the visitors, and in May 1929 the new lodge banner, worked by the Women's Institute members, was on view. Bro. George Borlase, tyler from October 1927 until his death in 1947, was succeeded by his nephew Bro. Cecil Borlase who continued for 30 years. The start of the 1930s brought the first ladies night, and in March 1933 there was a visit from the oldest lodge in the province, Love and Honour, for a ceremony, and exchange visits. In November of that year detailed plans were put forward "for a new temple on the first floor.....together with an anteroom and new staircase". The W.M., W.Bro. J.E. Tredinnick said he was prepared to complete the scheme within a few months for £197, and the temple was opened in March 1934 by the Provincial G. Secretary, W.Bro. F.A. Rawling, and dedicated by Bro. Revd C.G. Rolfe-Sylvester, Past Provincial G. Chaplain. Over 60 attended - with visitors from nine lodges - in October 1936 when the W.M., W.Bro. J.R.S. Bennett initiated a candidate and W.Bro. W.T. Hosking, W.M. of Druids Lodge and officers worked a ceremony. Exchanges between the preceptor's classes have continued to the present.

Lodge Histories

The first reference to the 1939-45 war was not recorded until September 1941 when terms were arranged with the county education authority for the use of the upstairs anteroom as a classroom for evacuees. In January 1942 Petty Officer C.Parrish R.N. was balloted for and initiated on the same night "cause of urgency, probably going on foreign service." That year it was decided to send an annual ten shillings Christmas gift to members in H.M. Forces. In December 1943 another candidate Mr. A. Windsor, a Merchant Navy officer, was balloted for and initiated on the same meeting and at an emergency meeting in December 1944 Mr. R.G. Trewhella, serving in the Royal Navy, was initiated by his father W.Bro. H.J. Trewhella. With an Army camp and two aerodromes close by, the adult population increased but, apart from a cinema, recreational facilities in the village were limited, so the downstairs hall was in great demand, and became a popular venue for the troops and a money-raiser for charities. Trevaunance Mark Lodge was consecrated in June 1945 and Trevaunance Royal Arch Chapter in 1973. In 1951 W.Bro. A.S.B. Sawle, secretary for 21 years, and W.Bro. R.W. Warren, treasurer for 17, retired. In 1959 brethren were involved in the founding of St. Piran's lodge at Perranporth, and there were fundraising events with Boscawen, Tregullow and Trevaunance. Major improvements were carried out to the lodge premises, a lodge benevolent fund was formed in 1973 to achieve a full contribution to the 1981 Festival: the fund continued for the 2002 Festival. The Deputy Provincial Grand Master W.Bro. H.I. Dingle attended the 50th installation ceremony in April 1974 - when Bro. T.D. Blight was installed - and an appeal launched to raise £1,000 for a fully equipped kitchen. The Provincial Grand Master R.W.Bro. Col. E. Perry Morgan attended in August and W.Bro. W.H.J. Pearce (W.M. of Boscawen) presented a charity box from the 'mother lodge' to mark the half-century. The consecration of daughter lodge Breanick (the earliest known name for the village of St. Agnes) came in February 1975, and the following year Trevaunance bought the former British Legion building and land in Rosemundy. W.Bro. R.C.A. Hooper, who retired as secretary in 1991 after 19 years service, later received Grand Rank. The close working of the freemasons at St. Agnes led to the forming of a masonic club in 1986, with a bar built into the dining hall. By coincidence this was 60 years after the resolution restricting entertainment in the building! In that year the new lodge banner was dedicated by the Provincial Grand Master R.W.Bro. the Hon. Robert Eliot. It was a replica of the original - incorporating parts of it - and the work again carried out by members of the St. Agnes and Breanick Women's Institutes, who were invited to the dinner after the lodge meeting. The 75th W.M., W.Bro. S.R. Walters was installed in April 1999 and the anniversary marked the revival of the lodge with a number of new members.

ST. LEVAN LODGE No. 5134, PENZANCE.

The 70th anniversary of the consecration of St. Levan Lodge was in October 1999. It had become clear in the 1920s that, with membership of Mount Sinai Lodge in the town being between 200-300, there was the need for another lodge. In April 1929 a meeting was convened of those Mount Sinai members interested in its formation. Thirty-four attended and resolved that the name be St. Levan Lodge, and that the R.W.Bro. Brigadier-General Lord St. Levan, the Provincial Grand Master be invited to become the first W.M. Among the matters agreed were that: the lodge pay Mount Sinai £30 per annum for the first three years and lodge night be on the first Wednesday in each month (it still is). Five members of the provisional committee met the Provincial G. Secretary on 13 May for advice and the founders met nine days later. It was agreed, among other things, the founders fee be £5.5s and each founder present the collar and jewel of his first office.

The first S.W. was W.Bro. Canon H.R. Jennings and J.W. Bro. Samuel Carter. The art master at Penzance School of Art, Bro. J.W. Lias was asked to prepare a sketch for a founder's jewel and he also prepared sketches for a lodge banner. Everything moved rapidly: the warrant was granted in August and the consecration arranged to be at St. John's Hall on Friday 18 October. Many played a part in the consecration preparations and this great day arrived less than five months from the first meeting of those who had expressed an interest in a new lodge. A total of 320 signed the register: all lodges from the province except two were represented and lodges from Plymouth to Ebbw Vale, South Africa, America, Bermuda, Detroit, Newcastle and Liverpool had members present. The consecrating officer was V.W.Bro. Sir Colville Smith, the Grand Secretary and Deputy P.G.M. He said it had long been felt that, owing to the increase in membership of some lodges, some of the junior brethren had been debarred from obtaining Mastership, which was the ambition of every mason, and so what may be called 'overflow lodges' were almost necessary.

The founding Master, Lord St. Levan, presented three tracing boards during the first year. W.Bro. Trenoweth presented a set of silver and ivory working tools and W.Bro. Dunstan a D.C's wand. There were three candidates for initiation and seven joining members.

In 1937 Provincial Grand Lodge was held in Penzance under the banner of St. Levan Lodge, at his Lordship's especial request, while he was still able to perform his duties. He held the view that "a good Mason could not be a bad citizen". The Cornish members felt that even if he was only able, owing to his health "to watch the activities of the Province from the summit of his rocky fastness at St. Michael's Mount, they wanted him to remain as P.G.M., and hoped he would preside over their destinies for many years to come." Lord St. Levan died on 10 November 1940: during his lifetime he had lived up to the family motto "Exact in Himself". Each successive Master brought his own individual contribution. Only one died in office, W.Bro. W.J. Kerswell, 18 days after his installation. In memory of her father, The Hon. Hilaria St. Aubyn presented one of the jewels worn by him: this memento decorates the collar of each succeeding W.M. The personal standard of the founder-Master and P.G.M. was also entrusted to the lodge and has been framed and hung on the north wall of the temple. The lodge was invited to sponsor a lodge on the Isles of Scilly (where there had been one from 1768 - 1851). In December 1961 the Godolphin Lodge was consecrated by the Provincial Grand Master R.W.Bro. Col. E.N.Willyams. The original Master's chair came back into use and St. Levan contributed the two Wardens chairs. St. Levan Chapter No. 5134 was consecrated in June 1977 and two years later came the 50th anniversary of the lodge with the Provincial Grand Master the Hon. Robert Eliot attending. Bro. Ian Lentern, the son of the secretary of the lodge, was initiated on this occasion by the P.G.M. Prior to the setting up of the Penzance masonic premises committee in 1984 the temple was repaired and decorated on a voluntary basis, with members of the three lodges taking part. There have been extensive refurbishments in recent years. The diamond jubilee was celebrated in 1989, with an initiation, and service at St. Mary's among the events.

Many provincial honours have been conferred on members and in 1999 Bro. S.G. Jolly was awarded the Provincial Grand Master Certificate of Service to Freemasonry. That year brought the 70th birthday and the Master, W.Bro. Philip Southwood and his wife arranged a visit by 14 to the United States, with welcomes at Madison Lodge in Grass Valley, California and Nevada City Lodge. It is hoped an annual exchange with Dundas Lodge in Plymouth will continue: it began in 1996 with 15 members making the trip to Plymouth. In 1997 W.Bro. Paul Leggo, who had emigrated to Portugal, became W.M. of Prince Henry the Navigator Lodge and invited brethren to visit: five from St. Levan and one from Lyonesse made the journey there.

Lodge Histories

ST. LUKE'S LODGE No. 5371, CAMBORNE.

It was in 1928 that the membership in Mount Edgcumbe Lodge in Camborne reached 200, and to enable younger members to reach the W.M's chair in a reasonable time the need for a new lodge in the area was necessary. It was thought the new one should be based in Illogan as there was a parish population of some 9,000 and this was believed sufficient. Mount Edgcumbe Lodge gave its full support, sponsored the application, and eventually supplied the new lodge's principal officers. There was, at that time, the opinion that the parish church in Illogan was dedicated to St. Luke as the parish feast day was held on the Monday nearest to St. Luke's Day. It is now generally agreed that the dedication is to St. Illogan and the church authorities have approved St. Illogan as the proper title of the Ecclesiastical Parish. There seems little doubt that had present knowledge been available the lodge would have been called St. Illogan. Indeed, the associated Royal Arch Chapter has that distinction. St. Luke's was warranted on the 22 June 1932 and consecrated on the 5 September 1932 by the Provincial Grand Master R.W.Bro. Lord St. Levan assisted by R.W.Bro. Sir Philip Colville Smith the Deputy P.G.M: The ceremony was at St. George's Hall, Camborne. In its life the lodge has had three homes; first in the heart of Illogan parish at Trevenson church hall in Pool, then at the former Primitive Chapel in Tuckingmill, and, since 1971, sharing premises with Mount Edgcumbe at the Masonic Hall, Cross Street, Camborne. In 1936 the lodge obtained a banner which was dedicated by W.Bro. F.A. Rawling the Provincial G. Secretary.

Trevenson church hall was a multi-purpose building and it was necessary for lodge furniture and equipment to be stored in another room and brought out each time for meetings. Unfortunately, the storeroom was poorly ventilated and during winter months when the heating was on, the carpet, damp through storage, used to emit clouds of vapour which added considerably to the mystery of freemasonry. The lodge started with 24 members but by 1940 this had risen to 73: the hall was no longer adequate and the chapel in Tuckingmill, still just within the boundary of Illogan parish was empty and available. The building seemed ideal for the purpose and the purchase price of £300 was paid. In 1942 came the move to Tuckingmill where the lodge enjoyed sole use of its quite spacious premises and made good use of the fine two-manual pipe organ which had been built by Fleetwoods of Camborne. It is still in use by the Christadelphian Church which now owns the former lodge premises. It was alleged that the blower came from a mine and when first switched on sounded as if knives were being sharpened. One prospective member waiting in the dining room on being told this by several passing brethren turned quite green and had to be reassured. Seating for Past Masters and distinguished visitors was on tip-up seats loaned by a P.M. who owned a cinema.

The 1940s and 1950s saw membership increase to over 150. Perhaps because of the pipe organ the lodge has always enjoyed music and singing. Several members have been associated with local church and chapel choirs as well as local male voice choirs. The Christmas meeting has always been rather special, business kept to a minimum and the meal followed by carol singing: these always include some by Thomas Merritt, the 19th century Illogan organist and composer. The Tuckingmill temple was said by some to be haunted and one distinguished brother swears this to be true. At Tuckingmill, because of the building's former use as a chapel, the lodge was considered to be teetotal but one visitor attending a Ladies' Night observed that he had never seen so many teetotallers with glasses in their hands. One of the lodge's greatest assets is its benevolent fund, a registered charity, which enables its trustees to furnish the lodge almoner with funds throughout the year. In 1971 it was decided that the financial burden of maintaining a separate building was too great and the lodge moved to Cross Street, Camborne where it happily shares premises with its mother lodge. The premises are vested in trustees but are managed by a joint committee.

In 1982 the lodge celebrated its golden jubilee and a record of the first 50 years was compiled by a small committee and written by W.Bro. Peter Holman: W.Bro. J.H. Toy made and presented a tapestry commemorating the jubilee which has pride of place on the W.M's pedestal. From its small beginning in 1932 the 1999 provincial year book shows the lodge to be the second largest in the province. There is a very happy relationship between the two local lodges. In company with many Cornish lodges, St. Luke's has had members who have emigrated to the U.S.A. or served in the forces. There is one who has become the W.M. of a lodge under the Scottish Constitution in the Caribbean. The lodge Bible is a gift from one member resident in the U.S.A.

Lodge Histories

TRURO SCHOOL LODGE No. 5630.

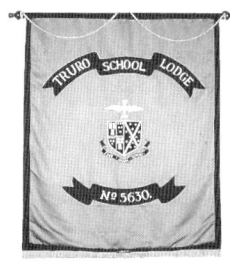

A meeting of Past Masters of lodges who were Old Boys of Truro School was held at the school on 27 October 1935. The object was to "petition Grand Lodge to form a craft lodge in connection with the school." This was unanimously agreed and membership was restricted to Old Boys, past and present masters of the school and governors, with the cost kept as low as possible. The consecration took place in the school hall on 24 September 1936, performed by the Provincial Grand Master R.W.Bro. Lord St. Levan, assisted by his officers. The organist was Bro. F.G. Ormond (organist of Truro Cathedral): an anthem was sung by the choir, under his direction. W.Bro.Dr. E.H. Magson, L.G.R., was installed as the first W.M. by the Deputy P.G.M., R.W.Bro. Sir Philip Colville Smith (Bro. Ormond, who was not an installed master, remained in his seat during this ceremony, apparently undetected by the provincial officers!). A founder's jewel was presented to each of the 21 founders: the late W.Bro. W.C. Argall, gave his to the lodge.

Fourteen of the founders became W.Ms of the lodge in the ensuing years. Gifts to the school lodge at its inauguration were gauntlets for the principal officers, silver square and compasses and a cushion for the Bible. Subsequent gifts included a silver alms plate and a cushion for the working tools. It was first decided to hold five meetings a year and in 1942 six. Whilst at Truro School the lodge normally met in the school hall but there were other venues: during 1938 some meetings were held in the new science block. At the advent of the 2nd World War an edict from Grand Lodge suspended all masonic meetings, but the ban was lifted in November, enabling a belated installation to take place. During the earlier years of the war when the number present was small and there was a blackout of the school hall; some meetings were held in the prefects' room, the boys' common room and the art room. Dr. Magson retired in March 1946 and, as his successor as headmaster was not a mason, an approach was made to Phoenix lodge, where they were welcomed.

When meeting at the school - a Methodist Foundation - no alcoholic refreshment could be served. From September 1950 the number of meetings was increased to ten per year (each month, except December and August). From June 1957 the lodge moved - as did Phoenix - to become tenants of Fortitude Lodge at Union Place, where meetings continued until 1972, when the move came to the new premises at Cyril Road. The first meeting here was in November 1972, and the number of meetings a year was reduced to six (alternate months).

It has been a feature of Truro School Lodge that any installed master should be permitted to initiate his own son. Seven of the masters or P.M's have performed this ceremony; W.Bros. Dr. E.H. Magson (twice), E.S. Vincent, A. Mutton, T.R.E. Trenerry, J.O. Roberts, W.H.L. Pearce and E.F.J. Purkis. By courtesy of the reigning W.M., W.Bro. W.L. White (Phoenix) and W.Bro. J. Ogden (Fortitude) also had this privilege. W.Bro. Trenerry also installed his son, Roger in 1974. A letter from the secretary of the Old Masonian's Lodge in January 1952 asked if the lodge would undertake to make Bro. J. Armitage, a master mason. Squadron Leader Armitage, D.F.C., was on sick leave in Cornwall and would be unable to attend his own lodge: the ceremony was held in the following March. In July 1993 the lodge was honoured by the attendance of the officers of the province for the dedication of its first lodge banner, given by Bro. Tom Lilley Past Provincial G.St.B. Some members of the lodge have received Grand Rank: Dr. E.H. Magson, P.A.G.D.C. (1940) and The Lord Bishop of Truro, Dr. J.W. Hunkin, Grand Chaplain (1942). On the occasion of Dr. Hunkin's appointment the lodge voted "a sum of 20 guineas" for the purchase of both full and undress regalia for his use. A.J. Roberts, P.J.G.D. (1951), who was Provincial G.Secretary 1945 -52, and Deputy Provincial Grand Master 1952 - 64. E.P. Adams, P.G.Std.Br. (1952), Provincial G. Secretary 1952-58.

W.Bro. E.S. Vincent, P.A.G.D.C. (1960) wrote 'A Record of Masonry in the Province of Cornwall 1751 to 1959'. It was published as a limited edition of 300 copies. C.W. Cook, P.A.G.D.C. (1941), was the longest serving Provincial D.C., from 1933 to 1954. From 1968 until W.Bro. A.R.G. Vigus, P.A.G.D.C., became a joining member in 1982 there were no Grand Officers who were members of the lodge. Pride of place for long service goes to Bro. B.S. Davey, Past Provincial G. Tyler, who was tyler of the lodge at its consecration and until he retired because of failing health in 1973; a total of 37 years. In appreciation of his long service the brethren presented him with a gold watch. W.Bro.E.S. Vincent, the first secretary, served continuously - except for war service - until his installation as W.M. in 1961. W.Bro.E.P. Adams was treasurer from 1936-1940 and 1944-58: in 1943 he became Worshipful Master. W. Bro. J.R. Slater was treasurer from 1958-1984, W.Bro. J.S. Vincent, secretary from 1961-87 and W.Bro. G.J. Hendra, organist 1963-73 and 1979-85.

W.Bro. Peter Roberts (lodge secretary for over 16 years) was appointed to PGStB in 2001.

Lodge Histories

TEWINGTON LODGE No. 5698, ST. AUSTELL.

The lodge was consecrated at the St. Austell masonic hall by the Deputy Provincial Grand Master the Hon. Sir Montague Eliot, on 22 March 1938, with the first W.M., W.Bro. W.P. Northey installed by the Provincial G.Secretary W.Bro. F.A. Rawling. Twenty-nine other lodges were represented. At the first regular meeting the following month three candidates were balloted for as candidates and nine joining members proposed. In May, Herbert John Brown Wilson was the first initiate. Not until 1959 was the number of meetings reduced from 12 to ten a year. Because of Grand Lodge instructions no meeting took place in September 1939, and during the war military uniforms were confirmed as acceptable clothing in lodges. In July 1940 meetings were again suspended and not resumed until October. A typical wartime emergency meeting came in February 1942 when the candidate was a Sub-Lieutenant in the Royal Navy, Bro. William Francis Clarke "who may be moved to a distant part at an early date." Some time later the candidate was Bro. H.B. Daniel, on leave from the R.A.F: between 1941-45 the membership increased from 38 to 55. There was no record of any brother being a war casualty. In peacetime came combined lodges of instruction with Peace and Harmony, the mother lodge, and the regular annual exchange meetings from 1953 to today. Founder-member W.Bro. L.A. Richards, preceptor, was a great influence on the high standards achieved: in 1967 he was promoted to Grand Rank as P.A.G.D.C.

By 1953 membership was 94 and by 1958 increased to 106 but since then there has been a decline to 101 in 1974 and in 2000 only 61. This has not been due to a lack of candidates - although with fewer meetings there were three candidates each year instead of four - but probably due to the resignation of older members and to the number of younger ones leaving the area. Since the 1960s greater emphasis has been placed on fundraising for local non-masonic charities, thanks to the social committee. Of great help in maintaining the old and imposing Victorian lodge building and temple has been the building committee of the four St. Austell lodges, working in co-operation with the trustees. In 1988 Tewington held a ceremony and dinner to celebrate the 50th anniversary, feeling that the tenets and spirit of freemasonry have been upheld, and giving confidence to maintain these in the future.

A special ceremony for Freemasons at St. Austell for the new Masonic Hall.

Lodge Histories

COLVILLE SMITH LODGE No. 5738, FALMOUTH.

The Colville Smith Lodge was named after R.W.Bro. Sir Philip Colville Smith, who had been Grand Secretary (1917-37) as well as Deputy Provincial Grand Master from 1899 until his death in November 1937. The lodge was consecrated in October 1938 by his successor, R.W.Bro. Sir Montague Eliot, and among the founder members was Lieut. Col. Sir Hugh Protheroe Smith, formerly Chief Constable of Cornwall, and brother of the late Sir Philip. Sir Hugh Protheroe Smith remained an active member of the lodge for a number of years until his death in 1961 at the age of 90, and his candidate, W.Bro. W.J. Roberts, went on to be W.M. in 1962. The founder members of the lodge have been a major influence for many years. The first W.M. was W.Bro. W.H. Laity, P.G.St.B. who was an active member until his death in 1968; the first secretary W.Bro. R.A. Truscott, and his assistant who became W.M. in 1943, W.Bro. G.B.H. Aggett between them served as secretaries until 1960: The J.D. was Bro. R. Jory who became W.M. in 1945 and was the last founder member when he died in 1979. Two years earlier, in 1977, the Grand Secretary, R.W.Bro. J.W. Stubbs visited the lodge in Falmouth, which he found particularly interesting as he had been made a Master Mason by Sir Philip. The lodge has celebrated its consecration, and honoured the memory of its founder members on a number of occasions, including its 21st, 50th and 60th anniversaries. The first took the form of an anniversary festival held on 15 April 1959. Its 50th anniversary in 1988 was particularly poignant as the W.M. was W.Bro. A. Jory, son of a founder member. The lodge was honoured by the company of the Provincial Grand Master R.W.Bro. Nicholas Barrington to a luncheon on the day of its 60th anniversary and to a working of a ceremony on the following Tuesday.

As befits a lodge from the 'Packet' port, it has been pleased to receive visitors from overseas and learn something about their foreign constitutions. In 1966 V.W.Bro. F. Wills. P.D.D.G.M., from Ontario was welcomed and in 1977 W.Bro. J.A. Bendix, P.M. of Sincerity Lodge, Maryland U.S.A. In 1984 the lodge was honoured by the visit of a large number of brethren from the Netherlands Constitution who were welcomed by the Provincial Grand Master R.W.Bro. the Hon. Robert Eliot. The lodge was still relatively young during the 2nd World War, but a contribution was made to the Mayor's Spitfire Fund, and a resolution was also passed to send a hundred cigarettes to each of the brethren who were serving in the Armed Forces. On a lighter note and to show that the lodge has always been forward looking, a resolution was passed as early as November 1968 to convert the subscriptions in the bye-laws to decimal currency, despite the fact that decimalisation was still over two years away. Two of its brethren have been promoted to Grand Rank. W.Bro. R. Fiddick, who was Provincial S.G.W. in 1975 and received the P.G.M's Certificate of Service to Freemasonry, was given the rank of P.G.St.B. in 1977. W.Bro. B.C. Beattie who was Provincial J.G.W. in 1985 was also given the rank of P.G.St.B. in 1991 and further promoted to P.J.G.D. in 2000. No history of the lodge would be complete without also mentioning the contribution of W.Bro. W. 'Harman' Pearce, Past Provincial J.G.W., who served as secretary for 23 years and gave immense support to the lodge and encouragement to the younger brethren until his death in 1994. The Colville Smith Lodge enjoys a close relationship with its mother lodge, Love and Honour No. 75, and was pleased to extend the family tree in 1990 when it helped launch Cornish Maritime Lodge No. 9374.

Lodge Histories

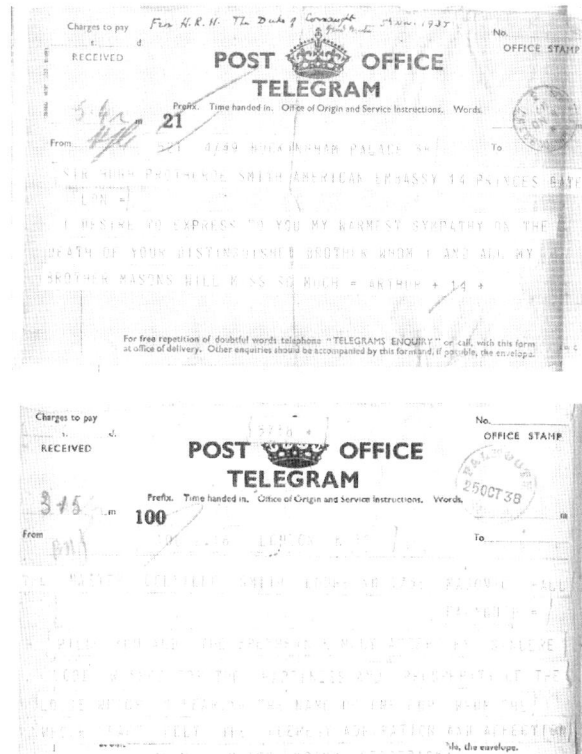

Copies of two telegrams, displayed in the menu card at the 60th anniversary luncheon of the Colville Smith Lodge, Falmouth, No. 5738 in October 1998. Sir P. Colville Smith who was Grand Secretary for many years, was Deputy PGM of Cornwall for nearly 40 years.

One is from the Grand Master HRH The Duke of Connaught to Lieut-Col. Sir Hugh Protheroe Smith (formerly Chief Constable of Cornwall) on the death of his brother in 1937: "I desire to express to you my warmest sympathy on the death of your distinguished brother whom I and all my brother Masons will miss so much."

The other is from the Grand Secretary in October 1938 conveying wishes for the happiness of "the lodge which is bearing the name of one for whom the whole craft felt the deepest admiration and affection."

Lodge Histories

LYONESSE LODGE No. 6014, PENZANCE.

This lodge consecration in 1945 was the first in the province since the outbreak of the 2nd World War. It was a time of great shortages, reflected in the fact that it was four years before the lodge had its own collars, jewels and working tools. There was no banquet after the consecration by the Provincial Grand Master the Earl of St. Germans, at St. John's Hall, Penzance, on the 19 April. With food rationing in force the brethren and provincial guests were entertained to tea. The P.G.M. said the ceremony was remarkable proof of the flourishing conditions of freemasonry in West Cornwall, for it was only 16 years since the second lodge (St. Levan) was consecrated in the town. The Provincial Chaplain, the Revd C.H.S. Buckley, Vicar of Gulval, spoke of the name. According to legend a cable tow's length from the cliffs at Land's End began the ancient land of Lyonesse. Near there was the valley of Avalon in which lay the remains of King Arthur. Great difficulty was experienced in acquiring lodge furniture and regalia. Brethren wore whatever colour clothing they possessed. All the regalia houses were approached for the supply of a banner - but the shortest time quoted was six years! As a result of this, one of the founder members, W.Bro. Frank Latham, who was an amateur artist as well as the Penzance borough surveyor, designed and - with the assistance of his wife - made the banner. The only material available was course hessian on which he painted the scene. The pole was found in the loft of a founder member's building yard: the frieze, cord and tassels were supplied by Mrs. Latham from old curtain fittings, and she also did all the needlework. In the foreground is the expanse of ocean and bordering on the ebbing and flowing tide is a rampart, encircling a paved lodge of the King Arthur's type in plan. The setting sun is closing the day and the rays of the Longships Lighthouse come into view.

At this time men were coming home from the Armed Forces, resuming normal life, and many wished to join freemasonry. During the first year of Lyonesse 16 meetings were held, 18 members were initiated. In each year 1946 - 50 there were eight initiates. These were busy times and in the first ten years the membership rose to 106 and in twenty years to 129. In 1957, however, the Past Masters decided that unless some restraint was exercised the membership would soon exceed 150. It was decided to restrict candidates to one per lodge meeting and the intake restricted to three per year. This policy has continued, but there has been a reduction in membership since the heydays of the 1960s. Because of the poor quality of wartime ink, in 1959 the warrant of Lyonesse had to be returned to Grand Lodge to be re-written. Similarly, because of the poor quality of wartime paint, it was agreed the banner needed refurbishment, and in 1980 this was carried out by amateur artist and member W.Bro. Tim Hawes. It was in February 1949 that a representative of the regalia firm of Cashmore attended the lodge and brought with him the collars, jewels and working tools ordered early in 1945. He also presented a set of wooden working tools for the pedestals and a poniard for the use of the Inner Guard. Until this time all the regalia, furniture and tools in use were loaned by Mount Sinai No. 121 and St. Levan No. 5134. Lyonesse has been honoured to have many provincial officers and Grand Officers among its members. The latter are founder-Master W.Bro. W.J. Hosken, P.A.G.D.C; W.Bro. L.E. Perkins, P.A.G.D.C. - a founder and lodge D.C.; 1952 - 76, W.Bro. R.D. Williams M.B.E., P.A.G.D.C; and the present senior member of the lodge, V.W.Bro. S.J. Pearce, P.G.Swd.Br., the Deputy P.G.M 1986 - 94. He was initiated into Lyonesse in August 1945.

An important milestone came in 1995 when W.Bro. E.C. Downing was W.M. with celebrations to mark 50 years of Lyonesse: these included a service at St. Just parish church, and 50th anniversary jewels, the first of which was presented to V.W.Bro. Pearce. The celebrations were attended by the Provincial Grand Master R.W.Bro. Nicholas Barrington. To mark his 50 years membership of the lodge Bro. Percy Harvey was presented with an inscribed Dartington glass bowl in September 2000 by W.Bro. John Davy Asst. P.G.M., on behalf of the lodge. He was initiated in August 1950. His younger brother, W.Bro. Bill Harvey (W.M. in 1974) has been Lyonesse organist for many years: their father was a founder-member and P.M. Each year P.Ms are invited to work a ceremony and there is an annual exchange with daughter lodge Penwith.

Lodge Histories

ST. EUNY LODGE No. 6025, REDRUTH.

The lodge was consecrated in the St. Andrew's Church Crypt on Thursday, 17 May 1945. The consecrating officer was the Provincial Grand Master R.W.Bro. the Earl of St. Germans. The lodge was born out of Druids' Lodge of Love and Liberality No. 589. The reason for forming a second craft lodge in Redruth was that Druids' at this particular time was very large. Many of the younger brethren were keen to progress to the chair, but because of the great numbers they had little chance. When the matter was put the Past Masters of Druids' were totally against it. However, the new lodge lobby was very strong and Bro. A.J. Paul, then a young member of Druids himself, was one of those keen to progress. He, representing the lobby went to seek the advice of the Provincial G.Secretary. W.Bro. Hall, who advised him to go directly to the P.G.M. This he did. To quote from the history of St. Euny, Bro. Arthur Paul says: "I did this and he (St. Germans) was in favour and sent me back to Druid's Lodge with his blessing. There was still strong opposition. However the P.G.M. gave me an ace to play. He said, 'Invite P.M. Thomas Shopland to be your first Master.' This was duly done and a goodly number of Druids' Past Masters and brethren rallied around in support and so St. Uny or Euny was conceived." "I say St. Uny or St. Euny", continues Bro. Paul, "because, when as acting secretary to my fellow petitioners, I submitted the proposed name I spelt it St. Uny, which was quite commonplace. I was promptly told by Canon Ladd Canney, Past Provincial G. Chaplain, and Rector of Redruth, that whilst St. Uny was used to spell the name of Redruth's patron saint, according to the old parish registers Euny is the correct way to spell it. This necessitated the sending to Grand Lodge a second request seeking to change the spelling. Things then ran rather more smoothly and the new lodge was formed.

The lodge crest, as used on the summonses was the creation of a Mr. A.C. Hambley, Bro. Paul's teacher at Redruth Art School. The crest depicts St. Euny, carrying a staff in his right hand, whilst in his left he has a Bible and psalter; also in his left hand he clutches a bag. This would have contained the

Lodge Histories

necessary for celebrating the eucharist. He would not have carried money. The crest also shows a number of animals around his feet. St. Euny, like St. Francis, was known to have a great love for animals. The year 1973 was important in the history of St. Euny Lodge and indeed of mother lodge Druids'. Until this time the Redruth masonic hall was owned and administered solely by Druids': all other lodges were their tenants. So in January, a joint committee meeting was convened to discuss the way forward, the result of which was the formation of a joint management committee, making St. Euny and Druids' joint and equal partners. In December 1976, St. Euny was presented with its first banner, made possible by the generosity of W.Bro. Charles Wilder, a joining member. The Provincial Grand Master Col. E. Perry-Morgan attended the dedication which was carried out by Bro. Revd F.R. Harwood, who also gave the oration. Two members became Mayors of Truro, W.Bro. E. Hockin and Bro. W. Flukes. In 1982 the lodge was presented with another representation of its patron saint. W.Bro. P. Phillips presented a large tapestry of St. Euny, taken from the lodge crest, hand-worked by Mrs. Phillips and was given to commemorate his year in the chair.

This 'portrait' of St. Euny was hand-stitched in wool tapestry and presented to the lodge by Mrs. Freda Phillips, the wife of W.Bro. Paul Phillips, to mark his year as Master of the Lodge.

Thread of Gold

Lodge Histories

TREWINNARD LODGE No. 6157, HAYLE.

The lodge was founded in response to the need for a second lodge in Hayle to relieve the pressure on Cornubian Lodge No. 450 and was the first lodge to be consecrated in Cornwall after the 2nd World War had ended. It was an act of faith on the part of the founders but their hopes have been more than rewarded.

The name Trewinnard is taken from one of the local landed families who also consented to the use of their Coat of Arms as a badge. To further cement the association with the Trewinnards a Bible was presented by W.Bro. Arthur Trewinnard P.A.G.D.C., at the consecration. The family maintained an active interest in the lodge and many of them were elected as honorary members. It is unusual for a lodge to be named after a family in this way, unless one of their members has been a P.G.M. or held high office in Grand Lodge. The lodge was warranted on 1 August 1945 and consecrated on Thursday 11 April 1946 by the Provincial Grand Master R.W.Bro. the Earl of St. Germans. The first W.M. was W.Bro. W.T. Blewett who along with the 23 other founders helped to lay the foundations of the lodge as it is today.

The lodge embarked on its masonic career with five candidates. During the first year the lodge was presented with a gift of £100 by Bro. T. Pascoe which was used to purchase collars and jewels for the lodge officers; and over the years other brethren have donated a number of gifts. In 1963 the lodge reached a milestone when it was presented with a patron's certificate of the Royal Masonic Hospital. Over the years the lodge has embarked on fraternal visits with other lodges and has had visiting workings with Tregenna Lodge No. 1272, St. Ives for many years.

In 1971 the lodge celebrated its silver jubilee, celebrated in some style, quite different from the 1946 time of rationing. The lodge was presented with a Loving Cup, to be used at installations, by W.Bro. and Mrs. R.H.R. Tilly. In 1970 one of the founders and stalwarts of the lodge who served as treasurer for 16 years, W.Bro. L.T. Roberts, died.

The year 1972 proved to be an important year for Hayle freemasons, for in April the Provincial Grand Master R.W.Bro. Col. Edwin Perry Morgan, accompanied by his wardens entered the refurbished temple in procession and re-opened the Hayle masonic premises. He mentioned this was the first occasion he had opened a lodge - other than Provincial G. Lodge - since he had occupied the chair of St. Andrew's Lodge in 1946.

Lodge Histories

W.Bro. F.M. Biggleston P.P.J.G.W., a founder of the lodge for 21 years was a guiding light as D.C. In 1973 he celebrated 50 years in masonry. In July 1975 the new Trewinnard banner, presented by Mrs. G. Taylor in memory of her late husband W.Bro. H.G.O. Taylor (Chaplain of the lodge when he died in 1973) was dedicated by the Provincial G. Chaplain, the Revd Canon Harmer. In 1978 came a change in the dates of meeting to the fourth Monday, January to November, excepting August and third Monday in December. In October of 1978 the new temple at Hayle was re-named "The Perry Morgan Temple" and the old temple called The Cornubian Temple in honour of the founder lodge in Hayle. In 1984 new cushions were presented for the W.M. and warden's pedestals by Bro. J.R. Middleton and a candle snuffer by W.Bro. E.P. Lashbrook. In 1985 two of the founder-members of the lodge died within ten days of each other, W.Bros. S. and C. Blewett.

In 1986 the lodge prepared to celebrate 40 years and in March W.Bro. R.J. Hosking gave a talk 'The First Forty Years'. The festive board was enhanced by the production of a cake resembling a Master Mason's apron, made by W.Bro. C.W.W. Maddern. In 1987 W.Bro. Steventon-Pinn was presented with a gift from the lodge to mark his 50 years in masonry; he in turn thanked the W.M. and brethren and presented the lodge with four officers' collars. 1989 was a landmark year in that W.Bro. L.T.F. Pascoe, the secretary, received Grand Honours with the rank of P.G.St.B. and the lodge presented him with his regalia. In 1990 W.Bro. Maddern resigned as D.C. after 17 years in office due to ill health, and was elected an honorary member and an inscribed watch was presented to him.

The early 1990s saw a number of senior officers retire from their offices due to increasing age: amongst these were the treasurer, W.Bro. W.K. Coombe and the almoner W.Bro. W.G. Rowe, both of whom were presented with inscribed watches. In 1993 W.Bro. F.L. James received the Provincial Grand Masters Certificate of Service. In 1994 the lodge was presented with a replacement organ by W.Bro. R.H.R. Tilly and his son Bro. J. Tilly, to replace the organ they had given to the temple some years previously. The lodge celebrated the first 50 years of working in 1996; from its inception the lodge has been a family lodge in every sense of the word, with sons following their fathers into the lodge and some even being fortunate enough to initiate their own sons into freemasonry.

Lodge Histories

FISTRAL LODGE No. 6258, NEWQUAY.

Prior to the founding of Fistral Lodge, masonry in Newquay had had its ups and downs. The first masonic lodge to be founded in Newquay had been Fort Lodge in 1875: this was followed in 1899 by St. Michael Lodge. Unfortunately Fort Lodge was by this time very weak and in 1901 surrendered its warrant. Masonry in Newquay had expanded and grown in the intervening years following the failure of Fort Lodge and by the 1940s it was felt that a second lodge in the town could be sustained. A joint committee meeting was convened on 15 December 1945, comprising members of St. Michael Lodge and founder-members of the proposed lodge when it was resolved that a new one would be supported under the name of Fistral. In January of the following year, a meeting of the founders was held to sign the petition and a sub-committee was formed to deal with any matters concerned with the launch. The secretary of St. Michael Lodge wrote to the province advising that in the opinion of the lodge a second lodge in Newquay could not only be sustained, but was desirable. On 17 May 1946, Fistral Lodge was consecrated by the Provincial Grand Master the Rt.Hon. the Earl of St. Germans, and the new lodge was duly launched. Fistral, being the second lodge, did not own the building in which they met so they did not have the problems associated with such ownership. They did, however, bring a new vision and a willingness to work hard to establish itself in the masonic world. Over the years it has supplied various artefacts which have been for the benefit of all the lodges who meet in Newquay. In 1954 the lodge became a patron of the Royal Masonic Hospital, a remarkable effort: to mark this the certificate was presented by W.Bro. Robinson, secretary - treasurer of the hospital lodge fund. In 1957 the P.Ms were invited to work the ceremony; this proved so successful this has now become a feature of the masonic year. The lodge continued to flourish, more than fulfilling the hopes and aspirations of the founders, and in 1976/77 held a special effort in its support of the Masonic Hospital and raised £465. In 1977,

the lodge achieved a notable milestone, in its history: it sponsored a Royal Arch Chapter so that its members could complete their masonry under the banner of "Fistral". All lodge members worked hard to make the 1981 R.M.I.B. Festival a success.

January 1985 proved to be a most unusual month: due to a very severe snowstorm the lodge meeting was cancelled. A dispensation for a meeting on 18 February was granted, but the weather was still inclement and only 15 members turned up. This was the first time this had happened in lodge history. In May 1986 the lodge applied to close during the months of June, July and August each year; this was the first major alteration to the bye-laws of the lodge since its consecration. The lodge has always worked very closely with the other lodges in Newquay and in 1988 agreed to pay £1,500 as its share of the bank loan incurred by the management committee for the building alterations. Many members of the lodge accompanied the Provincial Grand Master to Earl's Court in 1992 for the 275th celebrations. In that year the lodge acquired a new banner, dedicated by the P.G.M. and the provincial officers; the Provincial G. Chaplain, Bro. the Revd Michael Pearce gave the oration. In its short history the lodge has been fortunate in attracting masons of high calibre and this was recognised by the appointment of a number of them over the years to Grand Rank and senior rank in the province. W.Bro. J.J. Hoskin a founder-member and first secretary was appointed to P.G.St.B. in 1961; this was followed by W.Bro. C.J. Lugg in 1972 and W.Bro. A.C. Hooper in 1973 who both received the rank of P.A.G.D.C.

Consecrating officers and founders of Fistral Lodge No. 6258 in May 1948. In the front central group are the Rt. Hon. Earl of St. Germans (PGM), Wor. Master G.A. Bayley and Canon H.R. Jennings (Dep. PGM).

Lodge Histories

ESSA LODGE No. 6278, SALTASH.

In December 1943 W.Bro. Charles Devonshire M.C., was installed as W.M. of Zetland Lodge, Saltash and in his year of office some 26 ceremonies were worked, bringing the total membership to about 220. Initiates had little hope of reaching the chair in less than 25 years and it was felt that it was time to think about a new lodge. The end of the war and signs of rapid growth in the area accelerated the idea. Following a meeting in February 1946 a petition was submitted and a warrant was issued. The consecration took place on 25 September 1946 in the Saltash Guildhall with 170 brethren present. The Provincial Grand Master the Rt. Hon. the Earl of St. Germans conducted the ceremony and the Deputy P.G.M., V.W. Bro. Canon H.R. Jennings installed the first W.M., W.Bro. Devonshire. The new lodge was made up mainly of Zetland (the mother lodge) members with several from other lodges in Devon and Cornwall. In October 1949 Bro. G.H. Hopper became the first member 'from the floor' of the lodge to reach the chair and the most memorable meeting of his year came when he initiated H.R.H. Prince Chula Chakrabongse of Thailand. The Prince, soldier, diplomat, author, translator, racing car manager and television personality as a member of the Brains Trust panel, was a remarkable man. In pre-war days he and his cousin H.R.H. Prince Birabongse won many laurels in motor racing and was a very popular personality. He was never the W.M. of Essa but in 1960 became W.M. of his old school lodge, the Harrovian Lodge No. 4653. The clock over the door of the refectory at the masonic hall, Saltash, was a gift from him to Essa.

The decision to build the Tamar road bridge caused many changes for masons in Saltash when the masonic building in Lower Fore Street had to be demolished to make way for the bridge foundations. The July 1959 meeting of Essa was the last masonic function held in the old hall and a new site had to be found for future meetings. The kindness of Loyal Victoria lodge at Callington and Eliot Lodge at St. Germans saved the day when Essa were invited to use their temples: today Essa still exchanges visits with them from links forged in the 1960s. In October 1962 the newly installed W.M. W.Bro. A.J. Colville led a delegation of Essa members to the ceremony of laying the foundation stone of the new hall in Dunheved Road, Saltash and October 1963 saw the return of the lodge to the town, which was the first masonic meeting held in the new hall. In 1996 the lodge celebrated its 50th anniversary when the Provincial Grand Master R.W. Bro. Nicholas Barrington attended the dedication of the new lodge banner. He was accompanied by a team of his provincial officers including the Chaplain, Bro., the Revd S.W. Leach who delivered the oration.

Lodge Histories

It is ten-o'clock by this ESSA Lodge clock presented in November 1954 by Bro. H.R.H. Prince Chula Chakrabongse, of Thailand, a member of No. 6278. The clock hangs in the lodge refectory beside a plaque marking the gift and a photograph of Prince and Princess Chula.

Lodge Histories

TRENWITH LODGE No. 6309, ST. IVES.

The period following World War I had seen a general increase in the popularity of freemasonry, which led to the foundation of a Royal Arch Chapter and a Mark Lodge in St. Ives. In each case the prime movers as founders were already senior members of Tregenna lodge which was well over 100 strong and growing, with consequent very slow progress to W.M. One brother who had become a joining member in 1926 had risen to I.G. by 1946! Realising that interest would once more increase after World War II, much the same set of senior brethren decided informally in 1944 to test support for a new lodge, convening a meeting in January 1945. On 19th January 1946 "the Second Great War having been won", as the minutes put it, a successful meeting of potential founders was held and the petition signed. By June all arrangements were complete and the lodge was consecrated on 30 September 1946 in St. Ives Guildhall. The first Master was W.Bro. W.J. Jacobs, a P.M. of Tregenna and P.G.St.B. He was also the owner and editor of one of the local papers and saw to it that masonic occasions received full publicity, installations being well reported with lists of officers. Trenwith was the sixth lodge to be consecrated in the province within a period of 18 months.

A 'gentlemen's agreement' was reached by Tregenna brethren who became founders or joining members of Trenwith. They would confine their progress to one lodge only, thus clearing a log-jam and reducing to a manageable period the progress to the chair. The first seven Masters were all founders, the eighth a joining member from Tregenna and the ninth, W.Bro. R.E. May, was the first initiate to reach that rank, in 1954. During the first year there were seven initiates. A year later the W.M. expressed his appreciation of help from Tregenna for use of collars etc. and suggested that it was time that Trenwith provided its own: the new regalia was worn for the first time in August 1949. The collars have since been replaced but the jewels are still proudly worn, engraved with the names of those who presented them. Another item still in use is the lectern Bible presented by W.Bro. W.Sandrey, treasurer, in 1947, on behalf of his sister. This Bible had been given to her husband by his lodge Boksburg No. 2480, Transvaal, in 1925. The names of successive W.Ms are inscribed in this after their installation.

Lodge Histories

The premises were refurbished with new seating in the temple and rearranged accommodation downstairs, including for the first time a bar. Informal social events were the order of the day, and the first formal ladies' night was at the Porthminster hotel in 1954. Annual Christmas parties for children of the two lodges were instituted in 1958. In 1948 Bro. Peter Stevens, a joining member from Peace and Harmony Lodge, St. Austell, became tyler and for many years he and Mrs. Stevens provided refreshment after labour. Bro. Stevens, after many years as P.P.G.Tyler, was promoted to P.P.G.A.D.C. in 1984 and was made an honorary member of Trenwith: in 1993 he celebrated his jubilee in the craft in his mother lodge.

For much of its life Trenwith has had a steady flow of candidates, bringing its membership to 74 by 1956. On occasions when no candidate was available a lecture was arranged. A paper given by the Abbot of Buckfast to the Devonshire Masonic Study Circle entitled 'Our separated brethren - Freemasonry and the Roman Catholic Church' was read by the D.C. of Lyonesse Lodge in January 1969. The summons for that meeting added, 'No discussion of this paper will take place.' In 1978, Bro. E.V. Turner presented a set of working tools, made by him, which are still in use. Relations with the mother lodge were usually good, with exchange workings being quite frequent. For many years the summonses had printed 'Honorary Member: the W.M. of Tregenna Lodge'. This was at last ruled as unconstitutional and the title 'Guest Member' was substituted. The two masters retire from lodge together and occupy adjoining seats at refreshment whenever possible. During the celebrations of Tregenna centenary in 1970, Trenwith presented a set of gavels. Visiting between the two lodges adds much interest to proceedings as workings differ considerably. By 1991 Trenwith's jubilee was in sight and it was suggested that a banner would be an appropriate addition: a design by W.Bro. E. Cothey was accepted and a banner made by his wife, Win, was completed in time to be dedicated at the installation meeting in October 1992. The 50th anniversary came in 1996.

Lodge Histories

THE EARL OF ST. GERMANS LODGE No. 7031, WADEBRIDGE.

During the immediate post-war years discussions took place in Wadebridge over the possible formation of an additional craft lodge to meet the needs of the growing town and the surrounding rural area. Eventually the 15 founding members, of which one is still a member, signed and submitted the petition to the United Grand Lodge. This was granted and the date for the consecration of the new lodge was set for 18 January 1951, with the meeting held in the town hall.

The consecrating officer, the Provincial Grand Master R.W.Bro. The Earl of St. Germans, had graciously allowed the new lodge to adopt his name and the family Coat of Arms. This formed a bond between the Eliot family, the Eliot Lodge No. 1164 and the freemasons of Wadebridge which still exists. This bond was further strengthened when, in September 1960, W.Bro. F. Wilce and his officers travelled to St. Germans to perform a ceremony, a practice which continues with exchange visits taking place in May and September.

The years 1955–56 saw W.Bros. D.L. Lang and E.B. Davey as W.Ms: both were to take over from the original P.Ms in forming the future of the lodge. W.Bro. Lang, was for many years D.C. and W.Bro. Davey was elected treasurer of the lodge in September 1959, an office he held until 1987 and later he was invested as P.G.St.B. W.Bro. G.H. Gardner, the founder treasurer, was appointed and invested as Asst. P.G.M. in 1959 at the provincial annual meeting. From 1964 there has been an exchange working in January and February with the mother lodge Molesworth. The 1970s saw a concentrated effort to raise money for the 1981 Festival with such events as buffet dances, charity socials and a 200 club formed between St. Germans, Molesworth, One and All and St. Petroc lodges.

Despite losing some distinguished P.Ms the lodge continued to flourish throughout the 1980s, being in the forefront in supporting all the charities, with great emphasis being placed in helping at Cadogan Court (the R.M.B.I. home at Exeter) and in supporting the 2002 festival.

Lodge Histories

In 1991 came the introduction of a golf tournament held between the three craft lodges of the town to further improve good fellowship, with any surplus funds being equally distributed between the charity stewards. It was also decided that the charity stewards should work together for the 2002 festival. Also in that year, Bro. R.B. Radford retired as tyler of the lodge after 31 years of loyal service. In 1994 W.Bro. B. Tinker was appointed as Assistant Provincial G.Secretary, and three years later, Provincial G.Secretary. W.Bro. W.D. Gilbert was appointed to the rank of P.A.G.D.C. in 1995, and two years later W.Bro. Tinker to similar rank. The year ended with the sad news of the death of W.Bro. E.B. Davey, whilst on a cruise holiday.

The installation meetings for both 1998 and 1999 were milestones as the current W.Ms stood down to allow W.Bros. P.G. Lawrence and P.W. Collins to install their sons. In 1999 W.Bro. F. Wilce, the only surviving founder still a member of the lodge, celebrated his 90th birthday and to mark the occasion he was made an Honorary Member. In recognition of the honour he donated £100 to the lodge asking that it be used in some permanent way. It was decided to have a three drawer working tool chest made to house the silver tools bought as a result of a legacy from the late Bro. C. Ayles. The lodge celebrated its golden jubilee in January 2001. In that year W.Bro. Ivan Tregaskis (Editor of the Provincial Year Book) was appointed to P.AGDC.

Lodge Histories

KING ARTHUR LODGE No. 7134, TINTAGEL.

It would seem appropriate, whilst reviewing the history of the lodge, also to refer to the building and the development of the halls - as this much influenced the formation and progress of the King Arthur Lodge. Between 1929 and 1933, Mr. Frederick Glasscock who was a director of the custard powder manufacturing company Monk & Glass, instigated and funded the building of King Arthur's Hall at Tintagel. The hall was built as the headquarters of an organisation that he formed known as the Knights of the Round Table. The building was erected by local craftsmen using slate, granite, serpentine and greenstone from nearby quarries, and is decorated with 73 priceless stained glass windows - making it worthy of the description that it is one of the most beautiful masonic temples in this country. In the mid–1930's whilst returning from a visit to America to recruit overseas members for his organisation, Mr. Glasscock died aboard the Queen Mary and his family was not willing to continue his organsation. As a result, the hall then had limited use - especially during the war years. In the period 1950 to 1952 a number of local freemasons (who had been travelling to Wadebridge, Bude and Launceston to attend lodge) were aware that the trustees of the Glasscock estate were anxious to wind up the affairs. These brethren joined together and raised sufficient capital to buy the hall for approximately £7,500. The consecration was held on the 25 April 1952, the consecrating officer being W.Bro. A.J. Roberts, Provincial G. Secretary, 23 founders and over 200 visitors attended and were easily accommodated in the impressive large hall.

During the first year six new members were initiated and six joining members were admitted, of whom only two remain on the lodge register. During that first year, and for some years afterwards, each initiate and joining member was invited to make a loan to the lodge in order to reduce the bank loan. Several gifts of lodge furniture were made. After some particularly cold summer meetings, two senior members were instructed to purchase a heating system for use in both halls. Unfortunately both these gentlemen were deaf and at the official switching on of the new system so much noise was created by the fan arrangement that nothing could be heard of the ceremony that was taking place! The W.M. had to signal to the S.W. at the far end of the hall and one gavel pad was broken by the vigorous force applied by the J.W. to make himself heard above the din. Subsequently the heating system was switched off and the ceremony continued in a cold but quiet manner!

In April 1959 the loans made by the brethren to purchase the halls were repaid and a bank loan of £7,750 obtained to purchase all the shares in a company called King Arthur's Hall Limited. The shop area and hall visits were operated commercially by a shop manager. In May 1959 Provincial G.Lodge was held at the hall. During the same year members of this lodge visited King Arthur Lodge No. 6953 in London. April 1962 saw the first initiate of the lodge, W.Bro. E. Batten, installed: at the January meeting, due to the severe weather, the ceremony was cut short. During the year the Royal Arch Chapter was formed. Several members of the lodge paid a visit to King Arthur Lodge, Bournemouth in 1964 and during this year a new organ was presented to the lodge by W.Bro. Sprayson. The dining room was opened in 1976. As the commercial trading in the shop and hall increased during 1979, the company leased both ventures to a tenant. This arrangement has continued making the building self-financing, enabling the bank loan to be cleared and repairs, maintenance and new equipment to be paid for from the annual rental income. In 1981 the lodge suffered exceptional losses amongst the officers and brethren due to death and illness. W.Bro. Pat Rundle remained in the chair for two years, and together with the P.M. and officers helped the lodge to recover from a very low point, from which it has grown strongly. The lodge has two temples, one for summer and the other for winter meetings: visitors will understand why.

In April 2002 the lodge will celebrate its Golden Jubilee.

Lodge Histories

CARLYON LODGE No. 7392, ST. AUSTELL.

There was one lodge in St. Austell, Peace and Harmony, consecrated in 1844: due to excessive numbers and long waiting lists, Tewington lodge came into being in 1937. Numbers increased and the waiting time for prospective candidates became so long that a decision was made to form yet another. In November 1955, Carlyon lodge was consecrated in the Masonic Hall, Newquay, because of the large numbers attending. Sixteen brothers became founder members and in 2000 there were two founders still members of the lodge. There was a steady increase in numbers from 40 in 1955 to 56 in 1960 and now stands at a fairly constant 70. The lodge minutes, recorded by five successive secretaries, exhibit a constant state of virtually illegible handwriting and at first sight appear rather hum-drum and repetitive, but, at closer inspection, there is little variation in procedure revealed and a very strict adherence to the ritual.

So a very strong sense of continuity is achieved. The temple itself was built in 1900 and is a very good example of late Victorian architecture - cosy and intimate with an excellent atmosphere. It was thought at one time that, with road developments around the town, the temple might be subject to demolition. Because of its age, the fabric of the building has required re-embellishment and, as it is now the home of four lodges, a building committee has been formed and is responsible for repairs. The stained glass windows have been restored to their former glory. Fund raising is constantly in operation and over the years the Royal Masonic Hospital received generous contributions from the lodge: many other masonic and non-masonic charities are assisted. One of the proofs of the popularity of any lodge must be the number of visitors they attract: in this Carlyon is singularly fortunate: meetings are held on the first Wednesday of every month, July and August excepted.

ST. MELLYON No. 7422, MULLION.

Over a celebration drink at the Old Inn in Mullion, following the initiation of two men from Mullion into freemasonry late in 1954, it was suggested that a lodge should be formed there. At this time there were several members of True and Faithful Lodge, Helston, living in and around Mullion as well as several members of various 'up-country' lodges. Bros. A.H.E. Mitchell and L.R. Francis canvassed local masons and a meeting was held in February 1955 at the Polurrian hotel when it was resolved a lodge be formed and that other masons living in Mullion be invited to become founders: True and Faithful lodge was asked to sponsor. A meeting in March was attended by 17 prospective founders and it was decided to send the details to the Provincial G. Secretary. It was agreed to meet at the Polurrian and be a dining lodge, meeting the second Wednesday in October, November, December, January, February and March with the installation meeting in December. The petition was approved in September 1955.

There was great disappointment when it was found that Bro. Laurie Francis could not become a founder as he had not been a member of the craft for the required three years. In recognition of the amount of work he had done to bring the lodge into being it was unanimously agreed that he must rank as the senior of the prospective joining members. The lodge was consecrated in December 1955 by the Provincial Grand Master R.W.Bro.Col. E.N. Willyams, assisted by provincial officers. The lodge continued to flourish with two brethren being initiated each year and attracting several joining members. Because the lodge met only six times a year a double ceremony was worked at the March meeting. In 1971 the lodge was pleased that one of its founders, W.Bro. Bert Anthony, was appointed P.A.G.D.C. He was the first of several members to receive grand rank. In 1974 W.Bro. Francis was appointed Provincial G.D.C. and in 1976 P.A.G.D.C. In 1980 he rose to the rank of Assistant Provincial Grand Master and in 1981 was promoted to P.S.G.D. In the same year W.Bro. Stewart Hancock received the rank of P.A.G.D.C. In 1982 W.Bro. Francis received further honours when he was appointed Deputy P.G.M., and in 1984 promoted to V.W.Bro. with the rank of P.G.Swd.B. In 1989 W.Bro. Hancock was promoted to P.J.G.D., (he was Provincial G.D.C. for seven years) and W.Bro. Richard Church appointed P.A.G.D.C.

Lodge Histories

The lodge has a strong and supportive membership and candidates every year since it was consecrated: in 1974 four brethren were initiated. Possibly unique in Cornish freemasonry was the 'raising' ceremony by W.Bro. W. Minns of his two sons at the same meeting. Over the years members have raised thousands of pounds for charities.

Sadly, V.W.Bro. Francis died in 2001, after a long illness.

Trevaunance Lodge with W. Master, W.Bro. D.A. Hoskings and Past Masters in April 1989.

PENDENNIS LODGE No. 7520, PENRYN.

Pendennis Lodge was consecrated on 4 April 1957 at the Princess Pavilion, Falmouth: the ceremony was carried out by the Provincial Grand Master R.W.Bro. Col. E.N. Willyams supported by the senior provincial officers. The first and subsequent meetings of the lodge were held at the Masonic Hall, Falmouth. In January 1967 the lodge moved its place of meeting to the St. Michael's Hotel, and remained there until the hotel changed hands in 1976 when it moved back. In February 1985 the lodge transferred to the Masonic Hall, Penryn where it still meets.

Meetings are held nine times each year, excluding the summer months of June, July and August. Originally a full dining lodge, dining for members is now optional but it is the lodge tradition that evening dress is worn by the lodge officers. The original lodge officers provided the jewels of their office in silver and presented them to the lodge. Most of the lodge furniture was made by W.Bro. J.T. Paget and his two sons and W.Bro. Boaz, and much of it is now on loan to the Roseland Lodge, Veryan. Membership of Pendennis stands at over 40.

In 1991 W.Bro. Alan Groves was appointed to the rank of PAG Supt. of Works and received promotion to PJGD in 2001.

Lodge Histories

ST. PIRAN'S LODGE No. 7620, PERRANPORTH.

This history is unusual in that the members of the lodge built their own temple. Just after the 2nd World War suggestions were made that a lodge should be formed in Perranzabuloe, first mooted by some members of Trevaunance Lodge, St. Agnes, whose numbers were increasing. No positive action was taken until 1956 when it was considered that there were sufficient numbers for this. Trevaunance raised objections as it felt the new lodge might take away possible candidates so it was proposed that a lodge be formed in Perranporth.

Several meetings were held, culminating in one at the Ponsmere Hotel, Perranporth the owner of which was W.Bro. Jack Batchelor when it was resolved that the necessary application should be made. It would be called St. Piran's, and should be primarily for members living in Perranzabuloe.

The venue, for the time being, was going to be the masonic hall in Union Place, Truro (where Marks and Spencer now stands) until such time as a purpose-built lodge was built. A list of 24 proposed founder members having been agreed formal application was made to Grand Lodge and the warrant was granted. On the 22 January 1959 the lodge was consecrated by the Provincial Grand Master R.W.Bro. Col. E.N. Willyams supported by the provincial team.

In the meantime efforts were being made to secure land in Perranporth on which to build a lodge room. W.Bro. Gerald Keen was the owner of a confectionery business in Perranporth which faced on to Boscawen Road: behind was his garden and this was the land he donated. The lodge was fortunate in having among its members W.Bros. Horace Jose and Alfred Flamank (builders and contractors) Les Salmon (accountant) Maurice Bizley (bank manager) and Cecil Beer (treasurer). The site was cleared and levelled and foundations laid.

Lodge Histories

One of the master builders took charge of the volunteer workers. Several were taught how to lay blocks under the guidance of W.Bro. Flamank. Naturally the more expert work was carried out by those who were more capable. The roof had to be erected by professional contractors for insurance reasons. Eventually the stage was reached for the interior to be plastered, painted and got ready. Again all this work was by volunteer labour, and with materials, in the main, given by members.

One Sunday morning Bros. Flamank, Marks and Caddy were painting the lodge ceiling a very dark blue. The three were standing on a moveable gantry: one stepped back to admire his handywork and went off the back of the gantry and was left hanging in mid-air by one leg! Luckily he was not hurt.

At last the building was complete and in May 1967 the lodge was dedicated by the Provincial Grand Master R.W.Bro. Col. E. Perry Morgan in an "overfilled" lodge. Towards the end of the ceremony the heat was so great that a mist formed from ground level to about three feet high and in some cases brethren were unable to see the feet of those walking round the lodge! Of the founders and first officers the sole survivor is W.Bro. L.S. 'Pip' Phillips. The first W.M. was W.Bro. J.W. Batchelor. A banner was designed by W.Bro. Jack Price: two of the ladies whose husbands were in the lodge agreed to stitch the banner with gold thread, and all the other colours needed, Mrs. Phyllis Pearn and Mrs. Edna Caddy. In March 1959 the first candidate was initiated, Bro. Ronald A. Barley. The lodge has continued to grow in numbers and in the size of the building: an extension has been added to the dining room in recent years.

Lodge Histories

PENHELLAZ LODGE No. 7680, HELSTON.

By 1958-9 the membership of True and Faithful Lodge at Helston, one of the older Cornish lodges, was getting too large, in spite of a daughter lodge, St. Mellyon, having been formed in 1955. Eleven brethren attended a special meeting and decided to proceed with the formation of a new lodge. The resolution was "it should be Penhellaz in association with the local area", the lodge room being situated at the top of Penhellaz Hill and the word of an old Cornish language derivation. The word for court or palace is Hen-lys which became Hen-llys in Saxon times, changed to Hellys through usage, then the word 'ton' for town was added - hence Helston. Presumably to distinguish the court or administrative centre the Cornish name Pen (head) was added - Penhellys now Penhellaz. It was agreed the lodge should be dining and the officers wear dinner jackets. A petition was put before the brethren of True and Faithful lodge to sponsor this fledgling which met with unanimous approval and a warrant was issued in November 1959. The consecration took place at Gwealhellis C.S. School, Helston on 20 April 1960, which 250 attended. The Provincial Grand Master R.W.Bro.Col. E.N. Willyams was the consecrating officer and the first W.M. was Bro. A. Hawkes. The question of treasurer vexed the founders until Bro. Bree Thomas volunteered for the first year only: over 40 years on, he remains in that office. The lodge meets ten times a year on the fourth Thursday in the month, August and December being the exceptions, with the installation meeting on the third Wednesday of April, to avoid the date of Grand Lodge. In early years the festive board was held at a local restaurant, but from about 1975 the masonic hall has been used.

From the first meeting candidates became available on a regular basis until 1990 when for the first time in its history no one was forthcoming. This problem was not unique to Penhellaz but was disappointing for the W.M. and the lodge. The March meeting is a P.M's night and November regarded as the Christmas meeting when carols are sung. To mark the lodge's 25th anniversary in 1985, the provincial officers headed by V.W.Bro. L.R. Francis, the Deputy Provincial Grand Master were invited to perform the ceremony at the November meeting which attracted an attendance of 104. Continuing this

Lodge Histories

celebration, in December the ladies were invited to inspect the lodge room and receive a talk by W.Bro. Fred Shepherd followed by a festive board and dancing. Of the candidates, five have been sons of members, two of whom were brothers. The best known throughout the province was probably W.Bro. John Arthur, Provincial S.G.W. in 1985. D.C. in 1987. The two brothers were John and Paul Harris, sons of Wilf who was invited back into the chair to initiate Paul. When Paul became W.M. his father was D.C. and his brother Assistant D.C. On 22 January 1990 there was a storm when trees blocked roads, buildings were severely damaged and there was a total loss of power. It was also the fourth Thursday, the Penhellaz lodge night, due to perform a ceremony. Telephone connections were either non-existent or at the best sporadic, but in spite of these difficulties sufficient members made their way to the hall in the darkness. Two brethren have received high rank in another degree. W.Bro. Ray Goodhead was Deputy Provincial Grand Master of the Mark Master Masons, W.Bro. Frank Tonkin assuming that mantle upon Ray's death, and later becoming its P.G.M.

The Temple at Helston with pillars, furniture, and paintings before it was 'remodelled'.

Thread of Gold

Lodge Histories

TOWAN LODGE No. 7684, NEWQUAY.

Towan Lodge was consecrated at the masonic hall, Newquay on Thursday 25 February, 1960 by R.W.Bro. Col. E.N. Willyams, Provincial Grand Master and his officers. Of the 26 founders only one is still a member W.Bro. A.B. Henwood. The first candidate to be initiated was Ivor Anthony Start the son-in-law of the organist, Bro. J. Waterhouse, and the first joining member was Bro. William Alan Brown the son-in-law of W.Bro. C.E. Martin. These two brethren are still members. Towan has always upheld its family traditions and there have been several father and son members, father and sons-in-law, brothers and brothers-in-law and in one case father, son and grandson. Indeed in September 1964 Mr. D.H. Pollard and Mr. A.H. Pollard (twin brothers) were initiated.

When the lodge was formed it met on the fourth Thursday during nine months but in October 1972 the meetings were changed to the first Thursday monthly, except July - September. Apart from making their masonic charitable donations Towan members have always been very outward looking and have supported the local community with donations. The wives and families of members have given great support in organising various events throughout each year which enables funds to be raised and encourages a great fellowship among the brethren. The lodge is proud of the jewel presented for the support given to mark the 250th anniversary of the United Grand Lodge. The lodge is also a Grand Patron Lodge of the New Masonic Samaritan Fund. Towan has been in existence for just over 40 years so must be considered one of the younger lodges in the province and the present members thank the founders for their foresight.

Lodge Histories

GODOLPHIN LODGE No. 7790, ST. MARY'S, ISLES OF SCILLY.

The first record of freemasonry on the Isles of Scilly was that of the formation of the Provincial G.Lodge of Scilly and the adjacent isles. This was in consequence of a deputation from the Grand Master of Masons in England, James Brydges, Marquis of Carnarvon. In those 18th century years the word deputation did not have the same meaning as now, but that the Grand Master "deputised" someone to act, on his behalf. So, on 25 November in 1755, Isaac Head, the collector of customs in Scilly, was deputised as the first P.G.M. According to the provincial year book this was only four years after the first lodge, at Falmouth, was warranted and three years after the first Provincial Grand Master was appointed in Cornwall. The islands can therefore be said to be among the earliest centres of freemasonry in the Westcountry in the mid-18th century.

The following year, 1756, the Dolphin Lodge No. 365, was warranted in the Isles of Scilly by W.Bro. Head. Here, again, the islands acted as pioneers, as it was not then the custom to give names to lodges. They were generally called after the inn in which the lodge met. To jump a few years, the Dolphin lodge became the Godolphin Lodge No. 281, in 1783, and remained until it was erased in 1851. However, the by-law dated 1799 shows No. 235, and the returns to the United Grand Lodge in 1817 bear the No. 295. The Librarian at Grand Lodge states that there were many renumberings at about this time, due to lodges being erased and because of the amalgamation of the two Grand Lodges in 1813. W.Bro. Head appears to have been a very influential person in freemasonry and in the records is a very full account of the opening of a lodge at Marazion, in 1775, by him acting on a deputation from R.W.Bro. Bell, the Cornwall Provincial Grand Master. At Marazion the lodge was consecrated publicly with a procession through the town and a service at the chapel. The lodge on St. Mary's had a very similar procession to the church every year on St. John's Day, followed by the St. John's Day Feast.

Lodge Histories

Through his work on St. Mary's, W.Bro. Head would meet the Master of every vessel passing through these waters. Scilly was then the last and first port of call for many voyaging to the far corners of the earth, in particular to America. He was a man of fervour and endowed with a missionary zeal. The records of the lodge include many Masters and mates of the ships who were initiated into freemasonry in Scilly, but did not actually become regular members of the lodge. Such names appeared once, they paid their dues, and were not seen again! They were not normally resident at the islands, but came from such places as Gottenburg (the Captain of a Dutch East Indiaman), Hamburg, Denmark, Jersey, and from ports all over Britain, including Southampton, Bristol, Chichester and Plymouth. This seems to have been normal masonic practice. Shortly after the outbreak of the American War of Independence there must have been many privateers passing through the islands, and in 1779 there were nine initiations of officers of what were described as 'Private Ships of War.' One of the Commanders had the very local name of Jenkins. This was also the year of the death of Isaac Head. Four years later, the Provincial G.Lodge of Scilly seems to have lapsed, carrying on as the Godolphin Lodge No. 281.

Sprinkled through the records are the names of the officers of the Garrison, Master Gunners, and of Commanders of H.M. Ships stationed there. There were Lieutenants of the 43rd and 59th Regiments of Foot, and Ensign of the 22nd Regiment of Foot and the Captain of the Frigate H.M.S. Lark. The Steward to the Lord Godolphin, and the 'Chaplain to his Lordship,' were members of the lodge: one had to have reasonable means to be able to afford to be a freemason. In the middle of the 18th century the entire rental from St. Mary's was estimated at £300 a year, so that the lodge admission fees and other costs, a total of £2.19s.6d, was a sizeable amount to find. It was necessary, in the by-laws, to legislate against drunkenness, gambling and swearing, but many of the songs and poems found among the records place great emphasis on mirth and merriment. It is fairly clear that everything happened in the same room and what is now called the festive board continued after, or perhaps even during, the lodge meeting. It was normal to drink during lodge meetings, although smoking was discouraged! Contributions were made to the 'Board of Benevolence', the forerunner of our present-day Grand Charity. Petitions for assistance shed light on what life was like in those days. The first, dated 1821, was from Ann Tregarthen, widow of Bro. William Tregarthen, who was a pilot. While assisting a vessel a heavy sea broke, filling his boat, and he and all aboard perished. The boat was lost and the widow with eight children was left destitute. She was granted £10. The second was from Elizabeth Thomas, widow of Bro. Samuel Thomas, also a pilot. He was aboard the ship Scotia when he had a heavy fall during a gale. The ship proceeded to London and did not return to Scilly for a month, with him still on board, suffering from his injuries. He lingered for about four months, having to go once to Penzance for treatment, at great expense, and the widow being reduced to poverty. She was granted £5.

Well known Scillonian names crop up from time to time in the old records. John Badcock, gentleman, in 1775, Joseph Jenkins in 1779. Thomas Phillips, Steward to Lord Godolphin, was initiated in 1783 and the first Banfield (Daniel) described as a lander of customs, or land waiter, at Penzance, appears in 1785. In the early 1800s are found more Banfields. There was Alex (a shipwright), William (a ship Captain), Barnett (a merchant) and John (shipwright). The first Mumfords are also recorded: Clement (a ship's

Captain who later became a schoolmaster) and William (shipwright). Joshua Hicks, an innkeeper, was initiated in 1816, and Ismael, a pilot, in 1827. William Mumford did quite well for himself, for in 1836 he rejoined the lodge as a shipbuilder: he joined with the Provincial Grand Master R.W.Bro. Augustus Smith, Lord Proprietor of the Isles of Scilly, and John Smyth, described as Lieutenant Governor of the islands. There were many other fascinating members of the lodge in those days. These included George Whittaker in 1809, described as an itinerant hawker; Lord Viscount Neville in 1810 (Captain of H.M.S. Acteon) and Abraham Solomon in 1815, described as a pawnbroker from Falmouth. It took all sorts to make a mason!

Godolphin Lodge which celebrated its 40th anniversary in 2001, had its origin with a meeting of three Freemasons at Holy Vale Chapel. The new lodge was consecrated by the PGM RW Bro. Col. E.N. Willyams in December 1961.

The three were W.Bro. The Revd James Gillet M.A. (Chaplain of the Isles) who was the first W.Master and went on to become Grand Superintendent (1969-76) PAG Chaplain and was PDDGM (East Africa); W.Bro. Harry Hall PPAGDC (first S.W.) and W.Bro George Bailey. Three of the founder members continue in the lodge, W.Bro. Roy Wright PPJGW (who served as the founder assistant secretary) and was W.M. in 1966; W.Bro W. McFarland Mumford PPJGW (founder I.G., and W.M. in 1968) and Bro. Arthur Williams (the founder lodge Chaplain).

The lodge continues in its premises in Church Street: in recent years the Temple has been refurbished and the lower room acquired as a dining hall with a great deal of work carried out by members. W.Br. Sam Ellis made a cabinet containing the three tracing boards. This new dining room was used as an air-raid shelter during World War 2 - and the island siren was on the roof. A wall was knocked down to extend the room and the large fin of a bomb was discovered in a cupboard during the clearance.

Several members have served on the Council of the Isles of Scilly down the years, some as Chairman, and also played an active role in the success of the Steamship Company. One distinguished visitor while on holiday was the Grand Secretary, Sir James Stubbs, who gave an explanation of the Grand Certificate to a new member, pointing out among its many details "and this is my signature".

The long-serving lodge secretary W.Bro. Wing Commander George Leatherbarrow AFC, PPJGW. is the holder of the PGM's Certificate of Service to Freemasonry.

Lodge Histories

ST. GLUVIAS LODGE No. 7936, PENRYN.

The first record of freemasonry in Penryn was when the Peace, Joy and Brotherly Love lodge was constituted in 1782, meeting at the King's Arms hotel. The lodge was erased in 1809 but during its life another was started in 1799 under the name of Three Grand Principles No. 577, meeting at the Golden Lion. It lasted only 39 years. It was not until 1863 with the revival of the Three Grand Principles that freemasonry became firmly established in Penryn. The present masonic hall in New Street, Penryn, now occupied by four lodges, was erected in 1912. The Deputy Provincial Grand Master W.Bro. P. Colville Smith presided over the dedication ceremony. The cost of the hall was £846.10s and was built by the Barnicoat family. The father of the late W.Bro. C.C. Barnicoat, founder W.M. of St. Gluvias lodge, in 1963, had the task of completing the building.

In the early 1960s several older lodges had rather large memberships particularly Three Grand Principles then numbering 160. A petition was prepared and submitted, the lodge of the Three Grand Principles being the sponsoring lodge. St. Gluvias lodge was consecrated at the County Secondary School, Penryn on 2 November, 1963 by the R.W.Bro. Col. E.N. Willyams, Provincial Grand Master assisted by his officers.

Of the original lodge officers and members only W.Bro. A.A.E. Toye, the first Assistant D.C. and Bro. H. Rollason, one of the stewards, are surviving members. The first meeting was in November 1963 when Mr. D. Thomas was the first initiate: W.Bro. Price presented a Bible to the lodge. In May 1964 a lodge of instruction was formed and September of that year saw the first exchange working with Pendennis Lodge. Exchange workings with other local lodges have continued over many years. From 1965, with the support of the ladies of the lodge, the festive board has been held in the lodge ante-room.

The Provincial Grand Master the Hon. Robert Eliot, together with his officers, visited in 1980 to carry out an initiation ceremony; for the 1981 festival the lodge raised £9,355. In 1982 the founding W.M. reached his 80th birthday. The P.G.M., with his officers dedicated the banner made by W.Bro. F.W. Tresidder, the present almoner, coinciding with the celebration of the 21st anniversary of the founding of the lodge. W.Bro. C.C. Barnicoat was presented in 1985 with the Provincial Grand Master's Certificate for Service to Freemasonry and the following year celebrated 50 years in freemasonry. He reached his 90th birthday in 1992 when the lodge presented him with a framed certificate expressing respect and affection of all brethren. He died later that year.

In 1994 tribute was paid to the long serving almoner W.Bro. A. Stevens, when he was honoured by the Queen with the gift of Maundy Money. The lodge lost one of its most dedicated founder-members by the death in 1999 of W.Bro. L.C. Burton: he was for 25 years D.C. of the lodge. A further loss was sustained in that year by the move of W.Bro. A.F. White to live in Holland. He was Chaplain for 23 years and received the Provincial Grand Master's Certificate of Service to Freemasonry in 1991: he was made an Honorary Member of St. Gluvias.

No history, however brief, would be complete without the mention that on 13 December 1966 a Mr. N.J.F.C. Barrington, now the P.G.M., was initiated. He was installed as W.M. in 1974 and was secretary from 1976-1979. Members have watched his ever-growing commitment and progress through the levels of masonry with much pride and pleasure. During all this time he has continued to play an active part in the life of his mother lodge. (See special feature on Provincial Grand Masters).

Lodge Histories

ST. GEORGE'S LODGE No. 7953, EAST LOOE.

In November 1962 five brethren, four from the London area who had retired from business and come to live in Cornwall, were interested in forming a new lodge which was to be a full dining lodge. These comprised Bros. J.C. Charman, G.A. Ewer, A.R. Hallows, H.V. Aylward (London) and Bro. F.B. Mewis from Worcestershire. Bro. F.G. Bond, whilst working in his garden, noticed a pair of white gloves on the washing line of his next door neighbour, one of this group, and so he became another provisional founder member!

Other brethren were contacted and W.Bro. M.T.D. Weston (P.P.J.G.W.) of St. Anne's lodge agreed to join as a founder and assist in negotiations with St. Anne's No. 970 of East Looe regarding use of the masonic hall and temporary use of lodge regalia. Certification was granted for the formation of the new lodge, and two names were sent to province for approval: St. George's or Tremayne. The Grand Secretary advised in December 1963 that the petition was agreed and the name St. George's selected. The meetings would be held on the third Thursdays of October, November, January, February, March and April with the installation in April. The ritual used would be 'Taylors Working'.

The consecration took place at the Masonic Hall, East Looe on Saturday the 18 April 1964 led by the Provincial Grand Master R.W.Bro. Col. E.N. Willyams. The first W.M. was W.Bro. M.T.D. Weston (P.P.J.G.W.) As it was intended to use part of the old East Looe Coat of Arms in the lodge banner, the town council was approached and approval given.

At the consecration there were 126 brethren and 29 lodges represented. After the officers had been appointed and installed, three candidates were proposed, and to wish the new lodge a good start, an anonymous donation of £100 received. The date of the first regular meeting was altered because of a General Election taking place. The first candidate was Peter Denis Weldon, of Looe, who became W.M. in April 1973.

Lodge Histories

In January 1966 the first of the Past Masters' and founders' meetings was instituted followed by an Olde English Night at the festive board: it is still a very special and well patronised event. In August 1981 the wife of one of the brethren, W.Bro. Haywood, who was an accomplished embroidery mistress, agreed to embroider a new lodge banner: Mrs. Isobell Haywood produced the magnificent banner which hangs behind the W.M's chair in the temple. This was the frontispiece of the Cornwall masonic year book some years ago.

Two weeks after it was completed, the Provincial Grand Master R.W.Bro. M.R.V. Eliot carried out a dedication ceremony in April 1982. The lodge has gone from strength to strength with a total membership in 1999 of 54: numbers have been maintained for many years between 50 and 60. The lodge is proud of its charity record with the Olde English Night producing more charity revenue each year. The only active founder member remaining is W.Bro. P. Heathman. W.Bro. F.B. Mewis had the distinction of being in office from a founder member until his death in December 1989, having served primarily as acting secretary during the initial formation of the lodge, then as the first D.C. for seven years, then Chaplain and finally Organist. He received the Provincial Grand Master's Certificate of Meritorious Service to Freemasonry in April 1986.

Lodge Histories

ST. DENYS LODGE No. 8250, ST. AUSTELL.

St. Denys lodge is the youngest of the four craft lodges which meet at the masonic hall in St. Austell. The founder members came from Peace and Harmony, Tewington, Carlyon as well as the Duke of Cornwall at St. Columb. St. Denys is spelt the same way as the parish church of St. Dennis, a village between Newquay on the north coast and St. Austell on the south. The founding father and first W.M. was W.Bro. Len Richards, P.A.G.D.C. He was born in the village and it was hoped that one day the lodge would meet there. The founder members incorporated some of the workings from each of the four lodges to make up the 'St. Denys working'. They decided that much of the ceremony should be 'farmed out' to the members on the floor of the lodge and that the Past Masters should have their moment of glory once a year at the November meeting, to encourage the newer members to take an active part. It was also decided that Past Masters who held office for five years could volunteer their resignation, for much the same reason. The lodge usually invites the Duke of Cornwall lodge for an exchange working in May or June, and meetings are held each month except July and August (installation January). The consecration took place at the masonic hall, Newquay. On 18 January 1969. W.Bro. Richards and the founders decided that the festive board should be an extension of what went on in the temple and many a visitor who stood up to reply to a toast and decided he would 'tell a story' found himself cut off in midstream!

Bro. Frank Morgan, a founder-member, was a great benefactor: he gave the P.M's board and the lodge banner which was dedicated in September 1972. A dispensation was granted for the meeting to be held on the fifth Friday of the month to enable the Provincial Grand Master R.W.Bro. Col.E. Perry Morgan to be present. The prayer and address were given by the Provincial S.G.W., Canon G.W.S. Harmer. The Revd Michael Trezise was an example to all in his determination to overcome the physical disabilities due to his diabetic condition. He was a founder member of the lodge and its first organist in which office he continued (although registered as blind in May 1970) until he was appointed S.W. in 1973 and elected W.M. the following year. His year produced several firsts for St. Denys Lodge: few visitors realized that he was blind until they saw his notes in braille, though they might have noticed the absolute silence during lodge meetings apart from those who had to speak or move. He formed the St. Denys Lodge social committee and was the first W.M. of a St. Austell lodge to be given permission from the province for the ladies to view the temple. When founding father W.Bro. Richards died there was a memorial service at the parish church of St. Denys and when the church was rebuilt, having been gutted by fire, the lodge was proud to present a new pulpit.

Lodge Histories

A group of members of the lodge at St. Austell: an undated photograph.

Lodge Histories

CORNISH ACACIA LODGE No. 8302, HAYLE.

During the mid-1960s it came to the attention of the then area secretary of the National Association of Funeral Directors (W.Bro. R.J. Hosking) and others that many who regularly attended were also freemasons. It was decided to petition to form a lodge in which the members would be funeral directors and the P.G.M. gave his full support. St. Piran's Lodge, Perranporth agreed to sponsor and also to the use of the temple with meetings on the second Saturday of March, May, October and December.

At first it was expected that there would be a limited supply of candidates and the main object would be to have discussions and to receive lectures, but, in a later letter to the Provincial Secretary W.Bro. Hosking stated that it was felt that membership should not necessarily be restricted to funeral directors, but could include allied occupations associated with the funeral business. The first design submitted for the badge was turned down by the Grand Secretary as it was considered too similar to a P.G.M's jewel! W.Bro. Henry Mitchell re-designed the badge with a sprig of acacia on a sky-blue background in an oblong tablet.

The lodge was consecrated on the 8 November 1969 at the Masonic Hall, Perranporth, by the Provincial Grand Master R.W.Bro.Col. E. Perry Morgan, assisted by his officers. Sixteen founder-members and 80 visitors attended. The oration, given by Bro. Revd R.H. Cadman, was so much appreciated that a copy is affixed to the flyleaf of the first minute book. The Master-designate, W.Bro. R.J. Smith, was presented for installation by W.Bro. M. Kenyon, the W.M. of Acacia Lodge, Wandsworth, London. The founders and consecrating officers met in the morning for a rehearsal during which a great wind arose causing a sand storm from the nearby dunes. The brethren had difficulty in getting to and from the hotel for the celebratory lunch - all being covered in sand!

In the early years the majority of members were funeral directors: so strong was the connection that W.Bro. D.S. Farthing, P.M. of Felix Lodge, Ipswich (President of the N.A.F.D.) presented the 'Address to the Brethren' at the installation in 1971. It is therefore not surprising that the lodge acquired the nickname of 'The Undertakers Lodge' which continues to this day, although there are now few funeral directors among the members. In 1974 it was decided to increase the number of meetings to five a year and the introduction of an installation luncheon prior to opening was approved as a regular feature (replacing the usual tea and biscuits). The following year the installation luncheon for about 50 brethren was produced by the Hayle masonic premises catering committee staff and taken 20 miles to Perranporth, under the direction of Bro. T.C. Wakfer, and which, despite the distance the food had to travel, proved a success.

The decision was made in 1978 to move to the Masonic Hall, Hayle, and the installation of that year was the first time that an initiate of the lodge was installed as W.M: all of the work was performed by members of the lodge. It soon became absorbed into the masonic life at Hayle and was given much fraternal assistance. The number of applicants continued to rise and in February 1980, with only five meetings each year, two of which were taken up with election of officers and installation, it was found necessary for the lodge to be opened at 11.30am to work a ceremony. After lunch another was worked, this time by the Past Masters: this arrangement continued to the end of 1981. In that December a decision was made to become an equal partner in the scheme of the Hayle masonic management committee and in the following February new by-laws were adopted increasing regular meetings to nine.

In February 1982 a donation was made to the provincial fund for the Penlee lifeboat disaster and an immediate substantial collection in the lodge was also sent.

During the following November Bro. R.D. Balsdon said he had obtained a set of tracing boards from a retired Brother, recently come to live in the area. They were of excellent craftsmanship, painted in oils, of considerable antiquity and have been used regularly. A lodge banner was dedicated on the 28 February 1987 in a ceremony conducted by the Provincial Grand Master and his officers, with the oration by the Provincial Chaplain, Bro. The Ven. Tom Barfett.

In 1989 the first ladies festival dinner was held and proved very successful: the profit was distributed between the Royal Masonic Hospital, Hayle masonic museum and St. Julia's Hospice, Hayle. In July 1989 the secretaryship passed to W.Bro. F.B. Paddy: the post had been filled by W.Bro. Hosking for nearly 20 years. The W.M. presented W.Bro. Hosking, with a wrist-watch for his many years service. W.Bro. O.C.G. Harris relinquished the treasurership to Bro. P.C. Gallie, and it was revealed that W.Bro. Harris had made donations to the lodge, preventing financial difficulties. He was presented with a watch as a token of the high esteem and appreciation for his services.

At the installation meeting in 1992, although frail and in a nursing home, the lodge tyler, Bro. Frank Foreshaw, aged 94, was re-appointed, having filled this office for 20 years. The following year his death was announced.

Lodge Histories

In 1993 honorary membership was conferred on W.Bro. Hosking, the principal founder-member. He had suffered ill-health for some years and he died in June 1997. Honorary membership was also conferred on W.Bro. Revd C.A. Roach, P.P.G. Chaplain and Chaplain of the lodge for ten years, and on W.Bro. A.A.W. Doodes, W.Bro. J.H.D. White (founder member), W.Bro. S.F. Broom (the first charity steward) and W.Bro. H.W. Mitchell, for many years the Provincial Secretary.

The 25th anniversary of the consecration was marked by an informal festive board after the meeting in October 1994. The first annual social dinner was held in the following year with no speeches and only one toast. Wives and friends were able to view the masonic museum and the two temples. The lodge has led the way in following the wishes of Grand Lodge for Freemasonry to be more open. After the dinner Mrs. Margaret Triggs, (widow of the late W.Bro. Leslie Triggs sometime almoner of the lodge), presented a pair of mahogany Wardens columns in the style of the 18th century.

In the early days it was not unusual for a member to be called out from the lodge to attend to urgent business in connection with his profession. There were times when a call came from the police to recover a body from a beach brought in by the sea. Yet, it was not only funeral directors who were called out, for on another occasion the I.G., a farmer, answered a knock on the door from which urgent whispers were heard. He reported to the W.M. in his broad Cornish accent that his cows had got out of their field and he must leave at once.

In the West of Cornwall there is a distinct Cornish dialect which makes masonic ritual that much more rich and interesting; even if the inclusion of Cornish words and phrases may be somewhat baffling to some of the visiting brethren!

Lodge Histories

ST. BUDOC'S LODGE No. 8445, PENRYN.

The lodge was formed at a consecration meeting at Falmouth School on 11 November 1972: it was the 'brain child' of W.Bro. Frank Morris, supported by W.Bro. George Roberts. They were members of Love and Honour Lodge and felt there was a need for another in the town. Frank, a postman in the Budock area for many years was involved with the church and studied the history of the patron saint, St. Budoc.

He discovered that on his death St. Budoc had decreed that his right hand should be severed, as a sign of recompense to all those people that he may have wrongly excommunicated. This greatly influenced Frank in choosing the name, and the hand of St. Budoc is on the front of the summons.

The first meeting came ten days after the 1972 consecration, with W.Bro. Morris the first secretary and W.Bro. Roberts the S.W. W.Bro. Ennor was the first W.M. and the Provincial Grand Master R.W. Bro. Nicholas Barrington was also a founder, together with such distinguished brethren as the late W.Bro. Len Burton (D.C. for many years), W.Bro. G. Hubber, W.Bro. A.F. White, and others. Pendennis lodge of Falmouth became the mother lodge, but in March 1984 it was decided to move to Penryn (as did Pendennis). St. Budoc's has a membership of some 35.

HAMOAZE LODGE No. 8513, SALTASH.

The first choice of name for the new lodge, was Allerton but when this as rejected by the province the alternative name of Hamoaze was adopted. It is named after that part of the river Tamar, running alongside Devonport naval dockyard for one-and-a-half miles, and either side of the Torpoint ferry. The word Hamoaze means 'settlement by the water' and the badge of the lodge depicts the ferry crossing the river. It was formed with members from Carew Lodge, Torpoint, and members from Royal Naval Lodge No. 2761 meeting at Valetta, Malta, the latter being one of the lodges ousted from Malta and which now meets at Yeovil, Somerset. The prime mover was W.Bro. F.M. Jefferies, a P.M. of the Valetta lodge, and a member of Carew.

It was his perseverance in convincing most of the founder members, many of them from the original R.N. lodge, that the formation was a viable proposition. He remains a member of Hamoaze, and though resident in Sydney, Australia since 1978, he is still very interested in the fortunes of the lodge. Arrangements were finally completed for the consecration ceremony, but owing to the large number of visiting brethren expected, dispensation was obtained from Provincial G. Lodge, to hold the ceremony at the masonic hall, Saltash.

The consecration ceremony was on Saturday 9 June 1973, conducted by the Provincial Grand Master R.W.Bro. Col. E. Perry Morgan, assisted by his officers. The first W.M., W.Bro. F.L. Collins, was installed by the Assistant P.G.M., W.Bro. C. Andrew. A total of 116 brethren attended: of the founders only W.Bro. W.J. Burch, and Bro. A.H. Keenan are still members. In 1993, a number of brethren felt that the lodge would further prosper, if it moved from Torpoint to Saltash where it held its first regular meeting in January 1994. The lodge now has over 30 members.

PENWITH LODGE No. 8538, HAYLE.

Early in 1972 informal discussions took place among some brethren of the three Penzance lodges about the formation of a fourth in the area. Bro. T.C. Wakfer invited a number to a meeting in May and it was agreed in January 1973 that the formation should go ahead. As the temple in Penzance was not available it was decided the management committee of the masonic centre in Hayle be approached. The request was received very favourably and Penwith has used the Hayle centre for its meetings since its consecration. The petition to Grand Lodge was also presented at this time with the officers and brethren of Lodge Lyonesse making the recommendation. This kindness to the founders has meant that a very special relationship has existed between the two lodges, with an exchange visit and ceremony taking place each year. The consecration was on 29 October 1973 at St. John's Hall, Penzance by the Provincial Grand Master R.W.Bro. Colonel E. Perry Morgan, assisted by his provincial officers and the first W.M., W.Bro. R.H. Phillips was installed. A total of 148 brethren attended. The lodge meets on the fourth Tuesday in September, October (installation), November, January, February, March and April with Emulation working. From its first regular meeting the lodge has used the original Cornubian temple at Hayle, and many of the articles of regalia and equipment in use have been presented by past and present brethren. One special gift came in December 1987 when Mrs. Leonard, the widow of the lodge organist for some years, Bro. J. Leonard, presented an electric organ. The wives of the brethren were present at this presentation, which in itself made a special occasion in the lodge history.

It was the intention of the founders to provide a banner as soon as possible but the cost was found to be prohibitive and the idea was shelved. However, after many months of painstaking and skilful research and work, Mrs. Beryl Wright Matthews, wife of W.Bro. H.Wright Matthews, P.P.J.G.W., (the lodge D.C. 1973-89) completed a beautiful banner at the beginning of 1985. Its design was based on the map of the Penwith peninsula and contains representations of many of the natural features as well as the major masonic motifs together with the ancient burial grounds, the Longships lighthouse, St. Michael's

Lodge Histories

Mount, a mine stack and other aspects of the area. It was dedicated in November of that year by the Provincial Grand Master, R.W. Bro. the Hon. Robert Eliot and his officers. The relatively small size of the lodge, combined with its role as a dining lodge, has attracted more than 25 joining members since its formation. Some of these are also members of local lodges but a number of "immigrants" into the Penzance area have become members, and several have occupied the chair. The contribution to work in the province by many of the brethren of Penwith Lodge has been recognised. W.Bro. Phillips, the first W.M. of Penwith and a P.M. of. St. Levan was appointed Provincial S.G.W. in 1986-7. The P.G.M. awarded his Certificate of Service to Freemasonry to W.Bro. F.W. Shepherd, P.P.Supt.Works in 1988 and to W.Bro. H.Wright Matthews in 1990.

The Consecration of Penwith Lodge No. 8538, at Penzance in October 1973 by the PGM, R.W.Bro. Col. E. Perry Morgan and his officers. This was followed by the installation of the first Master, W.Bro. Herbert Phillips PPSGW.

After the investiture of officers of the new Lodge three proposals for initiates were made on behalf of the sons of three founder members.

The lodge meets at Hayle, using the larger Perry Morgan Temple for installations and other special occasions. The silver jubilee was in 1998

CARADON LODGE No. 8543, SALTASH.

Caradon Lodge was consecrated on Saturday 23 March 1974 at the Masonic Hall, Saltash, by the Provincial Grand Master, R.W.Bro. Colonel E. Perry Morgan. There were 27 founder-members, who came mainly from the two other Saltash lodges, Zetland and Essa. It was established as a dining lodge and for the past few years has dined at the St. Mellion golf and country club. The first W.M. was W.Bro. L.C. Marsh, and the S.W. Bro. C.J. Hamley, who became the lodge secretary in 1977, an office he held until his death in November 1991. At the consecration, in addition to the 27 founders, there were 92 visitors.

The first meeting after consecration was in May 1974 when Mr. Robert Hicks, later the M.P. and now Sir Robert, was balloted for and initiated: five brothers were also proposed as joining members. Since the lodge was consecrated there have been over 40 initiates, and some 40 joining members. There is one surviving founder, W.Bro. T.G. Preedy, who was the first secretary from 1974 - 77 and elected an Honorary Member in 2000. In November 1985 the lodge banner was dedicated by the Provincial Grand Master, R.W.Bro. the Hon. Robert Eliot. W. Bro. James Kitson, a member, was appointed Assistant Provincial Grand Master in 1994.

Lodge Histories

BREANICK LODGE No. 8610, ST. AGNES.

On the 27 February 1974 leading members of Trevaunance Lodge met to consider forming a new lodge at St. Agnes. After further meetings it was agreed the name would be Breanick, the ancient Cornish name for the parish of St. Agnes, and that the consecration ceremony be held on Saturday 8 February 1975 at the masonic hall, Newquay, followed by a banquet at the Ponsmere Hotel, Perranporth (supplied at no cost to the founders and consecrating officers by founder-member W.Bro. John William Batchelor, P.A.G.D.C., the hotel proprietor). The consecrating officer was the Provincial Grand Master, R.W.Bro. Col. E. Perry Morgan, with his provincial officers. The Provincial G. Chaplain, W.Bro. Revd James Gillett gave the oration. W.Bro. H. Whitworth was installed the first W.M. by the Deputy P.G.M., V.W. Bro. C. Andrew. In 1976 the lodge became a Grand Patron Lodge to the Royal Masonic Hospital, thanks to a donation bequeathed by the late Mrs. Tarrent, wife of W.Bro. W.G. Tarrent. At the May meeting in 1977 the new banner was dedicated by the Assistant P.G.M., W.Bro. the Hon. Robert Eliot and the provincial officers. The banner, the original idea of W.Bro. T.C. Ball, was produced in Hong Kong under the supervision of Mr. McArthey, from drawings by Mrs. Elizabeth Bennetts. At the October meeting in 1978 the ceremony was the first exchange working between Breanick and mother lodge Trevaunance: this exchange has continued.

"All beginnings are difficult", runs an old proverb: Breanick was no exception and at the end of the first decade although it had registered 25 initiates, 25 joining members and the 17 founders the total membership was only 44. There were few candidates for initiation or joining in the ensuing years.

At the September meeting in 1990 Bro. G.A. Nicholls (of St. Johns Lodge No. 347 S.C.), a friend of Bro. H. Smith, Past Provincial G.Std.B. presented a masonic orb to W.Bro. H.W. Mitchell, Curator of the Cornwall masonic museum. The orb, well over 100 years old, had been handed down from father to son for three generations.

Lodge Histories

ROSELAND LODGE No. 8734, ST. MICHAEL PENKIVEL.

The consecration of Roseland lodge on Saturday 30 October, 1976 was the culmination of several months' planning. The petition to found the lodge was based on three principles: the geographic entity of the Roseland peninsula bordered as it is on two sides by the sea and separated for some of its extent from the rest of the county by the River Fal: although Lodge Charity No. 223 was temporarily warranted in St. Mawes in the 18th century it moved back to Plymouth in 1799. Thus there was no lodge between Truro and St. Austell: there were some 45 master masons in the area who felt that they would like to form a lodge.

These brethren came not only from Cornwall but from Yorkshire, Lancashire, Gloucester and Essex. It was decided the lodge should meet on the first Wednesday of the month, that it should be a dining lodge - with dinner jackets worn - and to follow Emulation Ritual.

As no suitable property on the Roseland peninsula was available to rent or buy, the decision was made to meet in the Nare Hotel in Veryan. This made it necessary to acquire lodge furniture and furnishings. In the main these were rented from Pendennis and Boscawen lodges although a very fine set of tracing boards was presented by W.Bro. David Rowe, while the columns and toasting goblets were presented by W.Bro. R. Church, an honorary member. The banner was presented by W.Bro. R. Vigus and W.Bro. H. Whitworth (who also designed it). Recently the lodge was able to purchase its own carpet, mainly due to the generosity of W.Bro. Paul Strick. The meetings remained in the Nare Hotel until a change of ownership and plans for extending the hotel made a new venue essential.

The first meeting in a new location, Rosevine Hotel at Porthscatho, was in October 1989 but in January 1996 moved to the present domicile at the village hall (formerly the school) in St. Michael Penkivel, even though the 'purists' might argue it is not, strictly speaking, in the Roseland peninsula!

Lodge Histories

At present there are some 38 members, which is about the level of membership which Roseland has had from its early days. It was an honour for the lodge that the founding master, W.Bro. R.G. Vigus, became P.A.G.D.C. in 1977. W.Bro. Henry Whitworth M.B.E., became Provincial J.G.W. and received the Provincial Grand Masters Certificate of Service to Freemasonry. Several other brethren have received active provincial rank. Joining members have greatly widened the knowledge, enjoyment and appreciation of freemasonry: one even brought some ritual embellishments from the Grand Lodge of Ireland!

Most of the candidates over recent years have remained faithful members of the lodge and are now in progression towards the W.M's chair. The lodge is in a stable situation and very pleased with the meeting place in St. Michael Penkivel where the festive board makes the hospitality a pleasure both to offer and receive.

The Volume of the Sacred Law of True and Faithful, dating back to the mid–1800s at Helston.

A leader with his many honours displayed, wearing his Mayoral chain, together with his collar, cuffs and apron as Provincial Senior Warden and many medals.
It must have been an extremely busy year, holding these two demanding offices.

Saltash

St. Austell

St. Columb

St. Germans

St. Michael Penkivel

St. Agnes

St. Day

St. Ives

Tintagel

Torpoint

Tywardreath

Wadebridge

SIR JOHN ST. AUBYN LODGE No. 8839, HAYLE.

One of the younger lodges in the province, Sir John St. Aubyn received its warrant from Grand Lodge on 27 April 1978 and was consecrated on 9 June by V.W.Bro. Cyril Andrew as Deputy Provincial Grand Master in charge, whilst the installation of the first W.M. was performed by W.Bro. the Hon. Robert Eliot as P.G.M. designate. Cornubian Lodge, meeting in the same complex, sponsored the formation and the new lodge has used the Perry Morgan Temple from the outset. At the suggestion of W.Bro. Fred Shepherd the founders decided to form a lodge based on the findings of W.Bro. E.H. Cartwright, following his study of many rituals. Although it follows the main themes approved at the time of the Union this has different phrasing and perambulations to many other rituals in common use. Notable for the thoughtful freemason, this is an advantage for the brother undertaking the work, as few visitors know if he has strayed from the text or route! One of the features is that the installation has a more complete inner working, preserving characteristics now generally lost but at the expense of more work for the installing master. The original name proposed was Cartwright Lodge but the then Grand Secretary advised that he felt that Grand Lodge would probably not accept this title, as not being sufficiently eminent to the craft as a whole. It was eventually settled on Sir John St. Aubyn, named after the P.G.M. 1785-1839 (at 54 years, the longest serving on record in the English Craft), an ancestor of the present Lord St. Levan. In 1794 he presented the handsome set of silver gilt jewels still worn by the principal provincial officers, at the same time as Sir Francis Basset presented the provincial sword of state, also still in use. Meetings were originally on the second Friday in October, December, February, April (election) and June (installation). However, the steady flow of candidates not only required an extra meeting to be added in March (since discontinued) but also in the early days for double ceremonies to be undertaken.

Lodge Histories

W.Bro. Henry W. Mitchell, a founder and the first W.M., undertook the first initiation in October 1978. The W.M. stepped down for the second initiation in March, permitting the Cornish Masters' Lodge to follow their tradition and undertake the ceremony. The earliest installations were held on the second Friday in June. This date clashed with the Royal Cornwall Show, which was reflected in the attendance figures so the date was adjusted to the third Friday in May, a more convenient one that was likely not to be so hot in the low ceilinged temple. Each installing master receives a bound copy of the summonses, menu cards, notices, etc of his year of office. The annual lectures in April have covered a wide range of subjects presented by most eminent and talented lecturers including R.W. Bro. Michael Higham when Grand Secretary, V.W. Bro. Neville Barker Cryer, Grand Chaplain and W.Bro. John Webb, a Prestonian Lecturer and now honorary member. Although all were very memorable, the 18th century meeting presented in full period costume by the William Cobbett demonstration team is one to which reference is often made.

The very distinctive badge was designed by R.W. Bro. Sir Colin Cole, P.J.G.W., Garter King of Arms in the College of Heralds, combining those of Sir John St. Aubyn and the catherine wheel from the Cartwright arms. This badge has been incorporated in the banner embroidered by Mrs. Mona Peters, wife of a member. The original design is displayed in the Hayle masonic museum. Following each regular meeting, there is a formal dinner accompanied with toasts and masonic "fire." This fire, which often catches out the unwary visitor, uses miniature wooden mauls turned by the first secretary, W.Bro. J.W. Forward. A personal inscribed maul is presented to each new member following his initiation or joining. The ladies have occasionally been invited into the temple (after closure of working) to join the brethren and hear a brief explanation of some of the furnishings, etc., as well as to have the opportunity to ask questions. Annual ladies' nights are held and there have been trips to the Minack open air theatre at Porthcurno and the Theatre Royal at Plymouth. There have been several trips abroad, which, when possible, included a visit to a local lodge.

The tenth anniversary was marked by a detailed history compiled by W.Bro. Shepherd, whilst the completion of the second decade was marked by the promotion to the chair of the original, and then still serving, founding secretary, W.Bro. Jack Forward. During his term of office he completed 50 years in freemasonry, commemorated by the members with the presentation of an inscribed salver and other gifts. He also received the Provincial Grand Master's Certificate of Service to Freemasonry. The first W.M., W.Bro. Mitchell (a former Provincial G.Secretary) accepted honorary membership. The stalwart original treasurer, W.Bro. Owen Bartle, remains cheerfully in office!

SAINT MARY'S LODGE No. 8892, CALLINGTON.

In the mid-1970s it was felt by quite a number of brethren that the Callington area could usefully support another lodge. One of the reasons was that it was taking nearly 20 years to attain the chair in Loyal Victoria Lodge. It seemed superfluous to duplicate lodges such as Loyal Victoria or Cotehele, the two nearest to the area where they wished to meet, so it was decided that the new one should be a dining lodge meeting for only six months in the year. It was agreed at an early stage to ask Loyal Victoria to act as sponsoring lodge and to meet in Callington. Several names were mooted, but the one which gained acceptance was St. Mary, after the parish church in Callington. The founding secretary wrote the name in full and so it has remained. Saint Mary's Lodge was the first to be consecrated by the Provincial Grand Master, R.W. Bro. the Hon. Robert Eliot and the ceremony was on Saturday 15 September 1979. In the years since then it has had its "ups and downs": candidates and joining members have not really been in short supply, but because of the employment situation the "fall out rate" has been higher than expected. The lodge has, however, had a number of successes. The first of these was the visit of the Portobello Lodge No. 226 Scottish Constitution from Edinburgh to demonstrate the working of a ceremony in 1985. The lodge has also tried to include lectures as part of the programme for the masonic year and on occasions neighbouring lodges have been invited.

One of the founders W.Bro. Herbert Symons, who was also the first D.C., decided that he would like to donate a banner: he had done the same for Loyal Victoria some years before and felt that Saint Mary's should have one also. This was done in great secrecy, but on Thursday 15 March 1984, under the W.M., W.Bro. C.J.T. Willoughby, the banner was revealed. W.Bro. Symons had applied his artistic skills and painted a representation of St. Mary's parish church, the hands of the clock set at six o'clock, the time that the lodge meets, as well as a representation of the lodge badge. The banner was dedicated at a ceremony held by the Provincial Grand Master with his provincial officers: the Provincial G. Chaplain, Bro. the Revd Donald Richards gave the oration.

The first lodge to be consecrated by Rt. W. Bro. Robert Eliot, as Provincial Grand Master was Saint Mary's Lodge No. 8892 at Callington.

This was on 15th September 1979. Here is a group of the founders and consecrating officers, including W. Bro. D.P. Waterhouse (W.M. Designate) and V. W. Bro. Cyril Andrew the Deputy PGM., and W. Bro. Gerry Barton (Asst. Prov. G. M.), and several other familiar faces from the Grand Lodge and Provincial ranks.

Lodge Histories

ST. STEPHEN'S LODGE No. 9147, SALTASH.

The summer of 1984 saw W.Bro. Len Marsh P.P.J.G.W., as the prime architect and founding secretary, busy finalising the plans for the new lodge with his founder colleagues in Saltash. At about the same time nine expatriate masons, who had recently returned from Gibraltar to live in the Saltash area, met to consider which lodge they could apply to join to continue their friendship. At a meeting of Zetland lodge in the early autumn of 1984 the paths of these two groups converged and the opportunity of being part of a new lodge in Cornwall proved to be an exciting challenge. St. Stephen's was consecrated on Saturday the 9 February 1985.

As a means of expressing their appreciation to the founders who had so readily and warmly welcomed them as part of the new lodge, the Gibraltar expatriates decided to present a banner. Designed and painted by another Gibraltar freemason, Bro. Peter Wevill, this centres around a picture of St. Stephen-by-Saltash parish church, which has been adopted as the logo of the lodge. This was done with the assistance of Bro. the Revd Nigel Ashton the honorary Assistant Curate in the Saltash team ministry, who was later to become an honorary member of the lodge. Bro. Peter's wife Vicky, herself a Gibraltarian and daughter of a former Lord Mayor of Gibraltar, assisted with the needlework. In June 1989, the banner was dedicated by the Provincial Grand Master, R.W.Bro. Robert Eliot, and W.Bro. the Revd Raymond Wood, Provincial G. Chaplain, who gave the oration. A number of members of Sir John Hawkins Lodge, Plymouth, became founder members and continue to be a powerful source of support. The lodge now has a total of some 40 members.

Lodge Histories

ST. ENODOC LODGE No. 9226, WADEBRIDGE.

St. Enodoc was the 67th craft lodge to be formed in the province. It was proposed at a meeting on 6 November 1986 and consecrated only six months later. Although there were two other lodges in Wadebridge at the time, it was decided that there was a need for a dining lodge that did not meet in the summer for those who were unable to commit themselves to monthly meetings. It was agreed that members would wear dinner jackets and use the Emulation Working. It was later decided that no-one should hold office for more than five years - though some are reluctant to implement this rule! Because of the large number attending the consecration meeting on 30 May 1987, with 30 founder members and 145 visitors from 42 lodges, this was held at the large King Arthur's Halls temple, Tintagel, and, because of the popularity of the installation meetings, these also have been held there.

At the first regular meeting in October 1987, Mr Julian Darnell, the son of the senior steward, W.Bro. Roy Darnell, was initiated and six joining members were accepted. Bro. Julian became the first initiate to reach the W.M.'s chair in 1995. The founder inner guard, Bro. the Revd Raymond Wood, became the first provincial officer of the lodge when he was appointed Provincial G. Chaplain in 1988; he became W.M. in May 1989 in the presence of 125 brethren. In October 1989 a lodge banner, which had been presented by W.Bro. Bill Gilbert, was dedicated by the Provincial Grand Master R.W.Bro. The Hon. Robert Eliot and his officers. In 1989 the custom of having a Nine Lessons and Carols service in the Wadebridge temple for members and their families and friends was begun: this is followed by hot punch and mince pies! In 1990 the W.M., W.Bro. Peter Grundy presented a lodge board. The first three W.M's had the distinction of all being appointed Grand Officers a few years after having vacated the chair.

Lodge Histories

In October 1991 Bro. Archie Binding was proposed as an honorary member - aged 103! He was the father of founder treasurer W.Bro. John Binding. Bro. Archie was initiated in naval uniform in 1917, flew airships in the 1st World War and was awarded the Air Force Cross. He had not been through the W.M's chair but was active as an organist, charity fund treasurer, and trustee of Clevedon masonic hall. In 1991, his mother province, Somerset, honoured him with the appointment of P.P.J.G.W. The centenarian Archie was still astute enough to ask at the ceremony of investiture (held in his nursing home in May 1991), how he could be a past warden when he had not been a present one. He was informed that it is an idiosyncrasy of English Freemasonry; in Scottish masonry he would be a Honorary Warden. He was believed to be the then oldest English freemason when he died aged 105. In October 1998, W.Bro. Charles Matthews, who was installed as W.M. in May 1993, was presented by the P.G.M. with a certificate marking his 60 years in craft masonry. Bro. Charles was initiated into De Shurland Lodge, Kent, when he was a naval architect. In January 1940 he was posted to Hong Kong and joined Cathay Lodge No. 4373, a year before that colony was occupied by the Japanese and he spent the rest of the 2nd World War as a prisoner of war.

The origin of the lodge name comes from St. Enodoc church which is situated on St Enodoc golf links near the River Camel estuary. The golf course is of world renown, being of championship standard included in the top 40 in the world. The church which dates from pre-Norman times has a fascinating history significant to masonry. The church fell into disrepair and during the 19th century it was almost totally covered by wind-blown sand from the sea shore. Ecclesiastical law required the priest to enter the sanctuary of the church at least once every year. This he did, but the only way he could enter was through a hole in the north transept roof. There can be few lodge names that have been immortalised in poetry read throughout the English-speaking world. But when Sir John Betjeman wrote: "Come on! come on! This hillock hides the spire, all things draw towards St. Enodoc", he was thinking of this church he loved so much, and near which he is now laid to rest.

Lodge Histories

THREE SPIRES LODGE No. 9245, PERRANPORTH.

The lodge was consecrated at Newquay on 17 October 1987 by the Provincial Grand Master, R.W.Bro. the Hon. Robert Eliot. At the time the unusual nature of the lodge - where meetings are held in the mornings - was thought to be so revolutionary that it would not last. This has proved to be erroneous in that the lodge has initiated many candidates and attracted many joining members. Starting with 22 founders the present strength is now over 40. Two brethren retained their offices from the time of consecration: the organist Bro. Frank Pike (who died in 2000) and the almoner W.Bro. George Smitherman, still going strong. The secretary W.Bro. Roger Sprosen has also served for the whole period with a short break of a few months. The honorary member and tyler Bro. Bruce Brown also served constantly from the consecration up to recent times.

It was fitting that the lodge by its name should be identified with Truro: the cathedral has had strong masonic connections from the laying of its foundation stone in 1880. On 21 November 1997 the lodge banner was dedicated: the main space on the banner's design was taken up by the "Three Spires" with an embroidered Rose window in the centre spire, all representing the cathedral. The lodge originally met at the masonic hall in Cyril Road, and, pending the sale of these premises in 1997 when the various lodges meeting on the same site departed to other venues, Three Spires moved to Perranporth where it continues to enjoy its morning meetings which have proved such a success.

Lodge Histories

SIR HUMPHRY DAVY LODGE No. 9327, PENZANCE.

In the 1980s there was talk of forming a new craft lodge in Penzance, and when the Provincial Grand Master, R.W.Bro. Robert Eliot intimated that he would like to see 80 lodges in the province this was taken as a 'green light'. In 1988 a number of masons from the Penzance lodges met informally to discuss this. At a time when the masonic movement was not getting 'a good press', it was decided that a serious attempt should be made to maintain or even improve standards. Thus it was decided to meet formally in dinner jackets and also be a full dining lodge. Further meetings ensued and it was proposed, in order to maintain its identity, to use the Logic ritual. Twenty-three founder members signed the warrant and on the 16 September 1989, the lodge was consecrated at Mount's Bay School, followed by a banquet at Land's End Hotel. The first W.M. was W.Bro. Phil Vowles who was installed by the Deputy Provincial Grand Master, V.W.Bro. Sidney Pearce.

There is no record of Sir Humphry Davy having been a mason, but it was felt that the name of this illustrious son of Penzance would be a fitting one. "Davy lamps" are used in place of candlesticks at the Master's and Wardens' pedestals. The founder members, most of whom took office at the installation, donated their emblems and collar jewels. The lodge jewel was designed by W.Bro. Henry Mitchell (Past Provincial G. Secretary). The number of meetings was increased to five a year in 2000. A banner designed by W.Bro. Roger Veal P.P.A.G.D.C., was dedicated in November 2000 by the Provincial G. Chaplain, Revd Bro. Andrew Wilson. The Logic Ritual is an established one and coupled with the dining in the Trafalgar Room at the Union Hotel has proved popular among the brethren and visitors. It is thought the early lodges in Penzance met in a room which is now part of the hotel. The 1999 W.M., W.Bro. Richard Selby was the first of the candidates to come through the lodge.

Lodge Histories

TREVITHICK LODGE No. 9339, REDRUTH.

Trevithick Lodge was a wish and a longstanding desire of many brethren who were engineers, and members of other lodges, to one day form their own lodge, 'An Engineer's Lodge'. In September 1988 Provincial G. Lodge indicated that it favoured the formation of new lodges, suggesting that in the Camborne-Redruth area a mining, engineering lodge might be supported. A meeting was held, a committee formed, and the prospective members sought. Only five meetings were required to establish 'Trevithick' such was the resolve demonstrated by the founder brethren. Their wish came true on Saturday 21 October 1989 (warranted 14 June 1989). The lodge was formed by 33 founder members and the consecration, led by the Provincial Grand Master, R.W.Bro. the Hon. Robert Eliot, took place in the Refectory at Cornwall College, Redruth and was attended by over 90. The lodge was again honoured by a large number of brethren at its banner dedication in February 1993. The founder members chose the name after Cornwall's famous engineer Richard Trevithick, the 'father' of the steam locomotive, and many other notable inventions.

THE AGRICULTURAL LODGE No. 9342, ST. COLUMB.

At the Provincial G. Lodge meeting on 3 May 1969 the Provincial Grand Master, R.W.Bro. Col. E. Perry Morgan remarked that he considered some lodges were of such a size that progress to the W.M's chair was too slow. There were at that time 56 lodges in the province: this total increased to 66 by April 1979. During the 1980s the then Provincial Grand Master, R.W.Bro. the Hon. Robert Eliot continued to press for more lodges to be formed. During 1988 he approached W.Bro. M.H. Cock and W.Bro. K. Needham to research the possibility of forming a lodge for those connected with agriculture. It did not take long to get interest moving, for at the first meeting of 29 potential founders a committee was formed under the chairmanship of W.Bro. Cock. A name and logo were submitted and approved and the prospective W.M. was chosen. It was also proposed that it be a dining lodge. It was sponsored by the Duke of Cornwall lodge which offered the use of its temple for regular meetings.

Hence the birth of the lodge on the 25 November 1989: there were many masons from all parts of Cornwall at the consecration which took place at the masonic hall at Newquay. The oration given by W.Bro. the Revd Raymond Wood, Provincial G. Chaplain was of special note: he refered to the logo depicting a plough near to a stook or shock of corn, implying that as farming is dependent on help from the metal-worker and many other trades and professions, so each lodge benefits from its cooperation and harmony with other freemasons. The first W.M. was W.Bro. P.J. Pengelly, and two were proposed as candidates for initiation. The officers appointed donated their respective collars to the lodge. W.Bro. P.J. Pengelly, W.M. W.Bro. G.D. Stockwell, J.W., and W.Bro. J.R. Vian, S.D. presented the tools and W. Bro. M.H. Cock, D.C. presented the wands for the D.C. and Asst. D.C. A lodge banner was presented to the lodge in February 1993 by W.Bros. J.R. Vian, E.S. Williams and A R. Gilbert.

Three goblets were presented for the use of the W.M. and his wardens at installations and dining, by W. Bro. Needham, honorary member. Two offertory plates and a roll of honour board were presented by W. Bro. L.A. James, W.M. in 1998. At the first installation ceremony the Provincial Grand Master presented the founder members with their jewels. W.Bro. R.H.R. Tilly presented his son Bro. R.H. Tilly, who was also a founder member, to the board of installed masters at his installation in 1995.

Lodge Histories

At the meeting in December 1997, the W.M., W. Bro. D.A.L. Moon presented the gavel to W. Bro. T.C.T. Odgers, I.P.M., to enable him to initiate his son Mr. Paul Charles Odgers. He was the first 'Lewis' to have been initiated into this lodge the second being Bro. Martin Ivor Harvey, son of the late Bro. Ivor Harvey.

The first initiate, in December 1989, was Bro. William Davey, who became the first initiate to be installed as W.M. – in October 1999 – by W.Bro. Tony James.

The members of The Agricultural Lodge with their first W.M., W.Bro. Philip Pengelly, in consecration year of 1989.

Lodge Histories

THE CORNISHMAN LODGE No. 9350, HAYLE.

The idea for the lodge was conceived in the late 1980s when the Provincial Grand Master, R.W.Bro. the Hon. Robert Eliot encouraged the formation of a number of new lodges, and combined a pride and affection for Cornwall and its stalwart brethren. There was an initial reservation about the desire to form a lodge for 'Cornish Masons' particularly in the east of the province where the National Health Service arrangements invariably result in treatment or confinements within Devon. Accordingly the by-laws included the following: "As the name implies, this is a lodge of Cornish-born brethren with at least one parent born in Cornwall. There will be an exception to this rule if one is born outside the county because of the need to go to a maternity hospital in say Devon, or to any hospital for medical reasons, providing the parents are resident in Cornwall, or if in a service hospital, at home or abroad due to service in H.M. Forces, either parent having been born in Cornwall."

Experienced and enthusiastic masons from Hayle, St. Ives, Helston, Mullion, Camborne and the Isles of Scilly came together as 31 founders and one serving brother to form this new lodge and on 10 February 1990 The Cornishman was consecrated at Hayle School by the Provincial Grand Master. The first W.M., W.Bro. W.G. Jenkin, was installed by V.W.Bro. S.J. Pearce, P.G.Swd.B., Deputy P.G.M. The lodge meets at Hayle, where, in conjunction with five other craft lodges, it continues to grow at a steady pace; celebrating its tenth anniversary on 15th February 2000 with the installation of W.Bro. E. Nicholas as W.M., the first initiate to reach the chair. The lodge maintains close contact with The Cornish Lodge No. 2369 meeting in London and since 1997 an annual 'Olde Cornish Nyte' has been held at the November meeting when much hearty and enthusiastic singing is heard after the festive board (which consists of truly Cornish fare including, of course, the pasty) and funds are raised for masonic charities.

Lodge Histories

CORNISH MARITIME LODGE No. 9374, FALMOUTH.

It was in early 1988 that W.Bro. N.L. Marsh attended Penwith lodge to witness the initiation of a colleague who was an officer in the Royal Navy. He had previously seen two of his ex-naval colleagues through their ceremonies and was keen to see the third through. He was sitting next to W.Bro. H.W. Mitchell, P.J.G.D., and commented that if they had many more naval people as members they should change the title to the Maritime Lodge. Little did he know what the remark would generate. In a letter of November 1988, the Provincial Grand Master, the Hon. Robert Eliot wrote to W.Bro. Marsh, the gist of which concluded that he should form a lodge made up of 'naval types' but not a closed one. The first move was to circulate all the lodges, with the assistance of the Provincial G.Secretary and the initial response was encouraging. About 35 showed an interest after a lot of canvassing. The P.G.M. wrote again suggesting that he enlist the aid of W.Bro. F. Sowden as an ex-naval man, who subsequently became founder secretary, and W.Bro. L.C. Burton to act as chairman, because of his past experience in forming another lodge. Love and Honour agreed to be the mother lodge and all meetings would be held at Falmouth.

It was decided that it would be a dining lodge with Emulation working and the name finally became the Cornish Maritime Lodge, not because of the patriotism alone but to avoid confusion with similarly named lodges! Some 'founders-elect' dropped out, but still left the necessary number to proceed to the consecration. An item that generated lively discussion was the lodge logo and the banner. The brethren were invited to submit ideas and draft logos, and the decision finally rested with the design by W.Bro. T.W. Pusey which now adorns every agenda. The banner was not produced for some time due to expense and design details, but has now been dedicated. On the 26 May 1990 the lodge was consecrated and all the consecrating officers were made honorary members as was W.Bro. Burton for his services. A novelty is that red and green lights are lit (one either side, depicting port and starboard) and when the W.M. enters 'Eight Bells' are sounded. Fortunately, candidates were waiting, so there was no shortage of work for the new team. All initiates have progressed to the chair and there are five I.P.M's who were initiated in the lodge. The lodge was originally made up of masons from various lodges and rituals but has created its own identity, working together and holding its place with others in the province.

Lodge Histories

LODGE OF THE CHISEL No. 9398, ST. COLUMB.

In April 1989, after the appeal by the Provincial Grand Master, R.W.Bro. the Hon. Robert Eliot for help towards his goal of 80 lodges in the province, three members or ex-members of the teaching profession W.Bro. L.C. Marsh, W.Bro. J.W. Forward, and W.Bro. N. Hortop discussed the possibility of forming an 'Education Lodge'. An appeal for possible founders brought a limited response so the qualification for membership was widened. At a meeting in Truro in November that year it was decided to go ahead, to seek a base at St. Columb and to call it the Lodge of the Chisel. It was also decided that W.Bro. Forward should be the first W.M., W.Bro. D.G. Goldie treasurer and W.Bro. Marsh continue as organising secretary. Before the next meeting an offer of most of the collar jewels, gavels and wands for deacons and D.Cs was received from Bro. C. Stokes of Plymouth. This was gratefully accepted and he was invited to be a founder member. At this meeting the Duke of Cornwall Lodge offered a base at St. Columb and the promise to sponsor. Bro. R.M.A. Tempest-Woods was elected first S.W. and W.Bro. R.W.A. Holland the first J.W. A logo was submitted by W.Bro. Forward, which comprised an open book on which was placed a stonemason's chisel and ringed around the outside with the legend 'The Lodge of the Chisel' and 'By Which Means Alone'. The consecration was on 20 October 1990, at Newquay, by the Provincial Grand Master, R.W.Bro. The Hon. Robert Eliot, assisted by the Assistant Provincial Grand Master, W.Bro. Rollo E. Crabb and a provincial team. In all 102 brethren attended.

The first candidate initiated in November was Dennis Norman Howes from Rosudgeon, Penzance. At that same meeting a further candidate and three joining members were balloted for. Before the meeting in May 1991 the lodge suffered its first tragedy when the first S.W., Bro. Ronald Tempest-Woods died suddenly. At the next meeting W.Bro. Ray Holland was made Master Elect and installed the following month. Tragedy again struck the lodge in September 1992 when he died in office. W.Bro. D.J. Lewis, who had done fine work as almoner became Master Elect and was installed in October: he had received promotion to P.P.J.G.D. at that year's provincial meeting.

Lodge Histories

The lodge was presented with a P.M's board by W.Bro. A.L. James of Trevaunance Lodge, and the Agricultural Lodge. In May 1993 the meeting was enhanced by the presence of nine members from two lodges of the Grande Loge Nationale Francaise, Breiz 266 and Brittany 225. It was an experience for most of the members to hear greetings given in French and some of the French brethren were able to remain for the festive board and they, in turn, were intrigued by the 'masonic fire'.

The membership is spread throughout the length and breadth of the province which causes problems over rehearsals and social events. The tenth anniversary came in 2000: the founder-treasurer W.Bro. Derek Goldie became secretary on the retirement of W.Bro. Marsh.

Members and guests at the Newquay consecration of the Lodge of the Chisel in October 1990. In the centre are the W. Master, W.Bro. Jack Forward with principal guests, the P.G.M., R.W.Bro. The Hon. Robert Eliot and the Assistant P.G.M., W.Bro. Rollo Crabb.

Lodge Histories

BEACON LODGE No. 9425, BODMIN.

It had been felt for some years there was room in Bodmin for another lodge and in January 1990 fifteen brethren met and agreed to proceed. W.Bro. G.R.d'A Nadin P.A.G.D.C. was elected chairman and W.Bro. R.C. Johns the founder secretary. In March it was decided to form a dining lodge, meeting five times a year and to use the Emulation ritual. The founders wished the lodge to be called the Hubert Dingle lodge to commemorate the life of W.Bro. H.I. Dingle who had been a member of One and All for over 50 years and had served the province as a Deputy P.G.M., and had served Bodmin as a dental surgeon, magistrate and as chairman of the board of the Cornwall mental hospital. At the meeting in May it was proposed that W.Bro. Johns should be the first W.M., Bro. Sandercock the S.W. and W.Bro. Reed the J.W. It was agreed to work towards the 18 May 1991 as the consecration date.

The proposed 17 founders were informed that it was unlikely that Grand Lodge would accept the name as it was policy not to name lodges after anyone below the rank of a Provincial Grand Master so a resolution was passed that a letter should be sent to Grand Lodge: "the lodge should be called the Hubert Dingle lodge but that if that name is not acceptable to Grand Lodge then we will reluctantly agree to 'The Beacon Lodge'". This was finally agreed and King Arthur's Hall booked for May and the dinner at the St. Moritz Hotel. W.Bro. B.C. Treby, the treasurer, produced a logo. As the P.G.M. was in hospital, V.W. Bro. S.J. Pearce, the Deputy Provincial Grand Master was the consecrating officer and W.Bro. N.J. Barrington, the Assistant P.G.M. the installing officer. One of those named on the petition, W.Bro. W.D. Gilbert, had been appointed as a Provincial J.W. that April and was thus not allowed to remain a founder. After being made an honorary member, W.Bro. Gilbert became a joining member and after serving as the charity steward for several years was re-elected an honorary member.

The first meeting, an emergency one, was held in June when W.Bro. B.C. Treby's son-in-law, Andrew LeGrys was proposed as the first candidate, three joining members were received and officers not present at the consecration were appointed. Bro. LeGrys was initiated at the October meeting and became W.M in 1998. During the meeting in April 1992 the lodge banner, made and presented by W.Bro. Gilbert and his wife, was dedicated, and the oration given by Bro. the Revd Michael Pearce, the Provincial G. Chaplain. An occasion of note organised by the lodge was a demonstration in April 1999 of the building of King Solomon's Temple, by the Cleveleys lodge of Mark Master Masons No. 1196 from West Lancs. At the end of October 1999 there had been 16 initiates and 19 joining members. The lodge strength is about 40 members.

Lodge Histories

CORNISH ASHLAR LODGE No. 9446, CHACEWATER.

Founded 1991

The study and research lodge for the province began as the Cornwall branch of the Devon and Cornwall Study Circle in 1986. In 1984, the founders, F.W. Shepherd (1544), R.C. Jones, R.H. Hawke and N.D. Brown (all 331), first approached the P.G.M. with a request to form a study lodge open to all freemasons. This request was turned down as the Devon and Cornwall circle, although dormant, still officially existed as the research organisation shared between the two provinces. A Cornwall branch was allowed, some 20 joined the new group and the 'official' branch began on the 29 January 1986. The officers were; chairman W.Bro. F.W. Shepherd; secretary W.Bro. R.H. Hawke; lecture secretary W.Bro. H.T. Willis B.E.M., and treasurer W.Bro. J. Bowles.

The intention was to develop a Cornish organisation to encourage the study of freemasonry, form a core of local speakers and provide a base for visiting lecturers. The four meeting dates were originally chosen to miss all existing lodge dates; unfortunately, with the growth of both the Craft and other degrees, the dates now clash, leading to a reduction in attendance. The P.G.M. agreed that the branch could meet anywhere within the province. The first meeting presented a lecture on Robert Freke Gould by the late Bro. F.J. Cooper of Quatuor Coronati lodge.

Over the next six years, the branch was very successful, with meetings from Penzance to Saltash. The most popular proved to be a demonstration of a Dutch 2nd Degree. In 1990, the Provincial Grand Master offered the branch the opportunity of forming a new lodge with the stipulation that the initiation fee should be £1,000. The idea of a lodge did not receive universal acclaim and a compromise was reached in that a lodge was to proceed, but with an attached correspondence circle for those members not wishing to become full members. The founding W.M. was to have been the W.Bro. Shepherd, the horticulturist and masonic historian, the guiding light of the branch since its inception. Regretfully, he fell ill just before the lodge came to fruition.

The new lodge was consecrated at Newquay by the Provincial Grand Master, R.W.Bro. The Hon. Robert Eliot on the 19 October 1991. The first W.M. was W. Bro. Rollo Crabb, then Assistant P.G.M., the S.W. Lt.Cmdr. T.C.A. Waghorn, then Mark Masons P.G.M., and the J.W., W.Bro. W.L. Watters, then Deputy Grand Superintendent.

The founding permanent officers were: secretary W.Bro. Hawke; assistant secretary - lecture secretary W.Bro. G.A. Horner and treasurer W.Bro. J.P.D. Harry. The lodge meets officially twice during the year, and as the study circle on a further four. The circle meetings have taken place in an informal setting but attendance, which has never been large, has dropped in recent times. The lodge has been reviewing the format of all meetings in the hope that some way can be found to enhance its activities and encourage a wider participation.

Lodge Histories

The 50th Anniversary of Lyonesse in 1994-95 with W. M., W. Bro. E. C. Downing.

Lodge Histories

GREYSTONE BORDER LODGE No. 9449, LAUNCESTON.

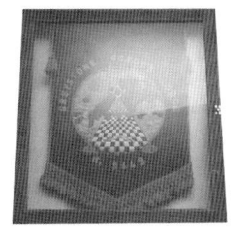

During the latter part of 1989, W.Bro. J.H.B. Parnall and W.Bro. F.A. Abbey met to discuss the possible formation of a new lodge in accordance with the general request made by the P.G.M. during his speech at Provincial G. Lodge in April that year. Whilst it was agreed that a new one, preferably a dining lodge, would be a welcome addition to freemasonry in the area, the two were uncertain as to the possibilities, especially from where the new members could be recruited. Two or three further meetings were held but with very little progress. Then during late 1990 W.Bro. Neil Hobday joined the other pair, and acted as a catalyst, for in January 1991 the three 'started the ball rolling'. It was decided the lodge be based in Launceston and a meeting took place with W.Bro. Roy Bailey, the treasurer of Dunheved Lodge to agree financial arrangements.

Dunheved were asked to become sponsors and 31 lodges within North Cornwall and West Devon circulated with the details of the new lodge; a meeting of all those interested was called. This was a great success with good fellowship very apparent. Many names were suggested but Greystone Border was chosen, representing the significance of the catchment area of the lodge across the Tamar Valley.

In July the draft by-laws were approved. Bro. Paul Wallis created a logo for the lodge incorporating the two counties shown as being linked by the Greystone bridge. Bro. Wallis, assisted by W.Bro. Nick Martin, went to the bridge to take accurate measurements to enable Paul to draw it to proper scale. The day of consecration arrived on 23 November 1991. After the first serious meeting of the original "Three", the lodge had been consecrated within ten months. The Provincial Grand Master, R.W.Bro. the Hon. Robert Eliot performed the ceremony and the Provincial G. Chaplain, W.Bro. Dr. the Revd P. Blackwell-Smyth delivered the oration. The Deputy Provincial Grand Master, V.W.Bro. Sidney J. Pearce officiated at the installation of W.Bro. John Parnall as first W.M. The banquet at the St. Mellion Golf Club was a splendid culmination to the day.

Antient and Honourable Fraternity of Free and Accepted Masons.

Provincial Grand Lodge  of Cornwall.

The Right Hon. the Earl of Mount Edgcumbe, R.W., Provincial Grand Master.
Sir Charles B. Graves-Sawle, Bart., Deputy Provincial Grand Master.

DEAR SIR OR BROTHER,

I have the honor to inform you that the **Annual Provincial Grand Lodge** will be held at the **Town Hall, Launceston, on Monday, 11th September, 1899, at 11.30 a.m.,** when the Masters, Past Masters, and Wardens of the Lodges in the Province, and all Present and Past Prov. G. Officers are summoned (and all Master Masons are invited) to attend for the despatch of Masonic Business. (See page 3)

At 12.30 o'clock the Brethren will walk in procession to the Parish Church, where the Annual Sermon will be preached.

At the conclusion of the Service the procession will be re-formed, and return to the Town Hall, when the Provincial Grand Officers will be appointed, and the remaining Business of the Province concluded.

By Command of the R.W. Prov. G. Master,

Yours fraternally,

BERNARD F. EDYVEAN, P.M., 330, P.A.G.D.C.,

Bodmin, 11th August, 1899.   Provincial Grand Secretary.

A LUNCHEON will be provided at 3.30 o'clock p.m., at the White Hart Hotel, at which the R.W. Prov. G. Master will preside. Tickets for the Luncheon (exclusive of wine) 3/6 each. Brethren intending to be present should make early application for Tickets to Bro. B. Parsons, White Hart Hotel, in order that proper arrangements may be made.

1st, 2nd, and 3rd Class Return Railway Tickets, at a Single Fare and a Quarter, will be issued by G.W. Railway at all stations in Cornwall where there are Lodges to Members attending the Meeting, on production of their Masonic Clothing—From stations west of Bodmin, to Wadebridge, and from stations east of Bodmin, to Launceston *viâ* Plymouth—the tickets to be available from the day before to the day after the Meeting. A special train (L. & S.W.R.) will convey the Brethren from Wadebridge to Launceston at 9.50, but at full fares. It will be necessary for Brethren from the West to avail themselves of the train leaving Penzance at 6.30 a.m.

HEARD & SONS, PRINTERS, TRURO.

A cover from a Provincial Grand Lodge agenda of more than a century ago: Launceston in 1899

Lodge Histories

EAGLE LODGE No. 9472, PERRANPORTH.

Eagle Lodge came into being on 30 May 1992 as a result of a conversation in 1989 between W.Bro. David Scarle, Bro. Nidrel Walsh, and W.Bro. John Watts that there ought to be a Royal Air Force Lodge in Cornwall. The Provincial Grand Master, R.W.Bro. the Hon. Robert Eliot, got to hear of it, thought it a good idea, but suggested that as recruitment may be limited, the foundation should be based on "an interest in aviation". This was expanded to, "require founders, candidates and joining members to have or have had a connection with aviation". The first founders meeting was called and invitations sent out, but there were apologies from all except the original three! The framework on which the lodge was based, was agreed between them. The name was proposed by W.Bro. Watts after much research into other RAF-type acceptable names.

The first letters sent out to prospective founder members were in fact headed with this and it was also proposed and agreed that W.Bro. Scarle should be the first W.M., W.Bro. Watts founding secretary and Bro. Nidrel Walsh the first J.W. With only three voting everything was agreed and set up! The number of meetings, where to meet and what ritual to use, were also agreed. Probably the most important item on the agenda was, from the list of prospective founder members, which offices should they be asked to take.

The proposed name Eagle was submitted to Grand Lodge for approval: W.Bro. Walsh designed the lodge badge which was also submitted. Everything was confirmed, together with approval for a red, white and blue ribbon. So, the founders jewels and now the P.M's have become collectable (V&A they would say in the R.A.F.) valuable and attractive. There were no problems and a very moving consecration ceremony: the venue, Newquay, was also to be 'home', with St. Michael Lodge the sponsor and mother lodge. At the first meeting the lodge was opened by W.Bro. Scarle who read, "Those who wait upon the Lord shall mount up with wings as Eagles, they shall run and not be weary, they shall walk and not faint". It has been part of the opening ever since.

Lodge Histories

In his first year in office, in preparing for Christmas and in organising his ladies night, W.Bro. Scarle obtained the copyright of the painting of the eagle which adorned the first Christmas and menu cards: painted by Dick Twinney, the wild life artist from St. Columb Major, it has been used ever since. Over the years among the most traumatic events was the change of venue from Newquay to Perranporth, but the lodge has settled into its new home. It is called "the high flyers" with a certain amount of pride. From an original 17 founders it rose, with just six meetings a year, to about 40 members with many initiates and candidates, a remarkable achievement.

In 2000 the first initiate, Bro. Geoff Burrows became W.M. The new banner, with the inscription 'Similis Aquila Actus' (Wings like an Eagle) was dedicated during his year, in the presence of the Provincial Grand Master, R.W.Bro. Nicholas Barrington. The lodge is indebted to both hosts for their acceptance and the use of their premises, regalia and furniture and has continued to maintain the by-law criteria in that everybody has a connection with aviation. Most, are ex R.A.F., but there is a Petty Officer in the United States Navy and members who are ex-Fleet Air Arm and civilian pilots. As long as the successful formula remains it will continue to recruit accordingly: Per Ardua Ad Astra!

Lodge Histories

THE CORNISH LINKS LODGE
No. 9481.

Founded 1992

The Cornish Links lodge was consecrated on 26 September 1992, at the Masonic Hall, Newquay, by R.W.Bro. the Hon. Robert Eliot, the Provincial Grand Master assisted by V.W. Bro. L.R. Francis, Past Deputy P.G.M. The first Master was W.Bro. B.C. Beattie. It was formed by R.W. Bro. Nicholas Barrington who invited brethren who had golf as a common interest, and as well as three meetings a year has broadened its horizons by playing annual matches against the brethren of Somerset and Gloucestershire. It is a lodge of 'no fixed abode', having a dispensation to meet at various locations.

Founder members of the Cornish Links Lodge in September 1992 with their first W.Master, W.Bro. Bernhard Beattie PJGD, and the present P.G.M. R.W.Bro. Nicholas Barrington (then Assistant P.G.M.).

ROBERT ELIOT LODGE
No. 9483.

The Most W.Bro. the Rt. Hon. Lord Cornwallis, Past Pro.Grand Master, led a star-studded team for the consecration of the 80th lodge in the Province, in 1992. This was a unique occasion for Freemasonry in the Duchy. The lodge was named after the Provincial Grand Master, the Hon. Robert Eliot, who was celebrating his 50 years as a freemason that week. For 14 years he had been P.G.M., and he became the first Worshipful Master of the new Lodge No 9483, with R.W.Bro. Stanley Hopkins, Provincial Grand Master of Somerset, as the Installing Master.

The Provincial Grand Masters of Gloucestershire and Devonshire also took part in the Consecration as well as a Past Grand Chaplain, the Assistant Grand Secretary, the Past Deputy Grand Director of Ceremonies, a Past P.G.M. and an Assistant P.G.M. "Their presence is an honour we all appreciate" said the new W.M. in thanking all who contributed to the success of the ceremony at Newquay Tretherras School on 31 October. The hall was crowded with 200 guests, Provincial officers, Masters and Lodge members, together with the 19 founder members of the Robert Eliot Lodge.

"The ceremony went as well as any in which I have taken part," commented Lord Cornwallis, who also stressed the comments of the Grand Master, the Duke of Kent, earlier that year at Earls Court, on the value of bringing the ladies more into the life of the Lodges. He considered this a "step in the right direction."

In his oration, R.W.Bro. the Rt. Revd Vernon Nicholls, Past Grand Chaplain and Past Provincial Grand Master of Warwickshire expressed his personal gratitude at being invited to take part. "Joy and cheerfulness, peace and unanimity, friendship and fidelity should be the foundation stones of every Lodge and of each of us. These are qualities which Masonry teaches and these are qualities needed so desperately in our world. If we live by these we can refute our critics and show to the community in which each of us lives, that Masonry has much to offer, that it is not a secret society but a society with certain important secrets. We are a society of men who have found a purpose for living, a faith in the great Creator God, and we have a desire to serve beyond the lodge room."

After listing the masonic record of the new W.M. he declared: "What a record of service to Freemasonry in Cornwall and how right you should honour him." Since 1978 he had consecrated 15 new lodges and as Grand Superintendent five new Chapters. The Chaplain added: "May the members of this Lodge carry the torch of true brotherhood and of hope and peace in this great Province."

Lodge Histories

THE MILLENNIUM LODGE No. 9708, PERRANPORTH.

Founded 2000

Cornwall's newest lodge was aptly named The Millennium, for its consecration came on 15 January, 2000, in a ceremony and celebration at the Ponsmere Hotel, Perranporth, led by the Provincial Grand Master, R.W.Bro. Nicholas Barrington assisted by his Deputy V.W.Bro. Frank Crewes who installed the first Master. The Provincial G. Chaplain, Bro. the Revd Tony Olivey gave the oration.

The first W.M. was W.Bro. R.L. Thomas, with W.Bro. P. Reed and J.H. Trewhella the Wardens. The consecrating officer carried out the impressive and moving ceremony and then dedicated and constituted the lodge.

The new lodge had 36 founders and meets on the second Thursday of January (Installation), February, March, September, October and November.

Lodge Histories

THE CORNISH LODGE No. 2369, LONDON.

Founded 1890

There can be little doubt that the formation of the Cornish Lodge in London at the beginning of the last decade of the 19th century was an event of more than ordinary interest amongst masons of that time. This was shown by the two-page 7,000-word coverage devoted to an account of the proceedings in 'The Freemason'. In the London of 1890, which was about to inaugurate its first electrified tube train service, some famous and distinguished men and masons were making their indelible mark upon history. Bros. W.S. Gilbert and Arthur Sullivan (Grand Organist 1887) were at the height of their popularity with "The Gondoliers" playing to enthusiastic audiences at the Savoy Theatre. The youthful Bro. Rudyard Kipling, having recently returned from India, had already attracted favourable attention with the publication of his short stories, as had the flamboyant writer and wit Bro. Oscar Wilde who, early in the decade, would achieve even greater affluence and fame with the publication and production of his plays. Retired London newspaper proprietor John Passmore Edwards, who was to be initiated into the Cornish lodge and whose philanthropy would later inspire a biographer to entitle him "The Cornish Carnegie" was about to open the first of his many endowments.

In Africa, Bro. the Rt.Hon. Cecil Rhodes, Premier of the Cape Colony, was masterminding the white settlement of those territories afterwards to be known as Rhodesia. A few years earlier, Bro. A. Cairne Hodge, a distinguished and widely travelled Cornish engineer and freemason, who later joined the Cornish lodge, had been exalted into the Royal Arch degree with Cecil Rhodes in what he described as "an impressive ceremony in a crudely furnished and appointed iron shed in Kimberley, S. Africa". It was against this background of events that, in April 1890 a petition was presented for the formation of the Cornish Lodge with the purpose of providing a masonic centre for Cornish freemasons resident in the London area.

Thread of Gold

Lodge Histories

The motivator was W.Bro. Nicholas J. West, P.Provincial G.Treasurer (Cornwall), P.M. of the Cornubian Lodge No. 450, Hayle, a civil engineer working in London at the time. Such was the enthusiasm that the petition carried 24 names including those of the Provincial Grand Master and Deputy P.G.M. of Cornwall.

The warrant was granted in May 1890 and the lodge was consecrated at Mark Masons Hall, Great Queen Street, on Saturday 19 June 1890 by V.W.Bro. Col. Shadwell H. Clerke, Grand Secretary assisted by Grand Officers. Attending were 21 founders and 42 visitors including the R.W.Bro. R.T. Walkem, District Grand Master of Canada, the son of a Cornishman. The banquet which followed the ceremony was held at the Freemasons Tavern and Bro. C. Greenwood, secretary, defined those eligible for membership as "all worthy men who might have been born in Cornwall, who were born of Cornish descent, or who had lived in Cornwall, or who had the wisdom to marry Cornish wives". It is now many years since a strict compliance with these qualifications has been required but, nevertheless, there still remains a genuine feeling of pride and affection amongst the brethren of the lodge for its Cornish heritage. The 'Cornish' met at Mark Masons Hall, then at Freemasons Tavern, the Holborn Restaurant, the Cafe Royal, and currently four times a year on Saturdays at the Central London Masonic Centre, Clerkenwell Green. With so many candidates going through in those early years, three ceremonies were often conducted during the lodge meetings. W.Bro. N. West presented the lodge with its first banner, as a memento of his year in office. Seventy-two years were to pass before this was eventually replaced by the present banner, which was commissioned from The Embroidery Guild, the cost being met from a legacy by W.Bro. R.W. George, P.M. The initiation of 70 year old Bro. John Passmore Edwards in October 1894 brought into the Cornish lodge one of its most notable characters. (See special feature).

The W.M's collar, with the names of all past masters engraved on sterling silver mounts, is the most highly prized possession. Presented in 1896 by W.Bro. Henry Sholto Hare, P.P.G.D. (Cornwall), many silver bars have been added and the collar material replaced from time to time. In 1963 a legacy from W.Bro. George enabled a major renovation to be undertaken and W.Bro. Douglas Wood, provided a new collar and arranged for all the silver fittings to be polished and re-mounted to commemorate the centenary year in 1990. With the gradual demise of the 'Cornish Member' from about the time of the First World War, the numbers of joining brethren fell severely from an average of three to less than one per year. W.Bro. Greenwood, founder and secretary for 13 years, became the first member to be honoured with the newly established "London Rank" in 1908 and his regalia was presented by the lodge. The early part of the century saw the emergence of some noteworthy family connections of which the most significant is probably the three generations of the Leete family. Bro. Joseph T. Leete joined in 1907 and was W.M. in 1916-17. A most active and influential member for 36 years, his two sons Bertram Joseph and Sydney John were initiated between 1912-14, "B.J." occupying the chair for the year 1921-22 and again 25 years later. Sydney, fell in action during World War 1. The third generation appeared in October 1929 when "B.J's" son, Bertram Douglas was initiated by his grandfather at a ceremony attended by the most distinguished lodge member at that time, V.W.Bro. Sir Philip Colville Smith. Twelve years later when 86 years of age, "J.T." again took the chair to install his grandson as W.M. "J.T." died in 1943: a fifth Leete, Sydney Graham, brother of "B.D." was initiated by his father in 1946: W.Bro. S.G. Leete, M.B.E. (W.M. 1954-5) the last surviving member from his family died in January 1997.

The tragic consequences of the war were brought home when, during 1917, the only sons of two lodge members, as well as Bro. Lieut. S.J. Leete were killed in action. There was a brighter side to the year when one eminent member, R.W.Bro. P. Colville Smith was appointed Grand Secretary and another, W.Bro. C.A. Hanson, M.P., was elected Lord Mayor of London. The Cornish Chapter was formed in 1925 with nine founders, all of whom were members of the lodge and six of them P.M's. The thirties were to prove the quietest phase in the lodge's history as there were but ten initiates and four joining members throughout the decade. If any one man has had more influence on the lodge than all others it is W.Bro. S.A. 'Tommy' Thomas; initiated 1913 and W.M., 1924-5, he held the office of secretary for 35 years, 1932-67. He made a record 200 consecutive appearances at the Cornish lodge of instruction and was honoured with the Grand Rank of P.G.St.B. in 1955. The last initate before the outbreak of World War II, and before its 50th anniversary, was W.Bro. Cecil H. Beer, P.P.J.G.W. (Cornwall), who was admitted in June 1939. On completing his term as W.M., in 1949, he presented a set of three gavels crafted in old Cornish oak from the 15th century belfry of Probus Church and with copper devices engraved by a Falmouth coppersmith. Two of these gavels are still used. The Cornish continued to assemble regularly during the 1939-45 war and only two meetings were cancelled. Meetings were opened at 2pm, the brethren having met for lunch an hour earlier. The 1940s produced many more new members than in the previous ten years. This upward trend continued for the next two decades, thereby restoring the losses of the 30s. Another three generation family connection was originated in 1945 with the initiation of R.T. Coward followed by his son-in-law, L.W.Carney, in 1947 and then, as a joining member in 1985, his grandson, W.Bro. Michael Carney, P.M.4452. The Hooper family also deserves special mention. W.Bro. William Hooper joined the lodge in December 1912 and his son, W.Bro. Harold T. Hooper, L.G.R., was initiated at the same meeting. A second son, W.Bro. William D. Hooper, was initiated six years later. They all became W.Ms., and "H.T." lived to complete over 66 years as a member. He shared his initiation with two members who also enjoyed long masonic careers; W.Bro. L. Penhall Phillips, L.G.R., just under 66 years and W.Bro. B.J. Leete, P.G.St.B. who completed 54 years. After the death of William (Senior), a solid silver alms dish was presented by his widow: sadly, the original was stolen but it has been replaced by a replica.

Brethren from the Cornwall province always receive a wonderful welcome on any visit and the lodge has made substantial donations to the province's appeal to its 2002 R.M.B.I. Festival. The brethren appreciate the welcome given when members attend the Provincial Grand Lodge annual meetings.

TRUE MASONIC NOBILITY
(an old masonic poem)

We deem a Mason manly
Who acts a noble part;
Who shews, alike by word and deed
He hath a Mason's heart;
Who lives not for himself alone,
Nor joins the selfish few;
But prizes more than all things else
The good that he can do.

We deem a Mason worthy
Who strives to aid the weak,
And, sooner than revenge a wrong,
Would kind forgiveness speak:
Who sees a brother in all men,
From peasant up to King,
And would not crush the meanest worm,
Nor harm the weakest thing.

We deem a Mason noble
Yea, noblest of his kind
Who shows by moral excellence
His purity of mind;
Who is, alike through good and ill,
A firm, consistent man,
Who loves our sacred Brotherhood,
And aids it all he can.

ANON.